PELLISSIPPI STATE
LIBRARY SERVICES
P.O. BOX 22990
KNOXVILLE, TN 37933-0990

Swingin' on Central Avenue

Swingin' on Central Avenue

African American Jazz in Los Angeles

Peter Vacher

ROWMAN & LITTLEFIELD
Lanham • Boulder • New York • London

Published by Rowman & Littlefield
A wholly owned subsidiary of The Rowman & Littlefield Publishing Group, Inc.
4501 Forbes Boulevard, Suite 200, Lanham, Maryland 20706
www.rowman.com

Unit A, Whitacre Mews, 26-34 Stannary Street, London SE11 4AB

Copyright © 2015 by Peter Vacher

All rights reserved. No part of this book may be reproduced in any form or by any electronic or mechanical means, including information storage and retrieval systems, without written permission from the publisher, except by a reviewer who may quote passages in a review.

British Library Cataloguing in Publication Information Available

Library of Congress Cataloging-in-Publication Data

Vacher, Peter, 1937–
 Swingin' on Central Avenue : African American jazz in Los Angeles / Peter Vacher.
  pages cm
 Includes bibliographical references and index.
 ISBN 978-0-8108-8832-6 (hardcover : alk. paper) — ISBN 978-0-8108-8833-3 (ebook)
 1. Jazz—California—Los Angeles—1921–1930—History and criticism. 2. Jazz—California—Los Angeles—1931–1940—History and criticism. 3. African American jazz musicians—California—Los Angeles—Interviews. 4. Jazz musicians—California—Los Angeles—Interviews. 5. Central Avenue (Los Angeles, Calif.). I. Title.
 ML3508.8.L7V33 2015
 781.6509794'94—dc23
            2015017034

∞ ™ The paper used in this publication meets the minimum requirements of American National Standard for Information Sciences Permanence of Paper for Printed Library Materials, ANSI/NISO Z39.48-1992.

Printed in the United States of America

For my family and all my jazz friends, past and present.

Oral history is a great art when out of the individuality of personal experience we detect a common humanity or common purpose.—Linda Grant

Sometimes ordinary speech is banal, and it is always repetitive, but if selected with art, it can reveal the inner life, often fantastic, concealed in the speaker.—V. S. Pritchett

Jazz, at the time, was a major part of the average black person's life. As a community, we were much more aware of jazz than we are now. For example, most of the people on the street then knew who Charlie Parker was, but if you were to ask now, most people wouldn't know.
—Billy Higgins, Los Angeles, 1984

Contents

Acknowledgments	ix
Introduction	xi
1 Andrew "Andy" Blakeney: Trumpet	1
2 Gideon Joseph "Gid" Honoré Jr.: Piano	33
3 George Robert Orendorff: Trumpet	45
4 Nathaniel Jack "Monk" McFay: Drums	59
5 Floyd Payne Turnham Jr.: Clarinet and Alto, Tenor, and Baritone Saxophones	75
6 Betty Hall Jones: Piano, Organ, and Vocals	95
7 McLure "Red Mack" Morris: Trumpet, Vibes, Drums, and Organ	105
8 Caughey Wesley Roberts II: Alto Saxophone, Tenor Saxophone, and Clarinet	129
9 Chester C. Lane: Piano	147
10 Isadore Leonidas "Monte" Easter: Trumpet and Vocals	169
11 William King "Billy" Hadnott: Bass	185
12 Norman "Norm" Leland Bowden: Trumpet	213
13 John Richard "Streamline" Ewing: Trombone	237
14 Charles L. "Chuck" Thomas Jr.: Tenor Saxophone	253
15 Jesse John Sailes: Drums	267
16 "Red" Minor William Robinson: Drums	281
Appendix: Snapshot	295

Notes	297
Selected Bibliography and Source Materials	305
Index	313
About the Author	331

Acknowledgments

I'm especially grateful to the musicians who allowed me to delve into their lives and careers. They were invariably hospitable and patient in responding to my inquiries. Their wives and partners plied me with refreshments and often contributed informal comments that added valuably to these stories. Above all, they were tolerant enough to overlook my ignorance and to forgive my lack of preparation. They lent me photographs and other ephemera, content to trust this stranger who had arrived on their doorsteps. Some stayed in touch by mail and telephone.

My friends Roger and Zoila Jamieson and attorney Bob Allen allowed me to camp out with them in Long Beach and Baldwin Hills, respectively, putting me up and driving me to appointments. They fed me and gave me the run of their homes. However often I pressed them to come over to London so that I could return their hospitality, they demurred. California seems like the best of places when you're there, I guess.

Others who helped by providing supportive information, leads, and photographs include the late Helen and Joe Darensbourg (who hosted me for several weeks while we were working on his autobiography); the late Harold Kaye for his generosity in sharing vital photographs and data relating to jazz in Hawaii; Franz Hoffman for his invaluable research into the black press; Steve Simon of the Fanchon and Marco Archive; Laura Risk and Anthony Barnett for their Ginger Smock expertise; the writer and LA expert Kirk Silsbee; the late Otto Flückiger for sharing his collection of Red Mack photographs; the always willing Howard Rye who made his "unpublished research on African American musicians in China and Japan" available to me, along with data supplied by Robert Ford; the gospel music historian Opal Louis Nations, who let me have scans of photographs of Monte Easter and Norman Bowden; Gary Lasley of Local 47 AFM and their archivist, Andrew Morris, who dug into the remaining files relating to the now defunct black Local 767; my long-term friend, the photo collector Theo Zwicky; researchers Bob Eagle and Eric LeBlanc; the Swedish researcher Bo Scherman, who gave me access to his interview with Betty Hall Jones; Steve Isoardi who opened his files; and retired drummer Dick Shanahan.

I'm also especially grateful to Tad Hershorn of the Institute of Jazz Studies at Rutgers University for his help with picture research and the provision of images. The same goes for Kelly P. McEniry of the University of Missouri–Kansas City University Library, which houses the Buck Clayton Collection, who found and supplied key images relating to Clayton's time in Shanghai.

Mark Cantor, Bruce Raeburn, Dave Bennett, Derek Coller, trumpeter Clora Bryant, bandleader/composer Gerald Wilson, Ernie Garside, Dan Barrett, saxophonists Vi Redd and the late Jackie Kelso, Danny Gugolz, Mark Berresford, the late Jean-Pierre Battestini, the late Ray Avery, Malcolm Walker, Tony Shoppee, bassist Bernard Carrere, the late Floyd Levin, and the late bebop drummer Roy Porter all gave willingly of their recollections and helped with photographs and leads.

Anne Bennett, Mick Beazley, and Peter Ryan applied their expertise to reproducing photographs and I'm especially grateful to them too. All the photographs that accompany the text are from the author's collection, unless otherwise noted.

Finally, I should thank Ed Berger of the Institute of Jazz Studies at Rutgers University for his initial interest and Bennett Graff at Scarecrow for his patience and faith in the project.

As ever, my wife, Patricia Vacher, was hugely supportive and understanding.

Introduction

It would be all too easy to dismiss these African American jazz stories as inconsequential and mundane. After all, none of the musicians gained international fame or achieved much more than local celebrity. Their recordings were largely low-key and, in some cases, frustratingly few. Most stayed close to home once they had settled in Los Angeles or its surrounding area. Only a handful ever toured in Europe more than once or moved regularly beyond California's confines, although Caughey Roberts Jr. did travel to Shanghai, China, in the 1930s and Andy Blakeney and Monk McFay worked in Hawaii for a significant period.

You could cast them as the journeymen of jazz: black Americans whose career trajectories took in territory dance bands in the South, theater and cabaret orchestras, minstrel shows, swing combos, rhythm and blues groups, and in some cases revivalist New Orleans music. You could also say that they represent the gamut of localized black music experience but largely excluding bebop and modern jazz. And it's in their precise placement in time that I believe their reminiscences have merit. Most of these players were centered in the pre-bop jazz world when swing was very much the thing and entertainment values mattered even when times were tough. Theirs are essentially untold stories, for only a few were ever interviewed and never at this length or with this amount of attendant pictorial material.

My initial desire to document these stories was prompted when I collaborated with the clarinetist Joe Darensbourg on his autobiography, *Telling It Like It Is*, which was published in 1987. Joe's recollections zigzagged between Louisiana, Seattle, and Los Angeles, taking in circus music, small group swing, R&B, and traditional jazz, the last most notably with Kid Ory and Louis Armstrong. Along the way, he moved between the white and black jazz communities in Los Angeles and provided some interesting insights into the confined world of African Americans in that city.

Joe introduced me to some of the surviving pioneers from the black jazz fraternity in Los Angeles, and I was able to interview them. These and the other interviews included here (mostly made on later visits) were essentially opportunist, relying on leads and referrals from friendly musicians and the cooperation of the interviewees themselves. Some were suspicious at first; others were obviously frail. In a number of cases my own preparations were inadequate and I was seldom afforded the chance to interview these people a second time, although I did revisit the testimonies of Andy Blakeney, Billy Hadnott, and Norman Bowden, and I know their chapters are the better for it.

Too often, musicians died before I could talk to them again. Looking back, I feel relieved that I caught some of their memories, however vague or abbreviated they are. Much more could have been done and should have been done to make some of the interviews more complete. In the early interviews, my questions were often subjective and ill informed—even so, I believe the stories presented here do add usefully to our knowledge of black jazz history as it relates to California.

These men (and one woman) represent a period in West Coast jazz history that is lost to us now, a faded memory for just a few survivors, when racial conventions confined them to a segregated lifestyle, performing in strictly circumscribed conditions and living in parts of the city zoned (by restrictive covenants) for African American habitation only. As will be evident from their reminiscences and the photographic evidence, their daily lives frequently overlapped. They were often in bands together, they lived near each other, and they joined all-black social organizations such as the Elks, Masons, and Clef Club together, while enjoying the protection afforded them through their membership of Local 767 of the American Federation of Musicians—which didn't merge with the all-white Local 47 until 1953—and often serving on its committees.

Some were on the inside, part of the select group of union members that was first in line for lucrative Hollywood film jobs when black musicians were needed for background or "atmosphere" purposes. Sometimes they obtained more prominent billing in films made exclusively for black audiences. Of course, they also encountered each other on Central Avenue, then black Los Angeles's "main stem," where African American Angelinos (and some whites) enjoyed the chance to shop, relax, and go about their business by day, then see the great stars of black show business and jazz in its myriad theaters, clubs, and dives at night.

Whole careers were formed and promoted on Central Avenue, including those of some of the early stars of bebop, like Dexter Gordon, Wardell Gray, and Teddy Edwards, whose stylistic intentions place them outside the scope of this collection, even if they did sometimes encounter and cooperate with players included here. Some of the musicians in this book spent much of their musical lives on the Avenue; others appeared there briefly and spread their wings more widely. They played jazz—it was their lingua franca—but they looked for breaks. When R&B became the music of the moment, some of them transferred their allegiance to this new and more lucrative field of work. Later on, they moved into Dixieland when that became popular with white audiences. They toured other parts of America, sometimes quite extensively, and in one or two cases tasted real success. For all that, much of their music making was confined to the black ghetto and went unreported (with only occasional mentions in national music magazines like *Down Beat* or *Metronome*, some reproduced here). They may have been well known in their community and their activities reported in the local black press, but they went largely unheralded in the wider world of American music. Their agents and promoters were African American, the hotels and bars they used were staffed by blacks, and their educational and religious upbringing was all contained within the narrow segment of the "walled" city that they occupied.

Of course, there were other black jazz pioneers that one would have liked to talk to, people like the resourceful trumpeter Jake Porter or the saxophonists Paul Howard and Elmer Fain, two men who made the transition from Local 767 to Local 47 and gained wide-ranging respect for their work. I never got to speak to Leo McCoy Davis, the saxophonist who had arrived in Los Angeles in the 1920s and was the president of Local 767 at the time of the merger, although I tried. I missed out on Teddy Buckner, Oscar Bradley Jr., Buddy Banks, and Maxwell Davis; on bassist Art Edwards and the drummer Bill Douglass, another who transferred ably to the postmerger union world. In most cases, I was just too late or they were out of town. Some I spoke to on the telephone and that was as near as I got. Others like Vi Redd, Gerald Wilson, Plas Johnson, and Britt Woodman were covered in one or other of my earlier books.

Each time I arrived in LA with a list of potential "subjects," it was to be thwarted by one kind of departure or another. Trumpeter Alton Grant was too busy looking after his ailing wife to see me; pianist Jimmy Bunn too embittered. I am sad to have missed trumpeter Dootsie Williams, a fascinating figure who started out as a Central Avenue sideman before becoming a bandleader and later a recording impresario who promoted the successful doo-wop groups of the 1950s. And so it went, all of which serves to emphasize why I think that the stories that I did capture are worthwhile.

Andy Blakeney was a valued player in 1920s and 1930s Los Angeles. He survived into his nineties and proved to be a lucid and illuminating commentator. His interview and those with George Orendorff and Norman Bowden link us to the pioneer musicians who helped to make jazz in California a reality. Trumpeters like Mutt Carey and Ernest Coycault from New Orleans and the legendary James "King" Porter were important early contributors.

Others like Claude "Benno" Kennedy, Bernice "Pee Wee" Brice, and Red Mack were also prominent. Only Red lived long enough to be interviewed.

Lesser-known figures like Monte Easter and Red Minor were never in the front rank for attention yet showed great integrity throughout their jazz careers. I am pleased to present their stories here. Among the trombonists I would have loved to talk to were James "Hambone" Robinson and Allen Durham as well as the trombonist-bandleaders George "Happy" Johnson and Baron Moorehead. No such luck. Although I was able to spend time with Britt Woodman in The Hague and in London, his father, the pioneer trombonist Willie Woodman Sr. (an early associate of Jelly Roll Morton), died too soon for there to be any chance of an interview. It was good, though, to get together with Streamline Ewing, something of a latecomer to Los Angeles.

The black jazz story in California has been underdocumented; individual autobiographies like those of Roy Porter, Horace Tapscott, Buddy Collette, Red Callender, Buck Clayton, and Marshal Royal are valuable, as is *Central Avenue Sounds*, but many of my subjects had already passed away by the time its instigator Steve Isoardi began his valuable oral history program. What is clear is that these musicians came from far and wide, from the Southwest and from Chicago, some arriving in the 1920s, others in the wartime 1940s, attracted to California for its plentiful work opportunities and ready to take their place in the black community. Doubtless they liked the climate and the sense of relaxed ease that California seemed to offer.

Their memories help build a picture of that world, now largely dispersed, when Central Avenue was the epicenter of black LA society, with stars like Louis Armstrong, Fats Waller, and Duke Ellington familiar presences on the street. It is my contention that these interviews help to partly right a wrong. It is commonplace for jazz histories to refer to West Coast jazz as if the early African American contribution to the music in California had little relevance. Emphasis is placed on groups of white players who settled in Los Angeles after having earned their jazz spurs on the road with bands like Woody Herman and Stan Kenton. These skilled musicians then became first-choice players for the burgeoning studio scene in Hollywood. While well-qualified black musicians like Benny Carter, Red Callender, and Buddy Collette were eventually able to cross the color line and make it in the studios, the greater mass of local black jazz musicians simply went on as they always had by making music in their community for their community.

This book is not a history of black jazz in California; that would be too substantial an undertaking. Rather it collects the reminiscences of a number of capable players who were rooted in the territory, played out their lives as performers there, and put their not-inconsequential mark on the music ahead of the change of styles that came with the advent of modern jazz. You'll notice that a few of these players express their puzzlement about bebop. It's also clear that there are discrepancies between some of these individuals and their recollections of particular incidents or events. For quite understandable reasons, there is also considerable emphasis on paydays and money matters.

I've retained their syntax as I heard it and tried to keep their speech patterns alive on the page, eliminating much of the repetition that is inherent in this kind of oral history, while adding appropriate corroborative details or occasional corrections to make their stories more accurate or coherent. I should add that I'm only too well aware of the limitations of the oral history process. The shortcomings of miniature tape recorders; the sometimes tricky acoustic situations where the recordings were made; the agonies of transcription as one deals with idiosyncratic speech patterns, half-heard asides, and the interviewee's tendency to deviate from the point or repeat statements all make for inconsistencies of interpretation.

For all that, I make no apology for these possible shortcomings. These people had something to say, and I'm pleased that we have been able to allow them their chance to say it.

Chapter One

Andrew "Andy" Blakeney

Trumpet

I first got to know the Louisiana-born clarinetist Joe Darensbourg when he came to London with the Louis Armstrong All-Stars. Our friendship led eventually to a book about his life. Later on, he became a founder member of the Legends of Jazz, a band of mostly ex–Kid Ory veterans assembled in Los Angeles by the expatriate British drummer Barry Martyn. Their initial UK tour took place in 1974, and I met up with Joe again at the band's hotel in Ealing in West London. His roommate was trumpeter Andy Blakeney—they knew each other well from their Ory days—and it was clear that Andy had quite a story to tell. Already in his midseventies, Andy was stocky and compact, his hair a mixture of salt and pepper, and he seemed keen to talk. I initiated an interview there and then, taking his reminiscences down in longhand.

That story eventually appeared in *Storyville* magazine (some of it is reprised here), and he later told me how surprised he had been by its accuracy, rather touchingly saying that he had framed the *Storyville* piece and placed it on a wall at home. Andy struck me as a man of considerable integrity, strength of character, and more than ordinary resolution. Evidently a durable lead player, he could also solo with commendable verve and power, yet had largely missed out on recording opportunities as he pursued his peripatetic career on the West Coast.

I carried out a final interview with Andy after he had retired from playing, at his comfortable condominium in Baldwin Park, Los Angeles, when he was ninety-one. I was gratified to find that his memory was still sharp even if his eyesight had largely failed and his physical health was in decline. As well as detailing his own career ups and downs, he was able to recall early players

Andy Blakeney of Andy Blakeney's Riverboat Jazz Band, 400 Club, Los Angeles, 1955. From the author's collection.

and their situations in both Chicago and Los Angeles, thus adding to our knowledge of those long-ago times.

Andy was clearly concerned about the health of his wife, Ruth, the fifth Mrs. Blakeney (her four predecessors had all died), yet they were still planning another visit to Las Vegas, this time to celebrate their twenty-fifth wedding anniversary.

Andrew Blakeney died at home on February 12, 1992; Ruth was too ill to attend his funeral. A fifteen-piece jazz band organized by Bob Allen and Roger Jamieson accompanied the mourners.

Andy Blakeney: Ealing, March 9, 1974; Basingstoke, March 17, 1974; Baldwin Park, May 9, 1990

Andrew Blakeney's father, "Professor" Thomas Blakeney, was a school teacher and part-time farmer in the small country town of Quitman, Mississippi, located two hundred miles south of Memphis, where his son was born on June 10, 1898, the eldest of nine children. Both sets of grandparents had been slaves, and Andy's father was born in slavery: "just two years before General Lee surrendered," he said. Although he took piano lessons (and could read music) while still in Quitman, Andy only decided to learn the trumpet once he had migrated to Chicago in 1917, after a year in St. Louis.

There was no future there in Quitman. I wanted to get a better way of making of living, so I decided to take up music. I had no college education, nor much school, so I went down and bought a secondhand trumpet and made arrangements to take lessons.

I started studying at W. L. Jackson's School of Music in Chicago in 1919—he was Erskine Tate's stepfather—where I was taught all the light classics. After I was attending three years I organized me a little high school band of my own, made up of youngsters of sixteen or seventeen coming up. I was the oldest. This was 1922 to '24. Called it the Utopia Orchestra. First time I got any money for playing was in 1922 out in Gary, Indiana, on Labor Day, a matinee dance job with a little four-piece group. Me and my wife were out doing the joints when this guy walked up to us on the corner of State Street, and he said, "Say, do you know where I can get a band? The band we're supposed to have disappointed us at the last moment. So now tomorrow afternoon, we need a band." "Yeah, I believe I have one of my own," I said. So we made arrangements to take my band out to Gary the next day. We'd been rehearsing, hoping for an opportunity like this. We played popular songs of the day.

The regular piano player we had in this little group couldn't make the job, so I went down to the union club that was open twenty-four hours a day, and they referred me to a man called Richard "Mynee" Jones. He was very popular. We found him, and he was available. The scale then was eight dollars a man, but he said, "Since you're going to Gary, that's out of town, I have to have more money. I need ten dollars." And he was wonderful. He could play a gang. He's the one who put us over. Lester Boone, he played sax that time, and Bill Winston was the drummer. He was just a kid; his father helped him with the drums on that job. They called us back out to the Gary dance hall a couple of times after that. By day I was a cooper, making barrels in the stockyards for Swift and Co. and living on Calumet Avenue. I'd have to get those barrels all full of meat, and I'd put the top on. Paid pretty good after a while. This was three or four steps above common laborer. In that Utopia band, I had various young guys like Shirley Clay on trumpet, Lester Boone, and the trombonists William Franklin and Louis Taylor. Like I said, on drums I had Bill Winston, who went later with Carroll Dickerson and Earl Hines. Then we had Lionel Hampton working with us later—he was about fourteen years old at that time.

We did party jobs and club dates, that kind of thing. We began to get better known, so I rented a hall on 37th and Grand Boulevard and ran dances there every Saturday night. This was in 1922. Promoted it myself with the same group. I took the door and split the profits with the guys after all expenses were paid. Had my brother in the checkroom, my sister and my wife selling pop, and my cousin as security. My mother-in-law sold the tickets and the violin player—we didn't need him—checked the tickets. Used to average 150 people. That's how I met George [Orendorff]. Les Hite and Lionel Hampton came by, too. We were reading everything. It wasn't jazz. We were doing so well that I thought I'd better give a matinee dance on a Sunday. So I went down to 57th and State and opened a dance out there. The same bunch and the same arrangement to split the profit with the band. The first Sunday it was fine. The second Sunday they had a free-for-all fight and broke up my dance. The police came and said, "You can't operate any more till you get a police permit." I decided it was too much trouble, so I quit trying to be a dance promoter and just concentrated on the trumpet.

I always wanted to go out to the joints to see what was going on, listen to the guys playing. So I stopped by this little after-hours joint, just a block from home, and there was no trumpet player. He was home sick. I said I play a little trumpet. He says, "Go get your horn and come sit in." This was about twelve midnight by now. I stayed there until six o'clock the next morning. When I got ready to go home, he says, "You can have this job if you want." That became my first professional steady job. Just four pieces. The Oriental Cafe at 3532 State Street. We called it the Funky London. I was working in the daytime at Swift's and I had to be there at seven o'clock in the morning and I worked until 3:30. Home at four. Went to bed. Ten o'clock I got up, took a bath, wife fixed my dinner, I changed clothes and walked five minutes to work. Midnight to six in the morning. Glover Compton was on piano, the drummer was Clifton "Snags" Jones, and we had Slocomb [Adam Mitchell] on clarinet, a real showman. Glover was an old-timer. He was a fair piano player and he could entertain too. He'd sing and recite Bert Williams tunes.

This was a third-rate joint, not even second-rate! I kept that job for six months. At first I kept on with my day job but after one week I quit that. So I was a professional musician from then on. This was 1924. Then I lost it [the Funky London job] to a little old redhead guy; he was a kid about twenty-one, named Reuben Reeves. Came up from a tiny town in Indiana and sat in. Blowed sharp and next week I got my notice. Finally a violin player around Chicago named Detroit Shannon organized a band and got an agency to book it down to northern Indiana, south Wisconsin, and south Illinois. Hamp [Lionel Hampton] joined us and I remember we were in Appleton, Wisconsin—that's a kinda resort town—and one day three of the boys borrowed a car: George McFarland, the piano player; Hamp; and a sax man. Anyway, they had an accident and Hamp was thrown clean out of the car in the collision but was unhurt. McFarland was concussed and died, while the sax player, who was driving, had a lucky escape with just a few scratches.

We came back to Chicago just before King Oliver opened at the Plantation Cafe with his Dixie Syncopators. This was in the spring of 1925. Tommy Ladnier had been with the band and he had a chance to go to Europe. He had to leave right away so Joe got me to take his place for a couple of weeks until Bob Shoffner, who was with Dave Peyton out at 65th and Cottage Grove, could come over. It was a big band with Barney [Bigard], Nick [Albert Nicholas] and Darnell Howard, Bert Cobb on bass, Luis Russell on piano, Paul Barbarin on drums, and George Filhe, trombone. I can still remember it. They had a heavy floor show there, one of the big road shows called "Plantation Days" and Joe would not play the first [trumpet] part for the show—he just played first for the dancing—so he gave the show book to the second trumpet player and since I was in Tommy Ladnier's place, he handed it to me. I called myself an upstart then, take on anything so I got on the stand for this big-time production but I couldn't handle it. I was too young and inexperienced. The show book was the toughest book. I had to give it back to Joe and he had to struggle with it. I could handle the dance book better. That was my experience with Joe Oliver.

I remember when Louis [Armstrong] first came to Chicago to join Joe. Joe had come in 1918 and Louis came in 1922. I wasn't really playing much then myself but soon after Louis arrived, I went down to the Lincoln Gardens to listen. Louis was a genius then; he just played second to Joe and Joe was playing the lead. Well, I enjoyed it. Joe and Louis gave me the inspiration to pick up the trumpet because at first I didn't know what I wanted to play. I'd started out on piano but I dropped that in Chicago and picked up the tuba. Joe Oliver hit it at a place called the Royal Gardens the first night he was in town, back in '18—it was in the papers that he was coming. King Joe. Shortly after that, they had a Battle of the Trumpets, him and Freddie Keppard at that same Royal Gardens and I was there. They said, "How did it come out?" and I said in my opinion, "It was a draw!" I listened to Keppard quite a few times. He had a sweet tone and he was powerful, just like Joe. Last time I saw him he was with Doc Cook. This was 1930. I was back in Chicago on a trip. It was a matinee dance at the Savoy Ballroom on the south side. He must have been on the downgrade because he was sitting over there, only playing a chorus every now and then. He would just hold his horn while the rest of the band was playing. In his early years, he was the featured trumpet player all the way through the band show.

I knew Jelly Roll Morton too, in Chicago. I first met him when I was working my first regular job in that after-hours place. He'd come and sit in. He was a good entertainer. To me, he wasn't much of a musician then but later on he turned out to be pretty good! He talked a lot, bragged a lot. I didn't work with him but I did rehearse with him. He had two trumpets, myself and Humpy [George] Mitchell, and [clarinetist] Omer Simeon too. I was gonna make a record with him and go on the road but I got another job before that happened so I never did make that record. He had a band; it was on the road with a show called "Burlesque Wheel"; they only worked in the summer and the wintertime, just played short seasons. He was just a big mouth fellow. He'd criticise any other piano player: "He can't play nothing—get me up there." That's the type of guy he was but it was just in fun.

Charlie "Doc" Cook and his Dreamland Orchestra had the job down at the Municipal Pier. This was a pier that was half-a-mile out into the lake. Big pavilion, could accommodate five thousand people, say, two thousand couples on the floor. It was a jitney. A nickel a dance. They had ropes, one on this side to let the people on the floor and one on the other side to let the people off. Everybody had to clear the floor after each number. Cook's boss who owned the Dreamland Ballroom where Cook played—that was a big ballroom on the West Side which was a white place—he had the concession for this Pier, which was only a summer job although it stayed open until after Labor Day. It would open around the first of May, and Cook's regular band from the ballroom couldn't get there because they had to work at the Dreamland until the fifteenth of June. Then they would take two months off from the Dreamland so they'd come down to the Pier and work there. Then they'd go back to the Dreamland in August.

Cook had to hire a substitute band to play for him, to open up and finish, and I was in that. This was twelve pieces and they put me on first trumpet. That was a really professional job. They called it Charlie Cook's No 2 Band—the director was [singer and violinist] Lawrence Harrison, the original leader of the Alabamians that turned out to be Cab Calloway's first band. That's when I first met Kid Ory. He stayed in Chicago for several years before coming back to Los Angeles. We were there for about two months to open before the regular band got there and to close but our regular trumpet *player got him another job and Harrison hired George Mitchell, put him on second. He was so good they put him on first and me on second. Ory had just hit town so we hired him to come in on trombone. This was around August 1925. The season went on a little longer and when we finished we played casuals with Joe Jordan.*

By then I was very popular. A lot of the big shots knew about me. I always liked big bands and I had the opportunity to take an eleven-piece band out. I was leader with Shirley Clay on second trumpet, three saxes including Al Washington, piano player Jimmy Flowers, and John Bell on drums. The violin player was Detroit Shannon. We were playing at a place called the Charleston Cafe. When the Lincoln Gardens [the former Royal Gardens] burned down in 1924, some gangster bunch from the West Side bought the place, restored it, and named it the New Charleston Cafe. The guy who got the music job was a friend of mine [Detroit Shannon?] *but he got in trouble with the union and they wouldn't let him lead the band so I took the leadership on condition I split the leader fee with him. He could play the violin in the band but I was the contracting leader. We did very good but I only stayed there about six weeks because I had this offer to come to Los Angeles. I quit it and turned my band over to Shirley Clay. That was my last job in Chicago.*

Verona Biggs, the president of the Chicago union [Local 208 AFM], *told me that Clarence Williams, a bass player out on the coast, wanted a good trumpet man. He'd asked for Joe Sudler, the famous trumpeter with Charlie Elgar, but he wouldn't go. Biggs said, "If you're interested, all you have to do is answer it" and handed me the telegram. At that time, Lionel Hampton and George Orendorff had preceded me in settling in Los Angeles so they asked these boys about me and as a result I called Los Angeles my home from then on. For personal reasons, I wanted to get away from Chicago because me and my wife at that time wasn't getting along so well and I thought a change would be good. They sent me a ticket and they told me about the band. Did I regret leaving Chicago? Yes, I did in a way. I had a good job and I gave it up to come out here. My wife criticized me. When I left she came to the station with me and I said, "I'm going to send for you as soon as I get settled." "No, you won't. If you want to see me you come back to Chicago. I'm not going to Los Angeles," she said. I arrived on Thanksgiving Day, November 1925. Lived on the West Side, had a fresh room with a private family. Three months later she was in LA. I had to work to save the money to send for her. The problem I had when I got here, that first year was kinda rough. I never could get settled. I'd get on a job and stay about three or four weeks, and then somebody would lose it. All that whole year.*

Blakeney had been summoned to Los Angeles to replace James "King" Porter, the star trumpeter with the celebrated Sunnyland Band.

He was the King of the Coast. A fine trumpet player, he was a powerful man. He ended up as a bum! Beggin' and stealin'. There was a misunderstanding. When I got here, I went straight to the ballroom at 15th and Main where they were playing. They weren't working steady at that time. They just had the Thursday night dance there. Had a full crowd out every Thursday night. This was a big ballroom, held about a thousand people. There wasn't no nightclubs for blacks here in Los Angeles at the time. They had eight pieces. They had Porter; Ash Hardee, trombone; Charlie Lawrence, sax; William Franz, sax; Buster Wilson on piano; Clarence Williams on bass violin; and the drummer was Ben Borders. He was a funny character with a bad eye like King Oliver.

I was surprised and disappointed Porter was still in the band, blowing up a storm but since I was here, they said, "We'll add you to the band. Make a second trumpet book." I didn't like that. I didn't come out here to play second trumpet but I made one job with them. Anyway, they asked me to take a solo and I wouldn't take an ad-lib solo. I played much worse than I would have ordinarily. I just played the melody so next day they had a meeting. I had disappointed them and they said they couldn't use me. They said I was too weak. Imagine me, being weak! I deliberately played weak. I didn't like my position, that's all.

I says, "You brought me out here; how about payin' my way back or payin' my expenses to go out and find another job?" I was a good friend of Reb Spikes, who was a big shot out here at that time; he had a lot of money, a lot of property, and had a band too. He said you can make them give you some money and he told me to go to the Labor Commission. They said, "Yes, you can make them send you back or give you something more." So I was going to take them to court to see whether we could compromise but by that time, somebody hired me. We settled it out of court. I asked for a hundred dollars. The Sunnyland were so powerful; they'd make as much as fifty dollars each man just on this one gig at 15th and Main. [Pianist] Buster Wilson was the musical director of the Sunnyland and did all the talking but he couldn't hire and fire. Porter was threatening to quit so much—that's why they sent for me but the only way to get rid of Porter was for every man to say "out." It was a cooperative band, see.

Spikes had a musical store [the Spikes Brothers Music Store opened at 1203 Central Avenue in December 1919] at 12th and Central. It was a kind of musical headquarters. They started the colored musicians union [Local 767 AFM] there. Reb would send bands out, two or three bands, on a weekend. And he had his own band. He told me one time, "I got a good job coming up at the Follies; I want you to play trumpet with me." This is August '26, but we went in October to Honolulu with Johnny Mitchell. Well, Reb finally got the job but I was gone. Still, I did make that record with him, Sheffield Blues. I had no dealings with Reb after that.

He sent for Lionel Hampton to come and play in a big band for a special job at Redondo Beach Ballroom. Lionel was only sixteen years old. This was the first black band in that area. And of course it was a setup. The band singer and the bass player had two teenage white girls to meet them at the hotel at 12th and Central. The girls went there, and when the two men got there, the police were already there. They got one of them, but the other player skipped out the back so he got away and ain't nobody heard from him since. Well, they lost their job. Big scandal for those days. And I got the news in Chicago. It soon died down. Nobody talked about this anymore. This was just before I got here.

Marshal Royal's father was president of the colored musicians union when I came here. They started the union before I arrived but membership was very small. "Montudie" [Ed Garland], he was already here; Sonny Clay; Herb Williams—he was a piano player, brought a band from Texas, and they were playing in a dance hall called Solomon's out on Grand, opened in '25—Curtis Mosby; Reb Spikes and his brother Johnny; and a few more. Can't think of them all. Mutt Carey was here and he was working in a taxi-dance hall. He was well known. He kept a steady band, never had more than four or five pieces. Ram [Minor Hall] worked with him; then Les Hite was with him for a little while, playing sax; and a little local piano player, Elzie Cooper, played with him. Elzie was raised up here, wasn't born here but he went to school here, and in the 1920s, he was learning to play piano. His teacher was Professor Wilkins. Elzie played in my band when I went into the Beverly Cavern. I didn't join in the union until the next year, '26, because I was a member of Local 208 in Chicago before coming out here.

When we amalgamated [with Local 47 AFM in 1953], Leo McCoy Davis was our president. He wasn't elected. He was vice president when the president—his name was Ed Bailey—resigned, and by Leo being vice president, he took over. I first met him in '27, soon after I got back from Hawaii. He had come from New Orleans. He said he had been in California before. He said he was raised up here and he went to New Orleans with his folks but came back in '27. We were good friends. The first group he worked with was from New Orleans; a piano player and her husband—he played trumpet, [Andrew] Kimball and his wife [Margaret]—they had a four-piece in a little hotel [The Gotham Hotel] on 7th Street between Central and Main, near downtown. That's when I first met Leo; he was with that group. He was first saxophone with [drummer] Curtis Mosby's Blue Blowers; they had a fine band. Curtis was about the biggest thing out here in the '30s. He was at Solomon's; they called it a penny dance. Then he opened the Lincoln Theater; that was in '27. The Lincoln Theater brought Broadway shows from New York and Curtis left Solomon's to go in the pit, backing the shows on the stage. Then a couple of years after that, he opened the Apex down on 42nd and Central. He quit playing because he was a big café owner then. He took his big band in there, ten pieces, Porter was on trumpet, Ash Hardee was on trombone, and Leo was in there for a while. When I got here, I made a record [for Vocalion, February 2, 1926] *with* [bandleader] *Sonny Clay. Ernest Coycault was the first trumpet player and I was playing second. He was with Sonny Clay then, and he lasted quite a while because I remember in '33, he was with the Georgia Minstrels. I was in San Francisco then, working with Wade Whaley. That's the last time I remember Coycault. Of course, I did a season myself with the Minstrels in '32.*

Twelfth and Central was the center for the black community at that time. You just stood on the corner of 12th and Central and by and by, you'd see somebody you knew pass the spot. Later it moved further down to Washington Street—that's the 1900 block south—and then it moved down to 42nd Street in the 1930s. That's where they built the Dunbar Hotel and opened the Apex nightclub. I played there and also the Dunbar Hotel too. In fact we played for the opening of the hotel [built in 1928 as Hotel Somerville and renamed as the Dunbar in 1930]. *I was with Leon Rene's band then. We played at the Open Air Dance Hall out on Whittier Boulevard, almost to Whittier. Little town called Pico. This was in 1928. Our drummer, Ben Borders, used to be with the Sunnyland band. Leon White, the trombonist, he was originally the drummer with the Black and Tan Orchestra in the early twenties, and we had Marvin Johnson and Charlie Jones on saxes; they were the main guys in the Les Hite reed section for years. Ceelle Burke was on banjo and steel guitar; this is before he worked with Les Hite and Louis Armstrong in 1930.*

Ed Garland, he had the One-Eleven band, playing in a taxi-dance hall [the One-Eleven Dance Hall at 3rd and Main]. *He must have been on that job about ten years until the Depression hit, right up to 1933. Back in the twenties and thirties, when I came here, most of the taxi-dances had black bands. After the Depression most closed up and then they started opening up again, and when they reopened, most of the bands were white. Fred Washington was always 'Tudi's piano player. He liked him because 'Tudi couldn't read and he was always at the left-hand end of the piano. He had a good ear for those modulations Fred could cater to him, and then you'd think 'Tudi could read. Somebody asked him one time, "'Tudi, why don't you learn to read?" "I don't need to read; I'm a jazzman," he said. I know one time we hired Fred as a replacement when we were working at the Lincoln Theatre and the pianist didn't show up on time. It was a Sunday thing and 'Tudi was off on Sunday, so Fred came in and substituted. He was a fine musician, could arrange. Another time I remember playing with him was on a cross-country radio thing with Barney Bigard. He had a job for Orson Welles so we went to his home to make this program. Ory had the job first but he couldn't get enough money so Barney took it. Naturally if Ory took it, I was going to play on it so when Barney took the job, he hired me and he hired Fred Washing-*

ton to play piano. Bass was one of the Prince boys, Wesley Prince, who finally went with Nat King Cole. Drums might have been Ram [Minor Hall]. Orson Welles had just married this young girl and they had a little baby, had it at home. We all had breakfast on the patio and he sat me at the table with his young wife and his young baby. We broadcast from his home. I never will forget that.

One big thing in those days was when Speed Webb arrived in Los Angeles. They opened up that Open-Air Dance Hall on Whittier Boulevard in 1926. He brought his big band here. It was a seasonal job, had to close in October. Then they came back the next year and opened up again, in '27, around April. He could only stay two, three months, because he had commissions back east. Harry Southard finished out the season for him. Southard was a trombone player. He'd been the leader of the Black and Tan. Not jazz, not like Ory, he just played straight melody. He owned a barber's shop; he put his horn down, just stayed with his barber's shop, had two or three other barbers working for him.

Then I went to work for a bandleader out here named Johnny Mitchell. This was from late 1926 through to New Year 1927. He was a local boy from here in Los Angeles, played violin and sax. This was at a nightclub, the Italian Village, downtown in Los Angeles, between Broadway and Hill on 8th Street. Johnny Mitchell and his Ebony Idols. Johnny was smart, you know. He would talk his way in, but if he kept talking he'd talk his way out. We had six or seven pieces, and we played the floor show as well as dance music. We used stock arrangements but with hot solos. This was my first real steady job in Los Angeles.

It was a 100 percent white audience. Los Angeles was a fairly segregated city, and what little mixing there was was in the colored section of town. Then we did a couple of months at a taxi-dance hall, the Plaza, a block north of Sunset, catering mostly for Filipinos in the Mexican section. It's worse now but it wasn't an elite part of town then. Mitchell had Les Hite on alto, Henry Prince on piano—Peppy Prince, the drummer, is his first cousin—and Lionel Hampton on drums, who stayed until the Quality Serenaders picked him. Hamp had been out of a job; he was still loafing from the Reb Spikes scandal. Strong band. The Italian Village job lasted until the spring of 1927, and our next job was at Spielman's Nightingale out in Culver City. This was a nightclub with one of the top colored shows called "The Creole Revue" starring Carolynne Snowden. We played the show and for dancing. The band and entertainers stayed in their special quarters—you couldn't mix with the audience. That really didn't seem unusual then. We were making pretty good money. I think we had a contract for about two or three months, but we didn't satisfy Carolynne Snowden and she let us go. She wanted her band and that was the Quality Serenaders. She and [Serenaders pianist] Harvey Brooks were sweethearts.

"Tin Can" Henry Allen, the drummer, was playing with Paul Howard's Quality Serenaders at the Alabam Tent and he came out to the Nightingale on drums. Hamp wasn't with us then but Ellis Walsh was. Hamp took Tin Can's place with the Serenaders. Then Tin Can got a job over at Frank Sebastian's Little Club for which he and [trumpeter] Mutt Carey were co-leaders, but Mutt and he didn't get along so Mutt only worked two weeks. Mutt told Frank, "I always had my own band. I never worked under nobody. I have to be at least co-leader." It didn't work so Mutt went back to his steady job at the taxi-dance hall. He could just quit and go back anytime he liked.

Tin Can Allen wanted a trumpet player so he came to me and begged me to go to Culver City with him. I was with this other band and I said, "No, I'm going to stick with this band." "Blake, if you come with me I'll give you $70 a week"—scale then was $63—so I said, "That's awfully good money." So I took it. I worked with him two weeks. The floor show was in Mildred Washington's name. Vernon Elkins, trumpet player, had worked for Frank at a nightspot in Venice called The-Hole-in-the-Wall and now he wasn't working and Frank thought he owed him. Tin Can Henry didn't want him because he wasn't strong. In fact, he got rid of him and wanted me back but I wouldn't go.

I also did two weeks, I remember, at United Artists in 1927 with bandleader Satchel McVea [Jack McVea's father] *working on the silent picture* Breakfast at Sunrise *with one of the Talmadge sisters, Constance Talmadge.* See, I got more jobs with the silent movies than after the talking pictures came in. We were there to inspire the actors while they were acting on the set. I went up to San Francisco around September 1927 with Herb Williams, a good piano player, to a place on the beach. He had a job up there, supposed to be six months. We got up there early: we thought we were going to open that night. Naturally, we checked into the union with our transfer cards and they said, "You too soon; the band has another week to work their notice out." Most of us were broke, don't know how we're going to eat and sleep for a whole week without working, and the union man said, "Don't worry, I got something for you. Out in Heywood, that's a suburb of Oakland, they want a band for tonight—this was on a Friday—and Saturday and Sunday. For these three nights you can make enough to hold you up until next Saturday night." After that, we thought we had this steady job but it only lasted four weeks. When we closed, the next day everyone packed up and went back to Los Angeles. I was ashamed to come back to Los Angeles. I was so disappointed so I went over to Oakland. I met [New Orleans–born clarinetist/bandleader] *Clem Raymond over there. I don't think he ever did leave Oakland. He wanted me to stay; he said, "You can get a job out here." I stayed around for about a week and finally decided I better go back. My wife was still in Los Angeles.

Then this same Johnny Mitchell got an offer to go to Honolulu with his original band and naturally he wanted me to go with him. This was October 1927. We had Gene Wright, piano; Lee Gibson on drums; Ceelle Burke on banjo; Elmer Fain on sax—he was the business agent for the union and when we amalgamated they gave him the same job with Local 47—and Mitchell playing sax and violin. I worked with Elmer for about fifteen days in 1930 one time on a theater tour, from here up to Salt Lake City, Idaho Falls, over to Portland, down to Sacramento, San Francisco and Oakland, and back to LA. Fitz Weston was our pianist, used to be with Speed Webb.

Ceelle passed for Hawaiian and called himself Joe Panouii; even tried to talk Hawaiian. He was a real character. This was a taxi-dance hall too. We played an average of three choruses, lasted about one or one-and-a-half minutes, mostly ten cents a dance. There were jitney dances too [jitney was a nickname for a nickel], where you bring your girl and dance for about three minutes. This was down at the Municipal Pier with about five thousand people dancing, all white with, once in a while, a colored couple. Men with ropes would clear the floor and then the next crowd comes on. We stayed over there three months and left in January 1928. When we came back we were playing three-night stands; we played the Venice ballroom three nights a week, then we'd go down to San Diego to the Mission Beach Ballroom and do the same. Gus de Luce played trombone with us for a little while. He came here with Joe Darensbourg. Joe left Louisiana and picked up this band [Hill and Vesthon's Original Dixieland Jazz Band] in Texas and they came to Los Angeles in 1926. That's the first time I met Joe, with that band. In fact they broke up soon after they got here. Gus put his horn down after he played with us. He could cook too.

When Ory's band went up to San Francisco working for Louis Landry's Swing Club, he was the cook. Gus and Landry got in a fight, argument anyway, back in the kitchen and Gus got this butcher knife and ran Landry out of the kitchen up to his office where Landry was going for his gun. I spent the rest of that year playing with local bands doing theaters, nightclubs, and dance halls. In January 1929, about the time of the stock market crash, we went into this burlesque house, the Burbank Theatre, on 6th and Main in Los Angeles. Stayed there all of '29 and played through to May 1930. Parker Berry, trombone man who had come out here with the Speed Webb band from Toledo, Ohio, and later arranged for Les Hite, was the leader. This was a twelve-piece band. I worked sixteen months in the pit—had a big show, biggest show I ever worked with. We had eighty-five people on the stage, had three sets of chorus girls. That was a different type of music altogether. Playing in the pit and watching them broads on the stage made it about the hardest job you could have. They changed shows once a week. They had a fine trumpet player named Jeff Smith; he was an older circus man, had a good reputation. Back in the early twenties, he could blow C above high C.

So they hired him and he hired me to play second under him, to take the hot choruses. He only lasted one week; his lip gave out, but as he was such a fine musician and could arrange, they elevated him and gave him a baton with a light in the end of it to direct us. They put me over in his seat and they hired another youngster to play second under me, but I still had to play the hot choruses and the straight lead too. They used to work me awful hard on that show. We had a violin player, a jazz violinist, and anytime they wanted a soft melody, it was supposed to be the violin, but this guy couldn't carry a straight melody so I had to put in a mute and play it and then go back to play the lead.

Johnny Sturdivant played lead sax, Edward Barnett played sax and clarinet, and we had another played third saxophone—I can't think of his name—had a fine bass player and we had a banjo; his name was Rupert Jordan. Of course, there was no jazz at all; we was just playing show music. Still, we made a good salary all through the Depression despite the fact the banks were going bust.

Now when Louis Armstrong first came to the Cotton Club in July 1930 [Armstrong performed at the club until March 1931], *the band was Vernon Elkins's. There was Elkins, George Orendorff, trumpets; Johnny Mitchell, William Franz, saxes; Lawrence Brown, trombone; L. Z. Cooper, piano; Ceelle Burke on steel guitar; bass was Reggie Jones; and Lionel Hampton was drumming. Leon Herriford, the first sax player, fronted the band. After they were there a few months, all the movie stars started coming out, business picked up, and the guys wanted a raise. Frank Sebastian, the owner of the Cotton Club, wouldn't agree so the band quit and walked out except for George Orendorff and Hamp.*

In came Les Hite as the band director and these two joined him. That was the fall of 1930. So Leon brought his band out on the street [Elkins had suffered a breakdown in his health]. *Lawrence Brown joined Curtis Mosby's Blue Blowers—Curtis owned the Apex on Central Avenue in the colored neighbourhood and right about then he opened a new Apex Club in San Francisco so he took his band to open the new place. He hired Leon Herriford to play at the Los Angeles Apex and Leon needed a trumpet player so that made room for me. Curtis stayed in San Francisco for six weeks and then switched us up there for eight weeks. The band was Milton Rousseau and myself, trumpets; Country Allen on trombone; a sax section of Leon, William Griffin, William France; with L. Z. Cooper on piano and Ellis Walsh on drums.*

When we came back to Los Angeles, the Apex had run down and Leon wouldn't go in there. Curtis Mosby had let Walter Johnson, his pianist, go, and Walter confidenced me to work at Jack Johnson's café. Jack was in and out, but he had somebody running it for him. He was kinda slow with his money too. This was for two or three months in early 1931. Leon then went into the Lincoln Theatre on Central Avenue with nine pieces. By that time, he'd hired Baby Lewis, a fine drummer, and we had Bud Scott on guitar, Reg Jones, Edward Barnett on sax, and he used me as the only trumpet; he let Milton go. The job lasted for six months until September 1931. In between the films there was a stage show and revue, and we'd back the acts and do presentations. We were on the stage there, but when the big show came in from New York, we had to go in the pit. The revue was Miller and Slater's.

About fall the Apex was taken over by some Italians and renamed the Club Alabam and we left the theater to go down there. That had a floorshow, the Four Covans Revue, and this went until the spring of '32. The Depression was slow hitting us out there. We were getting $40 a week—you could buy a good suit for $25 then. When business finally starting going down, Pete and Ben, the owners, wanted to cut our salaries. Leon, who had his own business and so was independent, wouldn't accept this so he just quit and pulled the band out.

There was nothing doing then so I jobbed around until the August. On one job I worked with Sonny Clay again, up in San Bernardino—this was in '32. They had a ballroom there, a big ballroom, and we played there Saturdays and Sundays, and then on weekdays, we did the small towns around there.

Sonny had a good trumpet player, his name was Doc Hart [Hart recorded with Clay in 1931] who came here from Arizona; he was an Army man. Good musician. He had a girlfriend and they had to live in San Bernardino. He would come back and forth, mostly every night; he had a fine new car. One night, in coming home from Sacramento back to Los Angeles, he hit a curve and didn't make that curve, hit something, and he died. So the next morning, "Big Boy" [Leonard Davidson]—he was playing for Sonny then—he came to my house early before I was out of bed. First thing he told me, "Doc Hart got killed last night and Sonny Clay sent me down here to see if you would come up there and take his place?" So I did but I didn't stay with him too long. Sonny? He had a kinda big mouth and talked a lot. He finally quit playing piano and went to [work for] the Post Office. He was a heavy drinker. The last time I saw Sonny, he lived in Watts; he was in the Post Office then, and I was with Kid Ory. This was in 1947, and we were getting ready to go to San Francisco. He wanted to talk to me but I was in a hurry because I was going to catch the night train. He knew I was with Ory and was making good money—I made better money with Ory than any other band—and he said, "Big shot, you ain't got time to talk to me." That was the last time.

George Bryant took over as musical director of the Georgia Minstrels, and I joined their combined brass band and orchestra in October '32 to play for their shows. George Bryant had wanted me to join the show from the very beginning, but I didn't want to work with no minstrel show. That was in the August so he hired Claude Kennedy instead. He was a powerhouse, almost like King Porter, and he had dentures; what was so wonderful about him being such a [great] trumpet player were those dentures! I heard he was out here earlier, quite a while before I got out here and he went back. When Claude came back later, I think it was in '27, he brought his own band from Texas, eight or nine pieces, something like that. Good band, too. His drummer was an eccentric type of drummer.

The Minstrels went out in Orange County to break the show in before they opened up at Loew's State Theatre in downtown Los Angeles for a week; then they played one-nighters up to San Francisco. By the time they got to San Francisco—this is October now—jobs were so scarce, I tell you what happened: we [Leon's band] were working what we called Little Teddies; it was paying us two dollars a night and those Little Teddies was nothing but moonshine, speakeasies, and soon as the police catch them, they had to close. Finally, Leon got a job at a little supper club in Huntington Beach. I said, oh, this is a nice club; this wasn't no speakeasy. There'll be a nice little salary on this job, and I asked Leon how much did it pay and you know what he told me? "It don't pay anything; we just working for tips." That was the last straw. I sent George Bryant a telegram: "I'm ready to join the show" and I went on the road.

It was very interesting. I really enjoyed it. George Bryant was a fine musician and he could write. Just say that you in the band and you ain't got a part. "You got no part?" "No, Mr Bryant"—we called him Mr Bryant, see—and after about a minute, you have your part. I think George Bryant did stay with the Minstrels. His last job before he retired. It was the first time I ever really traveled on the road. Right in the middle of the Depression. The show opened in Los Angeles under Fanchon and Marco's production, the big booking agents. They took over the Minstrels. They called the show "Fanchon and Marco's Idea." At one time, they had at least twenty-five groups on the road. We played all the major cities, the largest and finest Fox theaters wherever we went, traveled all the way up from Los Angeles to Vancouver, down to Chicago, Denver, across Canada and the northern part of the United States, down to Boston, New York, Philadelphia, and back to Los Angeles.

Shows are kinda boring, where you're playing the same thing every night, but this way it was different because you're playing the same show but it's a different audience every time. Maybe this audience is cold; that audience is warm. That made it interesting to see how audiences take to the shows. We had to ballyhoo before the first show, average three shows a day, and if they didn't have a house band then we played. We had forty people in the show; that's including the musicians and everybody. It was all men on the show. We had six blackface comedians; even those that didn't need it would put on blackface. We had tenor and baritone singers too, with songs like "Old Man River" and ballads. They catered to anybody in those theatres.

Before I went I had to go down and get a transfer from the union. Mutt Carey was our vice president, and he asked me if I was going to let the little schoolboy bands run me out of town. [Trumpeter] *Dootsie Williams* was cheaper than us and getting a little showing. I said I'd rather go out for $35 a week with the Minstrels than get a dollar a night in town. Transportation was included, but I had to pay my own hotel room. We stayed at cheap hotels, $2 a week, me and my buddy.

I quit the show in Bridgeport, Connecticut—we had about two months to go and I got enough of it. I was on the road with them for eight months and I quit. I got tired. I remember catching the bus in New York. Took six days. I left on Sunday night and it was Saturday afternoon when I got to Los Angeles. After that, I jobbed around with Leon again until September '33 when I got an offer to go up to the Capitol Theatre in San Francisco to join Wade Whaley. This was a burlesque theater right on Market Street where Ellis comes into Market. We stayed there six months. There were eight men in the band—four from Oakland, four from Los Angeles. Wade Whaley wrote me a letter and he contacted Ash Hardee and Doug Finis himself and he said, "Now, you bring whoever you want on the other trumpet." I picked Pee Wee Brice. He was already here [Los Angeles] when I came, working at Solomon's with the Herb Williams band; they came here from Texas. He was a nice little smooth trumpet player who'd been with 'Tudi [bassist Ed Garland] at the One-Eleven Dance Hall in Los Angeles. Douglas Finis was the piano player. Very, very good musician. Had to be good because we had to play that show. Went to the Post Office later. Ash, I remember him well. We played together quite often. He was a wino but he could play trombone. Made some good records. He lost his legs—had one of 'em amputated due to diabetes—and he died. His last days, I wasn't in touch with him very much.

Wade was a very nice man, quiet, sober, not the barrel-housey type. With us he just played clarinet. Wade was from New Orleans, and he and Clem Raymond were the two top clarinet men in the Bay Area. It was good music, background for the show. We'd play a popular number as an overture. Stayed on that job until '34. I never did see Wade anymore after that.

I got back in time for Leon Herriford to get the job at Frank Sebastian's Cotton Club, the big club in Culver City. We followed Duke Ellington [Ellington appeared at the Cotton Club April 5–18, 1934] who had followed Les Hite. When we went in, Lionel Hampton joined Leon from Les Hite's Orchestra and Peppy Prince took his place with Hite. The band was myself, Pee Wee Brice, and Red Mack on trumpets. Red did all the solo work and I was always the first trumpet player. Pee Wee wanted to play first but Leon was strict. He was pretty hard-boiled, an ex-Army man and a very good musician. He could always depend on me to hit that note, especially on the slow numbers. If I made a mistake, he'd eat me out. I had to be perfect. One time I let the second trumpet play the lead, and Leon turned around and said, "Who was playing the lead?" I told him Pee Wee was, and he said, "I told you I wanted you playing lead. No one plays lead unless I tell him."

We were playing big-time music. The Mills Brothers were on the show with us in '34. Leon was first sax, with Paul Howard, Emerson Scott, Willie Starks [replaced by Robert Garner, 'Tudi's sax man for years]; Buster Wilson, piano; and Ceelle Burke, guitar. Jonesy [Reggie Jones] was on bass and one day he was sitting with his feet up on the bandstand. Leon wanted him to sit erect. He asked him three times, "Take your foot down and sit up or go home." Jonesy, who had a short fuse, just got up, wrapped his tuba 'round him, and went straight out. We didn't see him again. Johnny Miller, who was later with the King Cole Trio, took his place. He was just a little youngster then. We tried Ory on the trombone playing in that band, but he couldn't make it because he couldn't read. We didn't play nothing by ear; we played from the book and Ory couldn't read it.

We needed a bass player one time and we tried 'Tudi; couldn't use him because he couldn't read either. Paul Howard took William Franz's place on tenor. He and I were pretty friendly and worked together a little bit later in the fifties. He was in the Shriners band when we went to the national convention in Denver, Colorado, in '53.

The band was called "Leon Herriford's Whispering Syncopators featuring Lionel Hampton." Leon was billed as "The Whispering Saxophonist" because he played a whispering sax. We played "Tiger Rag" every night for Hamp as a feature, and he'd go out and play drums on the tables all 'round the café. He used to get carried away sometimes. One night, Leon left him out there and started another song! We stayed there until February of 1935. After we were there three or four months, Frank Sebastian wanted to enlarge his place and go big-time. So he opened up the Lounge Room and he got Ben Pollack's band, which was the forerunner of the old Bob Crosby band, to open in the main room and he cut our band down to seven pieces, cut the show down, and put us in this Lounge Room. That left me as the only trumpet, with two saxes and four rhythm.

Frank had both rooms goin' at the same time. The Cotton Club was a big building and he was making money. Weeknights we'd close the room and make it smaller and then Saturday and Sunday we'd open it up. Ended up it was too heavy for Frank. When Ben Pollack's six-weeks contract was up, he let him go. He closed the Lounge Room and he put us back in the main room and enlarged our band again. Sebastian didn't use two bands again, but he wanted someone frontin' the band that was, say, Cab Calloway style. A showman. Leon wasn't that type of a guy. He was a good musician, a good director, but he wasn't a good front man for a band. So Frank went up to a club on Main Street, somewhere near 12th, and heard Charles Echols. He was one of those trumpet players that would lay down on the floor and play and throw his trumpet way up in the air. Looked good, too. Well-built, and *dressed in a nice white suit. Frank said, "That's the guy I want fronting my band!" So he hired him and Leon said, "What do you want me to do?" And Frank said, "Oh, just sit down there in front." So Leon said, "I ain't goin' to play under that dumb-son-of-a-gun."*

Echols wasn't much of a musician, and he wasn't too much of a trumpet player. He was up there just supposed to be acting the clown. Didn't play one note and he only lasted one week. We had a little trumpet player, his nickname was "Sarge"; he was a nice little trumpet too, could read anything but couldn't take off, just played third trumpet parts. Red took his place because Leon wanted somebody "hot" and Red Mack could go then. At that time, he was one of the best out here. Of course, when the big bands from the east, like Basie or Ellington, came to town, they'd have a jam session, they'd send for Red Mack. Then he lost his chops. Leon quit, took his instruments, and left. Lionel took over that band for eight months and that was his first band. We left the Cotton Club and went on the road from February to July. Mostly dance halls, one-nighters up the Coast, big ballrooms like Sweets Ballroom in Oakland, San Francisco, and some of the different ballrooms in the Bay Area around Oakland. We did play for black audiences in Oakland and San Francisco too, but mostly the audiences were white. After a couple of months, Red Mack jumped down and Herman Grimes came in. After six months, almost all the original guys quit; we couldn't make it with the money we were getting on the road. We weren't too successful so I left in July 1935.

From 1935 to 1942 I was in Hawaii. I left Leon to go to Hawaii. We were working a little nightclub out there at Vermont and Washington called Bud Taylor's. I remember working there with just only five of us at that time. With Leon I was making $15 a week. The job in Hawaii paid better. A piano player named Bernard Banks took a six-piece to Honolulu in October and invited me to join him. The offer was pretty good, and I just wanted to go back to Honolulu. I took my wife with me and sent for my daughter later. I was on the bandstand there for six years straight. I would call that my heyday. I was in top shape in Honolulu.

Banks's offer had come from a Chinese American businessman named J. T. Yung, who owned and operated the Casino Ballroom, a taxi-dance hall in central downtown Honolulu. Banks rounded up six musicians including Andy Blakeney and helped by the drummer Nat "Monk" McFay, an old school friend from Wichita Falls, Kansas, who had lately arrived in Los Angeles. Banks's band left San Pedro on the SS *Lurline* in April 1935 and was met by Yung on the dock and presented with leis, the traditional Hawaiian wreath of flowers. They started their job that evening, billed as Bernard Banks and His Five Clouds of Rhythm and playing without a break from 8:00 p.m. to midnight, six nights a week, and broadcasting regularly. According to McFay, they played "popular music for the slow dances but swung the hell out of them for fast ones." Racial prejudice was at a minimum: a welcome change from the prevailing attitude in Los Angeles itself, though some U.S. servicemen, especially those from the South, were troublesome. The band's personnel changed often, but Blakeney stayed until the end.

I shouldn't have gone because to tell you truth we were being paid starvation wages. Our wage was $27.50 a week plus tips. Tips would average a couple of dollars a night. Tips didn't mean nothing—we'd stop at the restaurant on the way home and between a sandwich and a cup of coffee and a half pint of liquor, it was all gone! Liquor didn't go to my head; I always controlled my drinking even when I used to drink heavy. We had Artis Bryant on trombone and a sax man from Washington, D.C., called Charlie [actually Charlie Wright]. I forget the others. Our leader suffered an automobile accident after we'd been there for a year or two and had to go home. He never did get straight after that—he was unconscious for three weeks. That's when I took over the band. Called it the Brown Cats of Rhythm. I think Monk [McFay] helped me find that name.

The original two or three guys left, and I had to reorganize with local musicians. I used some Hawaiians, a Portuguese piano man, Filipino sax and trombone, and a Japanese played second trumpet. I had no problems; we were working in a taxi-dance hall catering mostly to sailors. By then, we had one trumpet—that was me—one trombone, three saxes, and three rhythm. And a singer. We used to play stock arrangements, copied from records, like, for instance, "In the Mood"; that was made by Glenn Miller. We'd buy that arrangement, play it just like they played it on the record. I blacked out one time. We were playing this Glenn Miller arrangement, and on the very ending of this tune, where they got four trumpets and I'm the only one, after I got through that one high note, I blacked out. I'd had to play all the way through, just me.

Once an hour you'd make an announcement and play a long number and every girl in the house would have a partner. We'd do that just to help business. Usually the guys would wait until you'd play the introduction and if they liked it, they'd go get the girls. If they didn't, they'd stand there until you played something they liked. But for this long number they'd always grab a girl. That eliminated the boredom of just playing a chorus. That was interesting.

Trombone player named Happy Johnson came back from China with his band (in 1936) and stopped over in Honolulu for four days on their way back to Los Angeles. We needed a saxophone player so Kirt Bradford stayed on and worked with us. He was a fine alto saxophone. He could really play. After he left me, he came back to the States and worked with local bands and finally he went with Jimmie Lunceford. He took Willie Smith's place. Of course, we had Henry Coker on trombone who did so well with Count Basie later on.

My wife and I, and my daughter, came back to Los Angeles in 1937, stayed three months. Lee Young had a little job down on San Pedro one time, four pieces, that's all, with Buster Wilson on piano. I was playing trumpet and we had a trombone player, Thelma Porter's husband. He was a dancer and a performer who played trombone on the side. Can't think of his name. Later on, I reorganized the last band I had out there at the Casino. I sent for Bill Winston, the drummer, and Leon Scott on second trumpet, both from Chicago.

Down Beat, October 1, 1939
Writers Find Jump Band in Honolulu—The boys produce an uncommon jump and drive which should aid them immensely on the road to prominence. In general the band styles after Basie. It has been together about a year now and possesses a stellar drummer, Nathaniel [Monk] McFay who idolizes Jo Jones and whose work might easily be mistaken for Jo's. They were buddies once. Andrew Blakeney, trumpet and head man, is an alumnus of the old Les Hite band. Kurt [sic] Bradford, alto, is the other ace soloist.

Down Beat, April 1, 1941
Stuff Seems To Be On The Stir in Hawaii—This town's hot fans find their stuff at the Casino where a coloured crew managed by Andy Blakeney bats out the real thing six nights a week. Cecil Carter and Leon Shadowen [sic] play buckets full of saxophone and the leader gets a lot of Louis on horn.

Down Beat, July 15, 1941
Honolulu: At the Casino, the loss of the excellent trappist Monk McFay to "those people" [the law], Cecil Carter to a Sanitarium, and the truly fine trombonist L.C. Coker [Henry Coker] to the draft board put the skids on the town's top jive crew. But nothing daunted, leader Blakeney scuttled back to the coast and will return soon with more colored cats to fill the empty chairs. In the meantime, Rafael Greagor, Leon Shadowin, and Dewitt Ray sit sadly and play, trying like hell not to hear the substitutes.

We worked right up until Pearl Harbor [December 7, 1941]. I can remember that night very definitely. For a start it seemed as though everybody was in town. The place was crowded. They were all servicemen out there. Then suddenly, all hell broke loose. So naturally we lost our jobs. I never did have a chance to play anymore. It took us six months to get home. There was no transportation or ships; the government took over all the shipping. You had to apply for a booking and wait your turn. All the entertainment stopped so I bought and drove a taxicab most of the rest of the time, taking sailors to and from Pearl Harbor. That way I was my own boss. Most everybody else in the band had gotten a government defense job. I had my wife and child with me. My daughter was seventeen—one more year there and she would have graduated. When we left I went to Chicago because that's where I started out in the music business. I thought I'd make a fresh start but there was nothing there. I found that out in five days. So I came back to California but I wouldn't come back to Los Angles. I stayed three months in San Francisco before coming back down here. Somehow, I didn't like Los Angeles. I wanted to go someplace else. But things wasn't so good up there. I worked two or three gigs with some guys I knew, and I got a job in the daytime, went out to the shipyards. Finally my wife and I got here [Los Angeles] on the train, and I called the union and that night, before dark, somebody called me up, wanted me to go to work.

It was Carl Johnson who wanted me to play my horn on a steady job. Just four pieces. It was just a little supper-club club, around 45th Street at Vernon and Broadway. They didn't have no show. I had started to school to learn welding. I wanted to go to the shipyard here. Finally, after taking lessons about three or four weeks, they sent me down to Wilmington to work for Calship. They were making the Liberty ships and I was a production welder. Working daytime down there and working in this little club with Carl on drums [he was the son of the president of the union] I would get sleepy. It came to my time to play, I was too sleepy and he fired me after four or five months. "I better get somebody else; you working too hard." Floyd Turnham and two or three other musicians did that, working down the shipyard.

The Great Black Way: L.A. in the 1940s and the Lost African-American Renaissance, New York, 2006

Among the fired shipyard workers was a jazz trumpeter named Andrew Blakeney, a welder at Calship. Blakeney had played with Lionel Hampton, Les Hite and the cream of L.A.'s first generation of jazz musicians. He made a better living as a trumpeter than a shipyard worker, Blakeney told federal officials investigating the Boilermakers. But he was too old for the draft and he wanted to do his part for the war effort. Walter Williams had personally recruited Blakeney to lead a group that was suing the Big Three shipbuilders and asking for a temporary injunction against the ongoing firing of black employees who were refusing to pay their dues to the segregated union. While he waited for his case to work its way through the courts, Blakeney got his horn out and started practising again!

Ceelle Burke had the band out at the Bal Tabarin in Gardena. Eight pieces. Nightclub, they had a nice floor show, not as big as the one at the Cotton Club but still about fifteen to twenty people. It was the same producers who had the show at the Cotton Club the whole time I was at the Bal Tabarin. Caughey [Roberts] arranged some of it and Maxwell Davis arranged some of it, all special arrangements. We played a little jazz and Ceelle featured Latin music and Hawaiian music. He played the steel guitar. *Orendorff was with Ceelle Burke when I first came back when he had only one trumpet, and he tried to get the boss to hire me in addition but he said no, couldn't afford it, and so it remained until George* [Orendorff] *was drafted* [February 1943] *three or four months later. Ceelle came to my house one morning: "It's all set; you start to work tonight. Orendorff gotta go to the Army." So I went to work that night. I continued to do the welding job and play with Ceelle. For a whole year. The only way I was able to hold up with Ceelle, it was a little more interesting; there was a little more exposure to play with him.*

Orendorff went to camp and stayed to camp just one year, didn't go no further. He got discharged, couldn't do duty or something like that, and naturally the war was still going on and the boss had to hire him back. Now the boss couldn't pay for two trumpets but he liked my playing, see, so he wasn't going to fire me off the job so we had two trumpets. I was out there three-and-a-half years. Caughey Roberts worked in the band for a little while; Marvin Johnson too; Arcima Taylor, he was out there; Maxwell Davis was another sax; and we had one of the Erwing Brothers playing lead sax. Lee Gibson was playing drums, and we had a fine Mexican bass player called Joe Mendoza. We had several piano players, one was Charlie Lawrence, Charlie Davis another, and a couple of others. Joe Liggins one time.

The owner was a Greek guy with a bald head. Ceelle had been out there seven years and he said, "I'm tired looking at that old bald head. I want another job," and he quit. Curtis Mosby was trying a comeback. He had the Club Alabam again [Mosby had opened it as the Apex Nite Club at 4015 Central in August 1928 and it was renamed as Club Alabam in 1935] *and naturally he wanted Ceelle's band so Ceelle offered to go up there. We weren't up there but two weeks and Curtis didn't have the money to pay us. Finally, we stayed up there about four weeks altogether, and he was a week behind with his paychecks and Ceelle said, "I want my money or I'm going to quit" so Curtis said, "I'm gonna give it to you" but he never did. Ceelle called the union and Curtis Mosby already had another band ready to take our place and cheaper too. The union said, "He can't hire no band and put it in front of you guys until he pay you off in full," and that was how we got our money. So then Ceelle's band broke up. They had no place to go.*

That was in '46. Curtis owes me some money now. Mosby was crooked; he had spent two years in McNeil Island, the government prison up in Washington State. Then Ceelle formed a big band and we made some nice records [Burke's orchestra with Blakeney accompanied Ivie Anderson on Exclusive in 1945–1946]. *It was a swing band on the Benny Goodman style: three trumpets, two trombones. Sixteen pieces. We worked around the coast and in nightclubs with floorshows right on until I retired. We had Caughey Roberts on alto and Floyd Turnham in that band. Floyd was another good musician. If you wanted good music, then Floyd could do it. He should have been better* known. I later went with Lena Horne's piano man and arranger Horace Henderson for a spell. He was one of the top arrangers, and his trumpet section was myself, Jake Porter, George Orendorff and Teddy Buckner. I remember leaving his band in 1946 and deciding to retire from music. I felt I'd had my day. I was getting close to fifty, and there was a lot of good, strong musicians coming up.

I needed a steady income, a regular paycheck, so I started at the Los Angeles Board of Education in September '46. I was a tool keeper, in charge of the tools, issuing them out. I never was a janitor like some people said. I had started work first with the Board of Education in '43, worked there for about four or five months. I took examinations and they hired me as a sub—it was during the summer when the guys were taking their vacations—and when everybody was back to work, they didn't have a permanent job for me so they sent me down to the warehouse and that was all right for a while. They said then, "We gonna send you as truck driver's helper," and that was a nice job. But this happened to be an ash truck. This guy would go out to the different schools out in the Valley and empty the incinerators. I said, "How you gonna empty them?" "See those shovels back there?" he said. "Shovels? Put me out; I ain't going." So I quit. The music job paid twice as much as I got at the Board of Education. When I first started my salary was $153 a month. I was getting about $65 or $70 a week with Ceelle. I didn't go back to the Board of Education until 1946. Somehow or another they kept my name on the payroll so my seniority started from '43 right up to '64 when I retired. My retirement took in twenty-one years with the board.

From September '46 until May '47, I didn't even have a gig because I'd been out there so long with Ceelle some people in town thought I was still in Honolulu. I didn't put down my horn. The day job wasn't enough to pay my expenses. Anyway I struggled through until Kid Ory and Bud Scott came by and picked me up that May, I think it was. I was living in South Central and they came to my house. They wanted to know what I was doing. I said, "I ain't doing nothing!"

They asked if I wanted to join Ory's band. He had a lot of gigs lined up. It was just a casual thing at first, dates around Los Angeles and San Francisco. Ory made good money, you know. Something like $20 or $25 a gig instead of $10 like the others paid. When Ory reorganized his band, he had Mutt [Carey] playing, but he and Mutt didn't get along so Mutt quit. I came in after Mutt Carey left to organize a band of his own. First he got an agent and they sent him to New York City as a soloist. Then he came back and he liked to compete with Ory, but it didn't work. His drummer was named Everett Walsh—he'd worked with 'Tudi at the One-Eleven, had a good voice—and the clarinet player was Leonard Davidson [he went into the real-estate business later] and the trombone was Leon White. Buster Wilson was the piano player. Mutt just gigged around town and he didn't live too long after that

[Carey died in September 1948]. *Davidson, called him Big Boy, he came over one night and said, "I got a gig for you. Mutt has passed. We need a trumpet player to play this gig." This was in the Ory times, but I wasn't doing anything that particular night so I played the gig for Mutt. It was Mutt's gig, somewhere on Avalon Boulevard.*

We [Ory's band] *played the Blackshears on Fillmore in San Francisco, run by an ex-heavyweight fighter, for two months, September to October 1947. This was a big place and they needed two bands. Then we opened the Club New Orleans across the street from the Blackshears. This was in December, just before Christmas 1947. Stayed there two months. They paid a big salary: $125 a week. Of course he didn't pay everybody that. Scale was $67 a week. The owner was from New Orleans so after two months he says, "I'm getting tired of working for the band." He wanted to cut us down to union scale. Ory said no. So we left. He got a local band. Two months later we had to go back because the crowd just dropped down. We went back twice. The first time we opened with Buster on piano. The next time we had Dudley Brooks on piano. The last time we were there we opened with the third one, Charlie Lawrence. We worked steady at the Rendezvous Ballroom* [Balboa] *in '48, with Buster.*

From then, I ran steady with Ory. Barney Bigard was with us when I first started with the band. He was just out here; he had quit Ellington, thinking to form his own band and trying to get started on his own. Joe Darensbourg was sick or something and he finally joined the band later. We played the whole music for a picture: Crossfire [RKO, 1947]; *we're not in the picture but the music is our music. We played "Winding Boy." Bud Scott was in the band then. We'd go back and forth to San Francisco, and for a while, I commuted up there for weekends. I said, "Ory, I have a steady job. I can't depend on your job." He said, "What do you say that you come up and play with me every Friday, Saturday, and Sunday? When you get off work, you catch a plane, come up here and play, and Sunday night, you catch a plane back." I did that for a couple of weeks. There was another place in San Francisco* [Blanco's Cotton Club, December 1948] *where they cooked steaks right in front of the bandstand. Ory and I was working at that place. Now, I'm also working with the Board of Education and I had to be at work on a Sunday morning, and we had two nights before the job was up so I sent a telegram to Los Angeles to Winslow "Winnow" Allen to come up and work those two nights for me. Winslow had his own plane—he could fly—so he flew up to take my job.*

Winnow had his own band around here for quite a while. His brother Country and I were buddies in Herriford's band—we roomed together when we was on the road. Country could pass [for white]. *One time we went to Ventura, that was when we were with Lionel, he slipped off to a white place to get him a drink. Evidently the bartender knew this black band was in town.*

He must have recognized Country and he wouldn't serve him. Country came back and told us. Humiliation is good for you! He was grouchy, a type of guy who wanted to argue, and Leon wanted to fire him but he couldn't get anybody to play them [trombone] parts! He was here when I came. He was working with Curtis Mosby, with the Blue Blowers; that's when they were at Solomon's Penny Dance down on Grand Avenue. That's when I first met Country and Winslow was up in Oakland somewhere. He came down to Los Angeles later.

To tell the truth, I didn't take to it [Dixieland] so easy. I got a kick out of it for a while, but it was kind of monotonous. I never had confined myself. I played in marching bands, concert bands, community symphony orchestras, minstrel shows; I'd play anything in music, but Ory confined himself to Dixieland and I didn't like it so well. But money rules! I made good money so I made myself satisfied. One thing about Ory's band, you could dance to his music. The white bands played too fast. I remember the Ory band played opposite Les Brown for a college prom. They played one set; then we played. We had people on the dance floor. We were used to playing with good bands. One time, we played a jazz concert at a big ballroom and had a parade from the Biltmore Hotel out to Venice. Tommy Dorsey's band was in front on a truck and Kid Ory was on a coach between them and Benny Goodman's small group. Benny Goodman wouldn't ride on the truck. There was a dozen bands in that.

We played the same things over and over. Ory liked the trumpet not to go too far away from the melody. He'd bring me back if I went too far out. If I faltered with that lead, then Ory would leap in and play lead instead. He was very particular about this, and he had a big book of lead sheets for the band. Funny thing is he could never play "Ory's Creole Trombone" himself, although every time he got drunk he tried to play it.

It's a lot of fun thinking back to my experiences with the band, like when Montudie and Ory had that fight. They didn't fight on the stand like some people said; they got off the bandstand and said, "We'll go outside and fight." Ory was stationed at the Beverly Cavern for six months straight, and that was right near my home so I could manage my day job and work nights with him, taking my annual leave and sick leave for the out-of-town jobs. I couldn't go to New York when they did the national tour [April 1948]; I was afraid to take the chance. Looking back, I'm so glad because that's how I'm living now, on my pension. You see, I retired from my Education Board job in February 1964, but I never stopped playing. I retired early because my wife was very sick. She died in the October.

Anyway, at the Cavern, I got aggravated with Ory and thought maybe I'd leave and then Ory walked out. I'd been getting kind of evil on the bandstand, kind of bored with the band and the type of tunes. That was very narrow for me. See, Ory didn't play for no big shows in his life. Ory was a *nice fella to me. I got along fine with him until the end. He'd call out numbers and I'd groan. And I says, "Blakeney, you better quit," so I did. It was my fault.*

I was with Ory over two years. Teddy Buckner took my place. The owner of the Cavern [Dan Rittenberg] *was disappointed with Ory suddenly giving him notice to quit because Ory was still going big, so he sent me a telegram and wanted me to go in straightaway with a band to take Ory's place. I brought him in a band with Willie Woodman on trombone, Jonesy* [Reggie Jones] *on bass, Alton Redd on drums, and Arcima Taylor on clarinet. I thought mine was a better band than Ory's, but I just didn't have the personality he had. This was '49, around Thanksgiving. I was there four weeks.*

The first week we opened Albert Nicholas came to town and right away I hired him. Arcima had said he would go as soon as I found another man. But just before the week was up he changed his mind. He said he wanted to work another week and I'd have to pay him or he'd go to the union. I was going to hire Nicholas regardless so I did hire him, but I had to pay Taylor for the extra week, out of my own pocket. I never did enjoy being a bandleader. I preferred being a sideman. The bandleader thing was thrust on me. I met Alton Redd when I first came out here. He was working with Charlie Echols at a taxi-dance and then he worked with Les Hite, too, for a little while. He couldn't read; he could spell a bit. I worked with him quite often. Nice, friendly guy. We were good buddies. We had a kind of agreement: "Anytime I get a job, I'm gonna hire you" and vice versa.

Then a little later, I went in [to the Beverly Cavern] *with another band, a good band. I had Bob McCracken on clarinet, Smitty* [Warren Smith] *on trombone, Gideon* [Honoré] *on piano, Alton was on drums with that for a while. He was just playing jobs around town, in night clubs, small groups. He never did play in a big band, couldn't read the parts, see. Alton was in some kind of official capacity with the union before amalgamation.*

After leaving the Ory band, Blakeney concentrated on playing Dixieland (despite his reservations) with any number of revivalist bands, some of them under his own name. He also performed for twenty years with the Los Angeles Urban Concert Band under Millard Lacey, initially as first trumpet alongside his longtime friend Leo Dejan, playing union-sponsored concerts in the city's public parks and playgrounds every Sunday in the summer and with the Elks and Thomas Waller Lodge No. 49 marching bands. As he was at pains to point out, "I played all kinds of music." He was a stalwart member of Southern California Hot Jazz Society and participated in its Resurrection Brass Band playing parties, parades, festivals, and funerals under the leadership of Gordon Mitchell and Al Rieman with his trumpeter "pal" George Orendorff.

Down Beat, November 3, 1949

Beverly Cavern continues exclusive presentation of red-hot jazz, as expertly played by ANDREW BLAKENEY'S BAND.... Sidemen are L.Z. Cooper [piano], Frank "Devil" Dandridge [bass], Alton Redd [drums], Arcima Taylor [alto sax] and William Woodman, Sr. [trombone].

Down Beat, December 2, 1949

Andy Blakeney, former Ory trumpeter and his Chicago Dixielanders holding Beverly Caverns stand, with operators dickering for George Lewis New Orleans band.

Down Beat, March 24, 1950

Albert Nicholas launched a new band at Virginia's, Colorado Boulevard spot between Pasadena and Glendale. Has Andy Blakeney (t), Alton Redd on drums, L.Z. Cooper, piano, and Reggie Jones, bass.

I went back to the Cavern several times with George Jenkins, drums; Arcima; and trombonist Streamline Ewing [his first experience playing Dixieland]. From there, Teddy Buckner recommended me to take over from him at the 400 Club [1955]. I had Streamline; Phil Gomez, clarinet; L. Z. Cooper, piano; 'Tudi on bass; and Ram Hall, drums. Later on, about 1956, George Lewis was at the Cavern, and Rose Steadman, the manager, asked me if I wanted to work. She suggested I bring in Warren Smith [trombone], Bob McCracken [clarinet], L. Z., 'Tudi, and George Vann on drums. I stayed until Al Dietsch took over. We packed the place. That was when I built my new home in Pasadena. October 1956.

Bob Allen: *Andy Blakeney hired me on my very first professional gig. It was 1961 at the Beverly Cavern every Friday and Saturday night. The union scale was $16. Andy didn't know that at that time I was in the Navy stationed out at Los Alamitos. On a couple of occasions I ditched my duty station to play with the band. Besides Andy, it was William Woodman on trombone; Arcima Taylor, clarinet; Johnny St. Cyr, banjo; Austin McCoy, piano; Syl Rice on drums; and me on string bass. What I was doing there, I'll never know.*

Melody Maker, May 1, 1965

Keith Smith just back from Los Angeles says he "played with Johnny St. Cyr, Ed Garland and a nice clarinettist Caughey Robert in a parade for charity. Andy Blakeney, George Orendorff and myself were on trumpets, Dick Cary on alto horn and Alton Purnell was Grand Marshal. Andy Blakeney is the king out there, a darned good musician and very underrated."

Dan Barrett: *Andy was the one who met me at the musicians union—this was Local 47 in Hollywood—when I was about 16* [1971] *to support me for my audition for membership of the union. Another time, Andy came to my high school. We had a project for our U.S. history class where we had to come up with some kind of presentation. Mine was on the history of jazz, and as part of it I got Andy and some other New Orleans–style musicians to come in. Frank Demond played piano, Andy played trumpet, I played trombone, and we had a clarinetist, banjo, and bass. We set up in the band room and marched the U.S. history class down there. Then we played "Hindustan" and a couple of other tunes. Later, I got to play many times with Andy. Those were great days.*

Coda, July/August 1971

Los Angeles—On May 31, Memorial Day, Gordon Mitchell and his Southern California Hot Jazz Society marching band held the spotlight in a four-band thing put on for that occasion. This authentic band originally conceived by Gordon Mitchell in the mid-fifties is recognised as the only authentic group of its kind outside of New Orleans. New Orleans veterans Mike DeLay, Andy Blakeney and Grand Marshall Alton Purnell are, and have long been, a standard part of the cast. Another traditional jazz band patterned after the Kid Ory style is making some headway here. Led by local trombonist Roger Jamieson, the New Orleanians drew a responsive crowd on a repeat performance at the Exclusive Palos Verde Country Club in Palos Verde Estates just south of Los Angeles. The July 17 affair included Jamieson, trombone, Andy Blakeney, trumpet, Ron Going, clarinet, Alton Purnell, piano, Montudie Garland, bass, and Sylvester Rice, drums.

Coda, February 1973

Los Angeles—Frank Demond's Salutation Tuxedo Band recently opened up for a four nights a week gig at the Club New Orleans in Orange County. The cast included Demond on trombone, Andy Blakeney, trumpet, Ron Going, clarinet, Alton Purnell, piano, Vince Saunders, banjo, and Lee Wedberg, drums.

During all this time, I had a bar and restaurant in Altadena. I opened December 1, 1965; kept it up until 1971. I leased it out for a single year; he couldn't keep up the payments so I closed it up. My niece drug me into that. She and her husband had a bar in Milwaukee. She was separated and she wanted to go into business for herself. I lent her money and I had the license. Eighty percent of the money invested was mine so I thought I might as well take over so I did. We made money on it. I was the first black man up in that area in business. Then came some competition with a chicken shack and a whiskey place. At the same time, I was playing at Disneyland on the riverboat [the *Mark Twain*]. *I had a hard time getting away from there. If I had wanted, I could have stayed. I didn't want the job, but I was just asked to* come out there to take Mike DeLay's place. I wanted to quit. I had my business; I had my investments.

Blakeney's final (musical) hurrah came with the formation of the Legends of Jazz in 1973, a band of veterans assembled to play Ory-style jazz by the British drummer Barry Martyn, then resident in Los Angeles. In conjunction with his original partner in Crescent Jazz Productions, the businessman and writer Floyd Levin, Martyn created a program of wide-ranging U.S. and European tours, often combining the Legends with other established artists such as Benny Carter and Barney Bigard. Their touring show, *A Nite in New Orleans*, was successful in Europe and brought many other elderly musicians, including the powerful trumpeter Jake Porter, into belated public prominence. After Louis Nelson, Garland, and Darensbourg left the band, Blakeney stayed on, even though he was sometimes at odds with Martyn over musical matters. He recognized, as did Darensbourg, that Martyn and Levin rewarded the band members well and cared for them.

Barry did my career a lot of good. Financially as well. It was enjoyable at first. We got on fine all the way through, except we argued a lot and sometimes our arguments were so intense I thought they were going to fire me. Barry and I were buddies off the stand but not on the stand. He wouldn't swing. Ory swung and he was Dixieland. Barry did not swing. I wanted that four-beat danceable rhythm, and Barry wanted that two-beat, show-type rhythm. I said, "I can play better to that kind of rhythm rather than that old slow, lazy beat." See, 'Tudi was a great one on four beats—man, he'd sit in the back and go boom—but later when he got older, he got lazy and he didn't swing. Barry wanted to play in the old-time New Orleans style, two beat, and he was serious about it. I'd argue with him and I'd put it up to four but he'd insist on just beating two.

I feel I was way on the downgrade as a trumpet player when I started with him. My highlights would be all them early days in Los Angeles because I've had some very important positions, playing in different bands. Barry had heard the records I made with Ory. He wanted to repeat them. One was "Snag It," but I couldn't make it. Another was "Maryland My Maryland." Same thing. I was always more pleased with the records that I made with Ory. Better than what I did with Barry.

I guess I would have stayed with Barry longer if I didn't have that bad accident. That's what did it. I was up in Lansing, Michigan, with Barry, and I wanted to visit some people from my hometown and told the guys I'd see them at the concert. Anyway, I got lost and I was asleep at the wheel when I crashed. Unconscious. Passer-by woke me up. The car was demolished. He got me to the hall and Barry told me, "You going to the doctor," and Floyd Turnham's wife took me there. They said I had no broken bones so I took another tour to Florida, but I began to feel weak, couldn't get on the band-

stand. Back home, I had a stroke, fell out of bed unconscious. Paramedics took me to the hospital, and they found I had a blood clot on my brain. So they operated and I didn't know anything until I came to the next day. That whole year, 1982, I was off. I didn't play at all. They paid me seven months' compensation. I was making almost as much as when I was playing.

It was around September when I got to where I could play again, and Barry had this big guy, Herbert Permillion, playing trumpet in my place. "Now that you can play again, I'm going to have both of you. I'm going to have you go out on one trip and I'll take him out on the next trip," he said. So he took me out in January of '83. When I come back, Barry didn't have nothing until April and then we were getting ready to go to Pennsylvania. I had bought another car, and on my way home, something happened; I lost control and ran into a building on a busy street in Pasadena. Hit a lamp post and I was injured. They had to take me to the hospital. I had to call Barry right away. That's the last time I toured.

Despite these setbacks, Blakeney carried on performing with trombonist Roger Jamieson's New Orleanians, playing local residencies and making the occasional recording date. When he felt the moment was right, he introduced the female trumpeter Clora Bryant to Jamieson to take over from him. "I was losing my lip. I was dissatisfied with my playing. I know how I used to play. I knew what I could do. Now, I can't do it. I'm sensitive, see. That made me feel bad," he said.

Andy Blakeney Appreciation Day was held in March 1987 in Downey to mark his retirement from active music, with many of his musician and jazz club friends on hand.

Louis was my favorite man and trumpet player. He and Ory were friends, and we played on a lot of programs together, his band and Ory's band on the same stage. I can remember at the New Orleans Swing Club in San Francisco when Louis was working with the small band, the All Stars, up there and we'd get off before he did, and every night he'd come down. I remember his tune that I liked the best was "Dippermouth Blues"; they called it "Sugarfoot Stomp." I copied his solo note for note and could play it just like he did or that's what I thought.

I never heard Charlie Parker and Dizzy Gillespie [their quintet opened at Billy Berg's in Los Angeles on December 10, 1945]. *The only one* [bopper] *I heard was another trumpet player bebopping during that same time, Howard McGhee. I used to listen to him. Howard McGhee was playing at a nightclub a few doors down from the Alabam, right on the corner of 41st and Central, and I went in there several times to listen to him because he had a nice little group. I was just a customer listening to them. I enjoyed them playing bebop. I enjoyed listening to it.*

> *His drummer used to be with me in Honolulu. Monk McFay. Monk couldn't play for them beboppers. His type of drumming was for men like me. So Monk didn't stay with him too long. Those other guys, I never did hear them. Well, it was a strange type of music. I couldn't play that style or that type of music. You know, I never was a musician at heart. What I was interested in as a young man was making money. That's why I got into music. I have known musicians; they didn't want to do anything else but play. If they couldn't make it as musicians when times got tough, they'd go nuts. That wouldn't bother me. I'd go out there and get a job, sweeping the floor, anything.*

The late Canadian jazz writer and *Coda* magazine editor John Norris summed up Andy Blakeney's special qualities in 1977 like this: "His smoky, hot tone, excellent intonation and clean articulation provided the kind of lead trumpet that this music needs but which is so rarely found today. He is also a powerful, well-rounded musician who seemingly can handle any material—whether trite or interesting. It is a misfortune that he has chosen to live in Los Angeles—a city which does little to laud its talented residents."

Chapter Two

Gideon Joseph "Gid" Honoré Jr.

Piano

Driving from Woodland Hills down into South Central Los Angeles on a sun-lit October day in 1979, I was surprised when clarinetist Joe Darensbourg, my driver, leaned over to trigger the car's central locking mechanism. It was a precaution, he explained, as we entered the city's reputedly crime-ridden African American section. Happily, nothing occurred subsequently that seemed remotely threatening.

Joe had arranged for us to meet two of his long-term associates, the drummer Sylvester Rice and pianist Gid Honoré at the latter's house on Brighton Avenue, a tree-lined street that seemed almost eerily quiet. Surrounded on all four sides by a metal-mesh safety fence, the Honoré's single-story home was a pink stucco confection, set among other distinctive properties. Its living room interior was equally striking, dominated by a white grand piano and with its own huge, walk-in bar. The décor was pink, and the furniture quite fancy; even the telephone was pink. The Honorés were welcoming, Gid quickly dispensing the first of several Budweiser beers, and my initial interview with Rice went well.

When I broached the idea of an interview with Gid himself, he bristled, saying that he would need at least $1,000 in payment before he could consider such an idea. Hearing this, Joe absented himself speedily on an unspecified errand, muttering that this was between Gid and me. Without the funds that would have enabled me to comply and with a sinking heart, I thought on my feet and mentioned that I had recently completed an interview in Holland with drummer Wallace Bishop who I knew to be an old Chicago hand. With that the atmosphere changed. "You know Bish? He was one of my best

Gideon Honoré and the Andy Blakeney Band, Beverly Cavern, Hollywood, California, 1956. Courtesy Andy Blakeney.

friends." Gid smiled. "I knew everyone in that family, his mother and his sister, too."

The interview done, despite a moment of concern when a minor earthquake (4.1 on the Richter scale and the second of the day) set the living room chandelier rocking, Joe and I were entertained to a Louisiana-style lunch of red beans and rice, with salad and cornbread followed by Jell-O. Relaxed and gracious, Gid and his wife, Beulah, a former dancer, reminisced about working in Chicago's gangster-owned clubs, emphasizing their collective view that the likes of Al Capone and Capone associate "Machine Gun" Jack McGurn were "all kind and great for musicians."

A true New Orleans Creole, born in the Crescent City on January 8, 1904, Honoré had relocated to Chicago in his teens and quickly gained a foothold in that city's busy, segregated entertainment scene, living at 6045 South Park, before making for Los Angeles with his family after World War II. Along the way, his recording opportunities were few, just four official sessions, a fact that didn't appear to concern him at all. In a career littered with club engagements in the United States and Canada, some quite short-lived, Gid seems never to have been out of work. Just to list the prominent soloists with whom he performed is ample testimony to his qualities. I was not privileged to hear him play, but it was clear that he was a well-prepared musician, able to adapt readily from solo to trio to combo work, before returning to his New Orleans roots when the Dixieland revival suggested it. Arthritis hastened his retirement from active playing in the 1980s, and Gideon Honoré died in Los Angeles on September 15, 1990.

Gideon Honoré: Los Angeles, October 17, 1979

My father was of a French origin, but not my mother. She was a seamstress and played mandolin. When I was about seven or eight, after my father died, I was going to school and taking lessons from Professor [William J.] *Nickerson. He was very famous and then came Mrs. Massey. She played the organ, but I didn't want to play organ; I just played piano. Well, now, they said piano players was playing in these dives and people didn't want their children to be associated with that kind of life. It was supposed to be a low life* [laughs]. *I thought this was all wrong and I wanted to change it, from what they were saying to what I thought it should be.*

And that's why I started to taking music, associating with the different people that aspired to be good musicians. See, there was [pianists] *Steve Lewis and Red Cayou—he was very good; he died some years ago. They weren't from my neighborhood; they were from downtown. I grew up with players like Earl and Anatieve Wiggins, Napoleon Kiko* [or Cato]; *he was a pianist, also very good. I knew Freddy Keppard and King Oliver, Baby Dodds and Johnny Dodds, then all the different piano players like "Tink"* [Xavier Baptiste], *Son Swan, that's all I remember right now. Yes, I had a musical gift. I used to play parties and come home with two or three dollars that people give me for playing. I got to the place where I said I'm going to work, and when I thought I was able to play good enough, I just went on out for myself. That would be when I was around twelve years old.*

Then when I came to Chicago in 1921, I started taking lessons from Kenneth Anderson and he taught me quite a lot. I started to read very good, and I was playing all the different numbers like "Dizzy Fingers," "Flight of the Bumblebee," and "Prelude in C-Sharp Minor." I wanted to play a variety. Then I went to the Christenson School of Music. That was down on East Jackson Boulevard, and I paid a dollar and 25 cents for the chance to practice in the practice room and I took a jazz course. That gave me the use of different techniques that I hadn't been accustomed to. Like harmony and fingering. Later I used to teach in Chicago myself. Not out here [LA]. I had about four or five students that used to come to me and I'd teach them different variations. After that, why, I started playing different jobs. I had a job at a little wine room, Tony's Wine Room, on State Street, between 34th and 35th. Jelly Roll Morton used to come in there all the time. He was a heck of a piano player in those days. He was a flash musician, fast, you know. He was very inspiring but he was a braggish kind of cat. He was working on "The Wolverine Blues" at the time, and he used to say, "Come with me. I'm gonna take you, when I go to make some records; we'll get together and we gonna make some money, you watch." When the time came to go, he had sneaked off and that told me about him. I looked for him and he'd be gone. "Where were you, man? I came to see you and I couldn't find you," he'd say. I said, "I was right here."

Then I went to work at the Cascades Gardens; this was at 4950 Sheridan Road. I was playing relief piano there, playing for a couple of singers, and we worked there Friday, Saturday, Sunday. It was a white club and the fellow that had the job, his name was Dave North [pianist North recorded with Bud Freeman in 1928]. He had about three or four musicians. I can't think of their names now but anyway, I played intermission. This was 'round 1925.

This was my profession, what I wanted to do, so I started out with a little band of my own. I can remember Jack Valadiche [?] playing trumpet with me, Red Pinkney was playing drums, Wilbur Steward and Alan Bentley was playing saxophones, and I was playing piano. We played little engagements around. We started to playing in a little hotel called the Huntington Hotel [the projects are there now] which was at Cottage Grove. We paid for the hall; it was a cooperative deal where we split up the money after the dances. We did pretty good there for a while. After the guy saw how we was doing so well, he wanted to raise the rent so we had to find another place. We went over to the Lakewood Hall, and I played over there with my group for about three or four months; then we went off to Van Buren Avenue. That's where Lionel Hampton used to come in on Sunday evenings [Hampton relocated permanently to Los Angeles in 1927] and sit around or play drums. We couldn't get him up off the drums. That's why he's so great today because Hamp had such a lot of vim, vigor, and vitality. He had a lot of push.

Chicago was a place where musicians would come and they'd be learning and they'd go 'round to the different places to cut each other. See who could play the most. Earl Hines was around, Teddy Weatherford and Glover Compton [Compton moved to Paris in 1926], *too. Compton was working at the Dreamland; he would sit up there with a big cigar in his mouth and just play the piano. Trumpet player by the name of* [Natty] *Dominique was playing at the Paradise. He was a freckle-faced guy. The Pekin Theater was running and* [pianist] *Tony Jackson* [Jackson died in 1921] *was playing down there. He was just a flamboyant guy that was always very flashy. He was the one that wrote "Pretty Baby." I remember when Louis came to town. I'm telling you, Louis made a very deep impression on everybody that heard him play. He did something that no other trumpet player had ever done in the history of the instrument. The Royal Gardens* [where the King Oliver band with Armstrong played] *was a nice dancing spot for younger people, Sunday-evening-class-type people, to go out and have fun.* [Callwell] *"King" Jones was the first MC that was around there. He used to say, "Ladeez and gentle-men of the United States* [slow drawl], *no bodily dancing"—that was when they got to playing the blues—"don't get too close to my merchandise!" Oh boy. Those were some days.*

In later years, the Royal Gardens was changed to the Lincoln Gardens and then to the Café de Paris. Jimmy Bell directed the band at the Café de Paris. Ethel Waters came there. She was in Black Cargo, *I think it was* [probably White Cargo], *and the leading singers around there were Florence Mills* [with "Mandy Make Up Your Mind"] *and Josephine Baker; she sang at the Red Onion, right down the street from Mamie Ponce's place. Man, there were so many places to go. You'd leave and go to the Ascher, you'd go to the Pekin, you'd go to the Sunset, or to the Dreamland, to the Plantation, and then the Panama. You could go to any club and they were doing business and they all had a band. I was picking up everything I could hear, and I got to the place where I could just play anything I felt like I wanted to play. That would give you a feel of playing like Earl or Teddy or Gene Harpe or Clarence Johnson or Glover or any of them. The ones that didn't have anything to offer, why, you put them aside.*

In 1927, with François Moseley, we worked at the Hand, a place at Indiana Harbor that had a clientele of people that came in from the different outlying little cities to have a drink and do their shopping. They came in to listen to the band and then just go home. It was a live place. We New Orleans musicians had a certain beat, a rhythm the other guys couldn't get or they didn't try to get. It was too hard for them to comprehend whatever it was because it was a different swing. It's that brass band background. It gives you a feeling, I'm telling you. You have to be in front of it so you know that jive is coming out like it should. François worked for me in Indiana Harbor, but he got to the place where he had a day job and he couldn't make it. He lived a little ways out of town, coming in from Calumet to Indiana Harbor and he'd be sleepy and he just had to put it down. Later he formed his own band and they worked at the Swingland in Chicago. Punch Miller, trumpet player from New Orleans, was with him. [Drummer Moseley's band recorded as Frankie Franko and his Louisianans in 1930.]

I was playing then with [drummer] *Floyd Campbell. I had the job, but I gave Floyd the band because I didn't want that obligation to be getting musicians for different people. I just turned the band over to Floyd and we got Budd Johnson, Jabbo Smith and myself, and we had the best four-piece swing band in that neck of the woods; that's the South Side. That was '33, the year of the World's Fair.*[1] *Jabbo was a fine musician. All I can say he was just a wonderful guy. He'd come in, get his Chinese food, eat, light a cigarette and smoke it, and when he finished, he'd say, "Well, Gid, give me an A," and he'd get his horn in tune and he'd say, "Now we gonna blow" and he was ready to blow the whole night through. He had made records in opposition to Louis Armstrong. Of course, I don't know whether he had that quality, but he could make you think of Louis every time he blew. He was fast. He came there and upset the place.*

In what was a difficult sequence of engagements to put into any kind of order, Honoré also recalled working with drummer-bandleader Cecil White in Milwaukee at the River View Ballroom. "I was with him quite a while," he said, suggesting this might have been in 1930. There was also an association with singer Hosea Duff in 1933. "He used to sing and play drums. We worked together at different road-houses at different times." Gid spoke about performing in composer-arranger Jesse Stone's fifteen-piece big band in 1935 at the Club Morocco in Chicago and for country club dates, this quite an all-star affair, with Budd Johnson, again, on tenor plus his brother Keg Johnson on trombone; Al Wynn, trombone; Huey Long on guitar; and George Oldham, saxes. He cited this as "a very good band. We were blowing bubbles! Jesse used to make all the arrangements, taking numbers off the records, and never having to buy arrangements. We made a couple of transcriptions with Jesse. They got lost in the mail." There was also an entertaining stint with Eddie Cole's Solid Senders at the 5100 Club in 1937.

Eddie was Nat's brother. He was a pianist, he played trumpet, he played drums, and he played bass fiddle. He and I would do duets together. He'd dance and sing. He was just an all-round musician. He had left Noble Sissle and formed his own band. We worked that for a year. Then I went to work for Jimmie Noone. I'd known him before because he used to be around Chicago quite a bit and I'd go over to his house for dinner some times. His wife, Rita, was a very nice, hospitable person. I was working at the Sunset with Carroll Dickerson because they were putting together a big show at the time, and Jimmie asked me if I wanted to come with him. I told him yes and we went to work for Ray O'Hare—his brother Huck O'Hare had a band—and Ray was a booking agent. He used to get us all the work on the North Shore at different country clubs. Sometimes we had a seven-piece band, sometimes an eight-piece band. We had [Bill] Anderson on bass; [Ed] Pollock on saxophone; John Henley, Jimmie's nephew, on guitar; Leon Scott on trumpet; me on piano; Jimmie; and sometimes we had [Moses] Gant or Warren Smith on tenor. This was 1936. Jimmie was a very jolly, jovial guy. He was always open to suggestions. He didn't mind playing different songs that had come out. We'd get together, play a new song, and make an arrangement on it.

At first we were working at the Liberty Inn over on Harlem Avenue in Chicago, and we used to play all the different society dances around the city. After the Harlem Cafe we went to work at the Garrick Stage Bar. Jimmie said, "We got a job coming up and Fats Waller will be playing there [the Garrick]." We were to start playing in about a couple of weeks so we went down to see the place. I didn't think Fats Waller would be playing in a place like that. Well, they made a room for Fats downstairs—we were playing upstairs behind the bar—and that was one of the first good jobs I had playing in a pretty nice place in those days.

I stayed with Jimmie for about six years. He just had a very fluent style with different variations in control over his horn that the average clarinet player just couldn't get. Benny Goodman used to come 'round and listen to him. Jimmie was an influence on Benny. Also Johnny Lane plays just like him, same kind of tone. One time, after Jimmie had passed away [April 1944], I was playing an engagement with Johnny Lane and he did something on the horn, and I had to turn around and see it wasn't Jimmie.

Jimmie had a certain way; he'd put his reed on and if it wouldn't sound right if he made a cadenza he wanted to reach, he'd take it out and just throw it away. He didn't change reeds that often or be fixing his reed all the time like all those sax players and clarinet players do now. I was very proud to be working with him. He was a fine musician and a fine man to be with.

I remember one time we were broadcasting on a national hook-up, playing "You Know That I Know." It was cold as the devil and we were on the air and the engineer told us the time was up. Jimmie made a sign to me so I had to cut out of this number, change keys and tempo, and bring him into "Sweet Lorraine." I don't see how I did it but I did, and when I got through, everybody just said, "Man, who made that arrangement? You really did it." It was just spontaneous.

Having performed (and recorded in 1936) with Noone in his small groups, Honoré was on board when the clarinetist formed a big band three years later to play at the notorious Cabin Inn (formerly the Dreamland) with its all-transvestite chorus line. The band's vocalist was Joe Williams in his first professional engagement.

Down Beat, December 15, 1941

    Old Timers of Jazz Play At Chi Spot—New haven for followers of small hot jazz combos in the Windy City is the Sky Club on the town's far northwest side. Jazz clarinettist Jimmie Noone entertains in the bar with his own trio, made up of Gideon Honoré, piano; John Frazier, bass, and Jimmie himself.

Honoré also remembered partnering organist Tiny Parham during the American Negro Exposition, for the "Tropics After Dark" revue, held at the Chicago Coliseum on Wabash Avenue (July 4–September 2, 1940). "He played organ; I played piano. I didn't play with him; we alternated," he said. The same year Gid led his own quartet featuring the celebrated clarinetist Darnell Howard at the 4-11 Club, later working for Sidney Bechet's four-piece band at Club Rio in Springfield, Illinois, in early 1944.

Down Beat, June 1, 1944

    The Hot Box—Sidney "Pops" Bechet has been playing with his own group in Springfield, Illinois, for some time using Paul Barbarin on drums and Gideon Honoré on piano.

Club Rio was a nightclub, and they used to have gambling at the casino. We were there for about six months. Sidney was just a heck of a musician. He was a good clarinet player, a good tenor player, and he played a little piano and bass. Paul Barbarin was on drums. Sidney came to the house in 1949 and tried to get me to go to Paris. I didn't make it." [A two-week engagement in 1944 with bandleader Dallas Bartley became a yearlong stint.] *"I went there for two weeks and stayed a whole year. It was a night club named Joe's Deluxe* [6323 South Parkway Boulevard], *which was right in walking distance from my home. We had shows to play."*

Down Beat, June 1, 1944

    Chicago Band Briefs—Dallas Bartley returned, by popular demand to Joe's DeLuxe, 63rd and South Parkway, for a 16-week stay. Bartley has added Bob Merrell [sic], trumpet, Joshua Jackson, tenor, and Gideon Honoré, pianist, formerly with the late Jimmie Noone.

Down Beat, September 15, 1944

    Chicago—Dallas Bartley and his Small Town Boys recorded four originals Aug. 24 at the World Transcription studios here for Decca. Personnel on the date was: Al Atkinson, alto; Josh Jackson, tenor; Bob Merril [sic], trumpet; Gid Honoré, piano; Earl Phillips, drums; and Dallas Bartley, bass.

Down Beat, April 15, 1945

James Craig, after a stint in the navy, has replaced Gideon Honoré with Dallas Bartley at Joe's DeLuxe.

Down Beat, August 15, 1945

The Hot Box—Jazz Concerts: Jimmy [sic] Noone Memorial concert at Uptown Playhouse, Chicago given by John Steiner with Darnell Howard, clarinet; Boyce Brown, alto sax; Baby Dodds, drums; Gideon Honoré, piano (played many years in Chicago with Noone); Jack Goss, guitar; Tut Soper, second piano; Pat Pattison, bass. Sunday afternoon, August 5th.

Then I worked with Helena Jester; she was a dancer and singer. Very good. We had an act; a guy wrote a whole book for us. She had a preaching act and I had a few lines. Her line was "Gallivanting around all night, when I look for you, I can't find you." And I'd say, "I don't see what the hell you looking over at me for." That was my line. That's when curse words weren't supposed to be used on the stage, and it would bring the house down. Those were the days. We played different theaters and worked all the way out to New York and played the Apollo, the American Legion in Detroit, the Monogram Theatre in Chicago, too. Then she got a job to go to Russia, and when we got to the border, they were supposed to pay us off in furs. We were supposed to exchange them for cash. I didn't know nothing about furs so I didn't go with her. We worked together for about five, six months. I came back to Chicago after that. Played some jobs and then I went to Montreal as a single. I was playing in this nightclub, Lafayette's, and I looked up and who was stood there but Helena Jester. I got through playing and went over to talk to her and she says she was "pulling" a single at the Blue Angel and playing piano in her act herself. No, we didn't get together again. I played opposite Oscar Peterson in Montreal. He played down the street and I played down another street. Oscar said he wasn't feeling like he was ready to leave town [Peterson left Montreal eventually in 1949].

Chicago Defender, January 17, 1948

Music Box Lounge—408 East 63rd Street—The International Mecca of Bronzeville. Now Presenting Lil Palmore—The Queen of the Blues and Gid Honoré—The Prince of the Keyboard.

1948, July the 5th, we moved out to Los Angeles. I had been up in Pocatello, Idaho, on a job at Eddie McCann's. When we had a two-week layoff, I said I'll come down here [LA] and see my sister-in-law. This was before I thought of moving. While I was down here, I asked her if she could look out a place for me. My son was small then. In the meantime, after Eddie's, I was working at the El Capitan, Redding, California, and then I went back to Chicago. My sister-in-law found this place, where we are now, told us how much it cost and what they wanted for a down payment. She made a down payment for me, and my mother-in-law stayed on this side and I had that side rented out so this was just a good investment.

I had lots of work as soon as I came out here. Ory wanted me straightaway. One of the piano players, Walter Johnson, that was working out at the *Waikiki* [Mike's Waikiki Inn, 3743 S. Western Avenue] *passed on, and I went over there and took his place working with* [violinist] *Ginger Smock and* [pianist-organist] *Emile Williams. In the meantime, well, Kid Ory didn't have no work at that time. There was a blank spell for him, so I just kept working at the Waikiki. It was within walking distance from where we are now so Ory got another piano player. My wife told me, "Why don't you keep the job? It's close, the others have been there for eight years, and he's paying good," so I spent some time there.*[2] *Ory was a jovial type of guy, always cracking jokes and telling Creole stories. Him and Ram* [drummer Minor Hall] *and 'Tudi* [bassist Ed Garland]*. My style fitted all right with Ory. He said, "Just play those chords behind me." He never did bother you at all; he just said, "We gonna play such-and-such a thing" and we played. We got on well. We worked in San Francisco at the Venus Club for about two months in late 1948 and then at the Beverly Cavern in Hollywood. I was with Ory for about four or five months.*

Then [former Ory trumpeter] *Teddy Buckner and I worked together. We did quite a bit of work at the 400 Club. We just agreed to disband and I left the band. After that I was with Albert Nicholas's Quartet for three years, first at the St. Francis Room over here on 8th Street. We went to San Francisco and worked in the International Settlement; that's the red-light district. That was at the House of Pisco* [580 Pacific Avenue]—*that's where they had the Pisco Punch* [South American grape brandy cocktail]—*and we stayed there about three months. Albert was a good clarinetist, and we all lived like one family. We had a lot in common and everything was good.*

Down Beat, April 7, 1950

Albert Nicholas reopened at Virginia's after short lay-off while previous band returned on a contract adjustment. Has two new men in band, pianist Gideon Honoré in place of L.Z. Cooper, and bassist Leo Bibb for Reggie Jones. Still with veteran clarinet are Andrew Blakeney, trumpet, and Alton Redd, drums.

I liked to listen to modern jazz. I liked good execution. I used to study and concentrate on finger dexterity. See, I worked a lot as a single. I worked down there in San Diego for the Frederick Brothers. They had an eating place, a couple of blocks from Walter Fuller's place [Club Royal, 3rd and C Street]*. Then I worked with Walter Fuller, not in his group but alternating* *with him, on his night off. I also worked the Crown Lounge; that was another lounge right adjacent to his. I was there regular.*

I always want to play a variety of styles. I wouldn't want to be limited. I admired Art Tatum above all; he and I were buddies. He used to be in Chicago, but he died out here. Last time I saw him, he was on Western and Jefferson at the Safeway store, waiting for his wife to come out. I said, "Arthur, what are you doing out here?" He said, "Gideon, I'd know your voice anywhere."

Honoré spent his later years playing as a single (as in 1979 when he played at the Brussels Restaurant in Beverly Hills for five nights a week) or performing in a duo with bassist Rocky Robinson ("We stayed together for about five, six years") and with trombonist Roger Jamieson's Ory-style revivalist band, the New Orleanians. He was also Grand Marshall for the Resurrection Brass Band into the 1980s, alongside many other African American veterans, appearing at the traditional jazz festivals and gatherings that abounded then in Southern California.

You know, music has played a very important part in my life. Kid Ory, Jimmie Noone, Sidney Bechet, Joe Oliver, Fats Waller, all the different guys, every time I play I try to remember them. As for today's musicians, I'd like for them to keep their minds clear and not get clouded with what's happening with drugs, etc. You can play music without doing all that. I gave my son Joseph music years and years ago. He never did bother with it. He was in one concert and that was the end of that.

Chapter Three

George Robert Orendorff

Trumpet

That's where Sunshine Sammy lived, and just over there Bojangles [Bill Robinson] *had his place. Stepin' Fetchit lived around that corner. Of course, they're all gone now.*

We were standing on the balcony of George Orendorff's first-floor apartment at West 36th Place, his home since 1931, on a late October day in 1979, looking out over a quiet residential district in South Central Los Angeles and recalling his former neighbors, all past heroes of black vaudeville. Inside, it was shaded and still. George's wife lay chronically ill, and he liked to stay close to home.

George Robert Orendorff was born in Atlanta, Georgia, in 1906. As a child, he rode his father's horses at country fairs and liked the bands he heard, never thinking that he might make his career in music. Toward the end of World War I, after his parents had separated, he relocated to Chicago with his mother and attended the celebrated Wendell Phillips High School on the city's South Side, alongside such putative jazz stars as Eddie South, Lionel Hampton, and Wallace Bishop. George had experimented with the guitar before his mother bought him a cornet from a local musician. It cost her the equivalent of two weeks' wages, he remembered. He showed some talent for music and quickly attracted compliments for both the quality of his tone and his reading prowess.

George settled in Los Angeles in the 1920s and became a key member of the black music community, respected for his musicianship and his steadiness, and was best known for his lengthy association with bandleader Les Hite and for the fine recordings he made with Paul Howard's Quality Serenaders. He was later a trustee of the segregated Local 767 of the American

George Orendorff at a private party, Studio City, California, 1966. Photo by Perc Bond, courtesy Floyd Levin.

Federation of Musicians. After World War II, the demand for competent show musicians dwindled, and he joined the U.S. Post Office. In his later years, gentle George resumed playing and performed with Ben Pollack, Peppy Prince's Orchestra, and Gordon Mitchell's Resurrection Brass Band. He became disheartened after losing both his wife, Marian, and their only daughter, Joselle, in 1983. George died in June 1984.

George Orendorff: Los Angeles, October 17, 1979

I was away at the races with my father. See, in the summer time, I didn't go to school so when I came back, my mother had this horn sittin' up there on top of her sewing machine and my uncle said, "Sister, you just throwed your money away" and that made me mad right there. That was a challenge. I says, "Well, I'm gonna learn to play this horn," so this guy started to giving me lessons on how to read music, count time, and little things like that. He was smart enough to use psychology and not give me a lot of scales and stuff, but little simple pieces, like "Bluebells of Scotland," different numbers like everybody knows. I was fourteen.

So when I went to high school, the teacher told me to come up there and try out for the orchestra. What she's listening for is my tone, and then she said, "OK, you get in the orchestra." She liked the tone I had because I didn't play a brass band tone, and the trumpet had to play real soft for the different overtures. Then I got into the brass band. They asked me to go out one day and play with them. Well, I never walked in my life, and the guys in the brass band, they'd been playing those marches and they knew 'em by heart, and I'm out there, that mouthpiece jumping all over my face and hitting my nose. One thing led to another and then I got to playin' in the shows, like in the pit, for orchestras.

I used to go over and listen to Joe Oliver on Friday night 'cause I didn't have to go to school Saturday. Three of us would go to the Royal Garden Café [later the Lincoln Gardens, 459 East 31st Street] together. We had just enough money to get in there and 50 cents apiece left. That's a lot of money in those days. So together we'd have a dollar and a half and we'd give that to the waiter. Prohibition was on and he'd put a pitcher of water on our table 'cause we didn't handle no drinking but we could sit there all night long for a dollar and a half. One day I was going to school with my cornet and [Honoré] Dutrey, the trombone player in the band, saw me, so he said to me, "I want you to come over to the Gardens tomorrow. Little Louis is coming to town and join the band. He's the greatest trumpet player in the world." When he said, "The greatest trumpet player," I thought about Freddy Keppard who was blowin' the hell out of a trumpet, and Joe Oliver was hell, and Tommy Ladnier was coming through there, too. You know, Tommy could blow. Talk about the world's greatest trumpet players!

So I got over there to see Little Louis. Well, Little Louis weighed about two hundred and some-odd pounds! Had a box-back coat on and he had his haircut up like this. He looked like Sonny Liston. He wouldn't smile at nobody. In Joe's band, all that stuff they'd played, they knew it by heart. Louis was playing second trumpet, playin' way down low, some of the prettiest stuff I ever heard in my life. My God, I never heard nothin' like it before. He sounded like Coleman Hawkins on the tenor saxophone. I mean, the stuff he was playing. Guys from Isham Jones's band used to come down there, Louis Panico, Hoagy Carmichael and Bud Freeman, and all the other guys. They was goin' to "school," same as I was. I never heard of Louis 'til he came to Chicago.

Joe had a funny way of playin'. They would get to the first ending and he would make some kind of a run that they were gonna make in the next chorus. On the first ending they would run it through, so when they get to the next chorus, Louis had a second part to that son of a gun. He was playing *way down low, G, 'cause the band didn't swing real high like the guys screamin' now. That was the damnedest thing.*

The first time I heard Louis actually play was at the Oddfellows Hall one night. You know, Joe was one of them kinda guys that would get two more jobs than he could work on, so he sent Louis to play on the job and he was the only trumpet player this time. They kicked me out of the place 'cause I didn't have no ticket, but I stood on the steps and heard him play a piece called "Mandy Make Up Your Mind." I never heard so much damn trumpet in my life. The next time I heard him he was at the Dreamland.

I heard his [Oliver's] records here on the coast. They didn't sound nothing like the band in person. After all, in those days, you had to muffle the drums, and when Louis played, they had to put him way back. The band would drop way down like Basie's, where you hear the rhythm and the people's feet on the floor. Joe would just make a note and then drop out and that rhythm would carry the band. That was the damnedest band in the world. You had to hear Joe's band in person and you had to hear Joe in person, too, 'cause he was a great trumpet player. He could drop way down soft, and he played a beautiful lead. He would pick that mute and put it in there and scare everybody outta the place because of the difference in jumping from the real soft to the real loud.

I wasn't tryin' to play like they could 'cause I couldn't play like them. I was still playin' legit music, and sometimes a guy would get sick and they would call me. Like one night, Joe got sick and [trombonist] John Thomas came and got me out of bed. I was sound asleep. He says, "Come on, put on your tuxedo and come over. Joe's sick." That's like sayin' Mohammed Ali can't fight tonight; I want you to come over and fight in his place. So I goes over there and here's Tommy Ladnier, Barney Bigard, Fields [Filhe] on trombone, and Barbarin, this drummer out of New Orleans who wrote "Bourbon St Parade." I was playin' Joe's book. Tom was playing first trumpet and we had a show to play. Well, I played all that music and then they said, "Let's play 'Dippermouth Blues.'" Tom played lead but Joe [usually] played the solos. I could play "Dippermouth" because I'd been playing it with another guy named Bill Wilson. Now, Bill Wilson used to sub for Louis and he wasn't as powerful, but he was a helluva trumpet player on the type of Bobby Hackett, had a beautiful soft tone.

From playing behind him, I picked up things. So I played this solo in there, and I went over to Joe's place on Wabash to pick my money up and he says, "The guys tell me you played that 'Dippermouth Blues' last night. Well, that's my piece; lay off it!" No kiddin'! I didn't call it, they called it. They was razzin' him, sayin', "This kid come in here, blowed you outta this place." I was seventeen and a half, eighteen almost. It was a thrill; that's the greatest thing.

Most of my work was playing show music, in the pit. My teacher Raymond Whitsett played at the Grand Theatre, and he taught me how to play both ways. Of course, he was a legit trumpet player but he could play jazz, too, but not like those guys.

By 1923, George was a member of the Whispering Syncopators in Chicago. This band of youngsters was co-led by Will Walker and Thomas A. Dorsey, then a jazz and blues pianist who had been accompanist to blues singer Ma Rainey. Dorsey went on to become a celebrated composer and performer in the gospel idiom. Others in this eight-piece outfit to make their mark in music included drummer Wallace Bishop, saxophonist Les Hite, and violinist Detroit Shannon.

I came out here [California] *first in 1923 with a guy named Ben Harney, a white piano player who was supposed to be the originator of ragtime. We had five acts of vaudeville, but we didn't play for them. They had the pit orchestra for that. Harney closed the show. In our band we had a clarinet player out of New Orleans; we called him Firpo 'cause he looked like the fighter. His name was Parker. I can't think of the rest of the guys. Harney had a colored band; we was dressed in overalls. He would open up on the front and play 'cause the people wasn't used to that type of ragtime music, 'specially in the places where we played. We jumped from Chicago to Billings, Montana; now that's a helluva jump. Nothing but cowboys. We played a Saturday and Sunday there, and jumped from there to Walla Walla, Washington. This was on the Ackman Harris circuit.*

Harney was the star; he would come out and play piano with his tails on like Liberace, and then another curtain would come up and our band would be there with all these bandana hats on. We had another guy who played harmonica who was up in the balcony and he would come down the aisles. So all the cowboys was saying, "What the hell is goin' on?" Here's the band and here's some guys comin' down whistlin' like that. I was the conductor. We ended up in Long Beach, in September '23. Herbert L. Clark had a brass band there in Long Beach, and I would go out and listen to that band. Oh, my God! Anyway, I went back to Chicago to go back to school, and that started in September. You didn't have no plane to get back there then, so when I got my money, I got on the train. When I got back to Chicago, school had been started a week and a half. I was beat, anyway, so I said I'll go next semester, and I just laid out of school and got a job in the sawmills.

The next time I came to California was with Helen Dewey. This was in 1925. Now we had a clarinet player in there called Dodo Green, a helluva of a clarinet player! I mean a legit clarinet player. Our dressing rooms would be down in the basement, and that's the way the orchestras would come in the pit. So one day this Italian clarinet player was down there runnin' over some stuff in the book, and Dodo says, "You mind if I come and practice with you?" and the guy looks at him with disdain. Boy, Dodo played every damn thing in that book. He was like a Buster Bailey—this guy had everything in the world, but on our way out here he got sick and he had to call the doctor and they found out he was usin' a needle. The funny thing, he could always find out when we got into town how he could get that stuff. We went to San Diego; he had that stuff. He was a helluva musician, but dope got him.

Helen Dewey had a five-act show and George's boyhood friend Les Hite was with him in the band. When the show had run its course, they took cash rather than their return tickets to Chicago and stayed on in California. Both men began to play casual jobs with bandleader and music-shop proprietor Reb Spikes.

When I came to California the second time, I went to work with Satchel McVea [Jack McVea's father] and then with Reb Spikes out at Redondo Beach. He had a book that thick, and they wanted to see whether I could read. They got a number in there that's supposed to cut certain men in the band. I didn't know that, but I played the whole damn book through because all I was doin' was readin'. If you can transpose, then, naturally, you can play it where it is, so I played everything they had. Reb Spikes wanted a drummer, and we recommended Lionel Hampton, so Lionel came out here from Chicago to join Reb. I went over to Paul Howard's Quality Serenaders out in Culver City, at a small place called Louie's Nightingale [later renamed the Little Cotton Club when Frank Sebastian took it over]. This was 1925. The job folded up at Reb's place, and Lionel started giggin' round. I decided I'd just stay for a while and then go on back to Chicago, but I started to stayin' here and of course the Nightingale job was very good. Guys like [actor] Lon Chaney would come in there and Jack Dempsey. It was really a high-class place, you know. When we started the evening, Harvey Brooks was out front playin' piano; then we'd play a dance set; then [drummer] Tin Can Henry Allen and Leon Herriford and them would go round the floor and jive people, and we'd play for them; then we played the show with the chorus girls, the comedians, and the dancers.

The entertainers had a small piano for Harvey out on the floor. He was watchin' them 'cause the girls could slip that money, and he'd see they weren't stealing any. Just before the next show, the piano player would go out and have his dinner, and the band would play without him. Then after we played the show, Harvey would go back on the floor to play and we would go and have our dinner, so the music never stopped. You worked seven nights a week. We wore these red caps, like bell hops.

It was the Quality Four at first, and Doctor Nelson had a place down here called the Hummingbird. He was married to one of the Ziegfeld Follies girls. Then he moved the place out to Culver City and they had piano, drums, and a violin. Herriford went to Chicago and then he came back and rejoined the band. We played there, and then we went down to Mike Lyman's place downtown for a while. We came back when Frank Sebastian got the Green Mill in 1926 and changed it into the big New Cotton Club.

Tin Can Henry left, and we got Lionel in the band at the Cotton Club. On trombone, we first had Louis Taylor from Chicago; he joined us at Lyman's, but then he got sick and went back to Chicago and had an operation. While he was havin' that, we got Lawrence Brown from Pasadena. He could play so much it wasn't even funny! You see, his father was a minister, his brother was a piano player, he could play a little piano and he knew violin and he had a lot of things going. Lawrence was studyin' to be a lawyer or a doctor or somethin'. When we started, we only had two brass, trumpet and trombone, and then we added another boy. After that James Porter, who played with Curtis Mosby, came in the band; then Lloyd Reese came in. Now Lloyd, oh Lord! On trumpet, he was like Benny Carter. Lloyd was a clarinet player first, and he was studyin' law at this same school that Nixon went to out here. He was studyin' so much, he'd come to work and look in his trunk and his horn would be left at school or somewhere. Anyway, Lloyd turned out a lot of fine musicians. Some of the guys out of Stan Kenton's band and Gil Evans's band out at Balboa used to take lessons from Lloyd. He was a helluva trumpet player and a saxophone player. He could hit anything on piano, play "In a Mist"; he could tell you what you were playin' in your bass hand, standing way over there.

Porter came out of Chicago. He was a powerful trumpet player, who looked something like Joe Oliver. Every time Louis came on the stand, he would laugh and say to Porter, "You look just like Joe Oliver." Then Porter started takin' lessons from Doc Hyner. He had that non-pressure system, and Porter got so he could take his horn and play "When Day Is Done" in your ear and you could hardly hear it. It was beautiful. But he got away from his style of playing. See, he was a powerhouse trumpet player, but he got to playin' that sweet stuff.

I run into Mutt [Carey] a lot of times. Mutt worked right across the street when I was working at the Nightingale. He and Ram Hall and Les Hite played in there; they called it the Lion's Den, and it had sawdust on the floor. I'll never forget one night just before we played a show, I took intermission and went across the street because Les was playing in there and I wanted to hear him. I didn't want to go in the place 'cause I had to run back to play the show. They had the windows open, so I stopped out there and I listened. I never heard so much goddamn clarinet in my life. Turns out it was Benny Goodman. Ben Pollack was playing down at the beach and Benny stopped by and was playing clarinet with Papa Mutt. This was in 1925. I talked to Les the next day, and he said, "That wasn't me; that was some kid playing with Ben Pollack, down at Venice Ballroom." He sounded like Buster Bailey to me.

In Paul's band, Charlie Lawrence was doin' most of the arranging. He played saxophone and clarinet, but he was a helluva piano player, too. His uncle was Willie Grant Still, the composer. Earl Thompson, the trumpet player, made some of the arrangements, too. He was a nice trumpet player, came out of Andy Kirk's band. He got killed by changing a tire. Car killed him. Paul Howard's [saxophone] playing was more on the legitimate side. He was not what you call a hot player, but he had a very fine technique. You know, he was a trumpet player in the beginning. He came here from Ohio, before I came here, and he told me he played cornet. They fired him out of this band way back in the early days; then he changed over to saxophone. Paul played with the Black and Tan, too, for a while. He was a beautiful man to work for. We stayed at the Cotton Club for two years and made those Quality Serenaders recordings in 1929 while we were playing the Kentucky Club on Central Avenue. Stayed there a year. Then we played the Montmartre out here in Hollywood. I'll never forget that. The guy called it the Embassy Room; there were two rooms, with one big kitchen to serve both places.

Now Paul Whiteman had come out here to make that big picture, The King of Jazz, *so one night they brought his band in to eat on our side and they had tables all 'round the side. Everybody was there that night but Bix. Bix was sick. There was Bing Crosby and Al Rinker, the Rhythm Boys. They had their dinner. Then when they got through, they went on the other side and played, and I ain't seen nothin' outside smaller than a Rolls-Royce. There were chauffeurs out there for all those big movie stars. I thought for the time it was good; after all, he was trying to bring jazz in. Whiteman knew the types of guys like Bix, and he had Trumbauer, and he played "Rhapsody in Blue" and all that stuff. Henry Busse was in the band. A marvelous trumpet player, he could play real high.*

When the Kentucky Club closed in 1930, the Quality Serenaders broke up.

Every guy went different ways. I went to Les Hite's band but not right away. When Louis came out here to the Cotton Club, [trumpeter] Vernon Elkins had the band and he got sick. I wasn't working so I went out there to work in his place. Elkins was supposed to come back, but he never did get back. Marshal Royal's father was the president of our union and he said, "Somebody's got to be responsible for your Musicians Union taxes, so some of you gotta get together and find out who's going to take responsibility for getting this tax money in." Now, Leon Herriford was the one should actually have taken that over because he was the boss and called the shots. He wouldn't take it.

Earlier, Les Hite and Vernon Elkins had a band together at the Little Cotton Club. This was before they moved up to the New Cotton Club. Frank Sebastian always liked Les. Before he worked for Frank, Les had a band of his own playing out here at an open-air venue. Speed Webb's band was the first to play at both of Frank's places. Les had Charlie Jones and Marvin

Johnson, Archie Lancaster and Harold Scott with him at the open-air place. Baby Mac was singing at the Cotton Club and Les was married to her, so he used to come over to pick her up. Frank says to Les, "How about you coming in here and taking over the band? Otherwise they gonna pull the band out." Les said to me, "What do you think about it?" I said, "Don't come in here unless you bring your own band in here. When Elkins gets well, you gonna get kicked out of here, and you done lost your band. Then where you goin'?" So Les told Frank that and he said, "You pick the men you want to come in here."

Les kept Lionel; he was the drummer out there in the first place. He let Ceelle Burke go and brought his guitar player Bill Perkins in and he brought Harold Scott in, and he kept me because I was used to playing the show. I'd been there for two weeks, and I knew the show better than they did. I stayed 'cause Elkins never got better. He recently passed away. Les brought Harvey Brooks in and let Elkins's piano player go, and Sonny Graven came in on trombone.

Les wanted Lawrence Brown to stay, but he wanted to go to Curtis Mosby's band. Mosby played in two places, one in San Francisco, one here. Leon Herriford got one of the bands that went up north. Peter was paying Paul. I mean, Mosby was losing money here or losing money there: the one making money was paying the other. It got so he didn't make it, carryin' two bands like that.

The first night we opened up, Louis came to work early to help us out with the band stuff. He didn't have to do that because he was a star. That was very nice. Success hadn't gone to his head. He was just regular. He would come over to your house or to anybody's house, and he would always be helping. I remember Frank Sebastian wanted us to get on a truck and go down there on Washington, on Olympic and Grand. Louis didn't have to do this, but he got on the truck and played with us. I'll never forget he called "High Society," and half the band didn't know it.

Once, Lionel asked Louis to go down to Tijuana. That was a big thing then. Lionel took Louis and Gladys and my wife and me. Louis went down with his house slippers on, didn't put on no shoes, and he had him a ball, dancing on the floor. He was just a regular person. One day we were playin' the early part of the evening. I think it was a Monday or a Tuesday when business was slow, around 9 o'clock, and Louis was on the stand. We were running over some orchestrations. Frank had gone off someplace so the head waiter came down while we was playin' and he says, "There's a couple of men in front wants to see you." Louis says, "Well, I'm playing right now."

I'll never forget the last number he was playing, a piece called "Little White Lies." Then Louis says, "OK, I'm going up in front now," and here's these two detectives searching him, and they found a small roach in his pocket. Now, Vic Berton, the drummer who was working with Abe Lyman's band, had been caught first and he must have snitched on Louis. See, Vic Berton was the one that Louis gave this stuff to. They didn't bother Louis right then; they didn't take him down. When Frank came back, he was madder'n hell, 'cause Frank was almost like Al Capone out there; he run the town, but he couldn't fool with them guys. We didn't know what happened because we were still on the bandstand. Louis was mad, I know that.

I left about a week later to go to Chicago 'cause my father was sick. Red Mack came in and took my place. In Chicago, I went to see Earl Hines, and the guys in Lunceford's band, and Fletcher Henderson was in town, too. It was March; snow on the ground, it was so cold. When I came back in the band, Louis had gone. Now, I don't remember him doin' any time at all. He didn't go into jail. Red Mack's a damn good trumpet player, but ain't nobody gonna take Louis's place. Red was a melodic player, but he wasn't exciting, not like Louis. Nobody at that time could play like Louis.

Louis came out here twice. The first time, we made some records; then he went back east. When he came back again, we had Marshal Royal on saxophone. Les got so he didn't feel like he wanted to play anymore. He was happy fronting. We didn't make any recordings when Louis came back the second time. After Louis left, Fats Waller came in and played the Cotton Club. They gave him a dressing room the chorus girls used to have—a long room with mirrors all the way down. He had the whole room, and when he left there, there were whiskey bottles from one end straight on down to the other end. He could drink more whiskey than anybody and never get drunk. And eat. Boy, could he eat.

One night, he sat down at the piano and he start playing Bach and Beethoven. We didn't know he could play all that heavy stuff. Henry Prince was playing piano with us, and he told Henry, "You take a chorus; split it up." We had two pianos, and Fats played so much goddamn piano, this guy lost confidence in himself, although he was a helluva piano player. Fats was out here for about two to three months, I'd guess, and then Valaida Snow came in [summer 1935] with Ananias Berry and the Berry Brothers. Then another bunch came in. Henry Starr, from San Francisco, came for a while. He was quite a personality.

After we left the Cotton Club around '37, we did a lot of one-nighters up to Seattle. While Les was trying to regroup a band, I got this job out at the Bal Tabarin in Gardena with Ceelle Burke. One of the best jobs in town, seven nights a week, got paid $24 a week. This was when Lionel was working downtown as the leader, and I think he was getting $26 a week. I had to drive way out, but there wasn't no gas shortages at the particular time. Ceelle had a nice band, not a jazz band, playing for the type of people who came in and wanted "Deep in the Heart of Texas." Guys working the oil fields who'd got that type of money. We'd entertain, and they had good food in there. We had four chorus girls and a striptease dancer—it was a complete show—and two *saxophones and one trumpet. Caughey Roberts was on saxophone before he went with Basie, Charlie Jones was in there on saxophone and then Marvin Johnson came in when I went to the Army, and Lee Gibson was on drums. Had five or six different piano players. I was playing the lead, and Caughey said I was the only trumpet player out there that could play three shows that was as strong on the last show as I was on the first. Louis called me "Irondorff." I don't know about that, but I was good for playing shows. Later, Wendell Culley came in. He was a beautiful trumpet player.*

Down Beat, November 1, 1940

Ceelle Burke's Lineup Bared—The "mystery man" of those Decca records in recent weeks is Ceelle Burke, a young Negro vocalist and guitarist, whose platters of Trade Winds and When the Swallows Come Back are sensational clicks. Interesting, too, is that Coughed [sic] Roberts, alto sax star heard on many of Count Basie's early Decca waxing's, is in Burke's band. Others in the lineup include Charles Davis, pianist; Herschel Coleman, alto and trumpet; Vernon Gower, bass; Lee Gibson, drums; Charles Jones, tenor, and George Orendorff, lead trumpet.

Ceelle Burke was at the Bal Tabarin before I got there. I joined his band about '38 and left in '43 when I went to the service [on February 19, 1943] *and he was still there. When I came back, he got an Afro-Cuban band together and went out to a club in Hollywood where we had Pot, Pan and Skillet and Dorothy Donegan as the attractions. He had a bunch of guys in the band that were Cuban. Gaucho, the drummer, used to be with Katherine Dunham, and the first trumpet player had played second under Rafael Mendez. Everyone in the band spoke Spanish but me. A lot of times they would forget that. Ceelle had a rumba band like Machito's; he was over in the Islands for years, so he could play all that Hawaiian stuff as well. When I left the band and went back to Chicago, Karl George came in. Then the band broke up.*

In the service, they put me in the military police, which I didn't like because I figured I should be in the band. Rodger Hurd, saxophone player used to be with Les Hite, tried to get me in the band. My CO said, "No, he's not going anywhere until he's finished his basic training right here." This was doing judo, wrestling, and studying military law. There was only fifty-two of us attached to the Third Army, which was Patton's army. We didn't take any exercise until it was real hot. They'd give you so much water to drink and we'd go out on a bivouac. We had to march out there, see the place was clean, walk guard at night. Nobody liked the police. People don't like police around here, and they sure didn't like them in the Army. The Army took any ego out of me, if I had any, when they put me in the police because the band quota had filled up. That broke my heart.

When I got hurt, they sent me to Fort Huachuca, Arizona. There I got on the band with Captain Joe Jordan. He was a piano player. The first day they sent me out on parade. I hadn't been blowing a horn and I hit my foot against a rock and almost broke it. I didn't have no lip or nothing, but later, when they got a band together to play for the USO shows that came through there, I got in that band and played for Lena Horne and Pearl Bailey. Pearl stayed around and she used to come down to our barracks and rehearse. She had a girl who played piano for her. Nobody paid no attention to Pearl—she was nothin' then. Every time Lena come down, that band had to come out. Rochester came down; him and his partner Johnnie Taylor used to do a striptease thing. They used to come out dressed with long underwear or a big safety pin there between their legs like a baby. Because I had played all these shows, I was playing the lead, so the other guys could fall in behind it.

After Ceelle's band, I went to work for the Post Office. It happened because once a year you go down to the musician's union on New Year's Eve. If you don't get a job on New Year's, you know the handwriting's on the wall. All bands work on New Year's Eve. If you can't work, you ain't gonna work the first of the year. They said, "We don't have nothin'."

This was '47 so I went to the Post Office as a substitute. I says, "I'll stay here for a while 'til something happens." I went back to Ceelle and played with him for a while. Eight or nine pieces, chorus girls. Red Ingle's band, they came in there behind us, all that crazy stuff, and we played the show. It would be 4 or 5 o'clock in the morning before we'd get through, and I'd go on to work from there at the Post Office. Sometimes I was so tired I didn't know what to do, but I stayed with the Post Office because there wasn't nothin' happening around here but three-piece outfits, maybe a piano, a guitar, and a bass, in these small clubs. They wasn't using no big bands.

The music was changing; it was either small outfits or bop and I couldn't play bop. I didn't know bop, and I didn't want to play it in the first place. All those augmented sevenths. The last job I played was with Ceelle and we was supposed to open some place, and three of the guys on his band were bop men and I didn't know that. I played the first chorus and they played theirs and it was bop. The piano player was like that, and I said, "Oh, oh, it's time to get out of this band; I don't belong here."

Bop wasn't doing anything either. I was out at Billy Berg's the first night that Dizzy Gillespie came out there with Charlie Parker. I got in early and had me a complete dinner. I went out of curiosity. Eddie Heywood had just left there. He had a nice band, with Vic Dickenson. Dizzy came on with his "Salt Peanuts, Salt Peanuts," and the people said, "What's happening?" They wasn't used to that stuff; they didn't understand it. Other guys came in to listen, like Ernie Royal, who came down from San Francisco where he was in the Navy. He loved that kind of stuff because he was used to what was *happening in New York. Me, I like to hear the melody sometimes, somewhere!*

I did thirty years with the Post Office, and with my Army time, I get a little pension now. I came out in 1976. I practically gave up music. I made some recordings with T-Bone Walker. That was before I lost my teeth. I put my horn down for about two years. I started back when a guy came to me one day and said, "I got a New Year's job down here to Fort Waunienie, the Marines base." I was doing gardening work, and I said I didn't play anymore. He says, "All I want you to do is to play "Auld Lang Syne" and "Hail, Hail, the Gang's All Here" at 12 o'clock at night because they going to be raising so much hell in there you won't hear the band, because we only got two saxophones and a piano and drums." I went down there on the New Year's night and lo and behold, the brass from the Marines came in for "The Star-Spangled Banner." The piano player didn't know it, and I was out there playing by myself. I got through that.

Down Beat, January 25, 1952

Los Angeles Band Briefs—Calvin Boze [trumpet and vocals] heads eight-piece band at Central Avenue's recently-reopened Club Alabam. Has Floyd Turnham, alto and baritone; Curtis Lowe, tenor; George Orendorff, trumpet; Gene Phillips, guitar; Ralph Bateman, piano; Buddy Woodson, bass, and Bill Douglass, drums. Arrangements by Maxwell Davis.

Then I quit playin' again until Peppy Prince got a band together and called me; this was just before I lost my teeth. He said, "I want you to come out and just oversee the brass section, see they're phrasing right, and breathin' right." I went up there and they only had one trumpet; the other two didn't show. The next time, Parker Berry, the trombone player, came up and we got to talking together about going with the band. We wasn't making any money, wasn't even gigging. We'd get together on Tuesday nights and just rehearse. It was like a social thing. Then the band started building up, getting better and better. Peppy tried to get some formal jobs, but nobody would hire him because Sammie Franklin had everything tied up. Finally he got on his knees and they hired him for one of these damn jobs. We sounded pretty good and from then he kept goin' on and goin' on.

Peppy got Dootsie Williams to finance him to make some records. We had Doug Finis on piano and Leroy Lovett, who played piano with Johnny Hodges's small group, did some arrangements for us. The guys had such funny names, like Cat Head, Beef Neck, and all them kinda things. They were nice players but they weren't well-known. They all had day jobs. I haven't been with Peppy since about '73.

In addition to his 1930s recordings with Paul Howard, Louis Armstrong, and Les Hite, and those with T-Bone Walker, Ceelle Burke, and Peppy Prince postwar, George also recorded as a freelance with R&B artists like Kitty Thomas, Joe Evans, and Little Miss Cornshucks.

Along with fellow trumpeter Andy Blakeney, George was part of the Creole Jazz Band that helped his hero Louis Armstrong celebrate his seventieth birthday at a huge concert at the Shrine Auditorium in July 1970.

My view is that a guy should be himself and play himself. I never forget when I went to the studio once to do some recording. I walked in and the music was sitting up there on the stand. I told Charlie Lawrence, who happened to be on the session, "I don't know what to do on this," and he says, "Just be yourself." I started thinking, "Have I ever been myself? Who am I? I'm always trying to do this like somebody else." Hell, that was something that made me stop and think. It's just like you're going on the stage as an actor playing the part of Pagliacci or somebody. Somebody else. So just be yourself is my advice.

Chapter Four

Nathaniel Jack "Monk" McFay

Drums

Everybody in Los Angeles seemed to know Monk McFay, but locating him took awhile. We found him in August 1990 living in a rather anonymous but comfortable retirement facility on South Oxford in the Crenshaw area. Several elderly African American men were sitting outside, and they directed us to Monk's apartment. His greeting was warm and cordial. The living room was lined with jazz LP sleeves arranged at floor level like a continuous frieze. Lively in speech and emphatic, Monk explained that he no longer played although he retained his membership of Local 47 AFM. There was no sign of a drum kit.

He told us he kept in daily touch with his former bandleader and lifelong friend, the tenor saxophonist and Clef Club president Buddy Banks, then resident in Desert Hot Springs, where he held down a regular gig as a pianist, the tenor having been put aside. Monk put me on the line to Buddy who had nothing but warm praise for his old friend.

Monk had his true heyday in Hawaii as sideman and bandleader, gaining attention in the jazz press as much for his misdemeanors as for his musical prowess. Once back in Los Angeles, he was soon busy as a jobbing musician up and down Central Avenue, often with rhythm and blues combos. If his fame was largely confined to black Los Angeles, he seemed content enough with that. While he clearly enjoyed sharing these memories, however incomplete or sketchy, you sensed he'd love to be back on a bandstand somewhere, soaking up the adulation he recalled with such glee. That said, he seemed resigned to the need to watch his health.

He lent me a great number of photographs and was something of a jazz custodian, having hung on to all sorts of material. When I returned five years

Monk McFay of the Brown Cats of Rhythm, Honolulu, Hawaii, April 1940. Courtesy Harold S. Kaye / Monk McFay.

later, he was gone—to where, nobody knew. It took Howard Rye's research to establish that Monk had died the year before in Los Angeles, on either October 22 or 23, 1994, and that his family had taken him home to Oklahoma for burial.

Nathaniel "Monk" McFay: Los Angeles, August 27, 1990

I was born in Wichita Falls, Texas, 1908, June the 27th. A long time ago! We were poor, coming up there, so I worked as a dishwasher or shining shoes to make a living, just doing odd jobs. My father was a kinda rambler and he took off. The last time I saw my father, I guess I was between ten and eleven. The next thing I heard he had died of pneumonia so that ended that. Then it was just three of us, my mother, my sister, and me. I lost my mother the first of this year [1990]. She was ninety-seven years old. She fell and broke her hip, and then during her stay in hospital, she tried to get out of bed and she fell and broke the other hip. She never did walk no more.

She came out here [Los Angeles] in 1936. She was everything to me, God rest her soul. She was marvelous. Mama didn't do nothing; early days she worked as a maid before she got her family, and that's all she did. She married a couple of times, different husbands. We moved to Fort Worth, and we stayed there for quite a while until I grew up and came out of high school. Then we moved back to Wichita Falls. That's where everything happened.

My first instrument was saxophone and my favorite was Herschel Evans, but that didn't go too well. Herschel and Buddy Tate was playing alto then; Don Byas and Wallace Mercer, all the good players around was on alto. Buddy Banks, he started on alto, stayed on alto for little over a year. Of course, they all played tenor later on.

I did play with a white group in Texas. I was just a teenager. This was after we came back from Fort Worth. It sound like I was the only black man that ever played with a white group back then in Texas. This was at night at a roadhouse. He was a saxophone player; we call him Curly Robinson, and his wife played piano. He said, "What you do at night, when you come to work, you put on an apron and when we open up, when me and my wife start playing, you keep the apron on and play, and we tell everybody around that you supposed to be a waiter." So finally after working for them so long, the public were getting to accept me. We had a marvelous time.

When I left home, which was in '28, I got to go down to Amarillo. That was a trend then; it looked like everybody was leavin' my hometown and going to Amarillo. Things were good in Amarillo during that time. Plenty of work. Even during the Depression. See, there they didn't know about no Depression but they had it here [LA]. Back then, I was known as a dancer. My dancing, it wasn't professional. I was just a ballroom dancer. I used to have white couples ask me to come to their homes to show them some steps. One time I was getting paid for doing that. Then I start fooling around with music and I forgot all about dancing. I struck it lucky. I did very well in Amarillo.

My first job playing music, professionally, was with a bunch of musicians that had been with Gene Coy's Black Aces. Nineteen hundred and thirty, that's when this band was going to play a dance at Crook's dance hall in Amarillo for New Year's Eve and the drummer had left. They didn't have no drummer so they came to me and they say, "Well, Monk, you dance all the time; you can hold the time for us." I said I'd try and so I played this dance with them and upon completing the dance that night, we had a meeting. "We like what you did for us; if we get you some drums, will you stay with the band?" The bass player with this group was a former drummer and he began to give me lessons, so now I was in the band.

It was Roderick Thomas and his "Little Rod" Orchestra. Little Rod had been first trumpet player with Gene Coy back east. Gene was a drummer and I knew him well. I met him back in the twenties, he and his wife Ann; she played piano in the band. They had a terrific band. It was then I got my name "Monk"—my real name is Nathaniel. They said, "When you playin', you look just like a monkey. We gonna call you 'Monk.'" So I said all right and that started that. I'm stuck with it now. A lot of people only know me as Monk.

So I had to leave there with this band until we got to Nebraska. Scott's Bluff, Nebraska [the base for booker Vernon McDonald], *and that's where we ran into some other bands like Biagnini's Orange Blossoms, Sax Mallett, Smilin' Billy Stewart and his Celery City Serenaders—that was a famous band—and Gene Coy's Black Aces—that's one of the bands on the circuit with us. Then we got a telegram from Durango, Colorado; this fellow owned a big store there and he seemed to like us. We were doing all right, so we got away from McDonald's circuit and stayed in Colorado. That's where we got stranded* [laughs]. *That was one time I wanted to come home; me and Buddy Banks, we talked about catching a freight train so finally we got in touch with a fellow named Hickman in Amarillo. He had a car and he came to Durango to pick us up and bring the whole band back to Amarillo.*

Little Rod was a very nice trumpet man, but the best musician in the band was E. J. [Emmett] *Malone. He was a trumpeter and arranger in the band, and the one that taught Buddy Tate and all of them. Trombone man was fair; his name was Manzie* [Fanning]. *There was Tommy Holmes, third alto; Buddy Banks, tenor; and Mel Wright, first alto. Naturally, they doubled on clarinet and baritone. One-night stands, oh, we played so many of them, all of us traveling in a special Packard car. Played white dances too. When we quit McDonald's circuit, Nat Towles made it good for us, but with him it got to a place where we weren't making any money and Nat was spending all his money keeping us with food and places to stay. He said, "I'm gonna put you fellows on a basis where we'll give you a meal ticket that last a week." Finally that ran out and we weren't making* any *kind of money and he said, "I can't afford you fellows no more" and now we was on our own. I was so hungry, but that was the way of life; if you stranded, you just stranded.*

Finally when Hickman came and got us, we were so glad to get back to Amarillo.

The kid I was working with in Amarillo in Little Rod's band, [vocalist and saxophonist] *Bob Johnson, when the band out at the Ritz Ballroom in Oklahoma City heard about him, they called him and sent him a ticket. They said, "You gotta good drummer with you? We want to get in touch with him." By that time I had left Amarillo and came back to Wichita Falls to stay with my grandmother. So I got a telegram from this band in Oklahoma City saying they'd send me a ticket, and another friend of mine said, "There's a band came here lookin' for you; they heard about you and they want you in the band." So I said I'd think about it. My wife was still in school, but on her last day in school, I accepted the job and I told her, "Well, if the playing is all right, I'll send for you."*

We were Joe Brantley's "Spotlight Entertainers" Orchestra, at the Ritz Ballroom. It was a fine band. They were all good musicians, all sight readers. They could play and *read. They didn't* have *to have everything written. C. Q. Price was on alto; Pal Tillman, alto; "Popeye" Hale, alto—he was a good man. In the rhythm section was Abe Bolar, bass; Charlie Christian, guitar; Leslie Sheffield on piano; me, Monk on drums. Bob Johnson was our vocalist and the bandleader; Joe Brantley played trumpet, along with Leonard Chadwick and Miles Jones. A good band, no doubt about it. They rehearsed every day, even on Sundays; if they wasn't doing nothing, they'd rehearse. The band was tight; you couldn't put a pin between 'em. Everything they played, if a guy would pick out a solo, tenor man or alto man, or John White on clarinet, whatever tune it was, it was so knitted together. That's one band I enjoyed because there was just something about it that made me feel I was somebody. That was really the beginning for me. It got in my blood and I said, "This is it."*

My playing was goin' fine, to tell you the truth. I got to where my picture came out in the Down Beat *[in 1940]. They call me the "Krupa of Honolulu," but actually my favourite drummer before I met Jo Jones from Basie's band was Herbert Cowens.*[1] *He was a show drummer, and the next drummer I really admired was A. G. Godley.*[2] *He was the first drummer I ever did witness take drum solos. I dug him. Then came Jo Jones with Count Basie. That was it. I'm talking about personality, man, playing with that band. Basie never did have nothing but good drummers. See, after Jo got to be so famous, I'd sit in with the band, playing a lot of times but I never did go* [permanently] *in Basie's band. Basie was a beautiful person and he'd always tell me, "Come on, and sit in with the band."*

During my time with Brantley, I became a good support for soloists in that band. I never was a helluva take-off man. I could take off [solo]*, but I wasn't thinking about that. I was thinking about holding that time and keeping it going in a straight line. That bass drum meant something there.*

I learned a lot of little tricks, twiddling sticks and throwing them in the air, but well, the piano player stopped me doing that. I used to watch a drummer called Jimmy Westbrook.[3] He passed away here [LA]. They called him a "sensational" drummer. I got to where I was throwing up sticks like him, and Tommy Mitchell, the pianist in Little Rod's band and a very fine musician, gave me some advice and I got to thinking. He said, "You can't play no rhythm with sticks in the air." That opened my eyes and it's true. Back in those days it was showmanship, but they called it "sensational" drumming. Like A. G. Godley, who had a light in the bass drum, and when he'd be ready to take off, they'd darken the bandstand, and the light would be flashing on the drummer. I loved that.

Leslie Sheffield and myself were rooming together, and we had a piano in the room. Every time a band would come up to Oklahoma City, we'd have jam sessions. Lester Young would come over. Coleman [Hawkins] would come over. I wouldn't set up my full kit of drums; I would have a sock cymbal and a snare drum, a wire brush and a stick, that's all. Hot Lips Page from Texarkana, anytime he'd come to town, he'd always come to the room. We were all in there. Later on, Roy Eldridge came in. I played with him a lot of times. That's where you learned something off this or that guy. They'd be trying to cut one another, to blow, and then this cat would say that was a good passage but now listen to this and he'd take off. In those jam sessions, they'd want you, the drummer, to keep time, play some rhythm for them, not to take off. The take-off men was the trombone, clarinet and saxophones, and trumpets, and that's what they wanted, but I got the chance to play with so many good musicians that way.

At nights, when we'd get off work at the Ritz Ballroom, we'd come to one place, an after-hour joint called Honey Murphy's. That where all the musicians hung out at night. We'd jam all *night. This cat would take some, that cat would take some, and that's where everybody began to notice Charles [Christian]. He was my buddy. When Charles started playing, they would all stop and look at him. When this boy that played guitar with Andy Kirk, Floyd Smith, came in, they would hang up [play] and go for hours, but none of them couldn't seem to get with Charles. He was crazy about Lester Young, and he wanted to sound like a saxophone, like Lester. Finally Eddie Durham came there, and that was the only guitarist that I knew Charles would listen to. Back then, Eddie was playing trombone and arranging, as well as playing guitar. I had been knowing Eddie and all his brothers—they're from San Marcos, Texas—that's Earl Durham, saxophone and guitar; Joe Durham, bass and guitar; Roosevelt Durham, piano; and all of them could play. Trombonist Allen Durham—that's a different Durham family; they're cousins—and I worked with him in Eddie Christian's band in Los Angeles later on. Back then he was with Les Hite. He played before with Gene Coy's Black Aces, him and his brother Clyde, a tuba player.*

After about two years, Leslie Sheffield[4] took the band over from Joe Brantley; this was while we were still working steady at the Ritz Ballroom. We still had C. Q. Price, alto; also Charles Wright, tenor and alto and clarinet; and little Jack Washington on alto. Count Basie came and got him out of our band. We didn't have but four brass: three trumpets, which consisted of Carl "Tatti" Smith, Leonard Chadwick, and Miles Jones, and trombone was Artis Bryant, who went to Honolulu with me later. Charles stayed with the band until he went to Alphonso Trent. Next time I saw him, he had joined Benny Goodman.

So Charles left the band first and I worked a little over a year with him. C. Q. left next and then I say, "I believe I'll take off—I think I'll go to Chicago." Overnight I changed my mind to come out here to California. 1935. My sister was out here, and I knew some musicians out here. There was a lot of work; all the musicians was working. That was what I came out for. I got out here, and I knew a fellow that was working at the Club Alabam so I'd go every night. One night, I was sitting there watching, listening to the band, and they sound pretty good so I went over and I say, "Hey, man, let me play one," and the leader say, "That's not our tradition, but if the drummer agrees, it's OK with me." The drummer was Oscar Bradley, and he let me sit in on one. It worked out real nice so the next evening, they was playing a matinee there at the Elks Club, so I go to the club and they're playing some jazz that I kinda liked. It was Buddy Collette, Jack McVea, "Big Six" [Oliver Reeves], saxophone section; Red Mack and Teddy Buckner, trumpets; Bert Johnson, trombone; Vernon Gower, bass; Buddy Harper, guitar; Oscar Bradley and the leader, Lorenzo Flennoy, on piano. That was a good band. They were together, like they were real musicians. They weren't just honky-tonks. I told Lorenzo again, "I sure would like to play one because you sound real good," and Oscar said, "Come on, play one."

I wasn't working with nobody. I was just new in town, so I said, "I'm gonna show off a little bit" [laughs]. It was quite a hit, and when I walk off the bandstand, there's three different guys asking, "Who you work with? I got a job for you," so I went to work with Cappy Oliver, trumpeter, and a bunch of nice fellows. The group wasn't but six of us. The leader was Charlie Whitfield. We had two reeds, three rhythm, and one brass. Charlie played saxophone, a good little musician but he wasn't a helluva get-off man but he could take off. He died year before last, out in Las Vegas. Cappy Oliver[5] was one of the outstanding trumpet players here. He and Lloyd Reese, and Red Mack, they were the top trumpet players in LA. After I was here three weeks, Bernard Banks came to me—this was Buddy Banks's brother, who played piano. He said, "Monk, I didn't know you could play like that, man. I gotta job for you in Honolulu. I'd like you to go with me. A little friend of mine was going to go but I want you." I said, "OK, I won't accept any other jobs." I knew Bernard from school days in Wichita Falls; we were kids together, him and his brother and me.

April '35, and I made a five-day trip to Hawaii.[6] After I got through that boat ride, I was glad to get on land. The owner of the ballroom met us at the ship and took us straight to the [Casino] ballroom, which was on Nuuanu Avenue and Beretania Street in downtown Honolulu. I took my drums out and set them up, and then he's taking us to have food. We went home then, and he had our rooms all ready. So that night, they were all saying, well, we haven't seen nothing like that on that bandstand. They all were watching me, and I put on quite a little show for 'em. From then on, every night that place was full.

We had Andrew Blakeney, trumpet; Artis Bryant, trombone; Charlie Wright, saxophone; Bernard Banks, piano; Eddie Williams, bass; and me on drums. We were called Bernard Banks and His Clouds of Rhythm. Then about a year later, Bernard got hit; a taxi driver knocked him down. He loved to read, and when he got out of the taxi, he had his head back in that book, reading as he walked across the street, and this other taxi came around and threw him in the air. That was a sad moment. To show you what kind of friends we were, we were in diapers together, and I'd go to see him in the hospital and he'd say, "I don't know you. Who are you?" He wasn't no good after that. It affected him; he came back here [LA], but he wasn't the same and he passed away.

Blakeney became the leader. I'd been used to one style of trumpet; I'm not saying he couldn't play, but I'd been used to hearing Hot Lips Page. Blakeney was a good man, a good musician, but he wasn't exciting. He could hit them high notes, but he wasn't what we would say was a rough trumpet player. He just sat there, and the notes would be coming out. We always did get along; I call him now and I call him "Boss Man." He's a beautiful person. Beautiful mind and he's intelligent, but he just wasn't exciting like most trumpet players. There weren't any exciting players in Banks's band. That's why they watched me. They played all on me. It was something like a jazz or a swing band, but improvising in that band was mediocre.

I didn't have no trouble with the Hawaiian people. One incident that happened over there was with Tony Gora. He was Hawaiian American, a former boxer, and he owned the College Inn nightclub. So I was sitting in his place one day, talking with him while some customers were sitting at the bar having a little drink when some black sailors came to the door. He stopped them, "You have to have a pass to come in here," so after they left, I said, "Tony, why didn't you let the sailors come in?" He said, "Monk, I'm gonna be frank with you. Every time them colored sailors and whites get together in these bars, they start a fight. I'm not prejudiced, but I don't want my place tore up." When I first got there, there were only seven black people living in Honolulu. There weren't any black soldiers out at Schofield Barracks, but at

Pearl Harbor, there were quite a few black sailors, and anytime they got into town and got to drinking, they start fighting.

Nine months into their original engagement at the Casino Ballroom, a taxi-dance hall for sailors, McFay was contacted by Michael Angelo, who owned the nearby Casa Loma ballroom, to form a band. Armed with second-class return tickets, McFay, who had made for Oklahoma City for a playing vacation, persuaded tenor saxophonists Leon Shadowin and Ernie "Boots" Wilks, trumpeter John Ursery, altoist Kirt Bradford (from Blakeney's band), and pianist Ted Abrams to join him in Honolulu in summer 1937. After four months, McFay and the band moved over to the College Inn and later on to the Kewalo Inn on the Honolulu waterfront. Meanwhile, Andrew Blakeney had taken over leadership of the Casino band, now rechristened the Brown Cats of Rhythm, and modified the personnel, most notably by incorporating the fine alto saxophonist Kirt Bradford, who had stopped off in Hawaii on his way back from a playing visit to Shanghai with Happy Johnson's band.

Following the Kewalo Inn engagement, McFay disbanded and returned to the mainland on vacation in late 1938 before resuming in Honolulu, having selected new recruits for the Casino Ballroom band at owner J. T. Yung's behest: bassist DeWitt T. Ray, reedman Cecil "Count" Carter, and trombonist Henry Coker. By May 1939, the Brown Cats lined up as Andy Blakeney (t); Coker (tb); Cecil "Count" Carter, Bradford (as); Shadowin (ts); Ray Gregory (p); Ray (b); Monk McFay (d).

Down Beat, October 1, 1939

Writers Find Jump Band in Honolulu—The boys produce an uncommon jump and drive which should aid them immensely on the road to prominence. In general the band styles after Basie. It has been together about a year now and possesses a stellar drummer, Nathaniel [Monk] McFay who idolizes Jo Jones and whose work might easily be mistaken for Jo's. They were buddies once. Andrew Blakeney, trumpet and head man, is an alumnus of the old Les Hite band. Kurt [sic] Bradford, alto, is the other ace soloist.

Later on, we had Kirt Bradford in the band. Now, he was a very good musician. He had to be to go with Jimmie Lunceford and to take Willie Smith's place. I brought Henry Coker to Honolulu, that second time. He was a terrific trombone man, no doubt about it. He had been playing with Nat Towles's band in Omaha. I got him out of Nat's band. He didn't get the recognition he should have gotten. I don't know why. He was like you and me. They got their own ways, but to me you have to adjust yourself if you in another man's band; you gotta do what he wants you to do in his band.

Down Beat, June 15, 1940

Slingerland Drum Co—Advertisement with McFay photo
SLINGERLANDS ARE PLAYED THE WORLD OVER!
  In Hawaii—it's Nathaniel (Monk) McFay with the sizzling swing band, "Brown Cats of Rhythm." Currently playing at the popular Casino in Honolulu, the Brown Cats are easily the island's most well-liked band.

Down Beat, April 1, 1941
  Stuff Seems To Be On The Stir in Hawaii—This town's hot fans find their stuff at the Casino where a coloured crew managed by Andy Blakeney bats out the real thing six nights a week. Cecil Carter and Leon Shadowen [sic] play buckets full of saxophone and the leader gets a lot of Louis on horn.

Down Beat, July 15, 1941
  Honolulu: At the Casino, the loss of the excellent trappist Monk McFay to "those people" [the law], Cecil Carter to a Sanitarium, and the truly fine trombonist L.C. Coker [Henry Coker] to the draft board put the skids on the town's top jive crew. But nothing daunted, leader Blakeney scuttled back to the coast and will return soon with more colored cats to fill the empty chairs. In the meantime, Rafael Greagor, Leon Shadowin, and Dewitt Ray sit sadly and play, trying like hell not to hear the substitutes.

A white boy and myself, he was smoking [marijuana] and I was smoking too. I'd buy from him and he'd buy from me. I had connections with some friends who were bringing me some from India, Australia, and other countries. This was good, powerful stuff. I let him have it, what I had, and this had been going on for over a year. When they [the police] caught him, they told him, "You tell us where you got it and we make easy for you." See, I didn't know they'd caught him, so they let him out of jail and he called me. "I want about $60 worth" and he came and got it and the cops were with him. They parked where I couldn't see 'em. He got in the car and I noticed he didn't look right, but I had entrusted him and he had entrusted me so the minute he walked out, I put the money in my bathrobe pocket and went back in the bedroom and my wife said, "Baby, that car's full of police." They came in and they said, "Where's that money?" and it was marked. They knew the serial numbers. I said, "Well, I'll be damned." They said, "How did you get it?" I said, "I got it off the boat. Met some guys who bring it in and I picked it up." "How did you get it home?" "Put it in my car and bring it home." I knew that was a trap.
  They confiscated my car. The money I had in the bank, they confiscated that. I had money back in Los Angeles with the Bank of America and they confiscated that. The warden told me, "Monk, they cleaned you out." So I got nothing. You want to laugh about it. The judge said, "Monk, big a name as you've got and because I want to warn people, I'm going make you do fifteen months in jail." But I wasn't peddling no dope: I bought from him; he bought

from me. I was ashamed because everybody knew me and I was so well-liked. The [prison] *warden called me to his office, he say, "McFay, how did you get yourself into this predicament?" I said, "I got all my credentials. I was teaching; I was making money playing. I didn't need to do that," so he said he was gonna let my wife come and see me during the day. "There's a private room where you and your wife can talk." I thanked him. "While you're here, I tell you what you do. Bring your drums out here, and after you get through your work in the morning, you free to do what you want to do within the prison."*

The guy that told the cops about me, he was in there, and every time I looked at him, I said, "Don't you fool with him; he's no good." He knew he ain't got but a short time in here and then they let him out. Then the warden told me, "After you here for six months, you write in for compensation. I'll sign for you," so I wrote in but they wouldn't accept. I tried again more times. My own son was twelve-and-a-half years old then. I was there [in prison] *for Pearl Harbor* [December 7, 1941]. *I was about two blocks from Hickam Fields where the first* [Japanese] *plane bombed. Then Schofield Barracks, they got that, but the big damage was to the Pearl Harbor Naval Base. All the military installations, they got them all.*

My marriage came to an end after I got out of jail in 1942. See, I had been fooling around with Chinese girls, Hawaiian girls, Filipinos, Japanese . . . I'd go with all kinds. I had myself a ball. They seemed to like me. After I got out I ran into this Rogers guy, and I joined the band at the Royal Hawaiian Hotel [2259 Kalakaua Avenue, Honolulu]. *I showed up and played one. "We gonna let Monk play one with this white band," and when I got off the bandstand, Rogers, the leader said, "You gonna work here." They already had a drummer and me and him got along real fine, but he said, "Well, Monk, they really like you better that they do me." They fired him and hired me.*

So after I got me a little money, I told a friend, "Ain't nothing changed but I don't feel the same. Here I am a musician but I'm billed as a dope peddler so I'm gonna go back to the mainland." That arrest for dope, I'll never forget that. I had such a big name in Honolulu. Just smoking marijuana, that's all I was doing. Cocaine, opium, I'd been around all that crap. I'd drink like a fish and roll me some marijuana but that other stuff, oh, no. He said, "Monk, I'll tell you, so many people trying to get back to the mainland—see, this is during the war—but I'll go to see some of my friends and see what I can do for you." I said, "I certainly would appreciate that," so that night the phone rang, he say, "Monk, I got things fixed. You be ready to leave Saturday evening."

So Saturday evening I went down to the ship, and the second day out, they called, "Will the owner of the drums go to the purser's office?" I went up there and he say, "You a drummer? It's so dry and dull here. Will you help to entertain these people?" so he announced if there were any musicians on board would they report to the purser's office. Come to find out, I got hold of a bass player, two guitars, saxophone player, and a piano player. That was it. We playing all the way from out at sea until we got to 'Frisco. Got to 'Frisco and they had a write-up in the paper about me entertaining on the boat.

I came back on here [LA] from Frisco the last part of '42, and I went to work with Eddie Christian, Charles Christian's brother. He saw me and he said, "Well, you come to work tonight," and I started that night with Eddie on piano; Tony, Italian boy, played tenor; Basie [William Day] was on bass; and we worked a job down on Washington. After that, Eddie got this job at the Cricket Club [Washington Boulevard], which was with Allen Durham, trombone; Geechie Smith, trumpet; LeMon Thompson, tenor; it was six of us. We stayed right there until Eddie Christian, he taken sick and Buddy Banks got the job. Eddie was mediocre really, a good musician maybe. His original instrument was bass and he was a good bass player, but he switched to piano. Wasn't no take-off man. His chord structures weren't too great. After we disbanded, Geechie Smith put a band in there himself, but I was with Buddy Banks by then. The Cricket Club was a nightclub, and that's where I worked with Billy Eckstine, Herb Jeffries, and Billy Daniels. They'd be in maybe for two or three weeks at a time.

Monk played with Harlan Leonard's Rockets at Shepp's Playhouse in early 1945, the band's final engagement before Leonard disbanded and left music for good. It included Ed Preston, Norman Bowden, Miles Jones (t); Jap Jones (tb); Leonard, Earl Jackson (as); Jack McVea, Preston Love (ts); Arvella Moore (p); Bob Kesterson (b); and Monk McFay (d).

Down Beat, April 15, 1945
    McGhee Builds Own Combo On Coast, Los Angeles—Howard McGhee, trumpet player with Coleman Hawkins, has organized his own combo here and planned to leave Hawkins at close of latter's engagement at Billy Berg's Supper Club April 15.
    New McGhee unit includes Nat McVey [sic], drums; Vernon Biddle, piano; Stan Morgan, guitar; Eddie Davis, tenor sax. They expect to open at the California Theater Club Bar in San Francisco latter part of the month.

Metronome, May 1945
    Los Angeles—Hawk lost Howard McGhee, trumpeter, when the Shadow left for Frisco to form a five-piece band which features Monk McFay, drums.

Down Beat, May 15, 1945
    Los Angeles—Howard McGhee slated to bring his new band into the Down Beat club May 6.

The Capitol, June 1945

McGhee at Down Beat—Howard McGhee's new six-piece combo opened last month at the Down Beat club in L.A. McGhee plays trumpet.

I got Howard McGhee to join Buddy Banks's band because he wasn't making no kind of money. Bebop was just comin' in, and in Howard's new band was Teddy Edwards, tenor—Howard made him change from alto—Charlie Mingus, bass; Vernon Biddle, piano; Stanley Morgan, guitar; Howard, trumpet; and me on drums. I worked with them a while and we wasn't makin' no money on Central Avenue at the Down Beat club, and then Roy Porter, he come into the Down Beat while we was workin' and he asked me if he could sit in. I said, yeah, so during that time I turned in my notice, and Howard asked me, "How you think Roy Porter would work with us?" I say, "He's good. He fits this band good."

Monk was still with McGhee when the band, said to be the first to play modern jazz on the coast, made their debut recording for Modern Music in May 1945, but was replaced on later dates and live engagements by Roy Porter, a drummer better suited to the band's bebop style. "Howard wanted my drumming to be lighter. I had just been playing with a big band [Harlan Leonard] but Howard wanted to hear less of the bass drum," Monk told writer Ted Gioia.

After that I went back with Buddy. Everybody was talking about what a nice band he had. They liked that band. We rehearsed seven days a week, all through the day. We were together. *We had Frosty Pyles, very fine guitarist; Basie on bass—he passed away in Portland about five years ago—and Wallace Huff, fine trombonist. He just passed. We went out to Oregon; we went to Seattle, Washington, and to San Francisco, to Oakland, played up there six weeks at Slim Jenkins's club.*[7] *He had a liquor store there. It wasn't no rhythm and blues band, just nice, danceable music and listening music. Buddy sang, and we had a girl from New Orleans, Baby Davis, she sang with us, and another girl singer started out with us; her name was Fluffy Hunter. Buddy's style on tenor wasn't exciting, but he's very nice, he's cool, man, and his playing was beautiful. It wasn't rough. His style was rather like Herschel Evans. That was his influence. He loved Herschel.*

California Eagle, November 1, 1945

Buddy Banks and his fine Hollywood Sextete [including McFay] are currently supplying the Last Word café at 42nd and Central with correct atmosphere music. They are specialists at a variety of departments of instrumental musical entertainment. Their fine playing runs from quality dinner music through smooth boogie to hot lick jazz.

Then the same thing happened to me again. We were playing down at the Club Royal in San Diego in 1949, and this friend came up to my room and we laid down on the bed and the next thing, the cops were in there, in my room. One of the officers went into my clothes closet, came out with my coat, with three joints of marijuana. I jumped out of the bed and I said, "That don't belong to me." There were three of them and they pulled a pistol. The girl was naked; she's laying on the bed and they say, "Has he touched you yet?" She started to call them all kinds of bad names, and they pushed her back. "You sit down!" And then they took me to jail. This didn't make sense. I didn't have no marijuana, so a friend of mine got me a lawyer, and after I explained what happened, he said, "Monk, they were mad at you about the white woman because she was naked and she was laying on the bed and called them all kinds of bad names." The judge, when they took me to trial, my lady friend, she was there and she got pissed off. See, that marijuana did not belong to me. I didn't know nothing about it. Oh, yeah, I was still smoking but those joints weren't mine.

The judge said, "I see where you got another conviction for marijuana, McFay. Well, I don't know what to do with you, but I tell you what I'm gonna do. I'm going to give you six months in jail, and two and a half years on probation." I said, "Well, thank you, Judge," and I stayed in that one cell for six months down there in San Diego. They kept me locked in jail. Wasn't no get out and walk a lot, go here, go there. Couldn't do that. That second time, I was not guilty, I know that. First time, that marijuana was mine. I really had it then, but I never did deal in it. I tell you the truth.

Then I say, from when I got this [jail sentence], *I ain't gonna fool with marijuana no more; I'm gonna smoke a Chesterfield cigarette. After that I did a USO job. Played for the soldiers. Then I went back with Buddy. He had Charlie Blackwell, also Sam Joshua covering for me, and Sam was with the band when I got out of jail.*

I joined Joe Liggins in 1951 and I stayed with Joe almost two years. We made trips, tours, all down south, all back east. Joe was very popular. To tell you the truth about it, I was surprised when I joined him how in every town we'd go to, people would be in line waiting to hear that Joe Liggins Honeydrippers.[8] *He had a good band, but it wasn't as good as our band* [Buddy Banks]. *Joe's band was more like the John Kirby Sextet. He had Harold Grant, guitar; three saxophones, Jimmy Jackson—he was the original man—Floyd Turnham—a good musician and on top of it, a gentleman and a very nice fellow—and Brother Woodman; Bill Cooper, bass; Joe on piano; and me.*

The Seventh Annual Cavalcade of Jazz held on Sunday, July 8, 1951, at Wrigley Field in Los Angeles featured Joe Liggins's "new look" Honeydrippers R&B combo with Monk McFay on drums replacing Peppy Prince. Others on this all–African American bill included Lionel Hampton, Jimmy Witherspoon, Percy Mayfield, and Candy Rivers.

Monk recorded extensively with the Buddy Banks Sextete, accompanying singers like Fred Clark, Bixie Crawford, and Marion Abernathy, during the 1940s, later appearing with various Roy Milton lineups and as a member of the Floyd Dixon Trio and with Joe Liggins's Honeydrippers in the 1950s.

After Joe Liggins, I joined Art Foxall.[9] *Stayed with him for maybe ten years or more. He kept working all the time. It started out with just three of us, him on tenor, Dorothy Broil on organ, and myself. He never would hire nobody else. He only wanted a trio. He's from Houston, Texas, and he played tenor; he was an Illinois Jacquet, Arnett Cobb player. That was him; he sound like Arnett. I liked Arnett and I had worked with Illinois, before he left here; Coker was in the band [1948–1951]. I was in that band for quite a while. That was before Illinois got a big name. He left here [LA] and he didn't look back. His brother, [trumpeter] Russell Jacquet, went with him. I didn't go. That was before I went to Canada, sometime in the 1940s. Played different jobs, right here in town; this was before Illinois got to be a big star with Norman Granz with Jazz at the Philharmonic.*

Tahoe–Carson City Appeal, August 30, 1962
The Art Foxall Trio, playing nightly in Bill Fong's International Room is an aggregation of seasoned musicians, all stars in their own right. They have been playing together for 8 1/2 years and have had engagements all over the United States.

Monk McFay, drummer extraordinaire, has played with famous names from Johnny Ray to Count Basie, and is well known among all the musical greats. His gravel voice is said to be a "real Louis Armstrong sound."

We had a group called the Courtiers; that was in the sixties and we did pretty good. Eddie Williams—me and him left together to go to Honolulu—was on bass. He had a stroke. Frosty Pyles, from Buddy's band, he played guitar like Charles Christian, and Fletcher Smith was on piano. I talked to him yesterday. He toured with one of them Inkspots groups.

I retired in Art Foxall's band. We went to Canada. We were three months in one hotel, three months in another hotel, and we got back here and I say, "I'm tired of running around. I enjoyed everything but I'm hanging 'em up." I took a few off and on gigs with Buddy, and then I decided to retire completely. I could see where my breath was getting short, so I said, "Banks, that's enough. I don't want to overdo it." My drums are in a clothes closet. All my whole set. Other kind of work? No, that's it. I've taken no other kind of work. I go up there and draw Social Security. I'm living on my own and I have a couple of dollars saved. Live me a quiet life. I got no worries. I've enjoyed myself.

The doctor told me I'd been smoking too much—my breath was getting short; I had emphysema—and he said, "You better put the cigarettes down, put the alcohol down." Right on the bottom line. That was it. That's been twelve years now [1978]. So I put it all down, haven't touched none of it since.

Every now and then, I go out and they haven't seen me in a long time. "Man, where the hell you been? We haven't seen you. Make yourself known." I say, "I'm around and I made myself known years ago." They say, "Come on and play one." I say, "I'd like to, but no, not now." I can play maybe ten or twelve minutes, then I'd get tired. I can cut it, but I can't cut it long. It's still in my blood, but I can't cut the mustard no more. What used to be ain't no more but it has been. That's my line.

One of my finest jobs was in Santa Fe, Mexico, at the ballroom there. I played there with Little Rod's band for four weeks. That was one of the best jobs because we were stationed right there. I made a whole lot of money. I had so many friends there, Spanish people, so I took another job in Taos, Mexico, back in the thirties. Most of my jobs were good jobs, where you made nice, decent bread, and people were nice about coming to listen to you, take you out, and invite you to their homes, so you meet the people. I had a lot of fun.

Chapter Five

Floyd Payne Turnham Jr.

Clarinet and Alto, Tenor, and Baritone Saxophones

Floyd Turnham's jazz story is a tale of two cities, Seattle, Washington, and Los Angeles, California. He played a significant role in both places, initially as the scion of a musical family in Seattle and latterly as a busy sideman and soloist in and around Los Angeles. His recording credits are endless and cover everything from big band swing to combo jazz and R&B, his versatility and musicianship having allowed him to adjust to the changing fashions in local African American music with seeming ease.

I had already been in touch with Floyd by mail but was pleasantly surprised when he appeared in London in 1984 with British expatriate drummer Barry Martyn's reinvigorated Legends of Jazz. This sextet was due to play London's 100 Club on June 20, 1984, so we arranged to meet at Floyd's hotel before the gig for the interview that appears here. His deep-throated chuckle suffused the entire encounter as did his relaxed, laconic speech style. Seattle jazz historian Paul de Barros described him as a "lanky fellow given to naughty winks and stories, who was an amiable, slow-talking man," and that seems about right. His recollections were more or less random, each subject sparked by another, his second wife, Georgia, often adding her own observations, although other references confirmed that his recall was generally spot-on even if his remembrance of dates was often wayward.

Floyd's tenor playing when heard in person was a mixture of bustling drive on up-tempo numbers and Hawkins-like rhapsodic strength on ballads, always with swing in mind. Certainly underrated, he knew how to grandstand and build a solo with hoarse, simple phrases, cheerfully joining his companions as they paraded noisily around the packed club blasting away on "The Saints." There is a glimpse of this prowess on the band's 1979 recording and

Floyd Turnham Jr., Los Angeles, 1970s. Courtesy Floyd Levin / Crescent Jazz Productions.

rather surprisingly, on *Last of the Line*, a 1983 album with Barry Martyn's specially constituted Eagle Brass Band, with Andy Blakeney and John Ewing also among the personnel.

When I arrived in Los Angeles in 1990, it was to find that Floyd was now fully retired and living over in La Habra up near the Orange County line with Georgia and enjoying life. I was saddened not to be able to meet up with him again; more so when I heard that he had died in La Habra on May 5, 1991. He was 82.

Floyd Turnham Jr.: Mowbray Court Hotel, London, June 20, 1984

I was born in Spokane, Washington, January 23, 1909. Momma played piano and Dad played drums. They were just beautiful people. My mother was always a musician. She had played on the stage doing minstrel stuff before I was born. I got some old pictures and my dad was the black-face comedian on the end, and she's in one of them old-time mammy costumes. Every once in a while she would play them Indian tunes and I'd stand beside the piano and do the Indian dance. This was when I was about six or eight years old, even before I started playin' violin. Then I had a water hose, about a foot and a half long, and I used to hold it up to my mouth and blow through it and make tones. Later on, she had me playing violin before I got me a saxophone. I was about twelve, thirteen years old then.

Spokane, between Idaho State and Washington State, almost on the border line, was a small town, with two-story brick houses and not too many blacks and Indians. I don't think they had even four to five hundred of us there. My grandfather worked at Centennial Mill, and my dad worked at the Spokane Club as a waiter. He run into a violin player there, and the guy wanted to teach me violin so dad got him to teach me. I start takin' my violin to him. I couldn't bow then, but he'd hit me across my hand, and then finally, Momma got me a saxophone. After she put the saxophone in my hand, I start taking lessons from a fellow named Donovan in Spokane. I took lessons from him for a while. Later on, my teacher in Seattle was Frank Waldron[1] who taught a lot of Paul Whiteman's musicians when they came to Seattle in the twenties and thirties. He said, "Don't use no vibrato. Play a straight tone. Make it sound like an organ." When I practiced at home, I'd shake the reed to get a quality, but I knew I better not do that in front of Mr Waldron.

Finally, I start workin' with Momma. I was just a kid. Three pieces, with sax, piano, and drums. Momma got the charts, and in those days, music was mostly slow. Waltzes, little slow pop songs. Some of the notes I would write out and remember; otherwise she'd take the sax chart and mark down the fingering on some of the notes for me. That's the way I read the music. I had a sister, Frances; she start learning to play piano, but she went to dancing later on in life.

First we went to Tacoma, Washington, and then we moved to Seattle later on after I got to be fifteen or sixteen years old. We worked there playing shows and different rooms so we went from three to five pieces: that's trumpet, trombone, drums, sax, and piano. Chuck Adams was on trumpet; he was an old Army man from the 25th Infantry band. Man, when that cat played with the Elks band, you'd hear that trumpet all over that place. Strong, big tone. We kept on going and finally, my mother put on a program at James A. Garfield High School [on 23rd Street in Seattle's Central District]. *That's where I played saxophone in the school band, and after that, we got a band* together and hit the Orpheum Circuit[2] in 1927. We got some kids from the high school band and went travelin' to Winnipeg, Calgary, Vancouver, Seattle—where we did a week at the Orpheum Theatre—and on down the coast to Los Angeles. When we got back to Seattle, we was on the Pantages Circuit[3] coming down. That was in theaters where they had white acts. In those days, we'd just play waltzes, had a trio of violins, and had trios of vocals, singing. Not jazz, mostly melodies. Mostly section work. My thought when I was a youngster, coming from my mother's band, I said, well, I've hit the big time, what with the Orpheum Theatre and the Pantages Circuit; this is as far as you can go in show business!

Then we got the bass player; it was Joe Bailey. He went to Broadway High School in Seattle and later worked with Les Hite at the old Cotton Club after we come out to the coast. They [Pantages] had a booking at Salt Lake City, and we didn't go because they didn't get my mother enough of a contract to go further so we stayed in Los Angeles. This was 1927; I was about seventeen. We kept working around LA and finally, work got slack; then all at once, everything picked up. Jack McVea's dad [bandleader Isaac "Satchel" McVea] worked out at the studios, and he give my mother some work out there. The majority of time with my mother I was playing mostly for white people.

Everybody was crazy about the band on white jobs like the Dover Beach Club or the Café Duprit [Dupree?] and then we worked on Station KFWB [5800 Sunset Boulevard] and at KFOX; we were the staff band. We broadcast it five times a day on KFOX. We worked down at the Oaks Tavern where [pianist] Harvey Brooks worked for years and we were down there for years. All the music publishers, they'd bring in these big stacks of stock music. Everybody in the band could read and they all read that music.

We were called Edythe Turnham and Her Eight Knights of Syncopation [changed successively to the Black Hawks and in augmented form to the Dixie Aces] with Crawford Brown, trumpet; Ray Williams, trombone; me, Fats [or Floyd] Wilson, Lanier Conn, saxes; Creon Thomas, banjo and guitar; Floyd Turnham Senior, drums; and Joe Bailey, bass. Dad had a hell of a rhythm. He was solid. This was 1928. That band didn't do too much changing. We'd get some of the old standard tunes and we revived them. You can't do that no more because of the tunes they write now; in those days the lyrics told a story.

Teddy Buckner came in the band. He just did the same things in there. Just another trumpet player. He stayed with the band at Club Alabam. That was in competition with Frank Sebastian's Cotton Club over in Culver City. He was running the white people away from there, out to the Cotton Club, all the movie stars and everyone who used to come out to the Club Alabam. Anyway, we stayed on in Los Angeles and worked around town. Like when we worked the Deauville Beach Club [Deauville Castle Club, 1525 Ocean

Front Walk, Santa Monica, built 1927], *which was a big, fine castle place. They tore that down; it broke my heart. They had colored waiters there—that was a beautiful job—and then we worked a place upstairs, down on Wiltshire. Some prize fighter had it later on in life.*

Around 12th and Central, I seen so many colored people that I said, gracious, I never did check where they'd all come from [laughs]. *In Spokane, we was raised with white people. In that thirty- or forty-piece Garfield High School band where we had violins and violas, there was only one other black person in the band. He played trumpet. There wasn't that many black people in Spokane, but when we came to Los Angeles, we was frightened; there were so many blacks! Like on Central Avenue, with all the clubs, then later on, we blacks start migrating further out down to Slauson—you couldn't go no further than Slauson—and then later on we went out further. I remember the time, I'm trying to buy a property out there, and I couldn't buy it. Because I was Negro—we say black now—but when I was coming up it was colored.*

Dad first started out as a cow puncher. He left Texas and punched all the way up to Spokane when he was a kid, met my mother—she'd come from Topeka, Kansas—and they got married in August 1907. They had a boy before me, but they lost him at about six to eight months old, and then I came along and my sister came along. Then they had another baby who was deceased. He was in one of them little baby baskets, dead. We'd have been four in the family.

I lost my mother in 1950. I still have her baby grand piano in my house. She stayed in music all the time she was in Los Angeles. We lost Dad in '36, when we worked down in San Diego, and after that she just gave up the band and she start playing by herself, with three or four pieces. I had stayed with my mother up to '37, but then I started my own group and we went into the Cricket Club on Washington Boulevard. Nellie Lutcher worked there with us.[4] *Then I had a bigger band with Bob Dorsey, Andy Anderson, Leo Trammell, myself, saxes; Red Callender on bass; Fletcher Smith on piano; Oscar Bradley on drums, who had been with me in the Cricket Club. Britt Woodman was in the trombone section with Allen Durham, and Walter Williams and Forrest Powell played trumpet. We had a big band blow-out at the Elks Auditorium with my band and Vido Musso's band and my tenor men, Bob Dorsey and Andy Anderson, blew Vido Musso off the bandstand. We was blowin' so much music, man. I thought I was up there in front. I felt just as big as Duke or Basie, the way them cats played. Man, that trumpet section! Everything was drivin', drivin', and the drive came from Oscar Bradley. Oh, he's a helluva drummer. He travels with some group in the States now. I even got a write-up over that.*

See, we had a little color barrier in LA then. After we played against Vido, I was going to all the booking agencies and out to the studios, to William Morris, all the big agents, trying to get somewhere. I knew the band was great after I did what I did, and we rehearsed and had arrangements made. I was runnin' out there, runnin' out here, couldn't get nothing so that's when I start touring with Les Hite's band. The guy that was an announcer and booker around there, Al Jarvis, he booked us, but when I looked up, there weren't no jobs for big bands any more. You tried to keep groups together then.

Ceelle Burke band? I worked with him in '37 at the Bal Tabarin in Gardena. That's when I first got my Social Security card. We were playing ukuleles and we were singin'. It used to really get me though. Part of that deal was that he would play nothing but Hawaiian music. We played three groups of threes. We'd play a sweet song, then something with all the instruments, and then play a Hawaiian tune. Band had six, eight pieces. Orendorff was in there and boy named Charlie Davis played piano. Ceelle might have had a big band later.

Andy Blakeney recalled playing with Floyd in Burke's big band in 1945 or 1946, alongside Caughey Roberts, and recording with Burke and singer Ivie Anderson for Leon René's Exclusive Records.

Down Beat, January 1, 1940
 Les Hite Gets Break; Goes Out on MCA Tour, Los Angeles—Les Hite, sepia bandleader, steamed out of this port with a crew of 15 good men, headed towards Texas and, we hope, fame. Les has been playing around this burg for the past 10 years or more and is finally getting the break he has deserved. MCA has made plans for this unit to follow Count Basie on tour and build up a following.

Down Beat, January 15, 1940
 New York—Les Hite, colored band famous for many years on the Coast, finally came East to open at the Golden Gate January 9; they'll be followed on Jan. 26 by Count Basie.

That's when I went with Les Hite, seen all my men already there so I just went on with him. We had a tour to go down to Texas [September 1939] *and we went on to New York in January 1940. We run into some bad pianos down in Texas, and man, our pianist Nat Walker, he had to play in another key from us, in the black keys. We was always playing in the white keys. Nat used to cuss. You know, he had a pair of pliers and every time we'd run into a bad piano, he'd sneak them pliers down there in some way to cut them strings in two so the people would have to get a new piano* [laughs]. *When I first went down south, I'd see the black* [drinking] *fountains and the white fountains. Man, I'd rather not care about it. Bluesman T-Bone Walker was traveling with Les's band too, and one time we played down in Texas and they had a baseball screen up in front of the bandstand, with chicken-wire across there to keep people off the bandstand. And then some woman about four feet tall pulled out a pistol, and man, everybody start runnin'. First place they run was up on the stand, knocked the baseball screen down. I'm standing there with my horn in my hand and a guy wanted to grab the bass fiddle and break it up. Bassman had a lot of trouble guarding that bass.*

New York was all right. Just another town. We played the Golden Gate Ballroom and the Apollo Theatre. We all had other opportunities during that time with Les Hite. Basie wanted me to come with him when [alto saxophonist] *Tab Smith left the band* [spring 1942] *and I said no. I did play with Basie once. He called me "Iron-Jaws" because my horn was so far over the other saxophone players that I could keep up with the trumpets. I put an old Selmer 31 "cigar-cutter" neck on my new Selmer saxophone. You get the tone from the neck. The thinness of the metal in the neck makes a bigger quality in the sound.*

But I was with Les's band and I don't like to go from band to band, and anyway, I lived on the West Coast and Basie was an eastern band. He talked to my brother-in-law—that's Earl and Francis, dance team—and later on down the line, Coleman Hawkins heard me and he said, "Man, why don't you stay in New York? You just stay here six months and I'll give you plenty jobs." In those days, you had to be in town for six months to get your Local 802 card, but it was that East and West thing again. I wanted to play with Coleman when he came to the coast, but I never got to see him here.

Sometimes I do wish I had stayed. I'd probably have made a bigger name for myself, but I'm a person in my married life; I like to be with my wife. I was married in '32 [to Daisy Bush—their union lasted forty-three years] *on November 30, my dad's birthday. She was seventy-two when she passed. She stayed looking young for years, but then the cancer got to her. Back then I didn't have no money. I was working but I had no money at all. Anyway, my wife had some money in the bank and we bought a Model-A Ford coupe for $125. That was our transportation. I paid cash for that.*

Music is beautiful, but you got to have somebody. A lot of guys can have somebody and get away from them and be happy. I can't be happy without somebody. A lot of the musicians they'd go round jamming after-hours, but I'd be home. I know Art Tatum was there and I was there too, but I never did get to see him because I didn't hang out late at night. They had a gambling joint down there where all the cats hung out and the street would be just loaded with people.

Floyd was making his way in Los Angeles music circles at a time when many of the early African American pioneers were still around and looking for youngsters to play for them.

You talking about Mutt Carey? Oh, I played a gig with him at the ten cents dance hall. I went down and read his book off just like that, and Papa Mutt was surprised because I was a good reader then and played all his stocks. As for the five-cent and ten-cent dances, I didn't want none of them jobs. I think I played a few gigs around Papa Mutt on the weekends. I played one time with Johnny Sturdivant, sax man; he taught Papa Mutt. Winslow Allen, trumpet player, he played with my mother's band one time. Country Allen, his brother, trombone player, he's still living. Curtis Mosby, I never worked for him but he had a good band then too. Leo McCoy Davis, he's still living. He's about eighty-some years old. Alto player. He did a lot of arranging for Mosby. The Spikes Brothers, they kinda died out. When I got here [LA] *Reb Spikes was running a music store; I don't know whether he worked gigs or not. I never did work with him. Charlie Echols, he had a group; I think my mother played with him. Something happened there. They was running together and my mother wanted to get married, but my sister didn't want my mother to get married. Charlie Lawrence was a helluva piano player; when you talking about somebody getting some place, he should have made it. He was a great sax player too, but he went to work playing piano. Talk about playing, he worked with me too. Way back yonder* [laughs]. *Sonny Clay, I seen him out there in Watts one time, drunk.*

There was another trumpet player who played with Curtis Mosby's Blue Blowers called King Porter, little short, stocky, bald-headed fellow, real dark, and he played a lot of trumpet. First trumpet mostly. He was scufflin' at the end. I went to Lloyd Reese for about six months when I first went to the Brass Rail taking lessons on how to make high notes on the saxophone. He really gave me a helluva study. I had a copy of it to teach, but I lost it, and then I didn't feel like teaching kids. Man, so many characters squawkin', getting a bad tone on the high notes. Lloyd give me a method for each chord, how to get up there. He played a lot of saxophone himself, but he was known mostly for trumpet.

Les Hite was fine to work with. I enjoyed it. He had that automobile accident [in the early 1930s] *that kinda busted his lip up* [when Hite stopped playing regularly], *but talk about setting sax rhythms, he'd pick up a saxophone and set some riffs when the trumpet man's blowing; man, he was beautiful. One time in 1940 we had a booking to go to the Regal Theatre in Chicago. The guys went down to the Regal Theatre to see the sign-up for Les's band and they ain't seen nothing. Come to find out we got stranded there for six months.*⁵ *Les had a white lady friend; she had so much money she bought one of them great big buses and bought trumpets and saxophones for the guys in the band. She was the one that set up the booking agency with Hite in Chicago. Dizzy Gillespie played in the band with Les, and Dizzy's up there, standing back and clowning. Les said, "I can't go for that" because he's trying to have a class band and Dizzy's crazy.*

Britt Woodman: "In 1940 Les Hite met this rich lady, Mrs. Vera Crofton. She's the one who said, "Les, I'll manage the band. Let's go back east." In the winter months in Chicago, that was our first stay. We were supposed to do some one-nighters, but the weather was so bad. So for four weeks she paid our room rent and we went to a boarding place where they gave us some food. She also gave us twenty-five dollars a week" (quoted in Bryant et al., *Central Avenue Sounds*, 1998).

They paid the rent and food and everything. We stayed around there, just eat and sleep; we stayed at the Ritz Hotel. You couldn't work because of the Chicago union; you had to go out [away from the Chicago Local's jurisdiction]. *Gerald Wilson went down to the union about a job, him and I, and Gerald start blowin' his top at the union man. I had to quieten him up so the union wouldn't get hot at him. When the war broke out, everybody start leaving the band due to the draft, so I went to work down at the Lincoln Theatre in LA with Bardu Ali's band from 1942.*

Bardu was a fine person. He's the one that used to direct Chick Webb's band. He was a showman. They had a big show on at the Lincoln Theatre, with this boy that sings with Etta James, can't think of his name; Nat Cole come down there and [pianist/vocalist] *Charles Brown was there in the band. We had the girl trombone player, Melba Liston; I can't think of the others. Bardu had all of Chick Webb's music and he could direct the hell out of it, but when it come to the other stuff, the arrangements they had, I had to give a cue to the drums and the saxophones. We had three saxophones, two trumpets, trombone, rhythm section. It was a pretty good band.*

Funny part about it, Melba Liston turned out to be a helluva arranger after she met Gerald Wilson, who she was together with, but she used to write some little tinky arrangements at the Lincoln Theatre. I said, "Oh my God, what is this?" But as soon as she got with Gerald and knowed how to place the different horns, she was wonderful. I don't know whether Gerald taught her or not but she got on the ball, with them chords, got the trombones down there and the saxophones up here, and it was really nice. She was a little baby kid then.

Bardu's band just worked at the theater, nowhere else. That's during the rough times when I was working at the shipyards. I worked in the shipyards for about a year and six months.[6] *I didn't want to go in the Army. I didn't want to fight nobody so I worked like hell, out there by the beach. I could pick up steel. I was strong then. Them great big steel plates; I was picking them up. I first went down there with* [trumpeter] *Walter "Dootsie" Williams. Dootsie had the band down there, so we was going to rehearse and go play for the guys at lunchtimes. I was down there sweeping for a dollar an hour, and finally a white fellow there took a liking to me and said, "Floyd, why don't you try to train yourself up for welding," so I said OK and so I start doing flat plate, making a dollar 5 cents an hour; then he said, "It's time for you to get on the verticals" so I start getting on the verticals.*

Finally I made a good one but when it got overhead, miles up in the air, I couldn't do that. That was a dollar 30 but I got up to a dollar and a quarter. All this was when I was still working at the Lincoln Theatre which was just one show a night. I'd be at the shipyards at 8 o'clock until 3:30 or 4 o'clock in the afternoon. I'd come on home, eat dinner, get in bed, and get to rest before going to the show.

Finally, I got my induction papers. Bardu Ali told me to eat a lot of sugar before I'd go down for my induction so I did that. I went down there, and because I had fallen arches when I was a kid I missed it. They didn't take me for flat feet! Bardu told me what he did was act like a sissy—he was really a comedian like that. I just went on back home.

After I had learned how to weld, I went out there on the decks. I was putting bulwarks together—they go on the side of the boat—and taking a twelve-pound hammer and beating them with a wedge. It got easy. I'd run out of materials because the Mexican boy in front of me was doing seven or ten a day, and when I got on the job, I was doing eighteen or twenty, all to go on the ship, so when I'd run out of material, pikes and plates, I would just sit there. They'd say, "You gotta keep movin'." I'd say, "Are you kidding? I ain't movin'. I ain't got nothing to do. I ain't gonna be running around there. I ain't no fool." Some guy said, "Man, you gotta act like you do!" I said, "Hell, no." So finally they got a hydraulic jack to do the job and took me down to the deck-houses. I worked on the deck-houses after the stern casting. I didn't even keep my [welding] hood on! They had four fitters, four tackers, but when they got through I was the only tacker, with four fitters! I said I'm gonna get my lunch-pail and walk out of this shipyard and a trumpet player I knew was at the desk. We used to play together at the Orpheum Theatre in Los Angeles. He said, "You lucky, boy. If I walk out of here, they put me right straight in the Army." See, I had already made 4-F so I walked on out of that shipyard and I went on home. I said this is going to ruin my career; I gotta get on out of there. I was still working at the Lincoln Theatre with Bardu Ali then. I was supposed to work with Benny Carter after Bardu's band, but he wanted me to play baritone [saxophone]. I picked up my baritone, but I told him I couldn't make it.

It was in 1945 when I went to work with Gerald Wilson's new big band. We knew each other from working in the Les Hite band. We played Shepp's Playhouse here in Los Angeles, and then we had a nice booking and went to Club Riviera in St. Louis. We was there about two or three weeks [actually six weeks]. Anyway, we made a recording and our money was getting low and they was supposed to send us our money. It ended up we was up in our rooms and wondering. Anyway our checks came so after that we went to the club, and Ella Fitzgerald and Joe Williams was on the show. They had about six chorus girls and put on a big show. That's before Ella Fitzgerald got fat. Gerald didn't have a job within a month after that so I told Gerald, "I can't stay out here like this"—my wife was with me—so I cashed in all my defense bonds. My wife made about ten, fifteen pocket books for the chorus girls, so we got our money and we caught us a bus from Chicago to come back to Los Angeles. I ain't worked with Gerald Wilson since [laughs]*! After that, Lionel* [Hampton] *wanted me to come with him to play clarinet. I said to myself Lionel works too hard and I ain't gonna work myself like that, so I said no thanks.*

Floyd had recorded with Les Hite for the Varsity label in 1940 and then for Bluebird and Hit in 1941 and 1942 respectively. He soloed on Hite's *The Lick*. He remembered making "Soundies"[7] while he was with Hite. "We made those dates for machines where you sit over there and watch the band playing. Made a gang of them in New York."

Metronome, February 1945

Hollywood Periscope—Gerald Wilson's young outfit is scuffling again now that it's "at liberty" after a long run at the Playhouse. Wilson's trumpet, Jimmy Bunn's piano, Floyd Turnham's alto, Vernon Slater's tenor and Melba Liston's trombone add up to good music, along with scores penned by Wilson and Miss Liston.

Floyd's first session with the new Gerald Wilson orchestra for Excelsior took place on May 6, 1945, and was followed by several more for the label, including the first big band recording of Dizzy Gillespie's "Groovin' High," also in 1945. Floyd is featured playing alto with the Wilson band on a Melba Liston original "Warm Mood" for the Black & White label in 1946. He also recorded with Jimmy Mundy's all-star big band for an AFRS Jubilee program, broadcast from Los Angeles.

Around this time I went on the road with [trumpeter] *Jake Porter, with Joe Turner and Wynonie Harris. Made a trip down to New Orleans, and Texas, and on down. I used my own car for transportation. I think I got five cents a mile for my car so that paid for my phone—I sent my earnings home. I think that's about the best trip I've had. That was in 1946.*

Johnny Hodges and Lawrence Brown was leaving the Duke Ellington band [in February 1951]*, and Johnny was getting a little group together with Lawrence. Anyway, I went up to work with the band, didn't get paid for one night because of the union as the band before didn't get paid by the promoter; this is up north near Frisco. Sitting down there in the section, Duke had me play "Stardust" as my solo on alto, and then after we finished work, he was supposed to come by the hotel and talk to me about working in the band. We waited there two hours and a half, maybe three hours, for him to come back to the hotel. My wife said, "Come out here; Duke don't want you to stay.*[8] *You get the hell out of there," and she took me back to Los Angeles. Ain't no use regretting that. The reason of it is because it was an eastern* band. I didn't want to be blocked out east. See, Britt was single. If I'd been single, I'd probably have went on with Duke. I guess I was so in love with my wife that I wanted to stay home.

Britt's dad was William Woodman; he was a trombone player too. My mother didn't hire him because of his reading. See, Momma did a lot of reading. We had Montudie [bassist Ed Garland] working with the band for a while, but when they found he was a slow reader, that was it. Momma was a strong piano player. Duke heard her play piano at a club out here called the Plantation. We had chorus girls and a chorus line-up, everything. It was something like the old Cotton Club with a great long bar, each section went up in great big dance floors. Duke came out there and said Momma was the best woman piano player he had ever heard. She was very heavy [on the piano], heavier than a man. See, she started when she was three years old. She'd read all that Mexican music right off. She didn't have to rehearse. She just look up and read it all. I followed her when it came to the melody; I found looking at my music I could play a fraction of a second behind her [laughs].

Incidentally we made some recordings, Mexican recordings, with my mother's band. I don't know what the hell happened to those records. Some Mexican fellow came up to LA, and we went out there for a session and the technician messed something up. This was back in the thirties.

Next down the line for me was Joe Liggins's Honeydrippers with Little Willie Jackson, James Jackson, Peppy Prince, Frank Pasley, myself, and Eddie Davis, little short, colored bass player. I went on the road with them in '50, and that's the year I lost my mother. We made a whole lot of records with Joe—I wasn't on his very first records—and he added me on to the band. He made all new arrangements and we rehearsed in his house, and rehearsed and rehearsed. Down at the studio, the technician wanted something different, I'll be doggone, after all that rehearsing! That's what used to wear me out with Joe, playing all the rhythm lines on baritone.

Another one I recorded with was Johnny Otis [1950/1951]. I made a session with him. He'd give me the riffs—we made about eight records, something like that, on that session—and he'd sing the riffs. Honest to God, I'm playing, trying to remember. I said I ain't gonna do that no more. Nothing written down, just singing the riffs to me. For all the experience I'd had, my brain look like it was gonna be fried. Another time, I made a recording with Maxwell and he had a little tough part there for the baritone [Crown CLP 5050, made in 1959: *Tribute to Glenn Miller*] and I read that son of a gun right on down, but we rehearsed it so much, when it got to recording that part, I swear to God, I couldn't play it all. They went over it so many times; it just ripped me off [laughs].

One time with Joe, we stopped in Tuskegee at a gas station, and the vocalist, Candy [Rivers], went to the restroom and Monk [McFay] wanted to go to the restroom too. So when she come out, he went back there and went in the wrong [white] restroom. Man, that cat stopped pumpin' gas and he come back running. I see him with a pistol in his left hand. I jumped out the car, open the door, and anyway, Monk start running down the street. We had to pick him up down there. Like when we played at the Riviera Club in St. Louis for the colored taxi-cab driver—that's Gerald Wilson, Joe Williams, and Ella Fitzgerald—some guy pulled out a pistol right after we got in the hall. The show people run back into the dressing room and everybody else went to the floor. I'm on the bandstand by myself playing the "Star-Spangled Banner." Everybody left but me. What was the use of running? I just stayed there.

It was nice working for Joe. When I joined the band, I went to a Watts store and bought five uniforms, had to pay for 'em myself. We'd work for a while in one uniform, the next day change the jacket or something. After a while, the money got bad and Joe cut the salary and then never did bring it back up again. Every time I went out on the road with Joe, the band would go short but the money never did come back up. Still, we got along fine. I still do things with Joe. We played a Mexican dance; he had a baritone man and a tenor man, and this time I had my tenor. One cat, his name is "Eyes," he's the tenor man. Joe's retired, but every once in a while, somebody comes up and says play a gig and he gets his group together.

I went to Anchorage, Alaska, with Roy Milton. We was on our way there, and Roy said he didn't want no drinking. I always kept me a bottle for my tonsils disease. I'd always get a bad throat, riding at nights. So if your throat tighten up at night, you must be a lush-head, you understand? In the band before, some of them was fighting in the bus and that's why, I guess, I got the job. He had me come along with him so I went and bought this [baritone] saxophone for which I paid $567-odd and which is worth about $3,000 now. He didn't allow no drinking so I told Camille Howard I know I'm going to get sick; I like it just to keep the tonsils down and my throat clear. When I got to Alaska, I was as sick as a dog. We was on the bandstand; we'd got through playing and the valet come over and told me no drinking on the bandstand. I said, "This is my time," and I start blowin' my top. I respected him while I was working, but don't mess with me when I'm not working for you. Everybody quietened down and I got all loud and rough [laughs], saying the wrong things like, "You care for a taste?" The other saxophone was drinking, though.

They all say you have to stop [drinking] sometime. Like we used to meet at 55th and Central at the drug store and buy drinks after hours, staying out on the corner there, by the cars and drinkin' and talkin,' and all at once I'd feel that stuff hit me and totter home. I'd get on home while I could drive straight. I'd lay down on the bed and go to sleep for about 20 minutes, and everything start turning round. I'd be out of the bed and start heading to the closet!

I worked with Roy for about a year. Not too long. Roy wanted me to come with him in 1946 when I went with Gerald Wilson. He was working right 'round the corner from Shepp's Playhouse. I was happy in Gerald's band. I loved Gerald's band. Roy did all the singing and all I had to do was to play high. He had Camille Howard on piano. Oh, she's wonderful. He just added me on baritone saxophone. I sold my old baritone, which I brought down from Seattle, to [fellow Milton band saxophonist] *Jackie Kelso and bought me this one with the Low E and that's when I start doing a lot of recording with Maxwell Davis. We made some records for the Bihari's* [Modern Records] *with Roy's group. We did some for the René Brothers, and Googie René* [1959] *and I made a gang of records with the blues singers.*

Everybody that recorded with Maxwell with those blues singers could read [well] *so you didn't have to spend a whole lot of time rehearsin', and that was good because it was on a time schedule. All the tunes was his arrangements. Maxwell wrote stuff out on all the tunes. I never seen such a great man. Great skill. I never worked with him on jobs, only on recordings. He was an able tenor man too.*

I loved the big bands. Basie and Duke knocked me out. I'm so tired hearing everybody singing. I want to hear some music. I did enough singing as a twelve-year kid when my mother used to take me to a club down in the basement there on 12th and Jackson in Seattle. I'd sing "At The End of a Perfect Day," and tips would just fly like mad out there on the floor. But I can't sing now because that got away from me. With mother's band, the tenor man for her, Fats Wilson, he did a style of Bing Crosby and he could imitate him, and Frank Pasley, he did the rhythm and blues songs; rock songs we call them now. Frank played steel guitar; talk about playing good steel guitar, him and Ceelle Burke was in competition on steel guitar. Frank was a real fine person. Like when I was with my mother, I did just a few songs but I didn't do too many. The best for me was to stick to saxophone. We left my vocals out unless I demanded it. I probably could have but I'm not that type of person. I hold back. It's like when the guys go to jam sessions, I didn't try to overblow. Just want to play. A lot of tenor men, they try to outblow each other. It's like when I had my big band, my band would play like mad, and those tenor men, Bob Dorsey and Andy Anderson, they'd get drunk but still played good.

I started working in burlesque. Jesse Sailes and I worked together. I played burlesque for about three or four years at the Lake Club [17227 S. Lakewood Blvd., Lakewood], *and I worked the Brass Rail on Vernon and Broadway for six years with* [novelty dancers] *Pot, Pan & Skillet, Wanda* [snake dancer LaWanda Page], *and a comedian. This was around '58. This was with three pieces, organ, sax, and drums. Sir Charles Thompson, he worked with me on organ. It was my job, but I wouldn't take leader's fee because I'd always let the organ player get the melodies from the shows. I'd just get the sideman's pay. I kept it going that way because I didn't want all the arguments. After the place closed at night, we rehearsed until 3 or 4 o'clock in the morning putting in a new show. I had about seven organ players and about forty drummers* [laughs].

I changed from alto to tenor saxophone when I started playing burlesque shows. I was playing alto and clarinet all the time up to then. When I first started, the bartender says, "Broad wants to buy you a tenor if you can't buy a tenor. Tenor's comin' in," so I say, "Well, I'll see what I can do." I talked to my wife, and I went and bought me a tenor so now I had tenor, alto, and baritone. That's when I really started playing my tenor. Now I've learned flute. I probably might have went further but not playing flute held me back. I tried it years ago, and I said, well, there's no business for flute. They didn't have no flute parts in music then. They had clarinet parts so I said what's the use of me learning flute? Further on down the line they started writing the first saxophone with flute parts. It didn't end up my way!

We worked at the Lake Club, Chuck Thomas and myself, so when he'd get tired of going out there, I'd go out and work in his place for a while, and then they had a great big burlesque place—that was in 1950—called Strip City in Hollywood, where I worked with Jesse Sailes on drums. They had girls dancing out there, taking their clothes off. We had to play little jump tunes, and they appreciated what we were doing. I knew the numbers. They had about four or five different girls to play for. It was a lot of fun. I worked there with Jake [Porter], *and he's so hard-headed that I quit. He'd say, "I blow this way," and I got mad so I turned my notice in. He finally conceded and wanted me to stay, so I stayed and he started the same mess over so I quit. I did some recordings for his little place.*

Porter owned a home studio at N. Virgil Street and issued recordings made there on Combo Records, including five singles by Floyd's band.

Down Beat, January 25, 1952

Los Angeles Band Briefs—Calvin Boze [trumpet and vocals] heads eight-piece band at Central Avenue's recently-reopened Club Alabam. Has Floyd Turnham, alto and baritone; Curtis Lowe, tenor; George Orendorff, trumpet; Gene Phillips, guitar; Ralph Bateman, piano; Buddy Woodson, bass, and Bill Douglass, drums. Arrangements by Maxwell Davis.

Central Avenue just died out. They tore Club Alabam down and left the Apex derelict. The car doors are locked when we drive down there. Where I lived [115th Street], *that's where they had the riots. "Why don't you get out of that place?" I said my house is all paid for; my wife's there. Why should I move?" I had a double lot on the corner. Bought it in '44, but then they tore all the nearby buildings down. They built some projects and that's when it* started going down. Riff-raff made the neighborhood bad. We finally sold my house in February this year.

Melody Maker, January 6, 1962
The Fletcher Henderson Band Lives Again by Leonard Feather—A new band with a great name made its first appearance in December, when the Fletcher Henderson Band, under the direction of Horace Henderson, began a series of dates in Southern California.

"I think I've lined up a personnel that will do justice to the library we've built," Horace said. "I'm very proud of the sax section. The altos are Floyd Turnham, who was a member of Gerald Wilson's band, and Melvin Phillips. The tenors are Bumps Myers—you remember him with Benny Carter and Chuck Thomas. Ernest Scott is on baritone. Our trumpets are Freddie Hill, George 'Diz' Goodin, and Garnet McLellan. On trombone we're featuring John 'Streamline' Ewing from Chicago—he used to be with the Hines and Lunceford bands. The other trombone is Pete Collins. We have two vocalists, a girl named Renee Sands and my singing drummer, George Reed, who's been with me for 15 years. The band is completed by Everett Evans on bass."

Horace opened on Dec. 30 at the Avalon Casino, a popular vacation resort, about 20 miles off the Californian coast. He has already cut some stereo tapes and hopes to make a deal for them to be released by a major record company.

Following his short-lived experience with Henderson, Floyd concentrated on trio engagements in Orange County restaurant locations from 1964 through to his first attempt at "retirement" in 1975. This apparently nonstop process kept him away from the jazz media limelight and seems to have extended well beyond 1975 and the confines of Orange County. There was a regular Sunday jam session gig in 1977 with drummer Rich Parnell and comedian Bob Day at the Gaslight Cocktail Lounge [Beach Blvd., Orange County]. Then in 1978, his Floyds of London group appeared at Hogan's East [2753 Broadway, Long Beach] Thursday through Sunday, and a year later, they were at Harry V's [1050 W. Valencia, Fullerton] for three nights a week.

In those ten years I only had about six weeks off, and I'm driving thirty-five miles to work and thirty-five miles back every day. That's before the freeway. I was glad that job finished when I hit sixty-five. I say, "Well, this is it. I don't have to drive those thirty-five miles anymore." My first job was a trio at the Odyssey Club with Roy Milton on drums; Lorenzo Flennoy, piano player; and myself. They wanted me to be leader of the band, but I said Roy Milton had a little bigger name than me, and then I called Lorenzo about an organ player and he said, "Well, I'll come" and here he was. We went down and played the job and kept going, and going; then Roy, finally, found another job and we worked out on this job only to find out when we left that Roy got *paid so much more money than us, $65, and when we looked up, Lorenzo got $15 and I got $15. So Lorenzo said, "To heck with this mess," so we let Roy go and got George Reed on drums.*

Roy was a nice guy until we found out about the money. He did carry on with his own band later on because he made a trip to Europe. Lorenzo found us another job, and we kept on going down there for a long time. These were little nightclubs, mostly dinner houses. We were just playing melodies for the people in my style, with George Reed singing. He did all the vocals, everything people asked for. Nothing far out. Being a sax player in the big bands in years past, I dealt more to playing the lead and keeping it strong. Standard songs, that's what you heard out there. I knew all the good tunes. Now, I don't know nothin'! When we worked together with Lorenzo, when there was no business in the place, in order to kill time, just a few people around, we'd try to fool each other to see which one would know a melody all the way through.

Lorenzo Flennoy, oh, he was a clown. He was about six foot six, thin as a rail, and he was really enjoyable to work with. Played just ordinary, swingin' piano. That first time down in Orange County, he had a piano, just a piano, so he says, well, yes, he could play bass on the piano, but if he got an organ he could do the same thing but have more volume. He found him an organ, and man, that organ was the best one they ever had in Los Angeles! I lost Lorenzo[9] in '71 when he passed away. Then we got Charlie Martin.

I bought the organ from Lorenzo's wife and I sold it to Joe Liggins later on, but I'm kinda sorry that I sold it. It was a Hammond B-3 with a Leslie speaker and the quality of the bass on this speaker was just beautiful So I took the group, his organ, and all that stuff, and we went down to the Royal Coach—it's called the Sheraton now—and the owners said we gotta change your name, so that's when they called us Floyds of London because their place was built to look like a castle.

Floyd never cast himself as a virtuoso and was in awe of technically advanced players.

Charlie Parker played too much for me! I can't make it, but I'd have to respect what he did. I've heard many tenor men, beautiful tenor men, and I say, "I can't do that." No use me trying. My heroes were Johnny [Hodges] on alto, and Coleman [Hawkins], Lester [Young], Don Byas, and Lucky Thompson on tenor. Don Byas came out to LA, and he played with my mother's band at the Plantation. He played a solo; man, he was flying all over that saxophone. I got to say he played too much. That wasn't the style then, but it came to be a style later on. That's too many notes for me. I like to play melodies for people that they know. One time we had a little gig at some guy's house, a little jam session, Lester Young, Lee Young, me, I can't re-

member who else. I was never in Lester's company except then but he was beautiful. I loved his style.

You need somebody down here who knows how to play music and make a sound for the average, ordinary people. I'd rather be 'round them than the people that got a whole lot of money. I want to let them know what music is about and play for them. I've always had that philosophy about music. Why try to get up to the top and the people that want to hear you can't hear you?

Working in Orange County, every time we opened up in a club, the doggone club owners wouldn't advertise. They went by word of mouth. You can't get no business like that. One place I played called Mandy's Pancake House, I was faced with five owners in six years. The club was sold five times, but the band stayed on. Then they called it The Cats and Cleavers and college kids came in. Had a load of people in the place. Then I played with Nellie Lutcher quite often around LA. She ain't changed a bit. Red Mack was with us, and he lost a tooth out front and I guess he wouldn't get it fixed. Maybe he don't want to play trumpet no more. He plays organ now. So we got [trumpeter] Clora Bryant to work with us. Clora is a very good player, and she has a wonderful voice of her own. She sings like Louis.

Floyd's final hurrah was with Barry Martyn's Legends of Jazz band, and he credited Georgia with persuading him to emerge from retirement to respond to Barry's approach despite having turned him down several years earlier. Floyd replaced Sammy Lee in 1979 and began to tour internationally, keeping in trim in between trips by playing Clef Club concerts and sitting in with tenor man-turned-pianist Buddy Banks at his regular gig: "He plays by himself so I'd go by his club and heat up my chops!"

Barry cited Floyd as "the best tenor player I ever worked with. He was also a fabulous man, but, by God, he could drink!"

The main reason I got in Barry's band was to go on the show [1000 Years of Jazz]. *See, I'd been used to reading music. Dixieland? I kinda like it in a way. I can play it, but I won't be able to do all those runs* [on the clarinet] *the cats do, but they're mostly rhythm things, obligatos, in this band and I can do that. Momma used to play some of those tunes, but she didn't care much for Dixieland, although "St. Louis Blues," "Tiger Rag," stuff like that, we played that quite a bit. Before coming in this band, I had stopped playing clarinet for years. It got away from me. There were so many clarinet players; they phased me out. I can play a little bit, but years ago, I could really play it because I was playing clarinet all the time. I have trouble with the clarinet now if I have to play too long. My chops won't hold up that long. I have to use my teeth on the clarinet. On my saxophone I use double embouchure like Johnny Hodges. I used to do slap-tonguing like Joe Darensbourg, rode two horns at one time. I pick up my alto now; it sounds strange. It's tenor all the time for me.*

This year with Barry has been the slowest yet. I still gig around with Billy Hadnott. Before coming with Barry, I was getting quite a few jobs, so I start turning them over to Billy and he start taking them up. Now, he took them over [laughs]*! See, I like to play where they don't work me too hard. With me going away, there wasn't no sense in trying to get jobs. Then being with Barry, when I would go back home, I would get my unemployment. This traveling is a hard deal. You got to have a solid heart. I thought I was through traveling, but Barry flies you everywhere and you have the best accommodation. He does everything.*

I'm still kickin'! I've been a musician all my life. A lot of cats got a whole lot more than I got, but I made a good livin', being just a musician. Money ups and downs, downs and ups. I've always run into somebody that has a job. It's been my luck. I'm not the type that want to run in, go here, and jam here. I always went home to my wife. Being at it and going through it and then meeting up with someone that makes me happy. That's the most essential thing for a man.

Chapter Six

Betty Hall Jones

Piano, Organ, and Vocals

Betty Hall Jones enjoyed her heyday in the 1940s, recording for Capitol and then later for trumpeter Jake Porter's Combo label. She had been prominent on the Central Avenue scene working with Roy Milton's Solid Senders for several years before Capitol signed her up, and then played with local combos before making it as a single entertainer, appearing in hotels all over the United States and touring for the USO, often accompanied by bassist Edgar Mason.

Vocally, she sounded like a cross between Blue Lu Barker and Nellie Lutcher, while her keyboard style had much in common with Nellie's blend of boogie-woogie and swing. Always resourceful, Betty developed an entertaining routine swapping increasingly outrageous hats as she played that seemed to go down well with hotel and cabaret audiences, this helping to prolong her career long after Central Avenue's glamour had subsided. As she said, "I've built my act on the visual. I can't sing the blues all night long because I'm not constructed that way."

Billed as "Miss Versatility," Betty's calling card cited her as "Entertainer, Singer, Pianist, Composer and Life Member Local 47 with a repertoire comprising KC Boogie & Blues, Calypso, Show Tunes, Hawaiian, Japanese & Spanish Songs, and most everything you request." I missed her only London appearance in 1986 when she stopped over briefly on her way back to the United States after a tour of Sweden.

By the time Roger Jamieson and I located her, she was in her middle-eighties and living alone in Paramount, California, in a mobile home park, her career largely in abeyance. She was welcoming and seemed comfortable, standing to play the piano for us, as she always had, only bemoaning that her

Betty Hall Jones, Los Angeles, 1987. Courtesy Grosvenor Productions, London.

third husband had recently "transferred his affections to someone else." Betty was still appearing occasionally with amateur musicians at one or other of the local jazz societies run by enthusiasts and told us she was considering offers to tour, although it is doubtful whether these ever came to anything.

Sadly, her recall of her musical career was patchy at best, and it was distressing to learn some years later that she had been diagnosed with Alzheimer's disease, spending her final days in a care home. Betty, who was born on January 11, 1911, in Topeka, Kansas, died on April 20, 2009, at the great age of ninety-eight.

Betty Hall Jones: Paramount, California, September 8, 1995

I was born Cordell Elisabeth Bigbee—Bigbee is my maiden name—my father was George Archie Bigbee and my mother's maiden name was Meyer. She was Gertrude Meyer. My grandfather was a slave of German people—he spoke German fluent. He ran away when he was sixteen. They got him, but before they could get him back, slavery was over so he was free. Because he had been treated so badly, he had a sorta mean streak in him. He didn't think much about women.

My father worked for the Santa Fe [The Atchison, Topeka and Santa Fe Railway]. *I said that one time and somebody said, "In Topeka didn't everybody's father work with the Santa Fe?" See, Topeka was a railroad town. He worked in the offices, which was a job where he didn't have to wear overalls or carry a lunch bucket, but it was janitor work just the same. My father played cornet. He belonged to the city band and had this girls marching band. He taught the wind instruments too. This was of course before I was old enough to know anything about it. He died when I was seven so my mother was left with me, and I had a half-sister. We had different mothers so her mother's people came and helped. My half-sister wanted to learn saxophone, but they were of a school that thought women should not play* [saxophone] *so they didn't let her. They made her take piano. She could sight-read better than I could, but she couldn't memorize or things like that.*

Discipline was a main thing. My mother taught school after she married Poppa, and we came out from Topeka and we went out to the suburbs. She got a job teaching at the rural school, and she found out the people were illiterate so they had night school. She taught them to read, and I can remember now they put on plays. They sold ice creams for a nickel deal, and they helped the boys to buy instruments. This was all at a little place called Pierce Edition, Topeka, Kansas. I started at her school when I was five. I think it was because Momma didn't want to leave me alone. Almost everybody in Pierce Edition was with the Santa Fe too. Then she left Topeka and went to Kansas City. She had taught at schools in Kansas City, Missouri, before she married my father. We went back there, and then some of her relatives moved to California and they kept asking her to come on to California.

I'd been playing piano since I was five. My mother's brother, Harold Meyer, started me, but he was a classical fanatic. He thought jazz was a thing of the devil. We weren't allowed to play ragtime stuff. That was taboo.

He would practice hours at the piano. Played organ, too. He had a job working downtown as a janitor, and I can remember he'd come in from this job and you'd hear him go over a Bach run over and over. It made him feel better. He was a perfectionist and they're never happy. Never! Nothing was good enough, see. He was knowledgeable about vocals; he helped with the choir at the Presbyterian Church where my father and mother were, but he was strictly a loner. He wasn't a good teacher for me because I could never stand anybody to rush at me. I would do something wrong and he'd say, "As you were, as you were." That's from his Army deal. I would sit and the tears would run down and he'd feel bad. Then he'd let me go. I was quite a crybaby.

I knew about that [other kinds of music] before I got to Kansas City. My aunt had a player piano, and they had a lot of ragtime on it. I used to push it and put my fingers in the notes. My father, he used ragtime with his band as a come-on. If they got to feel good, he'd let them have a ragtime piece. After we moved to Kansas City, I had music teachers—my mother's brother was married to a person who was musical. She did voice and whatnot, but the only time you played ragtime was when you sneaked it in to play it.

Then we came to California, of course—I was about ten or eleven when I came—I graduated when I was fifteen and I was in the tenth grade. My mother had cousins that were out here. They got her a job on a place, and the people let me come and stay. One job she got was out in the valley, and so a bunch of us used to catch that big Red Car. In that bunch I was the only black. The man that my mother was working for was some kind of a scenario writer out at Universal Studios. She wouldn't take a job on a place unless I could be with her. She had taken one job downtown, and my mother was very naïve. She found out this job was a house of prostitution and she was to be the maid, but evidently the maid before her had helped with the business too, because the guy started to make advances of her and so she was busted. She went to the owner and they said, "Why didn't you know that?" She stayed there one afternoon.

My mother was a terrific person. She had lots of airs. Always spoke properly. One time in San Diego I was working on a job where I stayed so long and she'd come down there. I'd ride back [to Los Angeles] and she'd be with me. This particular Sunday night, she was there and we'd had a good crowd, a lot of people. On the way home, I said, "Momma, how did you like . . ." "Well, you sounded all right, but I couldn't understand a word you said," she said. So after that I worked on my diction because I was selling words. I improved but that was her attitude.

There was only three other blacks in the Hollywood High School [1521 N. Highland Avenue]. A fellow and his sister and they were passing. He looked like a Mexican and she was fair, and the other boy was in the marching band. He didn't have anything to do with me either except we were in the same harmony class. I took harmony the last year I was at school. See, I didn't know what the school offered when I came here because I came from a black school. Even in Kansas City, I was in the glee club and we had some music, but it wasn't like it was when I got here. I didn't realize I could take harmony until I got almost to the end so I missed it. My family was so classical orientated, I was sort of squashed.

After my graduation, my mother went back to Kansas and I took one year at *Washington College* [7340 Leavenworth Road, Kansas City] where I was directing the choir in a Baptist church. I was Presbyterian, and they wanted a beat and I didn't have it. I wanted to play for them to sing by the note. I could rehearse on Friday night and they finally get to a place where I almost liked to hear it, but by Sunday morning it was going to go back to that full harmony. Sometimes I'd throw up my hands because I would hear things and try to give it to them, but they were always gonna put that beat on it. I wasn't brought up to that.

My uncle had the choir back in Topeka, and he was a stickler for them just doing what was on the paper. He knew enough about vocals, about shaping their mouths and saying their words clean and all that sort of thing. That's why if I played, even playing an exercise, I'd hear him say, "That's not written. That's not the way it is." He'd be in the kitchen and he could hear it. Everyone liked Ethel Waters and Mamie Smith, Bessie Smith, but the thing about it is I came from a family that sorta looked down on that kind of stuff because that was rough. A lot of black people who were into music didn't realize that they had a thing with [black] music. They were so busy trying to be classical with the white people they didn't realize they had a gift.

My first professional job was in Kansas City. I worked with Bus Moten. My children's father and I were separated, and my cousin told me he could get me a job. I left my oldest boy with my mother because she was teaching school in Topeka, and I took the baby with me and I went and stayed with my cousin Orville Demoss,[1] who played saxophone. His wife looked after my baby while we worked together on the job. I played the Reno Club. Bus hired me because of my cousin being in the band so he told me, "I want you to work the floor." I didn't know what working the floor was—he meant you go from table to table and you ask them for anything they want to hear, and if they want to tip you, they do; if not you go and sing anyway. I was just flouncing around and my cousin said, "You never did this before, did you?" [laughs] and I said no. They told me you always had to come back to the band with your hand open so they could see what tip you got and you put that in the kitty. So after I got the hang of it, it was all right.

Julia Lee was playing in another club, and they took me over and introduced me to her and she told me about singing songs. Julia and [bandleader] George Lee both were nice people—there wasn't any professional jealousy. Julia would come over and she'd give me lyrics, so that's the kind of person she was because I didn't know anything about that kind of stuff. I was young and ignorant. I didn't even know this world of nightclubs with people playing was going on at that time.

We'd play a job sometimes, and then there was another club and they'd go there and they'd sit in. At first, I couldn't sit in because I didn't know the scope. My repertoire was not big enough, and I didn't know what was going on. They had a habit, too, at that time, you could go out to a place and they would be jamming and you'd look around and there wouldn't be anybody left but you and the drummer. They didn't want to work with you. It was rugged. It was such a different thing for me. That wasn't the kind of music they taught me. I was there maybe a month, six weeks. Bus played the accordion. He was good, but it wasn't the instrument people wanted to hear. Bennie [Moten] was around when I was in Kansas City. I met him; Bus was his nephew. I think that's when he got his first big break on records and went on tour. See, I wasn't paying attention to things then. I had these kids to make a living for. As I always said, I had too much education to wash dishes and not enough to do anything else.

After I got married—I was eighteen—I didn't do much with the church. My children's father played banjo. He was an elevator operator, and he was from Louisiana. His name was George Hall, and my youngest son is named George Hall. We could get gigs and play, but he was so jealous he couldn't let anybody come talk to me that wasn't in that field. He would watch me. See, when you're in this business, people come up to you. He didn't understand that. He would figure that they were flirting with me. I wanted him to take up guitar and we would have made a nice duo, but he couldn't see it that way. We'd play for dances and clubs having parties. This was happening on the West Side [in LA]. People would call you to play and we'd have club dates. I worked sometimes with other musicians, but I didn't run in those circles much. They weren't people you would socialize with. Because I had children and whatnot, I didn't, like Nellie [Lutcher] and all those other people, go out at night and do things because I had the kids and I didn't drive. I was real mature when I learned to drive but that was a case of necessity.

After my children's father and I separated when I was in my early twenties, I worked with a guy named Roy Milton; I guess for almost three years. I began to build up a repertoire. My style? I had a good ear—that you have to have—and I had a good sense of harmony. And I had good rhythm. That came from my father with the marching band. Improvising? I could always do that even with my exercises. It would sound good to me.

We had the black union then [Local 767], and somebody called Roy Milton and told him this place called Louie's wanted a band so we went out to audition. Roy knew about me from the union—he got my name from there—and we played little things, gigs that the union would send us on, and then we went out and made this audition at Louie's. We were there two years and nine months. Roy was on drums and Little Joe [Walker], he played clarinet and saxophone; I was on piano; and Fred Mason played trumpet. This was on Pico Boulevard. Just regular jazz. Luke Jones was with us later on [on alto] for quite a while when we played another place down the street for an Italian fellow.

We had a big repertoire because whenever anybody asked for something and we didn't have it, I would see if I could find it. [Local 767 financial secretary/saxophonist] Paul Howard, he was a lot of help because I could go and ask where to find this sort of thing. I did that because Roy was not a paper musician—he was a natural musician. We used to laugh at him. They had floor shows there and they'd bring their music up, and since he was leading the band, they'd bring it to him and he would be happy to give it to Little Joe or me because it didn't make a difference to me what was on there. I could read it. On top of that, too, with the help of Little Joe I did most of the arranging. Roy couldn't do anything with music, as far as notes were concerned. He didn't read. He didn't think he had to; he had natural ability.

Louie's had a bar and a dance floor and a bandstand. Louie was Armenian. It was definitely white audiences only; if any blacks came, they'd have to sit on the bandstand. There wasn't any mixing. We were making money for him so we were well treated. We were bringing the people in there. Luke Jones came in to replace Little Joe. Not much I can say about Luke except he played his horn. He was a barber otherwise, but he wasn't going to do any more than he had to. It's not that he wasn't a good musician; it was just that he took things as they came. He wasn't going to do a whole lot of pushing.

Roy had an aura where people couldn't help but like him. I used to get provoked with him because a lot of times I'd want to be serious, but the thing about it was he'd jive on me to get me off his back and I didn't understand that. I was the one that would find the music that people asked us to sing. I didn't know much about horns, but Joe would tell me what the clarinet could do in different keys so then I would put it down. We had another trumpet player [Forrest Powell] because Fred Mason left; I don't know why. That was before we played down the street for an Italian fellow, and then we went over to another place that was run by Miss Donnelly; that was the lady's name. She was one of these masculine ladies. She owned the place—she had a little girl who she didn't chastise at all. Some of the places we worked if we wanted something to eat, we could get it out of the kitchen, but after we started to work for Miss Donnelly, the only thing you could get there was a sandwich. She didn't serve a meal.

We weren't near Central Avenue, but I worked one time on Central before I got with the boys. I had not been a performer that could go before their audience. I always wanted to do something different. I did Mexican songs, Hawaiian songs, Japanese songs, and that wasn't as a rule what they were *expecting. I could play the blues, but with my background I guess I started to have my nose up at the blues. Only twelve bars and whatnot! Like I said with my father's band, the ragtime was something for relief after they had the marching music. It was a relaxation. A lot of people thought black people couldn't play regular classics, and that's why he worked so hard to not be like that.*

We went down to that other place with Roy, and we had a little altercation, so I just decided to go on by myself. I don't think I hurt myself by leaving. It made me independent. I had not been a social person like a lot of them. I went to work with Paul Howard out in Glendale at Virginia's. We had Ted Brinson, Buddy Harper, Willis McDaniel playing drums, and Eleanor Williams used to sing. Paul was on our union board. He was a nice guy and a good musician. Paul was all right for that time [as a jazz musician], but that's like the pot calling the kettle black because during that time I was struggling myself. We played just regular things and I did special material and the singer sang with the band. Well, on a lot of songs, I would add my own lyrics too.

Nellie Lutcher was instrumental in getting me on to Capitol Records [in 1949] because she had recorded for them before. We were friends from the union. Recording was something that scared me. I couldn't be free because we had to do the same thing every time and the songs I wanted to record, they didn't want me to record. They wanted me to be another Nellie and I wasn't. She and I were in the same kind of predicament. I had two children but she had one and no husband. She was always a little more flamboyant than I was. I would walk in and nothing would happen until after I started working. Well, I guess I'm a ham and it was nice; it was something when I was younger I never thought I could do.

I played on a job in San Diego for five years, working for the same group of people. It was a place called Top's—it's right on a highway. The Cohns—they were a Jewish family—they had a place downtown and then they bought Top's. I worked at the place downtown and then I worked at Top's for five years. This was the late 1940s—they were kind of like a monopoly. I was the intermissionist. The band was in the dining room and I worked at the bar. I was there for the overflow. Playing and singing as a single.

They had floor shows in there. At first, they just had a coffee shop, and then they made a big deal and put in a dining room with a floor show and they had the bar where I worked. The last time I was down there it was not only a bar but a motel too so they had all that. By that time my kids were able to take care of themselves. I didn't start really traveling until the 1950s. That was a good stage. I included songs l liked to play, and then people would bring me things and say, "Play this for me," and I had to learn that. I think being by myself, I could change key and stop when I wanted to. It just was relaxed. I wasn't the greatest musician in the world, but I could get to people.

I really think San Diego was the best time for me because I was there so long and I had friends.

After San Diego, I got an agent—I went wherever they sent me. I worked up in Seattle for six years from 1959, in Oregon, in Arizona, and in Alaska and in Hawaii, and I made a European tour.[2] *Back in Los Angeles, I was married to another musician, Jones, Jap Jones, trombone player. We lived on the West Side—I don't really know what caused us to break up but he lost his sight, you know. He went blind. I wanted him to do more, and my mother came to be with us and he resented her, but she wasn't the kind of mother-in-law that you think about. I think he was frustrated at being blind. We could have done something musically. He worked down on Central Avenue at the Dunbar Hotel with Curtis Mosby, and he played down there at Club Alabam. He stayed off the road while we were together. I worked for Curtis Mosby once, but I have not been a performer that particularly captivated black audiences.*

Jap Jones, he'd been around. He was a fine musician. He married again, but he died in 1986. They were getting ready to go on a trip. I used to make some kind of a nut bread, and when he married again after we separated, his new wife called me once and she said, "Would you give me the recipe for that bread? He speaks about it," and I gave her the recipe that I had and I thought it was pretty big of her. I understand that he died on the train—I'm not sure—they were coming back from someplace. I can see him now playing his horn. I was wanting one thing out of music, and he was wanting something else. I think it was the way we were brought up.

Now, I just do things when I feel like it. I don't go out at night unless somebody picks me up. I work with [banjoist] *Ray Lyon quite a bit. He sings too. Sometimes we do one or two things together. He's a nice guy to work with—he lets me do the things I want to do. When I play with jazz bands, they sorta let me go my own way. They tell me what they want to play, and we just do dance music and whatnot. I don't do a whole lot of special material with them.*

I like to progress and do things, but I've gotten lazy. I used to do new material, and I did keep up. I don't much listening now. Nellie was a good performer, but I never did cotton much to her style because it wasn't anything I could do with it. She's sort of flamboyant; she had personality and I'm not much of a personality person. I can go someplace and stay a long time because I have rapport with the people and I used to learn what they wanted to hear. When I was working alone back in the 1950s, I got the idea of making the hats bring up the type of songs I was singing. It was a way of killing time; I'd do Mexican tunes, Hawaiian things, and it just made my act a little different from somebody else's. With my bassist Edgar Mason, I never had to tell him the key. He didn't claim to have [perfect] *pitch, but when I hit the chord, he had it. He was a fine fellow to work with. We worked together for a long time. They used to laugh at him because Edgar was very close with his money, but he was a capable fellow to work with.*

I'm married [in 1981] *to a guy named Dick Beresford who is not a musician but he's a traveling man. He works in oil* [in fact, Beresford retired in 1972]. *He is in a nursing home now; this is about the third or fourth one, but recently at this last place he's gone into, he's become enamored of someone there* [laughs]. *I wouldn't make a big to-do about it; he hasn't been a husband to me in quite a few years as far as physical things, but we're married and I stuck by him and I still will. I feel sorry for him in a way because I realize he wanted to come home and he said I didn't want him home.*

Once before when he was here, he fell and I had to get help to get him up. He's a man over six foot tall and he can hardly walk. I have been going to see him, but I haven't been the last two weeks since he got this other thing. I just let it go at that. The way I'm situated here it would be awfully hard for me to take care of him. We're twenty years married. When I was on the road and things, he'd do some of the driving, and then he got to the place when he had the strokes; see, he had one or two at first. This is the fourth nursing place he's been in, and he's so tall they have to have special beds. Well, if I was just a housewife, it would be different, but being that I do get work if I want to do it, I can't find somebody to take care of him. [3]

I didn't make a whole lot of money, but I was happy to make what I did. Then on top of that I wrote a choral tune called "Gossip, Gossip." I was doing that tune while I was working in Hawaii. Jester Hairston [1901–2000] *that works with choral music, black fellow, he came in the place where I was working and he said, "Don't sing that song anymore," and I said why not and he said, "Because I'm going to publish it."* [4] *So he did. He published it. He added a verse to it. One thing I'm thankful for is he made the choral arrangement. I could have but it would have taken me a long time. We sold a lot of copies. He'd go places and get the people, churches and things, together and they'd do a big chorus. For a while I got quite a few royalty checks from that. When he was on the road, the choruses he was conducting, they were buying it. That was nice.*

It's possible that I might go back on the road again. Sometimes things come up out of nowhere just when you think this is it. Still, I've enjoyed what I've had. I wasn't famous, but I made a lot of people happy. I never drank or smoked. For the most part, I've been pretty fortunate.

Chapter Seven

McLure "Red Mack" Morris

Trumpet, Vibes, Drums, and Organ

Red Mack took some tracking down. He was always about to go to court to pursue a recalcitrant tenant and put off our interview more than once. His real estate interests seemed to take up a lot of his time, but finally we drew up outside one of his properties in West Los Angeles on a scorching day in 1990 and there he was.

Red was standing in front of a side door, wearing cut-down denim shorts, stripped to the waist, his chest disfigured by a livid scar, the aftermath of a heart bypass operation. The setting was like something out of the L'il Abner cartoon strip. To the front of the house on the burned-up grass there was a wrecked car and an abandoned Dodge truck. On the drive there was a shabby RV (recreational vehicle) of doubtful vintage, the hood up, its battery being recharged, with cable trailing back to the house. This was impressive in size if neglected in appearance, comparing unfavorably with the neighboring properties, their lawns trim and gardens neatly maintained. Set to the side was a padlocked fence with a door labeled "McLure's Castle" and in a more childish hand, "Grand Daddy Mack's Castle."

This led into Red's music room, more like a vast lean-to, where his celebrated jam sessions took place. At the entrance was a whiteboard signed by Nellie Lutcher and many others, some of them former Cotton Club showgirls. The walls were lined with show business photographs, press cuttings, and album sleeves. A Hammond B-3 organ occupied pride of place at the center of the room.

Red was genial and served us champagne in the sunshine as we settled down to talk on the patio. Very much a survivor, he was a recovering alcoholic. Red talked about his career in somewhat haphazard fashion, repeating

Red Mack, Los Angeles, 1940s. Courtesy Otto Flückiger.

stories several times and often losing the chronological thread. It was possible to see him as someone who had lived a chancier life than most, its picaresque quality quite evident in the account he gave us in the August heat.

That Red Mack played an important part in the musical life of black Los Angeles is irrefutable. He was in demand for film appearances and worked with a number of significant jazz figures when not fronting his own groups in local clubs. Had he been recorded more often in his 1930s and 1940s prime with his peers, it might have been easier to understand Buck Clayton's assessment of him as "the champion trumpet player in Los Angeles."

Red Mack died in Los Angeles in June 1993.

Red Mack: Los Angeles, August 30, 1990

I was born one, eighteen, twelve [January 18, 1912], *at Shelby County, Memphis, Tennessee. My people* [James and Emma McLure Morris] *came out here in '13 when I was one year old. They were from Mississippi. My mother was a McLure and my father was a Morris so they named me McLure Morris. Red Mack? Old Ted Merriman, the booker with Gene Coy, he gave me that name later. Well, yes, I was sorta red-complexioned, had reddish hair.*

As far as I can remember back, when we first come here we picked cotton in Imperial Valley [southeastern California]. *I remember they didn't have no clock to tell the time so when the sun got straight up, everybody stopped pickin' and they'd feed. After that, we came to Los Angeles and my father got a job as a janitor. We lived down on 9th Street, and I went to the 9th Street School. Then Poppa got a little barbershop.*

In those days, the colored people was on Central Avenue down as far as the Market—that's 7th and Central—and then we worked up to 12th and Central. We lived then on Burke Street right across from Lafayette Junior High. Really what happened, good and bad ran together; the war [WWII] *did a lot of people good too, because it brought a lot of them out here that never would have been here and they never did go back. The war broke down a lot of prejudice because naturally, we had to get together to save ourselves. There's good in it. There's bad in it. Somebody's goin' to get killed but somebody's goin' to advance. I remember we finally worked* [further] *down Central Avenue and the Rosebud Theatre was about on 20th and Central. That's where* [guitarist] *Buddy Harper's brother got killed. Police officer shot him. In the early twenties they built the Lincoln Theatre—that's on 23rd and Central—and then we worked on down and they built the Dunbar Hotel* [originally the Somerville Hotel] *at 42nd and Central. Curtis Mosby played drums and he had a band, called it the Blue Blowers, and they opened up the Lincoln Theatre.*

My grammar school was the Nevin Avenue School at 32nd and Central. Miss Tibbits was the principal. The old train tracks used to run down there and on that side was the rock crushing. I was tickling with the piano, I would say, but if you could hum it, I could pick it up. We'd go to church [Church of God in Christ, 20th and Driver Street] and the sisters would be singing some song, and I'd go on piano and try to pick it up. Every Friday at school, we'd all go to the auditorium, and I would play when they come and march in.

The great [trumpeter] Claude Kennedy came in from Texas with an outfit, and in them days they would go ballyhoo in the neighborhood: "Big Dance Tonight! Big Dance Tonight!" They'd stop on the corner and play some, and everybody would get around. Claude would just lay back and blow. Man, that cat could blow. Right then, I wanted to play trumpet. I was inspired by him. He went [died] the same year as Lloyd Reese. He had an appendix; that's what got Lloyd too.

In them days, if they sent you to the [school] office, they would paddle you. I got sent to the office pretty often, and Miss Tibbits says, "McLure, what's wrong with you?" I was cryin', "Miss Tibbits, I want to play trumpet." She says, "If I get you a trumpet, will you be good?" So I says, "Yes, ma'am." She got me my first little cornet in a little bag, and boy, I clasped that brother and ran home at 12 o'clock. We had but twelve 'til one for lunchtime, and I'd go home, polish my horn, and blow in it. I kept that horn so nice. I'd practice and practice. I got so I could blow "Taps" for the raising of the flag. When everybody came in and she'd say, "Raise the flag," I blowed the "Taps."

Then I got with Alma Hightower—we called her Aunt Alma—she had a child's dancing school and she taught music. I got with her when I went to Lafayette High School at the seventh grade. That was [drummer] Alton Redd's real aunt. I'd drive for her, drive her Chandler car, and run errands for her. She really taught me music. She played jobs on Fontana. Blind Willie [Jackson]—we called him Willie the Weeper—played saxophone and Mrs. Sturdivant played piano for Aunt Alma, and I would drive them. Finally, she said, "Mac, you can bring your horn." My first job I ever played, Marshal Royal was playing banjo with us. He wasn't playing saxophone then. We had Willie the Weeper on saxophone, Aunt Alma on drums, and Mrs. Sturdivant on piano. They gave me a dollar apiece, and boy, I ran home and gave that money to my mother.

Aunt Alma taught me the foundation of how to build a scale and about the different scales. You take the instrument apart so the key won't mean nothing to you. You got to get above key. So you play one tune in one key and then you play the next key and the next key. It don't make no difference what the key is and that frees you. It will make you fast on your instrument. You know, a lot of musicians ain't learned that yet. If you change key on him, you got him fucked. You can tell what kind of musician he is; he can't cut it. Don't *play in just one key; play in all the keys. Lloyd Reese taught me some too. He was great. Lived on 23rd and Central. He used to come to my house and give me my lesson on the back porch here on 22nd and Compton. That's when I was going to Nevin. He played saxophone and trumpet. I tried saxophone too.*

I played with Aunt Alma, and I wouldn't leave her. Joe Lewis, the guitar player, he came after me. In them days, you know how musicians are, you jam, and he wanted me to go with him on a gig. I said, "No, I ain't gonna never leave Aunt Alma," and Joe Lewis kept coming after me and he got to Aunt Alma. She said, "Mac, go ahead. It's all right. That's what I taught you to do." I cried, but I finally did leave her. I loved Aunt Alma. She was like a mother to me. I went with Joe Lewis, and that's when I started to getting into music. First gig I played with Joe Lewis, I was missing from school. I did graduate from junior high, and I went to Jeff [Jefferson High School] *in the tenth grade, but I got stretched out in music, running up and down the road with raggedy bands and getting stranded.*

I'd call Mother, and she'd send me a ticket and get me home. That's why I didn't finish high school, because of the music. "I'm gonna be a star," I said. Finally, she put her foot down. She said, "OK, you don't want to go to school, don't call me no more." So when they [the bands] *came after me, the first thing when I got there I would get some money. I learned to save. I sent money home to Mother. Elmer Fain, the walkin' delegate* [business agent] *from the musicians union* [Local 767], *he sent me over to get a gig. So we was playin' for this kiddie and then Elmer said we got to get a raise. The boss told Alma, "You come in and you check the cash register and see I can't pay you no more." So Elmer pulled us off our gig, and we ain't got nothin'. We out on the street, and he ain't got no gig to give us. That's the other side of the coin. The union is good and the union ain't good. Unions ain't good for this country.*

Red's first significant [if short-lived] association was with bandleader Sonny Clay, a key figure in African American music in 1920s and 1930s Los Angeles. Clay, a pioneer pianist and organizer, had already recorded by the time he enlisted Red for a new band that he formed in 1929 or 1930 for a residency at the Creole Palace in San Diego. The band is known to have made some film sound tracks.

Sonny Clay, oh yeah, he was a wheel. He played the big ones. When I went with Sonny, he had to get permission from my mother because I was under age. He was supposed to look after me and he did. We was playing at that hotel [the Creole Palace], *and we used to live upstairs. The café was downstairs. When I got down to San Diego and I got to drinkin', I goofed up. I was young and didn't know how to drink, and me and Sonny got into it. He said, "Man, when you goof up, you apologize." I thought it was unmanly to say* sorry. When you're young, you got that old shit in you, you know? I remember I said, "You ain't my father. You don't tell me what to do." Anyway he took me upstairs and locked me in my room. It's a wonder I didn't kill myself because I got out through the window, and when he looked 'round, I was back downstairs. Him and I had it again, so I cut and I got on the train. I was pretty near home when I start to straighten out. I wanted to come back, be with the gang again. Oh boy, we had some times. See, I learned from Sonny. He'd say, "Mac, you know you got drunk last night," and I'd go back and I'd say, "Well, I'm sorry," and get another chance.

Teddy Buckner was in that group, and Juanita Moore and Emma Priestley, chorus girls. I don't remember making any recordings with Sonny, but we did get a gig in the MGM studio. I made a tip of $500. Ooh, that was good. That's when my mother made a down payment on a little place I still got over there on the East Side. $500, that was a lot of money then.

Around that time, I worked with Reb Spikes. Lee Gibson was on drums. Reb had the music store on 12th and Central. He was a good musician but from the old school, way back. Sorta like Papa Mutt [Carey]. We used to play those walkathons when you go all night and the ones that dance the longest win. I was in San Diego and I went with Reb to Bakersfield, playing a walkathon. I'd had my hair gassed [straightened] with lye; in those days we used to call it gas. The guy didn't wash it out good, and I went up there with Reb and pretty soon, it start bubbling and goin' down all over my head. My whole head was a mass of sores. I'm blessed it didn't start running in my eyes. Reb took me and put me in the hospital. He was great. They laid me back, and the doctor had to wrap my whole head and just left the eyes [uncovered]. All night long, this nurse would come in and pour this salve on me. Man, I didn't have no eyebrows; I didn't have no hair; my whole thing [head] was plain like a newborn baby's butt. I went back on the gig, and I used to wear a little cap. Oh boy, I went through it, but Reb took care of me, put me in the hospital, looked out for me, and brought me back.

Another of the "raggedy bands" that attracted Red was that of the Seattle-based bandleader Gene Coy. Something of a nursery for talent, Coy's band was rated highly by musicians though it never achieved more than a local reputation. Red is listed in Coy's band personnel in 1932 alongside fellow trumpeter Carl "Tatti" Smith and trombonist Allen Durham.

Gene Coy came to town and I joined him. I must have been in my teens then. We went up to Sacramento and got stranded. Ain't got a quarter in the whole outfit. That's why I learned how to save a buck. I don't go nowhere without putting a buck in my pocket, baby. I took my horn and I went down to a taxi dance. It wasn't for us, I mean, all white, but they had a colored band in there. I went in and I saw him [the leader] and he said, "You blow horn?" He let me sit in. In them days, you blow a chorus and then you go back to the *bridge and get out, and the girl takes a ticket from the kiddie. The girls laugh and they buy them tickets. I started packing up and said, "Thank you," and the guy says, "The boss likes the way you blow" and I got me a gig. When Gene and them got enough* [money] *to get some gas and get in the cars, I said, "No, man, I'm stayin'." That kid looked after me, got me a room. His wife was a maid in a hotel. Sacramento is the capital of California, and politicians was turning tricks with the girls in the sporting houses. All first-class houses. We was making $15, maybe $17 a week. That was good money.*

When Louis Armstrong was arrested in early November 1930 for marijuana possession while appearing at Frank Sebastian's New Cotton Club in Culver City, Red was brought in to cover for Louis while he was in jail awaiting trial. He played Armstrong's solos and sang his vocals; according to Buck Clayton, "He sounded so much like Louis that many people hardly knew the difference." Red later played at the Cotton Club with Leon Herriford—"He was real particular"—and stayed on when Les Hite assumed leadership of the band after Louis returned. He recorded with the band on one of Louis's sessions before working with trumpeter Charlie Echols and then rejoining Gene Coy's Happy Black Aces.

That marijuana, Pops smoked so much of that stuff. He got caught, and Stuff Crouch took the rap for him—he wasn't in music; he was in nightlife. In them days, they was more serious [about marijuana] *than they are now. I was a regular member of the Les Hite band, played with* [trumpeters] *George Orendorff and Harold Scott. This lasted until Louis Armstrong came out to the coast, and the Mills Brothers came; Broomfield and Greely had the show. Lionel Hampton was playing drums because Louis liked Lionel; they'd do that long ending together.*

We had fifteen minutes on the air. You had that little radio time. You didn't get no solo; all you was doing was background, setting riffs underneath, in a mute. Pops would be blowing "I'm a Ding Dong Daddy from Dumas," and we'd go on the air blowin' that and we come off there, we still playin' the same tune. Oh, Louis, he was something else. I'd go up in his dressing room and talk to him. He gave me a lot of pointers. Sebastian had a kiddie to undress him and take his shoes off and rub him down. Pops was a star, but the poor man didn't have no freedom; he was booked solid, way up into the next year. When he did come down, he didn't have time to drive his car down the street. When you get up there, every time you look up, it's show time. Somebody say, "Go back, man; you ain't up to it so go out and take something to make it. I'm payin' you to play. I don't want to hear your chops is down; you making that good money." The way I see it, sometime you think you want something, but when you get it, you're a slave. That's show business. I'm so glad I'm free.

I got back with Gene Coy [in late 1933]. *The trombone and the bass player were brothers. Clyde Durham played tuba, and Allen played trombone. Gene's wife, Ann, she played piano; Gene played drums; Ike* [Ken] *Young played alto; and then we had a tenor man out of Seattle, from when we had played up there, that was Dick Wilson. We played up and down the coast, Sacramento, Santa Barbara, Frisco. There was an agency who would get us gigs. Robinson was the agent. You contact them and they'd brew something up for you, but sometimes you got stranded. Then we had Ted Merriman; he'd go in front in a car, set things up, and get us goin'. Sometimes, the bookings would fall through, so when we get there, they'd closed the place up or something. You're up and down the road; we called it barnstormin'. No bookings sometimes. Wherever the car broke down, that's where we slept. In the car. Then we'd pawn something to get money to get the gas.*

I must have worked with Gene Coy around six months to a year. We went all the way to Chicago, and Ted said we got a lucky break and we played the Savoy Ballroom. It was only six of us, saxophone, banjo, and bass tuba, plus me, Ann, and Gene. Erskine Tate had a big band, fifteen, sixteen pieces, they was up there in tuxedoes, everything first-class, and we was playing intermission for them. We didn't have no uniforms, just little waiter jackets that we washed ourselves. I tried to imitate Pops. Imitatin' Pops got me a whole lot of breaks. I got to do my feature numbers; I'd do "Shine" and "Ain't Misbehavin'," and they be clappin', do my long ending like Louis. That's what got me a break with Erskine. He said, "Boy, you around? I might be able to use you." I say, "Yessir," and he gave me his card. So next day, I called him.

Erskine Tate enjoyed a prominent position in Chicago's segregated music scene. Louis Armstrong had been a featured performer with Tate's orchestra in the 1920s. His band played regularly at the Savoy Ballroom in the early 1930s, and Red was on Tate's payroll in 1933. Tate later opened a music school.

Erskine had two or three bands working under his name, and his mother was teaching piano. I went and saw Erskine, and I joined him. I wrote my mother and she gave me the address of a cousin, Aunt Bessie, so I got to her and she took me in. I rehearsed and rehearsed with Erskine. He would send a kiddie to pick me up and take me to the gig. I didn't know about it at the time, but Erskine took care of me that way. This was not his main band, not his big band, so we'd play the gig and he'd bring me back. Finally, Erskine went to the union for me, took me there with him. The president, a little short fella, said, "No, hell, no. He can't play here. He's gotta be around six months." Anyway, Erskine took care of me until he finally got me in his main outfit, and we opened the old Vendome Theatre on State Street. We had five brass,

Vernell Yorke [recordings with Zutty Singleton for Decca, 1935] *was on trumpet with me.*

Vernell was on that dope; he was smokin' that marijuana, and I was drinkin'. This bypass [operation] *come from drinkin'. When I had this I was up to a fifth a day. That marijuana was something else, no wonder they get hooked on it. We got so we had a connection; I would bring it one day, and then he* [Yorke] *would bring it the next. When they said, "Show time!" you get ready to hit; that's when I would take my three draws, and ooh, man, I could blow! I'd get up there* [high note ending] *and bring the house down. Everybody be clappin'.*

We was smokin' brown stuff; it was wrapped in brown paper, and I thought I had it captured. I knew just how much to take and boom, I'd be right there. This night he brought some black stuff and I'm taking my same three draws, but I ain't never got on stage. They said, "Red, you upset the whole theater." They had to drag me back in the dressing room, and when I start coming 'round, the doctor was standing over me. Erskine had called the doctor, and he mixed something up, looked like soapsuds to me. They was all standin' 'round, but they was way off in the distance. I could hear this doctor, "Who's this boy's people? You better call his people." I ain't got no people; I'm by myself, and you talk about prayin'? You ain't never prayed like I prayed. He said, "Well, don't move him." I slept in the theater all night, and the musicians and the watchman, they was all lookin' out for me. I promised the Lord, "Let me get up now and I'll go straight home."

Next morning, when I start to coming 'round, I said I'm going home. "Oh man, you just had a bad trip," they said, but I made up my mind. I had saved enough to get on the steam train, so I packed up my horn and walked off. The union fined me and put me out because you supposed to play your notice out. I came home to Los Angeles to my parents' house, got off that choo-choo train at 1st and Alemera. I was stupid to try that stuff. See, I thought I was in love with a chick, and she was on it. I was trying to get her off it, and I wound up trying it. Oh, them was days.

When Red returned to Los Angeles in 1933 or 1934, he rejoined Charlie Echols, first as the band's drummer, at the All American Ballroom, before taking his rightful place in the trumpet section. Red played with pianist Lorenzo Flennoy's group at the Rose Room, a taxi-dance hall in downtown Los Angeles, for six months before going into the Club Alabam with Flennoy in the middle of 1934. This band broke up when Echols formed his new "star-studded" big band to go into middleweight champion boxer Billy "Young" Papke's Harlem Nite Club in 1935. According to band member saxophonist Jack McVea, this "was one of the finest bands ever to originate and work in Los Angeles." Aside from Mack and McVea, it included trumpeter Buck Clayton, trombonist Tyree Glenn, and saxophonists Herschel Evans and Don Byas.

We opened up a ballroom downtown. I wanted to play drums and Charlie said no, so I quit. I went and got me some drums. Put them up in my garage and start practicin'. I was going to play drums with one hand, trumpet with the other. I might have had it in mind to do a single. I got that from the Sweethearts of Rhythm. Charlie came and said, "Yeah, you can play the drums, but bring your trumpet." So I rejoined him playing drums and I played trumpet too.

Then we opened Papke's on 18th and Main. Upstairs on the second floor. Papke was a fighter, and it was a boxing club, like a hangout for fighters. They'd all sit at the bar. Charlie had a lot of nerve himself. He'd go over there to the playground and train all the time. Oh yeah, he loved to fight. He had a lot of nerve too, like he'd be there with Papke and say, "I bet she got on blue panties" and go over and pull up this girl's dress.

It was Claude Kennedy, me, and Bernice Brice—they call him Pee Wee—playing trumpet at Papke's. Buddy Banks was playing the saxophone at the time. He played piano later. Jack McVea was there and Alton Redd on drums. Bert Johnson, Cee Pee Johnson's brother, was on trombone with A. J. Williams; he was an ex-fighter. They was all older than me, looked out for me. I couldn't drink—that's where I goofed—but I learned a lot. Charlie Echols blowed trumpet, but he didn't know the horn. He wasn't a musician. He'd scream high, on the end. It didn't have to be the right note, just as long as it was high, that's what he said. He'd direct the band and knock us off, set the tempo. He was bad kiddie; boy, he's been gone a long time. We played a gig down in Long Beach, and that's where we made our money, from the soldiers and sailors. When the fleet came in, we'd make more in the kitty than we was getting paid. This sailor gave him the money, and Charlie started putting on his gloves. He went downstairs to the restroom, and we went on playing. Soon he come back and got up on the bandstand. He hit that kiddie and knocked him clean down them stairs. Charlie was a tough guy.

When we got to the Cotton Club, Charlie couldn't cut it because he didn't know his instrument that way. Him and Lionel [Hampton] got into it; that jealousy always gets in there. After we left the Cotton Club, Lionel organized a band of his own and we went to Frisco. We got stranded in Frisco, didn't have a quarter. It was rough! Gladys [Hampton's wife and manager] cooked a big pot of red beans and rice and fed the whole band. She was great, the brains of the outfit. She was more of a businessman than Lionel was. We was in the hotel, and we didn't have no money to pay for the hotel. They finally cooked up a dance and we made about $15, $20 apiece. That was good money. So we went down and got the Studebaker started and we split. Came on back to Los Angeles.

In 1935, saxophonist Eddie Barefield came to Los Angeles with Cab Calloway's orchestra to appear in a film with Al Jolson and to play the Cotton Club. Enamored of the climate and at odds with Calloway over money, he decided in early 1936 to stay on in California, working with Echols before forming his own big band with Red in the trumpet section alongside Leroy "Snake" Whyte (from Cleveland) and Pee Wee Brice. Tyree Glenn (trombone), saxophonists Don Byas and Jack McVea, bassist Al Morgan, and drummer Lee Young were also in Barefield's outfit. The band worked at the Cotton Club for nine months (without Red apparently) and then toured. Its recordings, made by the disc jockey Al Jarvis, have never surfaced. The band broke up in late 1937 having lasted a year.

We rehearsed all day; man, the morale was so good. Eddie could write! We didn't get nowhere with it, but we did work at Club Alabam. It had been the Apex but the government got [owner] Curtis Mosby for the income tax and they put him in San Quentin. They let him out to die and he did die. Ben and Pete Rosardi, gangsters from back east, they came out here and they got it, named it the Alabam because it was in the colored district. I worked there for them after that. Leo Davis had the band. I think I worked at the Arrowhead Inn, but I don't remember working at the Cotton Club with Eddie. Anyway the band fizzled out and Eddie went back east, and I got into doing my own thing. The Brown Sisters had an after-hours place down in Watts. You could sit in. They just jammed. Curtis Mosby had an after-hours place across from the Apex, and then Miss Brown had an after-hours place right across from the Alabam. She bootlegged; she was selling whiskey there.

That Don Byas could blow his can off, and he could blow circles 'round Ben Webster because he started young; his father was a musician, and he was brought up in music. When Don went to Europe, he cut Ben Webster, and Ben jumped on him and beat him up. That Ben was bad actor. Down here on Washington, just the other side of Vermont, there used to be a club— Sammy Davis and his father had a dance team on the show there—and we all used to go down there and jam and Webster was gonna jump me. I had my gun in my car and I started getting close to my gun. Later in '41, I had a club called the Ritz on Vernon and Central. Whiskey was hard to get, and I used to drive to Hollywood to get one fifth of whiskey and cut it and put it in half-pint bottles and sell it after-hours. That's where I made my money, bootleggin'. Anyway, Ben Webster came in there and he jumped on a guy in my place. He was a bad actor.

The Barefield period enabled Red to sharpen up his reading.

He could write and do special arrangements, and you had to read them. There was a piano player who played the Cotton Club with Les Hite where they used to have shows by Bloomfield and Greeley, and this guy would use a lot of classical music in his shows, "Rhapsody in Blue" and a lot of stuff in 12/8 time and 6/8 time, and we couldn't read it. He'd take it bar by bar and teach us. Then I finally learned how to read, and when the war came on, I got a lucky break at MGM for recording. This [other] *kiddie got called to the Army. You had to read. They put the part up and they would tap it off to run through it to see if there's any mistakes in it. If you couldn't cut it, you wouldn't have it. You had to cut it. I cut it. I got so I could read 'round the corner. Read two or three bars in front.*

Nat King Cole came out to the coast with a show [in 1937], *and they got stranded because this fellow ran off with all the money. So we took Cole on our gig. I was playing with* [saxophonist] *Buddy Banks on the Pier here at Long Beach. That's where we made that big money when the fleet was in, and them whores, they'd come in there and just throw it in the kitty. King Cole played so much piano, we let him jam with us and we split the kitty with him, gave him a taste. Oh, he was somethin'. Later, I played with King Cole with his own outfit.*

There was lot of kiddies then that couldn't get off [improvise]. *They could read, but they couldn't ad-lib. Lloyd Reese could do it because he studied. We was learning so you play a pet solo or you copy somebody's solo, but you wasn't free to make up your own, to go up and down the horn. See, music was changing like everything else. All I hear now is people blow blues, but in them days you had to play a melody line. You take "Stardust"; how you gonna blues "Stardust"? They're bluesing everything now. I get so sick and tired of bluesing. I want to play some melody lines, different than just 1-4-5; three changes, that's all there is to the blues. You got three chords to run up and down, but you take "Stardust," you got to know how to get off against the melody. Then you take a tune like "Body and Soul"; it's got a bridge to it, in the last half, so when you go to ad-libbing, you can put some blues in it, but it ain't the same as a blues. The way I see it—this is just my opinion— they're not the musicians they were yesterday. You change key on him* [today's musician] *and see if you don't hang him up. The musicianship ain't there. The young kiddies nowadays, they don't tell a story. I like to play like Pops, and I remember his solo so I play his solo. It had more meaning in it, like a melody line.*

After working with the entertainer Cee Pee Johnson's band at the Paradise Club in 1938 [replacing his early hero Claude Kennedy, who had died suddenly from a burst appendix], alongside saxophonists Buddy Banks and Jack McVea, Red formed the first of many small swing combos in 1939, with Lady Will Carr on piano, to play at the Streets of Paris as well as Billy Berg's club.

That lasted quite a little time because we did Billy Berg's on Pico and La Cienaga, right next to the Bank of America. When we got off the stand for intermission, man, she'd play and we had a time getting back on; they all wanted Lady Will. She could play some piano. Her mother taught her when she was just three, four years old. She knew the instrument. I went downtown and bought "Rhapsody in Blue." I was going to trick her, and she put it up there, and you know, she ain't miss a note. She read fly-shit; she read 'round the corner. She was something else.

She got to drinkin', poor Lady; the only time she wasn't drinkin' was when she was asleep, couldn't get it up to her mouth. She went fishing with some people, and they'd been up all night drinking, and she got drownded. When they found her, the body was in such bad shape, at the funeral they just put a picture on top of the casket. She wasn't all that old, might have been in her fifties.

Oh, we were doin' it. We had it sewed up. With that rhythm behind me, I could play what I want. Bert Brooks was the drummer. Did you ever hear of Brooks Bathhouse? His father had a bathhouse on 28th Street way back when we was going to grammar school. We all went to grammar school together. Dudley Brooks played piano, Alford Brooks played trumpet, and Bert Brooks was the youngest; he played drums and violin. When I was home on 22nd and Compton, their father was a bootlegger before the liquor came back. He had a still in the backyard underneath the chicken coop. Don't how he got it in there, but he did, and he was bootleggin', but the government got him. Then he had the bathhouse; that used to be a meeting place with women, after hours. Alford went to China with Happy Johnson's outfit; Luke [Jones] was in that band too, but I was back east at that time. They all gone now.

The California Eagle, September 2, 1939

Floyd Turnham's Rhythmaires Ork—Among local bands that are forging to the front is the Rhythmaires under the direction of Floyd Turnham. This aggregation, recently organized, has just completed a successful engagement at Café DeParee, swank downtown café. Members of the band include Red Mack, trumpet; Bob Dorsey, Luke Jones, Andy Anderson, Floyd Turnham, reed section; Fletcher Smith, piano; Red Callender, bass; Oscar Bradley, drums.

Central Avenue then was like Harlem to me. It would jump all night. Some of the movie stars would even come and see us on Central Avenue. Bing Crosby came over there.

Jazz Information 1, no. 18, January 12, 1940

Los Angeles Jan. 3—There are a few spots where unknown talent can be heard. Best right now is probably the Onyx Club where Bob Dade, the white New Orleans vocalist, has successfully introduced a colored band and Harlem-type entertainment into Hollywood. Band features Ceepee Johnson and his "Torrid Tom-

toms," but real kicks come from the trumpet of Red Mack and the singing of Marie Brian [actually Bryant].

Down Beat, June 1, 1941

Les Young Joins Brother's Band on West Coast; Los Angeles—Lester Young packed up his tenor and migrated out here from New York last month to join his drummer-brother, Lee Young's band at Billy Berg's Club Capri.

With the ex-Count Basie star on tenor, others in the band are Arthur Twine, piano; "Bumps" Meyers [sic], sax; Red Callender, bass; Red Mack, trumpet; Louis Smith [actually Louis Gonzales], guitar, and Lee on drums.

I went with Lee and Lester at Billy Berg's. Charles Mingus was playing bass. He was good. He played with the Erwing Brothers at one time, too. He played with Louis, didn't he? He's out of Watts. He must have died young. Lester? Oh, he was great. He was OK, easygoing. He could sure blow. He knew his horn. He knew his instrument.

In the autumn of 1941, the singer and bandleader Will Osborne, who had been playing dates around California, recruited new players to his dance band to go east, playing one-nighters, adding Red as "hot man."

Down Beat, November 15, 1941

This Osborne band is easily the best Will's ever had. Spotlighted are the heated solos of Red Mack, Negro trumpeter, who took Brodie Shroff's chair and who played with the Duke Ellington "Jump for Joy" show [in fact, Mack did not play in this show].

That's the biggest break I ever got. I was workin' for Billy Berg, but he let me go. He told me, "Red, you ain't gonna like it there," and I did catch that prejudice when we went down through Texas and up through Chicago, playing one-nighters.

See, California is nothing but a big old country town, and I wanted to go and get my stamp—"oh, he's from New York"—you ain't nothin' until you get your stamp. If you played New York, you got it. In Los Angeles, I was makin' it, but this was my break. I hadn't hit the big time before.

African American soloists like Red with Osborne or Roy Eldridge with Gene Krupa faced constant racial harassment and prejudice on the road.

I damn nearly got lynched in McClure, Illinois. I never will forget it. We'd played a one-nighter, and I was riding with Dales Jones, the bass player, in his car. Two or three of us. We went down through Texas, and Dale went into a gas station to gas up. We didn't know where to eat so Dale asked the kiddie, "Say, can you tell us a good place to eat round here." The guy kept looking at me. I had my hair gassed. The guy said, "Why you go down there ... but don't take that nigger with you." So I said, "Some shit's starting, just like Billy Berg said."

We went on up to Illinois, and we got in early where we was supposed to play. This was a first-class place, off the road, with big white posts, like a plantation. Anyway, we was the first ones to get there. When I joined Will, he laid down his law; that's when we learned how to make time. He said, "I want your music in order, don't want to hear your chops are down"; then when he come on the stand, one, two, that band hit, man.

So we went in there. We didn't ride in the uniform, but Will said you supposed to be in your uniform early so we got dressed, sat around playing cards, just settled in. This kiddie must have thought I was the flunkey or the valet, and by the time it come to hit, the manager's saying, "He gonna play here? Oh, no, you can't. Oh, hell!" Boy, him and Will had it, and finally, I was to play but I wasn't to take no solos. I was to sit back, behind the band.

About twelve or one o'clock, this guy was dancing and dancing, the ladies in evening gowns and men in tails and tuxedoes, and he stopped and said, "I'll be damned!" Then he start pulling old Will around, and I said, "Here's that shit again," and pretty soon, two or three more had stopped and they started shouting, "There's a nigger up in that band." Big Dale says, "Come on, Red," and we went out the back door, took my horn, and got in his Lincoln Zephyr and we split. We had to come around from the back to get out. By that time, everyone was causing a commotion, like a riot. "There's a nigger up there!" This was in McClure, Illinois; that's my name!

Eventually, in December 1941, Osborne's band made it to New York City and played the Strand Theater on Broadway. Drummer Dick Shanahan, who joined Osborne a week before this prestigious engagement, remembered Red as "a good player and a nice guy. Red and some of the others went back to California."

See, I was imitating Pops, making them long endings, doing my feature numbers. Everybody clappin', just me and the drums. I thought I had it made. With Will, you didn't have time to do nothing but go to the hotel and back to the theater because when we got there in the morning, they'd be lined up for the show. We'd do five or six shows a day. Sometimes we'd clean the theater out and do another show, back to back. You're making that good money, but you don't have time to spend it. I'd send my money home to my mother, and she bought me a down payment to help me own this house. Lionel [Hampton] was at the Apollo with Marshal Royal and Jack McVea and Dexter [Gordon]. All kiddies that I knew so I went over there and sat in with them. Pow-wowed a bit with Lionel.

Then they bombed Pearl Harbor. The news media upset the country when they put on the news that the Japanese were going to invade. Said submarines seen off the coast of California. New York went upset. The Army was up and down the street. The band broke up, and it took me about a week before I could get out of there. They had the trains all tied up. I had my wife and kids here [Los Angeles], and I had to get back. When I finally made it back to the Coast, we had [electricity] blackouts here. Believe me, the U.S. wasn't ready for this. It upset the whole country. If they had come through, they would have got us, but that Roosevelt, he said, "Don't worry; we gonna get ready," and we really did.

I bought this Ritz Club, this after-hours place, and I went into business. I had music in there. Musicians would come in after hours. I was bootlegging too. They finally got me for that. Someone brought a young chick in there, and I sold them whiskey. They got her drunk, and they were going to do their thing with her so they carried her out of there. The police got 'em and she was under-age. The police asked her where she got drunk and she named the Ritz, so that put the thing on me. I was gonna go straight because I was tryin' to save for a beer license. Cost around $500 at that time.

Anyway, the Juvenile Department summoned me. I was scared to go down there by myself, so I went to Walter Gardner, a heckuva attorney, and he said, "Bring $500." I was supposed to go to court down on 12th and Broadway. I met him at his office, and we got in the car with some other parties; he had two or three divorce cases he had to do. Juvenile Department had her there, this little teenager, with her mother, and pretty soon Mr. Gardner came into court and put the girl on the stand and he criss-crossed her. Had her crying. "Where did you say you were?" "Where's the Ritz?" And whatnot. Her mother started crying, and the judge said, "Case dismissed for lack of evidence." All my money had gone—$500 was a lot in those days—but it worked, didn't it? I didn't get the beer license. I went back and bootlegged more than ever. I didn't stop playing. I think the war was over when I finally gave up that place.

Red and his brother Joe Morris (who owned and operated the celebrated Plantation Club at 108th and Central) were determined to avoid the military draft.

I wasn't going to no war. My brother and I said no to that, but they got my youngest brother. I was trying for 4F [excused duty]. They put out that farmers didn't have to go, so we was going to claim that we was farmers. Joe had the Plantation then, and at the back was a big lot of space, an acre or two of land. We got us a plow and a horse, and we plowed it all. We got some chickens, bought these baby chicks and an incubator, but we didn't know anything about raising no chickens. We put in we was farmers, but they finally got us. Sent me my final "Go for Induction" letter. I made it down there on 5th and Main, got in a line, and they looked at me, and then they said, "Son, step over there. You can't make it; you got a murmuring heart." I played like I was so sad, but I was so glad. I ran all the way home. I left the car and everything. They put me in 4F!

I had to go to defense. It was a shipyard, by the beach, towards Long Beach. I was riveting and we was building ships around the clock. That's when my wife, Esther, left me. She put in for a divorce. She left me with the kid, Julie, my youngest daughter. I had to take Julie to school, go to work, come home in the evening, get her and take her to my mother's, come home again and change clothes, and get ready to hit at nine.

I blew my horn all night and worked in the defense all day. I was always going to the tool room, and I'd slip off, go in the bathroom, and get me a nap. I was just beat. Couldn't get no sleep. The foreman said, "Morris, if I catch you sleeping anymore, I'm gonna let you go." Finally, they did catch me and they put me out.

Then I got a job at the school. Puss Waide—he played saxophone—he got me that job. He was the janitor there. I could take Julie there, but I didn't get off 'til five and the kindergarten would close around three. So I'd go get her and put her in that sand pile and let her play until I got off. Then I'd take her to Mother's, go back home, and get ready to hit at nine on the gig.

Red worked for five months at the shipyard and then resumed his varied musical and property interests. He told an interviewer that he bought a grocery store around this time, but that is unsubstantiated. As are his statements that he operated a gas station and a beer bar. The Ritz Club was an after-hours joint, which allowed him to play at other local clubs as well. During the day, there were studio calls for movie appearances, and Red also participated in a series of novel short films made for the Edgar Bergen organization.

Down Beat, July 1, 1942

Jam Sessions Begin in Hollywood; Los Angeles—Series of jam sessions, scheduled to take place every Sunday afternoon from 4 to 7pm, were launched at Hollywood's Trouville Club last month.

Sponsor and financial backer of the affairs, is Norman Granz, who works for a Beverley Hills brokerage company and hobbies at hot music. Line-up for the opening session included Les Young, tenor sax; Nat Cole, piano; Oscar Moore, guitar; Wesley Prince, bass; Lee Young, drums; Red Mack, trumpet; Eddie Barefield, clarinet; Taft Jordan, trumpet; Joe [actually John] Ewing, trombone.

The same year, Red appeared with a short-lived band fronted by Barney Bigard at another of Billy Berg's clubs. This interesting unit included altoist Jackie Kelso (later a key member of Roy Milton's band and subsequently the lead alto with the Count Basie Orchestra) and the young Charles Mingus on bass. It also gave New Orleans trombonist Kid Ory something of a career revival.

Down Beat, August 15, 1942

Los Angeles Band Briefs by Hal Holly—Barney Bigard debuted his own quartet at the Trouville. With Barney is Red Mack on trumpet, a top man in anyone's band.

Down Beat, September 1, 1942

Kid Ory Comes Back to Bizz; Los Angeles—Barney Bigard, whose new seven-piece combo was scheduled to open August 20 at the Trouville, sharing the spot with Stuff Smith, will have on trombone none other than Kid Ory, who is coming out of retirement to take a last fling at jazz before putting his old horn away for good.

In addition to Ory, Barney has Red Mack, trumpet; Jack Calso [sic], alto and clarinet; Henry Tucker, drums; Charlie Engels [sic], bass; and Garland Finney, piano.

Down Beat, September 15, 1942

Los Angeles—The small band spotlight is shared by the new combos launched here last month by Barney Bigard and Murray McEachern. Barney has backed his clarinet with Kid Ory's trombone, Red Mack's trumpet and an alto sax. Barney takes his band to the Capri this month.

Metronome, September 1942

Kid Ory returns to active duty as a member of Barney Bigard's new seven-piece band, currently at the Trouville. He is now fifty-two years old, and hasn't been heard as a regularly active musician in many years.

He's killing the cats in these parts. So is Barney, of course, who left Duke [Ellington] recently. Also in the band are trumpeter Red Mack, altoist Jack Kelso, drummer Tommie Tucker [actually Henry Tucker Green], bassist Charles Ingles [actually Mingus] and pianist Garland Finney.

Down Beat, November 15, 1942

Los Angeles Band Briefs by Hal Holly—Red Mack, trumpet player featured with Barney Bigard's erstwhile band at the Trouville, has stepped out with his own combo of Local 767 cutters at Central Avenue's Club Plantation. Sitting proudly and ably at the tubs [drums] in Red's new band is Local 47's Walt Sherman. Hat's off to a boy who recognizes only One Big Union for musicians—the Musicians' Union.

Later Red played with Cee Pee Johnson's band again at the Trouville and took an outfit to Victorville with Dorothy Broil on piano. By then Red was playing vibes and drums as well as trumpet. Few of these short-lived combos recorded, and it's hard to pin down dates and durations for many of these engagements. In 1945, he made a USO tour to Alaska with his old friend altoist Luke Jones in his band, plus dancers Earl and Francis and comedian Nick "Nicodemus" Stewart.

I took up the vibes; that's what got us the gig to go to Alaska for the USO. They had bands tryin' out, and when I tried out, I played like Lionel Hampton and we got the gig. I had the band. Luke Jones was with me. We went to grammar school [Nevin] together. We were musical buddies. Sam Joshua was on drums and a kiddie out of Chicago on piano. We flew to Anchorage, got off there, and we went 'round all the Aleutian Islands there, Cold Bay, Dutch Harbor, Umnak, Adak. It was pitiful, some of these poor souls, when we played the hospital. This was the end of wartime. You get on some of those islands and the weather changes, and you can't get off because the ship can't get in or the airplane can't get out. You run out of liquor, you run out of cigarettes, and man, you really have it. A tough time.

You really in the Army when you in the USO. We all got down to the base to get off, and the man gave orders for everyone to get back to barracks. We stuck on the island. On some of them islands, they had a wind blowing so strong it'll blow you off into that ocean. They only give you three minutes. You gone, if you fall in there. That's so cold. We had them big parkas on, and they have a rope from one dugout to another. If you go from one to another, you hold on to that rope; otherwise you'll be blown away. Some of the soldiers on there, they got some stuff they make out of potato peel, call it "Black Lightning," and you drink that stuff, man, you be drunk for three days. That's all they got!

Red was also a member of Jimmy Mundy's 1946 big band that entertained servicemen in hospitals and at military bases around Los Angeles.

We played shows with Jimmy Mundy down at some Army bases. I made some recordings with him, I remember that. I also made some records with a guy named Smoky Joe Whitfield, and then I wrote a tune called "Give Me Some Skin, My Friend." Jimmie Lunceford came out here [1945] and he played the Cotton Club, and we'd been jamming with his tenor man, Joe Thomas, and he took this tune of mine to Lunceford and he had someone make an arrangement of it. Rehearsed it and got it ready with some other tunes they was going to record. Got to the studio to record it, and they said, "Whose name we gonna put on it?" and Lunceford said, "Lunceford," so I said no, and that's where I made my mistake. I should have had it as Red Mack and Lunceford, but I wanted it as my tune. He tore it up and threw it out. I should have let him make it. We could have got a hit.

I had a band with Luke and we got into it about who's the leader, whose outfit it was. I'd say, you take the band; it's your outfit. I'll stay. The leader gets more money, gets the recognition, and calls the numbers. All bands have trouble with leaders. Jealousy always seeps in. I guess I might have had in mind then to do a single one day. Later on I did a single and I enjoyed it. I didn't have nobody to worry about but me. I could do my thing. Have more happiness and more peace.

The California Eagle, August 30, 1945

Red Mack and Music Pleases—Thoroughly capable of playing music both sweet and hot is Red Mack who leads a little band here in Los Angeles that is currently wowing lovers of dance music. Red's combo is now doing double duty, playing at Little Joe's Café [corner of East Jefferson and South San Pedro] from 8 to 12 midnight and at the Rhythm Club from 1 a.m. until 5 a.m.

The musicians who make up the band are Sonny Heard on drums; [Marshall] Hicks on bass; Leon, tenor sax; Alfonso [Anderson] on piano and McClure Morris, better known as Red Mack on trumpet and vibraphone.

This little aggregation is an up-and-coming group which is already catching the eye of music experts and predictions are numerous that they will hit the top of the heap in the near future.

I didn't get with that bebop. I kinda got with Pops's style. Dexter and Teddy Edwards, they turned it around, but I didn't take out on that. I left it to them.

The Capitol, February 1946

Howard McGhee's band is out of the Streets of Paris in Hollywood, moved to the Back Stage club in San Francisco. Red Mack's ork and singer Kay Starr took over the new show at the Streets.

Red's memories of the postwar years were hazy, although his continuing prudence over money was a constant thread in the narrative, as was his day-by-day involvement with his real estate interests. Although he recorded often for small local labels, it's clear that he played less often as his property affairs became more pressing. He mentioned that he had sent money home when he was in Chicago in the 1930s, a habit he maintained while he was on the road with guitar star T-Bone Walker twenty years later.

We went all down through to Texas. Texas is so big you can play a different place every night and still be in Texas. Then we went on to Louisiana. T-Bone went up to Chicago and Detroit, and I left him there. Lloyd Glenn had the band, and we had to go and get a room at a motel. They'd be jumpin' off going into motels. I slept on the bus. [Saxophonist] Big Pete Peterson spent a lot of money playing with them chicks and drinkin' and ballin'. Them chicks will take you, but I didn't want to spend all that money. I would send the money home to Mother.

Every time I'd save up $500 or $1500, she'd put a down payment on another place. I wound up with a four-family flat over here on Risley Drive; I had a four-family flat over on Virginia and Adams and another on 48th and Central, and I had a house down here, the first house next to the corner, and I still got that one over there, the little house plus I had a place on 51st and

Broadway. A lot of places. So what happened was, I start taking care of these places. What ruined me was bad tenants; every time you get trouble with tenants payin' rents, you gotta go get your attorney. So that's more money.

I got so I could do it myself. I could make my own papers. I still got my typewriter. Write and go file. It takes you time to get in court; you can't just go down there. You gotta get in line, to get on the list. By that time, bad-assed tenants done taken you for another payment, another month, and when you get there [to court] *the judge goin' give him another month. You losing all the time. You don't own the place; you just got a down payment, and you got to make your payments! You got your taxes to pay, then you got your upkeep, and this son of a gun is living there on you. Pretty soon, you into foreclosure. Once you get in foreclosure, they come in with "money shouts," I call them. "I'll give you so much and I'll take this over" because the bank ain't gonna wait for their money. If you don't make them payments, you in trouble, so what I did was I take one from over here and claimed that one, and then I run to the bank and borrow $5000 because your credit's good. You can borrow all the money you want if your credit's good. They keep on saying, come in and get some money. So I run back to the bank and by the time I get that one* [loan], *I take the rent from over here and save that one over there. I don't want no more incomes out of that. I'm just putting people out over there on that last one, and they talking about they gonna sue me. I only got one* [rental property] *left. All you can do is take what they give you and get out! If you stay there, you won't get that, unless you want to shoot it out with the marshal. When the marshal comes and put that thing on there and say you gotta be out by a certain day, you want to stay there and shoot it out? I ain't gonna do it.*

Down Beat, January 11, 1952
    Club Alabam, Los Angeles. Floor show and dancing with Calvin Boze band. Red Mack (trumpet) and combo headline Monday night sit-in sessions.

Red's association with Kid Ory in the Bigard band led eventually to a short-lived involvement with the legendary trombonist's revivalist Creole Jazz Band in the middle 1950s. Red performed with Ory in *The Benny Goodman Story*, shot in Hollywood in 1955, although New Orleans trumpeter Alvin Alcorn played on the sound track. Incidentally, Red denied ever appearing in the film.

I worked with Papa Mutt Carey, just a few gigs, but Kid Ory taught me Dixieland. It was [with] *Barney Bigard's outfit that we played at Billy Berg's. Ory started to rehearsing and then he got me into it. He started showing me Dixieland. Dixieland, at that time, I would say, had a sorta corny-like staccato. I remember laughing, "I can't play that." I thought it was sad. And he say, "No, that's it."*

In autumn 1963, Red headed for Europe, pausing in Paris for an unexpected reunion with his old friend Buck Clayton, who persuaded him to try his luck in Switzerland. Red crossed to London with Buck where he was interviewed by *Melody Maker* writer Max Jones and then returned to Switzerland for a two-month engagement in Basel concentrating on organ, with trumpet on the side.

I was doing a single, backgrounding myself with the organ, playing trumpet with one hand. That way you get all the money; you got all the kitty. You play what you want when you want. You ain't got nobody to say, "Hey, man, that's in the wrong key." It's beautiful. And you get all the sex, all the love, everything. I did that in Switzerland.

I had a bad love affair, thought I was in love, but we broke up. I always wanted to go to Europe, so I locked up and let my sister take over the real-estate stuff. I got on the plane and went straight to New York; then we jumped across and I got off in Paris. Didn't know a soul. Myself and my horn. But I had my money, enough to come home. My trouble was I couldn't speak French. I sat in the station there until finally an Englishman came by and I asked him, "Sir, I want to go someplace where there's nightlife." He called a cab for me; the cab took me to this hotel and I got me a room. I didn't want to go out because of the money I was carrying. I know how you get to drinkin' and you goof up. I found a Bank of America, put that money in there, got me an English paper out of London. It said, "Joe Turner . . . someplace . . . in Paris," so I said, "Big Joe is over here—well, I know Joe; I played with him."

I got sharp that night, took the ad out with me, and the cab took me there. I settled down, had a few drinks; pretty soon this kiddie walked in and he wasn't no Joe Turner that I knew. But he was named Joe Turner,[1] *doing a single there on piano. He came over to my table, and we got to talking about music, different bands, and who was doing what. We talked about Basie and Joe happened to mention Buck Clayton, and I said, "Yeah, I played with Buck before he was famous." He said, "Well, he's over here," and he told me where he was. That's why I say musicians and entertainers are the greatest people in the world. You travel anywhere, look for the musicians, the nightlife, and man, you got contacts.*

Buck was playing with an English band [Humphrey Lyttelton] *out of London, and he was the only colored guy with them. I got there and sat at the bar, and Buck was sitting with a chick. He put me in a hotel with this chick, and man, we had a time. Didn't do anything but ball and eat. I sat in with the band and blew with them. Pretty soon, Buck said, "We're going to Switzerland to play concerts." I said, "Yeah, get me a ticket; I'm going too." They played a concert, and after the concert we had a jam session with a lot of musicians and I played a couple of tunes on piano. When we got back to the hotel, Buck said, "Man, do you want a gig? This guy wants you to play in this café." So I met the guy and told him I wasn't good enough on piano to do a single. I said I could do it with the organ—like my Hammond B-3 that I bought from Lorenzo Flennoy—and told him what kind of organ I played. So we left and flew to London. Buck got me a hotel and they played some concerts there, and Buck said they were going to Canada, I think it was. London is beautiful. First place I saw a double-decker bus.*

Melody Maker, July 20, 1963

Trumpeter-singer Red Mack (real name: Maurice McLure [sic]) who played behind Louis Armstrong at Sebastian's Cotton Club in 1930 is now in London. He hopes to stay here for a week before a two-month Swiss engagement.

Then this guy called and he'd got an organ for me. I put Buck on the plane and went back and found me a place where I could practice the piano and get me a little rep together, eight or ten tunes that you know you know. If you go to play by yourself, you don't want to goof. I flew to Switzerland to take the gig, and, man, I had a ball. They put me upstairs over the club, and I'd get sharp and come downstairs to play. I loved that place. On the days off, the agent would send me on another gig. I'd get on a train and go to some other town. Told that agent, time after time, "I can't play nothing but a Hammond B-3"; heel and toe, that's all the rhythm you got. I remember going on a gig one Sunday, and when I got there, they had them little organs. I started foolin' around, and pretty soon, this kiddie came in and, man, he could play the hell out of that little organ, so I grabbed my horn—it was my gig—and I started blowin' and he went on back.

Then what happened, the union guy came by saying that I was takin' their gigs. I felt uneasy because I was by myself. So I said, "You better get out of here." I was going to get my money and split, but they had my passport. I went to the American Embassy. "Mr. Morris, we'll get your passport," they said and they did. The agent got me a gig in Rome, and then I got on the train and went to Spain. Fell in love again, had a good time, and flew from there to New York. That's where I saw Ben Webster. He had an outfit at that ballroom, the Renaissance, and I sat in and blowed with his musicians. We got a gig, but I didn't want to play with him; I was going to do my single with the organ. I got me a gig, but they wouldn't rent me no organ because they burn them up; guys put cigarettes on them and whatnot. I wanted to see New York, so I got me a map, walked around, learned to look out for myself. I like to walk and look and see, go in a café and rest. Stayed there about two weeks. Finally I got a plane and came on home to Los Angeles.

After that I got back on the real-estate thing, but my sister was taking care of it so I started cutting out. I'm not goin' to stay here until the bell rings. I plan to get out and see the world. I want to go to Australia and so many other places. I had this heart attack—that was in '86—so my blowin' days is over, but I still plonk on piano and organ. We have jam sessions here with a lot of younger guys, the new ones, and I belong to this Performers Club, and they give a bash here. Roy Priestley, he plays saxophone; George Mason, he plays bass. We do our thing. They bring their drums, their guitars, and everything. Willie Covan, taught some of those stars to tap dance out at MGM; he had his birthday party over here. He's gone in [died] *now. Got to be daytime because I can't stay up late no more. I'm having a time, see, because I built it* [Red's music room] *and I didn't have a permit. I ain't gonna tear it down. I'm gonna fight.*

I had my turn and I really enjoyed it. It's been beautiful. The best time was when I was younger, like when I made a picture with Bette Davis [Marked Woman, 1937]. *To me, music is happiness. You're putting out happiness. I think I still got a lot to do. You only got so long; it ain't forever. My brother went, and he didn't make but sixty-two and I'm seventy-eight now. I want to get into composing. Writing some real tunes that tell real stories. Communicate. Be happy and carry on with the show.*

Chapter Eight

Caughey Wesley Roberts II

Alto Saxophone, Tenor Saxophone, and Clarinet

The alto saxophonist Caughey Roberts's brief employment in the Count Basie saxophone section in 1937 and again in 1942 has ensured him a minor footnote in jazz history. Despite this and his subsequent association with Fats Waller (which also led to recordings) and his more extensive periods with rhythm and blues bandleader Roy Milton and traditionalist Teddy Buckner, he remains a shadowy figure, his status as a respected teacher and active sideman largely overlooked in the jazz encyclopedias. Never an assertive or strident figure, Caughey enjoyed the respect of his peers in the Los Angeles black music community even if the wider public knew little about him.

In 1990, when this interview was made, he was living in shabby retirement on his own in a drab area set between Central Avenue and Avalon Boulevard, his house strewn with papers and in very poor order. He told us that he no longer played or taught, though he did sing in a Methodist church men's chorus. He seemed content enough.

By the door, locked and barred against intruders, there was an ornate trophy inscribed to

Caughey Roberts
Master Musician and Dedicated Teacher.
With Appreciation from his Students. 1930 to January 9, 1989.

Although his circumstances appeared much reduced, Caughey was welcoming and gracious, if uncertain about his chronology. Laconic at times, excitable at others, yet vague about personal details, he was a bright-eyed sprite of a man who laughed often and was generous in lending us photographs and

Caughey Roberts of the Teddy Buckner Dixieland All-Stars, Los Angeles, 1950s. Courtesy Caughey Roberts.

providing information, even though his memory sometimes let him down. Although he seemed relaxed when talking about his own achievements, I sensed that he was exacting on himself and serious about the profession of music. Here was a man who thought deeply and had his own ideas even if his explanations sometimes seemed diffuse and a little difficult to follow.

Caughey died in December 1990, just three months after our meeting.

Caughey Roberts Jr.: Los Angeles, September 3, 1990

Caughey? Well, that was my father's name too. It's spelled one way and pronounced another. When I was going to school, most of them would say "Cor-gie" or "Cor-ey." I got tired of saying that's not it, so I quit correcting 'em. It's spelled "c-a-u-g-h-e-y" but it sounds phonetically as "c-o-chey." Correct is "couchie"—just like the couch you put in your house. A lady got real interested in the name so she start backtracking, and the closest she got was it was from India. Now, I don't know whether she's right or not, but that's what she say. It's different [laughs]*!*

I was born in Boley,[1] *Oklahoma, 1912, August the 25th. This particular place was an all-Negro town. Regular farming, stuff like that. My mother was a housewife, and she worked with us five kids. Dad was a baker. He went to Tuskegee. I gave his diploma to my nephew, my sister's oldest boy, who has the same name. He's Caughey Harris. Tuskegee was very important at the time.* [Tuskegee founder] *Booker T. Washington was well-liked, and I read that book of his all the way through. I always remember one thing out of that book: "Drop your bucket where you are." You know, that makes sense: why worry 'bout going way over somewhere to make some money; why don't you make it where you are?*

Actually both my parents liked music but just never had the opportunity to study it. One time my father wrote a song and had somebody write it out. Course, it never got nowhere, but my point was, he was interested enough to sit down and figure out some lyrics on it and a melody, although he couldn't write it. For myself, I just learned a little bit about music in that little grade schoolhouse they had there in Boley.

When my sister got ill, they decided to come to California. She had something [wrong] *concerning the spine. The doctors in Boley didn't know enough, so that's the reason we came out here. We had some relatives already living out here. My other brothers came out first, and then I came out by myself. December 1926. I was fourteen years of age. It takes a little time* [adjusting] *after coming out of a one-horse town out in the country, but I just took in my stride. We started* [living] *on the west side, moved to the east side and back to the west side* [W. 35th St.]. *Central Avenue was the hub even then. Blacks were already well-established. They said you should go to Jefferson High School, about two blocks down on 42nd Street, so I went over there. I decided I wasn't going to college. First place, I wasn't going to work my head off day and night and then try to study. That's for the birds.*

I'd had the clarinet all that time, so I start practicing two and three hours a day. The way I got interested in clarinet was they used to have a vaudeville show on tour and this guy had this clarinet, corner of this band they had, and he was playing the heck out of that thing. This is in Oklahoma. So I said maybe I'd like to play the clarinet. For some reason I did know it was a clarinet, so I asked my dad, "Will you buy me a clarinet?" and he got me a Sears-Roebuck one from the catalog. It was an Albert System. I was trying to learn that thing on my own, and I couldn't understand how you could make a note in the lower register and push that octave key and get an entirely other note, twelve notes away. On the sax, when you press the octave key, it'll jump an octave. How come this son of a gun, when I press the octave key, it jumps and it's another note altogether? I had no problems with the reed. It was the sound jumping that got me; that's what messed me up.

There wasn't any teacher [in Boley], so when we came to Los Angeles, this guy had a band, named LeBlanc. Called it LeBlanc's Boys Band of L.A. He was a real nice person, always having kids, so I said, "I want to get in the band," and he said, "Yeah, come on." One guy there knew more about clarinet than anybody else—his name was Paul Hanna—so he said, "Man, you need a Boehm System; nobody don't play these things." Some of the old guys did, and they played the heck out of 'em. So I finally got one [Boehm] and that's when the trouble started [laughs]! That's a world of its own. That's why so many guys don't fool with it. You either play it or you don't play it. There's no middle ground. You can jive on a saxophone, but you can't jive no clarinet.

Well, he got me started. I give him credit for that. The LeBlancs were on 22nd Street, off Central, about five blocks between Avalon and Central. Any kid interested in music could come in there. Anyway Paul quit, and in the meantime I'm practicing two and three hours a day so naturally I'm getting better. So by the time Paul quit, I had enough knowledge to teach them kids. So LeBlanc told me, "Go ahead and teach those saxophone guys and those clarinets." One family brought three boys in there, and all turned out to be musicians. One was Vernon Gower, played bass violin, and a little bitty boy played trombone and one [Martin Gower] played saxophone. His nickname was "Fuzzy," turned out to be a nice alto. They were small kids. Got behind with the payments. What we gonna do about that? No money. That's not the American system. You get left out if you drop your money. Wasn't that much, so he [LeBlanc] said, "Just go ahead and teach them."

In the meantime I'm going to Jeff, so I'm not going to worry about no credit, going to college, and all that mess. Every subject I could get to, that's what I was in. Jeff then was the melting pot. It was about 50-50 black and white, and I remember we had some Mexican guys on the football team. We had all nationalities. It was a real nice school. It had a good music program, and some great folks were teachers. Samuel Browne, he came in there afterwards, and all the guys will tell you how nice he was. I had no problem reading music—my problem was getting the fingers to play it [laughs]! My hands wouldn't go right.

This great big problem came up at school. The lady I had to see was Mrs. Gurnsey. It was for a clarinet, and I had transposed it and everything. Still couldn't play it so she asked a friend of hers to come in. He said, "I'll do that thing at sight." I said, "That's good; you do it, man." I kept on working until I could handle it. After that I was really interested in going into classical music, but I looked around and everyone's starving. Making no money so I thought I'd leave that alone. As a matter of fact they didn't make any money in Los Angeles until they joined [merged] the union. I'm talking to the classical now.

I wasn't paying that much attention to music around there. I was trying to learn that clarinet. I liked to rehearse rather than be playing, so it was just a matter of hard work until I finally got it together. When I got to the eleventh grade, come to find out they had given credit to the old-timers in the senior orchestra, and that made me graduate a whole half-year earlier. I was seventeen.

I had already decided music was it. I found out I had to learn something, so I just picked on music. I didn't start playing little engagements until I took out of Jeff. I can't remember the names of those little groups who used to play. Only one I can remember was a piano player. His name was Monroe Tucker. He had to be carried around as he couldn't walk although he played real nice piano. Little short guy. He played good. We'd just be playing little house parties so we made a little money, but we was playing because we liked to play. I must have had a saxophone by then because my mother gave me the saxophone for my graduation present.

The reason why I chose the tenor was because there was less tenor players than alto players. Seem like bandleaders were prejudiced towards clarinet. There was one clarinet player that always impressed me. He was from some island—they called him Slocum [clarinetist Adam "Slocum" Mitchell was from Martinique]—and I'd sit through these shows and all of them burlesque things and he'd play the same number, "Tiger Rag." The guy played so much clarinet. This was at the Follies [Follies Theatre, 337 S. Main Street]. First place, he'd got a nice sound on the clarinet and his phrases were musical. That's what I liked. To my ears, that guy was good. Told me I had to go back to the woodshed.

I didn't listen to records a whole lot. At that time there was a lot of radio. All the bands were on the radio. Besides I couldn't afford records anyway. I got in a group and played some symphony music; I never will forget that. The idea was to get a black symphony in Los Angeles, but they didn't get no black symphony because a lot of the instruments the blacks didn't play so they had to go get some other guys. We were practicing Haydn's Symphony Number

101 in D Major *and it's hard playing that stuff. It's all off-beat even when you're trying to hold that one note. One engagement and that was it. Like it is now. They've been folding up like accordions round here. Money, money, money, that's the American system.*

Leon René had a good little band there—he had a few good bands at that time. Ceelle Burke was his boy because he could sing. That's the first band I worked with that I made decent money when I first got my saxophone. I never forget we were making $25. This was at one of them places where they sold chicken. On the side, they had a little thing kids ride on, on playgrounds. Grown people like to come down so we went to work there. "Oh, now you have to join the union," so I said, "OK, let's get it over with." If you join the union, you get the best jobs.

Finally we found the guy in charge at the black union—that's Local 767—and he's underneath a car, working on a car. So finally he came out from under there. "OK, it's $25." "OK, here's my $25." He gave me a receipt, and I'm in the union. They got my $25. Johnson ran it when I joined, and the latter part of it, Leo Davis was the president. Had their place down on Central near 18th Street. Now and then they'd have cook-out things, barbecues, real nice. But I didn't socialize much after I started working unless it was some special thing because I stayed kinda busy.

I remember the first alto player that impressed me was Benny Carter on all those records he made overseas. They had reproduced them, and they were playing them a lot. I always admired the tone of that son of a gun on that alto. Really fine.

The band I really started making money with was the Erwing Brothers. One brother [Harris] *played alto, and he was very, very good. One brother* [Jim] *played piano, one brother* [Chester] *played the guitar, and they needed a tenor. They set the music up there, play that number, turn the page, and play the next number, and just keep on going. Harris, the alto player, played very good clarinet. His alto work was just superb, so a lot of people wanted him to travel with big groups, but he never did. Harris was the spark plug of that band. He had a lot of energy, and he played well. For that time, the Erwings band was considered a good band.*

This was at a taxi-dance hall. That's just what it was, at that time, mostly for Filipinos. They get a ticket and the ticket was good for one dance, so most of them had good jobs so they'd buy maybe about ten or fifteen at one time. Then they'd sit out and talk, buy a drink. At the end, the band would play a long waltz because otherwise there was just one chorus—that's thirty-two measures—but they'd play two choruses for the waltz, and that was considered a long dance so naturally they liked the waltz. Got a little more for their money. This place was downtown, can't remember the name of it. There was about three or four of them [taxi-dance halls] *down there.*

So we made them few little bucks. This was 1933; no, a little before that. I can't remember anybody outside those three brothers, but I never will forget the bass player in there. He's the only man I've ever seen who could go to sleep going boom, boom, boom, and bowing that bass and he's sound asleep. How did he do that? Edgar Mason, I think, was his name. He had some [bass-playing] brothers. One thing you'd learn [playing in a taxi-dance hall] was how to build up your endurance. Just keep rolling [laughs]. I didn't play too much clarinet because Harris would take all the clarinet solos. I got a few solos but no to improvising. Any solo would have to be on the short side because you never did go over one page. You'd just take a big old book, finish one number, turn that page, and go on to the next one. That was a learning process for me. I was with them a pretty good while.

I was living at home then, and in the meantime I started teaching. I'd been teaching for a long time, but then I'd go on the road and mess it up. I stayed with LeBlanc a long time. After I came out of high school, I swore I didn't know enough about music, although I had studied there. I guess it must have been with the two nice ladies in the music department there, Miss Behrens and another nice lady by the name of Smith, both of them good teachers. Anyway this particular day, she's explaining me the formation of chords. She talked for forty-five minutes explaining chords, how it was constructed so I came on home, and when I woke up the next day, I understood about the construction of triad chords because that's the basis, and I ain't had no trouble with them since. It took me a night to digest it.

Then I started studying with Professor Gray,[2] tremendous musician. He went to study with Miss Boulanger in Paris. She didn't speak English, but he was a linguist and he could speak French, so that made no difference. He was a black guy; he knew his music. He said, "I can't teach no one until I have about five [students] or at least three." So finally he got three guys. One was a bass player; the other guy worked with Les Hite's band, trombone player, and we had one lesson a week, two hours long. He gave us so much that when I came home, I'd put his book up in the corner of the house and I'd work on it that whole week. When I get back everything that was wrong, he'd put them red lines all through it. We tried to carry on until one of them decided he had to go somewhere and he quit. That broke up the class because Professor Gray wasn't charging that much so he was sorta wasting his time.

So in time I started teaching in his place. I went down to get my teacher license and filled out the application and made it like they wanted it, and I got my own individual teacher license. I didn't teach at home. Most of the time, Professor Gray had studios so that went on for years and years. When he died, his son had the property, so I said, "I'll just stay until you sell the property." So he stuck a sign up: "For Sale," and I said, "When he sells it, I'll worry about moving." Took him three years to sell it.

At that time, everybody was moving in with somebody. This company was merging with this one, this company was merging with that one, so I guess I'll merge too. So I went over to Eubanks, this school over on Crenshaw,[3] and said, "Well, I'd like to teach for you." I made out an application, and I had one student so finally I got two. Another teacher had all the good ones, teaching everything, and he was a good musician but she [Mrs. Eubanks] got mad at him about something and gave them to me. So here I am teaching five days a week. I didn't want 'em five days. Can't do the yard work, can't do nothing. I can't be teaching five days a week if I'm gonna take off. OK, I'll give you Thursdays and I'll take Mondays and that makes two. From then on, I was up and down. Class would be full and then it wouldn't.

Eubanks Testimonial
Caughey Roberts, saxophonist par excellence.
With deep appreciation.
We thank you for fifteen years of dedicated service as a distinguished and dynamic member of our woodwind faculty.
Thank you for sharing with your students your knowledge, artistry, love of teaching, your great humour and joy of life.
The Eubanks Conservatory of Music and Arts, Faculty and Staff.

She got on the plaque "fifteen years," but I was there twenty-two. Later when I was working at Disneyland [with Teddy Buckner] I couldn't teach late so hours would start at eight. I had to leave there at five, come home, and you'd never know how the traffic is. I got on that freeway, couldn't go forward, couldn't go backwards. The reason I know it was twenty-two years because when we started to work at Disneyland, that's when I started to work over there [with Eubanks]. Between you and me and the gatepost, the reason why she put fifteen was so she wouldn't have to pay me more money. She's paying by the hours so naturally the more years you get in the more money she pays. I did write a jazz improvisation course. Now Mrs. Eubanks didn't ask for it. She doesn't like jazz because she can't play it. I spend six months making up that course, and all told there were nine people going through that course.

After I left the Erwing Brothers, there was a guy by the name of Earl Dancer[4] had the band. He more or less put the big band together. Here we are starving to death and we did a week's engagement in one of the theaters downtown and everybody said, "Oh, man, we going to get some money—we sure need it." They had a show with the band so what Dancer did, he collected the money; it wouldn't have been no big deal, but I know they paid the man and we never saw it. Anyway he got Buck [Clayton] in the band so after he stole that money and went and lost it [gambling], the band was so shook up that we said we had to get another leader and everybody voted

Buck to lead the band. Earl Dancer was a good hustler, but he hustled too much, and you shouldn't hustle off the band.

Buck hadn't been there too long. When he first came here, we had a little band with that piano player, Monroe Tucker, who couldn't make it, so Buck says, "Well, I play piano," so he came to rehearse and he brought his trumpet. He picked up his trumpet and he played more trumpet than our trumpet player so we said, "Well, we'll have two trumpets." I don't remember the other trumpeter. Anyway, Buck was a natural. A very gifted musician. And he just kept on developing and developing. He could arrange and play real well. Always played tasty things.

The reason why we went to China was there was a studio job for black musicians out there, and this other band went and put black on their faces to get the job. I mean times were hard; nobody was making any money, so when this guy [pianist Teddy Weatherford] came looking for a band for China we said, "Let's go."[5] If they're going to have to put black on their faces, that's tough; that's a hard act to follow, but anyway that's the reason we went to China. The main thing was we're going to make some money because we sure weren't making it here.

Definitely an adventure, no doubt about it. It was interesting. Where we played [the Canidrome Ballroom in Shanghai's International Settlement] *all the best people of all the nationalities came to the place. It was a white club. Only rich people would come there.* Summertime, they might have a little matinee. Now we start making some money, we bought some tails. In the meantime, they sent for a band from the U.S. and they pulled a trick to get us out and we fell for it hook, line, and sinker. The show was on, and these guys came in and started a fight, so the management said, "Sorry, we can't use you anymore." I wanted to come home, and they said, "Man, you can't go before the rest of us get back." I stayed, but it was under protest. I stayed until everybody got their money, and we got a Japanese boat straight back to Los Angeles.

How good was the band? When we left, it was tops. Buck would get some outside arrangements, but he did most of them himself. Any number coming up sweet, Teddy Buckner got the solo. He had a beautiful tone. Happy Johnson was in the band, and when we decided to come back home, he brought another band over to take that job,[6] but I'd had enough of that. Bumps Myers was a tremendous musician, but of course, he drank a lot. He had a tremendous ear. Ask him to name a note, he couldn't name it. What difference did that make? He had the ear. Arcima Taylor was basically a good musician. He was just lazy, that's all. I said, "Why don't you practice sometime?" But he had some training somewhere because he could read real well.

Frank Pasley was the one who kept the band in tune. "Hey, man, pick that note," he'd say. Had a very good ear. Nice guy, too. Reggie Jones was an excellent bass player. Fantastic, in fact. He got stuck over there. Sure did. He *started playing in another band so he stayed there* [China], *and they put him in the concentration camp and he pretty near starved to death. When he finally got out and came back to Los Angeles, he said, "I'll have to get another job just to pay for my food bill!" He got mad at somebody, somebody upset him, and they put him in the stockade. He used to play tremendous tuba when everybody was in the process of changing over to the string bass so he kept flopping on that thing. He had a good ear so it was no problem for him with the change* [from tuba to double bass]. *Babe Lewis, that was the prettiest guy I've ever seen. He'd think he could make any woman over a half pint of whiskey. That's the man he was, but he wasn't no drunkard. An excellent drummer—he could sure kick a show.*

Shanghai was fun, but there's an old saying that there's no place like home. Back in Los Angeles, it [Clayton's band] *never did function as a band thereafter. Although we did play some jobs up in Oakland where we had Red Callender on bass—you know, he played with everybody—and Kid Lips* [Hackette] *on drums. He was a heck of a drummer. Show drummer. He could slide on his fanny across the stage and hit the bass drum, "boom, boom." Cee Pee Johnson got a lot of work, so if you get work, you can get musicians, and I went with him, along with some of Buck's guys. Cee Pee would work off and on. He played a lot of tom-toms. He had Bert Johnson, his brother, in there. We used to go down to San Diego all the time to work. I remember a lot of sailors coming in there to the Creole Palace. That was the place.*

With Lionel Hampton—this was summer 1936—only thing I know we got the small combo and we'd be playin' little jobs here and little jobs there, all the time. I never did go on the road with Lionel. It was a good little band; he'd buy them tight little arrangements. The band swung. *Soloists? Lionel, he took all the solos; anybody else get a solo, they just lucky. This guy that owns the Paradise on Main Street put us in one of his outlying places, and then he says, "You guys ain't got no business being here; you should be downtown at the Paradise," so he put us in there. I admired Lionel. He was a very original musician, but I felt he should hire a drummer if he wanted to play vibes all the time, but it was his band so he could do what he wanted. He was a nice guy, and he has a memory that's just fantastic. He can remember people's names: somebody he met twenty years ago and he'll walk up and call their name. He's something else. Paradise was mostly the show, very little dance music. Of course you know about the Benny Goodman thing; he'd just come in and be jamming. Close up the joint and they'd jam until three or four o'clock in the morning. That was the beginning of his quartet. Right there. It was just three or four of our guys and him. I thought Benny Goodman played good. He was always a good clarinet player. After Lionel left to go with Benny Goodman, Armand Hudson came in, young guy, on drums. He didn't play too much after this engagement down there.*

> Buck Clayton had disbanded and was going back home to Kansas, so he stopped off in Kansas City. In the meantime, he started working with Count Basie, and the guy that was playing first alto had just left. Everybody said he was a heckuva musician because he was writing lots of Count's arrangements. Buster Smith. "Prof," they called him. Count asked Buck did he know anybody could play first? Buck said, yeah, and that's when he sent for me and Herschel Evans. We left Los Angeles and went to Kansas City together on the train. I thought it'd be nice.
>
> Tremendous band. I'd heard of 'em. I think the leader [Bennie Moten] had just died, and it seemed like Count took over. We was working at that little Reno Club. All the best people would come down there; chicks hustling on the street, they'd come on in to listen to the music. When you get in a band, you have to learn how the band play and all that stuff. I was more or less interested in that. Lester [Young] was a tremendous soloist. I thought his sound was too light for tenor, sound like alto to me. But I put up with it. He was a jovial guy; you can't dislike him. He's just a good-humored guy. Everybody liked Lester. He always played well. Frankly, I didn't pay too much attention to it. He was a stylist. The contrast between Lester Young and Herschel Evans, I think that was the drawing card. The difference between their two styles. I had to admire Lester because he knew what he wanted. That's important because when you build up your own style, you listen to everybody you want to and then create a style of your own.
>
> It ended up he and Herschel took all the solos, so it was set up like that. How the alto came about for me was all the guys in Buck Clayton's band say, "You guys got the wrong horn, man, so Bumps should be on tenor and you should be on alto." That's the way it was, so I said, "OK, here's your tenor; give me the alto," and that's when I started playing alto. After that, I was on alto for a long time. So with Count, there was no room for tenor for me anyway. I was there over three or four months. Why did I leave? One day I woke up, I said I look so bad, I have to go get some cod liver oil, trying to keep up with those guys. Too fast for me. So anyway, that's when Earle Warren replaced me.

Roberts joined Count Basie and His Barons of Rhythm at the Reno Club in Kansas City in late 1936. Basie's enlarged orchestra then began to tour before opening at the Grand Terrace in Chicago in November and moving on to New York where they played the Roseland Ballroom. Roberts recorded with Basie for the initial Decca sessions on January 21 and March 26, 1937, but had been replaced by Warren by the time the band recorded again on July 7.

Basie sponsor John Hammond described Roberts as *"a bald, dour man"* and according to Gunther Schuller got *"Basie to fire Roberts,"* whereas Schuller considered that *"his somewhat pressed cool sound related much* better to Lester Young's and Jack Washington's than [successor] *Earle Warren.*"

Roberts was home in time to appear with Louis Armstrong in Paramount's *Every Day's a Holiday* (filmed in September–October 1937) as part of a parade band made up of Local 767 members. He had already appeared in Columbia's *Pennies from Heaven,* again with Armstrong, in July 1936 while a member of Lionel Hampton's Paradise Club band.

It was fun working with Basie's band because that sort of band, they don't tune up; they just wanted to play. All you got to do is listen, even the saxophones; the idea if it's cold, the mouthpiece go in. After it warms up, naturally you pull it out; otherwise you'd be sharp, so that's the best way to tune up. That's the only band I been in that never tuned up.

So I came on home, played a few gigs, and then Fats Waller sent me a telegram, "Coming to the Coast, such and such a time, play such and such a place." So everything's going on good, got a chance to make some money. This was with Al Morgan's band. That was just a freelance band. A small gig band. Well, it had two leaders; whoever got the job, that's whose band it was. Baron Morehead was on trombone, and he'd lead the band sometimes. This was an interesting band, I guess, because of Fats himself, just the way he works and his sense of timing. I just couldn't believe it; it was incredible. So we got this one job, nightspot, and he'd start that tempo, however many choruses you play, at the end of it, it's that same speed. Humans always pick up on time. We were supposed to go to that St. Francis Hotel. The most popular place to get suits made, the whole band went out there, got two suits each, went back for fittings, and the next thing you know Fats went and caught a train and went home. So that broke up the band and the new uniforms. He came out again, but he brought his own band. We never did get the uniforms out because he never did pay for 'em. Just ordered them and they sat up there.

Fats was tremendous, absolutely. He had to put on the comedy stuff so that the people would like him, but his musicianship was absolutely fantastic. We made a recording [RCA Victor, December 16, 1937]. *We'd never seen those numbers. Just go ahead. I think Ceelle Burke played on them, Al Morgan, Lee Young. I think the records were popular. Al Morgan had cut out from Cab Calloway, and he would be around musicians and he'd say, "Now in New York, fellers, we don't do things like that," and somebody would say, "Why don't you get a bus or a train and go back to New York?"* [laughs]. *Al was a nice guy who ended up doing a duo with* [tenorist] *Buddy Banks. They worked together for years and years. Always something goin', so if one of them had to go to the can, the other had to stay up there and work. Sometimes Al would be singing; sometimes he'd be playing bass. That was their philosophy, always something going on. He was a good bass player.*

Paul Campbell was our trumpeter. Tremendous trumpet player! Little, skinny son of a gun, wouldn't think he could play anything. Look like he needed to go get some food. He was so tiny. But he was a funny guy. I never heard anymore of him after that Fats deal. I couldn't figure how Fats could hold all that [liquor]. *How could a guy drink so much brandy? Oh, he'd drink so much.*

Down Beat, November 1, 1940

Ceele [*sic*] Burke's Lineup Bared; Hollywood—The "mystery man" of those Decca records in recent weeks is Ceele [*sic*] Burke, a young Negro vocalist and guitarist, whose platters of *Trade Winds* and *When the Swallows Come Back* are sensational clicks. Interesting, too, is that Coughey [*sic*] Roberts, alto sax star heard on many of Count Basie's early Decca waxings, is in Burke's band. Others in the lineup include Charles Davis, pianist; Herschel Coleman, alto and trumpet; Vernon Gower, bass; Lee Gibson, drums; Charles Jones, tenor, and George Orendorff, lead trumpet.

"When the Swallows Come Back" was written by Leon René and was supposed to be the hit number, but Sinatra came out with "I'll Never Smile Again" and wiped "Swallows" out. Ceelle always managed to get good jobs. George Orendorff was an excellent trumpet player and a nice person. Vernon Gower, one of the brothers that studied with me, turned out to be a good bass player. So anyway I joined the Count Basie band the second time. Somebody dropped out and that left it open. I can't remember the name, but I know I had to wear the same uniform. That's why I wanted to get back in there because they were making money, man.

Roberts rejoined Basie at some time in July 1942 supposedly to play tenor, playing a couple of local theater engagements. He recorded on alto with Basie on July 27 and appeared with the band in *Hit Parade of 1943* for Republic Pictures. Still single, he was drafted into the U.S. Army on August 13, eventually serving for four years.

Down Beat, August 1, 1942

Lester Young Nixes Basie; Los Angeles—Though Basie didn't get Lester, he did get a good man here in Couchy [*sic*] Roberts. Just which one of the present Basie tenor men Couchy would replace wasn't known here. Basie is en route to Los Angeles. He'll play the Orpheum theatre here and opens at the Trianon around August 15.

Down Beat, September 15, 1942

Basie's New Tenor Man Gets Call; Los Angeles—Couchy [*sic*] Roberts, the tenor man secured by Count Basie from Los Angeles just before the band headed west, has already left the band to don the uniform of Uncle Sam. Roberts left the band to be inducted during the last week of August shortly after the Count opened at the Trianon. Marvin Johnson, a local boy, was in as a temporary replacement.

I went to Fort Huachuca for a week and a half, and I requested to go with the band. When I got to Fort McArthur, the band had gone, but they were real nice and they found me a band in Papago Park. Sixteen miles out of Phoenix, Arizona. Prisoner-of-war base. I shall never forget it, hot as it was there. I was there close to four years, always as a musician, playing in the dance band and a small combo. They weren't the greatest musicians, but at least they tried. I think they did all right considering that they weren't going to make music their careers. Sergeant Willey was in charge of the big band, and the little band I was in charge of because I would make the arrangements for them. I'll say this, the Army was interesting. Very interesting. Took me a long time to make Sergeant. This is just like civilian life. Politics. Same old soup, warmed over. I never went overseas. It was segregation, more or less at that time. Other entertainers would come there.

They let me out, and after I spent the $200, I said I'm going to have to find me a job, so I got a job with this guy El Herbert.[7] *He got a good name. I say, "Man, the union say you supposed to take fifteen minutes out of an hour, and you don't want to stop playing, you want to play straight through. That ain't right." He was a trumpet player; he had his book. All the cities where he'd played and everything.*

So they come down there, "We look for a band to make some recordings," so I told them, "Well, you come to the right place, I say; this band can't play no recordings. They can't hardly keep their little jobs; we got to go to work, man." So we played our little tunes. Roy Milton called me that morning: "Hey man, we're making a record, want you to play alto. Be at the studio for nine o'clock." So I get there at nine. And here they come, all sleepy, because they got an after-hour job, and they sit down. The guy explains what he wants, "I want an original number and I want it to be fast." OK, let's play "Steppin' on the U Car"; that's for the U Car that ran up and down Central Avenue. I say, "Wait a minute, wait a minute, let me find out what intervals you using," so I figured out the intervals and I said now you can play as fast as you want. I hadn't seen these guys before and this was Roy Milton's band. Roy said, "That's what I want," so I said, "Well, call me; you got my phone number. Now you walk down on Main Street and play that mess." So in the meantime, Roy said, "Hey man, why don't you come and work with us?"

So I gotta give El Herbert my notice; it's not right to walk out of there without giving some kind of notice. I'll have to give him a week's notice; supposed to give two so I worked the week out and then I started with Roy. El Herbert was working quite a few little jobs 'round here. He was such a good hustler; he couldn't play that much trumpet, but he sure could hustle jobs.

Another good sax player came along and took my place in El Herbert's band. He just got out of school and he need money. His name was Bill Green.

With Roy, I'd go down, hanging on; that next week, wouldn't be nobody in there. But then about 2 o'clock they start coming down there. This was near San Pedro, around 7th or 8th, somewhere about there. Roy had a store of his own, too. I got to tell you this, they walked in there, all sleepy, so they looked up and the place is full and Roy says, "Show time." "What you talkin' about 'show time'?" Everybody woke up. The tenor player went that a way, trumpet player went that a way, and I stood on the floor and just laughed because I ain't never been in no band like that [laughs]. They were criss-crossing, doing an act, playing baseball, and all that stuff, while they were playing. This was the routine. That was funny. That's where I learned showmanship. I made one big trip with Roy, and then I told Roy, "I'm sorry man; I ain't gonna bob up and down no more." Being on the road, I didn't particularly care for it. I know some people in the band just loved the road. I got married when I was in the Army, so at that time with Roy, I was married. Roy made quite a few pop-up records. One I remember called "R.M. Blues," Buddy Floyd took all the solos; he set the style. He knew how to bend notes.

Roy was very likeable, a real nice person. He could sing well, had a real nice voice. Camille [pianist Camille Howard] *could sing well, too. The thing I noticed about Camille was she could sing in tune. Fantastic. Roy believed in showmanship. "Do sumpn', do sumpn'. Don't just stand there flat-footed"* [laughs]. *That tickled me. He was very successful. After that, Roy said, "Man, now I need alto player." I say, "I know alto player to go with you. You can't find one better in the United States." This is 3:30 in the morning, so Roy says, "Let's go wake him up," and that same guy, Jackie Kelso, he stayed with Roy many, many years. Jackie Kelso was one of my pupils at LeBlancs. He's the guy who gave me that trophy. He was playing with Lionel Hampton—he's in the upper echelon. I just helped him. He's the one who did the work. It seemed like a long time that I was with Roy, but actually it wasn't all that long because we did so much in that short time. Maybe about a year. It was just a fine band.* [Trumpeter] *Hosea Sapp, that's the craziest guy I ever laid eyes on. First place, he played sharp; tuned up all night and two numbers later, he was sharp again. So one night, Roy says, "If you move that tuning guide you got on that thing, I'm gonna fine you $50." "OK, Pops. OK," so he go behind Roy, pushing that tuning slide in, but he was a showman and he was a nice trumpet player. Wherever he'd been, he'd developed a lot of showmanship so he fit right in. We played exclusively to black audiences.*

That first week I worked with Roy like to kill me for endurance. He start playing—here's what he would do—play for two and a half hours straight. One number behind another. Take a half-hour break and come back and play the last hour. I finally figured out why he did it. If people come to a dance and don't hear the music, they figure nothing's happenin', so that was the idea. It was a lot of fun really. The money was nice, and the thing about it, Roy wasn't cheap. Considering he wasn't a big name. He was just a middle name.

The change to rhythm and blues, that's the way it seemed. As to bebop, well, I thought it was interesting. I knew it wasn't gonna make a whole lot of money [for musicians] playing it. I knew that. I remember when that stuff really got rolling because one guy bought the records and everybody's interested in this new music. Then Charlie Parker upset all the alto players, and [Johnny] Hodges, tremendous soloist, he got wiped out. Charlie Parker, I analyzed it. Absolute genius. I heard him in person at a dance hall on 15th and Main, somewhere along there. He used to play weekends up there. Guess who played trumpet that weekend? Chet Baker. I never dreamed of him playing bebop. He played it quite well. I was surprised. That's what makes it interesting. All these different styles. I met Charlie Parker, but there wasn't too many words. He bought a band in behind Roy Milton at this place. Everybody whispered, "That's Charlie Parker over there," so I went over to say hello. That's about it. I got a bunch of his solos, and I listened to his records. His prominent phrases I memorized. That guy was something else. Somebody said he didn't chord so well, but he was never lost. His sense of timing! Fantastic.

Roy Milton's band split up into two parts, and that's when the Four Cheers came into existence. A breakaway from Roy Milton, that's what it was. So we had a ring [circuit], took us a year to go 'round this ring. I told the leader, "You gonna have to get some new numbers as we come back to the same places all the time." Sure enough, a guy said, "Hey, man, you play the same stuff you played when you were here before." "See that, I told you." The leader was [bassist] Dave Robinson, and we stayed together for over three years. We kept working because it was strong entertainment-wise. Most of the places we played were sorta out from town. Clubs, mostly.

Teddy Buckner called me, "I want you to join the band." I didn't emphasize no Dixieland, so I didn't pay no attention to it. Before Teddy called me, I twice got offered a chance to join a Dixieland band. Around 1950. This was Mutt Carey, trumpet player. I just played a few engagements with him. Two or three times is the most I ever worked with him. Very nice, jovial and everything. He always had a sense of humor. I remember him because I played a job with him but he just wouldn't give me my money. I had to go get my money. I can't remember what type of music we played. I guess it was Dixieland.

Like I said, I hadn't played Dixieland before so I listened to two Dixieland programs every day for about six months. All the music I could find. When I first started, I had to write out these key sheets because I didn't know the numbers. Teddy had this job way out somewhere, so we stayed out there *about a week, and then we came into the Beverly Cavern. It took a little time to learn the numbers, but I finally learned the more important ones. After I got those numbers, I got tight. Real tight.*

Down Beat, September 27, 1962

Caught in The Act—Teddy Buckner—The Huddle, Covina, Calif.—In reed man Roberts and trombonist [William] Woodman Buckner has two rip-snorting associates. Roberts does the Sidney Bechet routine on soprano sax on Bechet's tune, *If You Could See My Mother,* but Roberts' forte is clarinet. He achieves a gutty, toughfibred sound.—*John Tynan*

I stayed [with Buckner] *roughly fifteen years. It was fun. We played all the best jobs. I met some nice people and got along OK with the guys. We had a good band. I thought Teddy's main thing was pleasing the people, and he did that so I would say he was a good leader. Well, if you don't please no people, you ain't got no band. He knew how to greet people. I thought he did the Dixieland bit quite well. Everybody thought he looked like Louis Armstrong. Teddy and Louis were good friends. They used to make a lot of pictures together a long time ago. I used tenor and soprano saxophones because Teddy was doing a lot of show stuff out at Disneyland. We had a vocalist out there, too. Jewel Hall. Real dark chick.*

Roberts had recorded regularly with Roy Milton for his Miltone label and for Specialty from 1946 to 1948 and with bandleader Floyd Ray, before he joined Teddy Buckner's Dixieland band in the late 1950s and participated in a series of Buckner's albums for Dixieland Jubilee and GNP from 1960 through to 1974 (including a session with folk singer Hoyt Axton in 1974). Roberts was present for the special tribute concert *Hello Louis!* held at the Shrine Auditorium in Pasadena on July 3, 1970, and the Buckner band with Roberts was also used on the sound track for the Billie Holiday biopic *Lady Sings the Blues,* made for Paramount in 1972, starring Diana Ross with the music issued by MoTown. Caughey was especially taken to be asked to record as a one-off in 1959 with the veteran New Orleans trombonist Kid Ory on his Verve album, *Kid Ory Plays W.C. Handy.*

Here's what happened. Ory was working in San Francisco, and he brought his band down here to make a record. He came in that night, and he say, "Hey, man, you want to make a recording?" The only one that played on the recording that he brought from San Francisco was the piano player, Cedric Heywood. I think he made the arrangements. The other guys didn't play well enough, so he used Teddy; Jesse Sailes, our drummer; and myself. It turned out to be a real nice session. When the record came out, they had somebody else's name playing clarinet. I thought it was funny. "Hey, man, give me a break."

I was so intrigued the way Ory was playing the trombone part. It was just interesting. The way he chose to come in, his decision when to come in fairly intrigued me. How he would make the fill-in at the proper spot. He's liable to wait ten measures before he'd come in, but that would be the right place. His sense of timing was fantastic. The place where he put that note, that's where it was supposed to be. Teddy had learned Dixieland under Ory. After he learned it, Teddy decided to get a band of his own.

I just felt stagnant; fifteen years, that was long enough. I kept on teaching, but I'm not interested in working anymore. I play with the James Judkins orchestra, but that's just practice. That's about as much as I want to do. I'm more or less retired. One of these days I'm going to start practicing. I got some more hard [tuition] books to work on. My philosophy was always to keep studying. You keep studying, you keep improving.

Roberts also played in the Los Angeles Urban Concert Band, conducted by Millard Lacey. "A swell person." This interracial band included such other Central Avenue luminaries as trumpeter Andy Blakeney, trombonist William Woodman Sr., and fellow clarinetists Bill Green, Jewel Grant, and Paul Howard.

Playing music? I enjoyed it. It was nice. Ups and downs, like anybody else. I don't care what you gonna do, you gonna have certain problems. Jazz now, it's a tough row to hoe, to make a living.

Photospread abbreviations (beginning on next page): [as] alto-saxophone; [b] bass; [bjo] banjo; [bs] baritone saxophone; [cl] clarinet; [d] drums; [el-b] bass guitar; [g] guitar; [kbd] keyboards; [ldr] leader; [p] piano; [sop] soprano saxophone; [t] trumpet; [tb] trombone; [ts] tenor-saxophone; [tu] tuba; [vib] vibraphone; [vln] violin; [voc] vocalist. Unk refers to unknown or unidentified players.

Lincoln Theatre Orchestra, Lincoln Theatre, 23rd and Central Avenue, Los Angeles, March–September 1931. L–r, rear: William France [ts]; Harold Brown [p]; Arthur "Bud" Scott [g]; Lloyd "Country" Allen [tb]. Front: David "Baby" Lewis [d]; Andy Blakeney [t]; Leon Herriford [as, cl, ldr]; Edward Barnett [as]; Reginald "Jonesy" Jones [b]. Photo by Avair Los Angeles, courtesy Andy Blakeney.

Capitol Theatre Orchestra, San Francisco, September 1933–February 1934. L–r: Ash Hardee [tb]; Bernice "Pee Wee" Brice, Andy Blakeney [t]; Douglas Finis [p]; Unk [d]; Wade Whaley [as, ldr]; Unk [ts]; Unk [tu]. Courtesy Andy Blakeney.

The Brown Cats of Rhythm, Casino Ballroom, Nuuanu Avenue and Beretania Street, Honolulu, Hawaii, 1941. L–r, rear: Andy Blakeney [t, ldr]; Alford Brooks [t]; Henry Coker [tb]; DeWitt Ray [b]; Unk [d]. Front: Ernest "Boots" Wilks [ts]; Unk [as]; Leon Shadowin [ts]; Ray Gregory [p]. Courtesy Andy Blakeney.

Kid Ory and His Creole Jazz Band, benefit for Bud Scott, Cricket Club Café, Washington Boulevard, Los Angeles, March or April 1949. L–r: Andy Blakeney [t]; Ralph Peters [g, hidden]; Joe Darensbourg [cl]; Minor Hall [d]; Edward "Kid" Ory [tb]. Photo by Ed Shaughnessy, courtesy Floyd Levin.

The Legends of Jazz, unknown location, Los Angeles, c. 1974. L–r: Ed Garland [b]; Joe Darensbourg [cl]; Andy Blakeney [t]; Louis Nelson [tb]; Barry Martyn [d, ldr]. Photo by Julius Adelman, courtesy Andy Blakeney.

Floyd Campbell / Jabbo Smith Quartet, Panama Café Nite Club, 307 E. 58th Street, Chicago, 1933–1934. L–r: Gideon Honoré [p]; Budd Johnson [ts, cl]; Floyd Campbell [d]; Jabbo Smith [t]. Courtesy Gideon Honoré.

The Celebrated Jimmie Noone Trio, Fox Head Tavern, Cedar Rapids, Iowa, 1936. L–r: Gideon Honoré [p]; Jimmie Noone [cl]; Mel Draper [d]. Courtesy Gideon Honoré.

Albert Nicholas and the Dixielanders, "That's A Plenty," The St. Francis Room, Los Angeles, 1948. L–r: Albert Nicholas [cl, ldr]; Danny Barker [g]; Gideon Honoré [p]; Leonard Bibb [b]. Photo by Bill Martin, courtesy Gideon Honoré.

The New Cotton Club Orchestra, with guest star Louis Armstrong, Frank Sebastian's Cotton Club, Culver City, California, July 1930. L–r, rear: Joe Bailey [b]; Luther "Sonny" Graven [tb]; Lionel Hampton [d]; Bill Perkins [g]; George Orendorff [t]; Marvin Johnson [as]; Harvey Brooks [p]; Harold Scott [t]; Charlie Jones [ts]; Henry Prince [p]. Front: Louis Armstrong [t, voc]; Frank Sebastian [Cotton Club owner]; Les Hite [as, ldr]. Courtesy mr.jazz Photo Files (Theo Zwicky).

Les Hite's Cotton Club Orchestra, City Hall, Los Angeles, 1933. L–r, rear: Bill Perkins [bjo]; Parker Berry [tb]; Lloyd Reese, George Orendorff [t]; Joe Bailey [b]; Henry Prince [p]; Marshal Royal [as]; Charlie Jones [ts]; Marvin Johnson [as]. Front: Goddard L. McDonough [supervisor, 2nd District]; Lionel Hampton [d]; Les Hite [ldr]. Seated, left: Dudley Dickerson [dancer]. Others unidentified. Courtesy mr.jazz Photo Files (Theo Zwicky).

Leslie Sheffield and His Rhythmaires, Ritz Ballroom, Oklahoma City, July–August 1935. L–r, rear: Nathaniel "Monk" McFay [d]; Abe Bolar [b]; Leslie Sheffield [p, ldr]. Front: Artis Bryant [tb]; Charlie "Little Dog" Johnson, Miles Jones, Carl "Tatti" Smith [t]; Charlie Christian [g]; Charles "Crown Prince" Waterford [voc]; C. Q. Price, Edward "Popeye" Hale [as]; Ernest "Boots" Wilks [ts]. Courtesy Monk McFay.

Bernard Banks and His Clouds of Rhythm, Casino Ballroom, Nuuanu Avenue and Beretania Street, Honolulu, Hawaii, late 1935. L–r: Charlie Wright [ts, as, cl]; Nathaniel "Monk" McFay [d]; Andy Blakeney [t]. Courtesy Monk McFay and Harold Kaye.

Buddy Banks Sextette, Excelsior recording artists, Los Angeles, 1945. L–r: Earl Knight? [p]; Bill "Frosty" Pyles [g]; Ulysses "Buddy" Banks [ts]; William "Basie" Day [b]; Wallace Huff [tb]; Nathaniel "Monk" McFay [d]. Johnny Robinson Agency Photo, courtesy Monk McFay.

The Blackhawks Orchestra (formerly Edythe Turnham and Her Knights of Syncopation), Seattle, 1928. L–r: Joe Bailey [b]; Crawford Brown [t]; Ray Williams [tb]; Floyd Turnham Sr. [d]; Floyd Turnham Jr. [ts, cl]; Floyd Wilson [reeds]; Creon Thomas [bjo, g]; Edythe Turnham [p, seated]. From the author's collection.

Les Hite Orchestra, Golden Gate Ballroom, Lenox Avenue and 142nd Street, New York, June 1940. L-r, front: Les Hite [ldr]; Sol Moore [ts, bs]; Floyd Turnham Jr. [as, cl]; Qudellis Martyn [as, cl]; Rodger Hurd [ts]. Rear: Allen Durham, Britt Woodman [tb]. Courtesy mr.jazz Photo Files (Theo Zwicky).

Gerald Wilson's Orchestra, Shepp's Playhouse, upstairs at First and San Pedro, Los Angeles, 1944. L-r, rear: Henry "Tucker" Green [d]; Art Edwards [b]; Teddy Buckner, Jack Trainor, James Anderson [t]. Middle: Jimmy Bunn [p]; Isaac Livingstone, Melba Liston, Robert Huerta [tb]. Front: Charles "Chuck" Waller [bs]; Odell West [ts]; Floyd Turnham Jr., Ed "Popeye" Hale [as]; Vernon Slater [ts]; Gerald Wilson [t, ldr]. Courtesy Peter Carr.

The Legends of Jazz, 1,000 Years of Jazz Show, unknown location, early 1980s. L–r: Adolphus Morris [b]; Floyd Turnham Jr. [ts]; Herbert Permillion [t]; Clyde Bernhardt [tb]. At rear: Barry Martyn [d, ldr]. Courtesy Barry Martyn.

Roy Milton and His Solid Senders, Mario's Café, Los Angeles, 1942. L–r: Roy Milton [d]; Luke Jones [as]; Betty Hall Jones [p]; Forrest Powell [t]. Courtesy Danni Gugolz.

Betty Hall Jones [p, voc] with Edgar Mason [b], unknown location, Los Angeles, c. 1950s. Courtesy Betty Hall Jones.

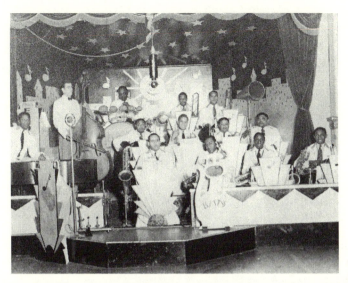

Charlie Echols Orchestra, Papke's Del Rio Club, Los Angeles, 1935. L–r, rear: Herb Williams [p]; Joe Mendoza [b]; Alton Redd [d]; Bert Johnson, Jasper "Jap" Jones [tb]. Middle: Buddy Harper [g]; Red Mack, Bernice "Pee Wee" Brice, Claude "Benno" Kennedy [t]. Front: Emerson Scott [as, bs]; Carleton "Puss" Waide [ts]; Ulysses "Buddy" Banks [ts]; Jack McVea [bs, as]. Courtesy Red Mack.

Will Osborne Orchestra, Strand Theatre, New York City, December 1941. L–r, rear: Vince De Berry, Jimmy? [t]; Dick Shanahan [d]; Dale Jones [b]. Front: Red Mack [solo t]; Unk, Unk, Bud Jenkins, Elmer "Moe" Schneider [tb]; Will Osborne [ldr]; Len Dody? [g]; Unk, Unk [as]; Joe Glazer [ts, bass sax]; Unk [bs], Unk [p]. Courtesy Red Mack.

Luke Jones and His Modern Recording Artists, Los Angeles, 1949. L–r: Luke Jones [as]; Red Mack [d, vib, t]; Dorothy Broil [p]. Courtesy Red Mack.

Buck Clayton and His Harlem Gentlemen, Pantages Circuit Theatre, Portland, Oregon, early 1934. L–r: George "Happy" Johnson [tb]; Jack Bratton [t]; Frank Pasley [g]; Joe McCutchin [vln]; Eddie Beal [p]; David "Baby" Lewis [d]; Buck Clayton [t, ldr]; Arcima Taylor [as]; Reggie "Jonesy" Jones [tu]; Hubert "Bumps" Myers [as]; Caughey Roberts [ts]. Photo by Davies, Portland, Oregon; used by permission of the University of Missouri–Kansas City Libraries, Dr. Kenneth J. LaBuddle Department of Special Collections.

Buck Clayton and His Harlem Gentlemen, Canidrome Ballroom, International Settlement, Shanghai, China, November 6, 1934. L–r: Teddy Buckner [t]; Joe McCutchin [vln]; Reggie "Jonesy" Jones [b, tu]; Arcima Taylor [reeds]; Duke Upshaw [tb]; Frank Pasley [g]; Buck Clayton [t, ldr]; Hubert "Bumps" Myers [as]; Jack Bratton [t]; Caughey Roberts [ts]; David "Baby" Lewis [d]; George "Happy" Johnson [tb]; Eddie Beal [p]. Used by permission of the University of Missouri–Kansas City Libraries, Dr. Kenneth J. LaBuddle, Department of Special Collections.

Roy Milton's Solid Senders, unknown U.S. military base, 1940s. L–r: Roy Milton [d, ldr]; Hosea Sapp [t]; Dave Robinson [b]; Caughey Roberts [as]; Buddy Floyd [ts]. A.N.P.S. (McQuain C.M.) photo, courtesy Caughey Roberts.

Jeter Pillars Orchestra, Club Plantation, St. Louis, Missouri, 1938. L–r, rear: Floyd Smith [g]; Vernon King [b]; Robert "Bobby" Ross [d]; Ike Covington [tb]. Front: Chester Lane [p]; Ted Smith [voc]; Hayes Pillars [ts]; Charles Pillars [as]; James L. Jeter [as]; Ralph Porter, Walter "Crack" Stanley, George Hudson [t]; Hayes Pillars [director]. Courtesy Chester Lane.

Chester Lane's Blue Jacketeers, U.S. Navy, Whiting Field, Milton, Florida, 1944. L–r, rear: Chester Lane [p]; Frank Motley [t], rear, extreme left, others unidentified. Front: Eldridge [b]; Hill [as]; Griffin [bs]; Leon [as]; Unk [as]; Timmons [ts, cl]. Official U.S. Navy photograph, courtesy Chester Lane.

Louis Jordan Orchestra, USA, 1953–1955. L–r: Johnny Kirkwood [d]; Bob Mitchell [t]; Bert Payne [g]; Chester Lane [p]; Louis Jordan [voc, as]; Thurber "Sonny" Jay [el-b]; Lowell "Count" Hastings [ts]. General Artists Corporation photo, courtesy Chester Lane.

Roy Clark and His Swing Band, unknown location, Los Angeles, c. early 1930s. L–r: Monte Easter [t]; Unk [d]; Roy Clark [as]; Fletcher Smith [p]; Unk [cl, as]. Courtesy Monte Easter and Opal Louis Nations.

Sonny Clay Band, Paradise Club, Los Angeles, 1937. L–r, rear: Unk [d]; Bernard Carrere [b]; "The Kingfish," Monte Easter [t]; Sonny Graven? [tb]. Front: Buddy Harper [g]; Unk, Ronald Wharton [vln]; Unk [voc]; Sonny Clay [p, ldr]; Roy Clark? [as]; Charlie? [ts]; Edward "Popeye" Hale [as, bs, cl, sop]. Courtesy Bernard Carrere.

Monte Easter Group, unknown club, Los Angeles, c. early 1950s. L–r: Alice Young [p]; Jimmy Delaney [ts]; Monte Easter [t]; Gabriel Williams [d]. Courtesy Opal Louis Nations and Danni Gugolz.

Down Beat Award Winners Concert, Philharmonic Hall, Los Angeles, January 28, 1946. L–r: Dizzy Gillespie [t]; Lester Young [ts]; Charlie Ventura [ts]; Willie Smith [as]; Billy Hadnott [b]. Courtesy Tempo Music Shop Collection and Kirk Silsbee.

Julia Lee and Her Boy Friends, Capitol Records recording session, Radio Recorders Studio, 7000 Santa Monica Boulevard, Los Angeles, November 13, 1947. L–r: Dave Dexter [Capitol Records producer]; Vic Dickenson [tb]; Samuel "Baby" Lovett [d]; Benny Carter [as]; Julia Lee [voc]; Dave Cavanaugh [ts]; Jack W. Marshall [g]; Billy Hadnott [b]. From the author's collection.

Louis Jordan and His Orchestra, publicity still for *Look Out Sister*, directed by Bud Pollard for Astor Pictures, Hollywood, 1948. L–r: James Jackson [g]; Aaron Izenhall [t]; Christopher Columbus [d]; Louis Jordan [as, voc]; Billy Hadnott [b]; Paul Quinichette [ts]; Bill Doggett [p]. General Artists Corporation promotional photo.

Nellie Lutcher Trio, "Piano Cavalcade," Louis B. Mayer Theatre, Motion Picture Home, Los Angeles, March 25, 1979. L–r: Billy Hadnott [b]; Nellie Lutcher [p, voc]; Gene Washington [d]. Courtesy Billy Hadnott.

Sonny Clay Band, Jack Johnson's Chez Paris, 41st and Central, Los Angeles, 1932. L–r, rear: Jasper "Jap" Jones, Andrew "Pat" Patterson [tb]; Sonny Clay [p, ldr]; "Pee Wee" [d]; Bernard Carrere [b]. Front: Norman Bowden, Monte Easter, Austin Williams [t]; John Sneed [g]; Maxie Thrower [voc]; Leo McCoy Davis [as, cl]; Albert Baker [as]; Jim Wynn [ts, cl]; Rodger Hurd [ts]. Courtesy Norman Bowden and Opal Louis Nations.

Boots and His Buddies, The Barn, Memphis, Tennessee, c. 1939. L–r, rear: Henderson Glass [voc]; Bill Johnson [g]; A. J. Johnson [p]; Walter McHenry [b]. Front: Charles Anderson, Percy Bush, Norman Bowden [t]; Samuel Player [bs, ts]; F. Shelby, Alvin Brooks [as]; Pepper Martin [ts]. At left: Eddy Eugene [band director] and Clifford "Boots" Douglas [d, ldr]. Courtesy Norman Bowden.

Jam session, unknown club, Central Avenue, 1940. L–r: Norman Bowden [t]; Eddie Williams [b]; T-Bone Walker [g]; Lorenzo Flennoy [p]; Carolyn Richards [voc]. Courtesy Norman Bowden.

Bardu Ali House Band, Shepp's Playhouse, upstairs at 1st and San Pedro, Los Angeles, 1944. L–r, rear: Eddie Lee Myart [p]; Monte Easter, Leroy "Snake" Whyte, Norman Bowden [t]; Unk [b]; Melba Liston [tb]; Henry "Tucker" Green [d]; Herb Flemming [tb]. Front: Prince Robinson [ts]; Floyd Turnham Jr. [as, cl]; Unk [bs, cl]; James Jackson [ts]; Bardu Ali [director]. Courtesy Norman Bowden and Opal Louis Nations.

Zutty's Creole Band, Capitol Records recording session, Los Angeles, June 30, 1944. L–r: Ed Garland [b]; Barney Bigard [cl]; Dave Dexter [Capitol Records producer]; Zutty Singleton [d]; Norman Bowden [t]; Bud Scott [g]; Freddie Washington [p]; John 'Shorty' Haughton [tb]. Capitol Records photo by Charlie Mihn.

Earl Hines and His Orchestra, Roseland Ballroom, 1658 Broadway, New York City, 1939. L–r: Walter Fuller [t]; John Ewing [tb]; Ed Sims [t]; Joe McLewis [tb]; George Dixon [t, as]; Alvin Burroughs [d]; Budd Johnson [ts]; Quinn Wilson [b]; Robert Crowder [ts]; Omer Simeon, Leroy Harris [as]; Billy Eckstine [voc]. Courtesy Tad Hershorn, Institute of Jazz Studies, Rutgers University, Newark, New Jersey.

Fletcher Henderson's Band directed by Horace Henderson, Avalon Casino, Catalina Island, California, December 30, 1961. L–r: Horace Henderson [dir, p]; Everett Evans [b]; Ernest Scott [bs]; Chuck Thomas [ts]; George Reed [d]; Floyd Turnham Jr. [as]; John Ewing [tb]; George "Goody" Gooden [t]; Melvin Phillips [as]; Pete Collins [tb]; Freddie Hill [t]; Hubert "Bumps" Myers [ts]; Garnet McLellan [t]. From the author's collection.

Teddy Buckner and His Band, Pasadena City College, Pasadena, California, 1960s. L–r: Chester Lane [p]; Art Edwards [b]; John Ewing [tb]; Jesse Sailes [d]; Teddy Buckner [t]; Caughey Roberts [cl]. Courtesy Chester Lane.

Al "Cake" Wichard Band, Club Congo, 4215 Central Avenue, Los Angeles, 1940s. L–r: Fletcher Smith [p]; Bill Davis [b]; Prince Stansel [g]; Forrest Powell [t]; Al "Cake" Wichard [d, ldr]; Chuck Thomas [ts]; Edward Barnett [as]; Bill Gaither [ts]. Courtesy Chuck Thomas.

Felix Gross Band, Cricket Club Café, Washington Boulevard, Los Angeles, mid-1940s. L–r: Eddie Cane, Chuck Thomas [ts]; Bernard Carrere [b]; Ernie Freeman [p]; Felix Gross [d, ldr]; Vernon "Smitty" Smith [t]. Courtesy Chuck Thomas.

Peppy Prince and His Rhythm Lads, Los Angeles, 1954. L–r: Warren McOwens [b]; Little Willie Jackson [as]; Preston "Peppy" Prince [d, ldr]; Chuck Thomas [ts]; Christine Chatman [p]. Courtesy Chuck Thomas.

Happy Johnson Band, USO concert for the U.S. Army, Los Angeles, pre-1945. L–r: George "Happy" Johnson [tb, ldr]; Jewel Grant [as]; William "Brother" Woodman Jr. [t, bs]; Maxwell Davis [ts]; Jesse Sailes [d]; Carolyn Richards [voc]; Ralph "Chuck" Hamilton [b]; Asher Sailes [p]. From the author's collection.

Maxwell Davis Band, unknown location, Los Angeles, 1950s. L–r: Art Edwards [b]; Willard McDaniel [p]; Floyd Turnham Jr. [bs]; Jewel Grant [as]; Maxwell Davis [ts, ldr]; Unk; Jesse Sailes [d]. From the author's collection.

Geechie Smith Band, Cricket Club Café, 1571 W. Washington Boulevard, Los Angeles, 1947. L–r: Fletcher Smith [p]; Unk [b]; Bixie Crawford [voc]; Louis Speiginer [g]; Freddie Simon [ts]; Minor Robinson [d]; Clifford Burton [as]. Courtesy Minor Robinson.

The New Orleanians, Los Angeles, mid-1980s. L–r: Mike Baird [cl, ts, sop]; Vic Loring [bjo]; Clora Bryant [t]; Minor Robinson [d, voc]; Roger Jamieson [tb, ldr]; Bernard Carrere [b]; Bill Mitchell [kbd]. Courtesy Roger Jamieson.

Chapter Nine

Chester C. Lane

Piano

As expansive in his manner as he was in his playing style, Chester Lane was a physically imposing man with a broad smile. He made us very welcome when we called, as did his wife, Lucille, and their son, speaking animatedly and at length about his time in St. Louis and lending us pictures from a capacious stock of memories. It was clear from his reminiscences that his was a story well worth telling. It embraced picaresque road tales, a lengthy engagement with the finest St. Louis big band, and a lively period mixing with the biggest names in show business while he was with Louis Jordan's Tympany Five before he and his family chose to settle in Los Angeles. Chester entertained us by playing "Just Friends" magnificently in his living room, and it was a delight to hear him perform just days later with his group at the 1990 Los Angeles Jazz Festival, complete with Lucille's lusty blues vocals and Johnny Faire's fine guitar work.

Chester had worked happily (and recorded) with Teddy Buckner out at Disneyland until the trumpeter opted to retire, and like the other musicians from Buckner's band, he was genuinely saddened when the engagement came to an end. I sensed that Chester was always his own man, well aware of his worth as a musician. He told me how he had turned down the chance to join the Louis Armstrong All-Stars when the salary offered was markedly less than Joe Glaser had been paying Earl Hines. "He offered me $50 a night with Louis. They had been paying $500 per week to Earl Hines. Five bills a week!" he said.

Lucille Lane [née Agers] was an integral part of his group, and it remains a matter of regret that the duo never recorded in their performing heyday. When we conducted this interview, the Lanes were living comfortably on

Chester Lane at the Stork Bar Lounge, St. Louis, Missouri, 1945–1946. Photo by Robinson Studio, St. Louis, courtesy Chester Lane.

West 20th Street but already voicing some concerns about the deterioration of the neighborhood. When I phoned Chester five years later, he was still leading his group and playing in Canoga Park with Dan Snyder. He had been out for a year following a hip operation, and in later years his health problems were compounded by emphysema. Chester Lane was born in Lexington, Mississippi, on November 18, 1912, and died on February 19, 2004, in Los Angeles, having been in a care home for a number of years.

Chester Lane: Los Angeles, August 23, 1990

My grandfather Edward Lane was a minister in Lexington. I wasn't too familiar with my father. Of course, nobody in my immediate family played any music at the time, but my aunt lent me an old organ so I started fooling around. Within a couple of weeks I was playing. When I got to be about twelve, the lady that my mother, Fannie Lane, worked for allowed me to come in and play some. She asked me if I knew popular music so I said no, and she gave me some music. Numbers like "Bye Bye Blackbird," "Yes Sir, That's My Baby," and I learned those.

I was fourteen when I played my first professional job. There was this little hometown band, the Jazz Nighthawks, and we went to listen to them and my mother spoke to them. She said I could play the piano so they turned the piano around and I played those numbers. They said, "What else do you know?" I said, "Well, I don't know any more." "Can you fake?" I said I was no good faking, and they said, "Well, we'll teach you," and they taught me some numbers and then they asked my mother if I could go play with them that Saturday night.

We went to Kosciusko, Mississippi, up in the hills there and we drank that moonshine [laughs]. *They would take their whiskey jug and put it over their shoulder and take a big swig and pass it on to the trombone player and back to the bass player and come back to the drummer and he'd take another swig and look at me and say, "What about that boy? He ain't drinkin' so well." "Well, he's only fourteen years old." "He sure is big for his age and he sure can whip that piano." I'd never been out after 9 o'clock before, and I got so tired by 10 o'clock, I was almost sleeping. Eventually we start to playing "Home Sweet Home" and that's when they pass the hat around. I don't remember how I got home or what time. I was supposed to make $10, but when I got up the next morning, I had three $10 bills in my pocket. That was so hot! That was all the money in the world.*

Lexington was just a small town with a square and a courthouse.[1] *It was mostly black people, and all the surrounding places was farming. We didn't farm on account of my grandfather being a minister. Back in those days, with him traveling with the horse and buggy to different churches, it kept us going. People didn't have much money to give you, so he would come home with a lot of smoked meat, and they'd fill up the buggy with groceries and other things they'd bring.*

The Nighthawks band was trombone, banjo, drums, and a violin and a tuba. The tuba player was named Big Boy, and Smollen [?] was the violin player. They're all long-gone now. They said, "Well, we going up to Greenwood, Mississippi," and I wanted to slip off with them, and they said, "No, we don't want that," and they mentioned it to my mother. She said, "If you want to go, go ahead, but we would like you to finish high school." I said I could finish it later. I was very smart in school and I would have finished it the next year, but I wanted to go with the band.

We went up to Greenwood and played in a place they call a pig-stand, like a drive-in. It was right on the edge of town, and they had the band up on a stand playing to draw the people in. Just entertainment. They had to come in and get food. We played there for about three weeks and then along came the sheriff and closed the place down because they were bootleggin' whiskey.[2] *So then they was out of work and they wanted to send me back home, but I told them I wouldn't go back. Give me the money and I'd stay, I said. "We promised your mother we'd take care of you." I said I'd call or I'd write. That's when I learned life can be pretty rough, and I wound up washing dishes. I was fifteen years old.*

Young Lane's first experience as a dishwasher and general dogsbody ended badly when his employer accused him, falsely, of stealing and sent him packing without pay. His landlady, evidently a kindly woman, found him another dishwashing job at a local Greek restaurant where he fared better.

Then here comes the band that I was working with. This time, they had a white boy with them, Mr. Morris, and he has a show and they say, "We'd like you to go on the show with us." Mr. Morris says it's $35 a week. and if things get better, "I'm gonna give you a raise." Finally the chef come out and he wants to know what's going on. I say, "Well these fellows want me to play with them." He says, "Play what? Why didn't you tell me? You should have been playing my piano and I had you washing dishes! You going, aren't you?" I said my week is not up until Sunday, and he reached his hands in his pocket and give me $5. "Go on and play music!"

Then the band kinda halfway broke up. Just some of the musicians—the tuba player, the banjo player, and the drummer—went on the show. It was called the Morris Brothers Show, and they had a little stage for the band. They'd show a movie under the tent and travel from town to town, all through the sticks. I stayed with them until they wound up in Philadelphia, Mississippi, where they closed the show down. They said Morris was running a movie without a license.

So of course, I went back home. I was all dressed up. I had about two suits of clothes, shoes, and everything. I felt like I had accomplished something. The Nighthawks thing had lasted about a year and a half. Then the guy that took us on the road, he had a place in Hot Springs, Arkansas, called Wilton's Café. This was a resort town, and at that time people from all over the country would come down there for those fairs. It was practically a wide-open town. From January to March or April, that was the season, so he took a band that came through Greenwood and picked me up with this band. This was a bigger band, but I can't remember too many of them. Those fellows practically faded away, and I never did see them anymore. The guy's name was Wilson. He wasn't a musician; he'd find a band and take it on the road so I joined the band. Eventually he wasn't giving us any money. He wasn't payin' us so the banjo player and the trombone player—they was from my hometown—they quit. This was in Warren, Arkansas. "We goin' back to Lexington, Chester. You got money, so let's go." I told them I never will go back as a failure so I stayed there.

It got pretty rough—you want to know about tough times? I start off playing the theater; the man was paying me a dollar a night, so I found *myself playing for movies. If it was a love scene, I'd play "Indian Love Call"; play "William Tell" for the drama. I worked Fridays, Saturdays, and then finally they cut me down to the Saturday and finally they cut me out completely so I didn't have any work. My landlady says to me—this shows you how luck would run with me—"Chester, I don't mean to make you feel bad, but the toe of your shoe is all worn out and your big toe is about to come out. I'll fix you your lunch and I don't want you to give me any money, but there's a truck going down to pick cotton so you go down and pick enough cotton to buy you some shoes." So I picked cotton from Monday, and on Friday here comes the man riding 'round to settle up. I couldn't pick cotton, wasn't used to it. Somebody got $20 for picking two thousand pounds of cotton and a girl got $25 and another fellow got $32, and finally he gets to me, "Who is Chester Lane? You got $4.85. Now don't you come back!" I felt kinda bad over it, and I didn't want to tell the landlady. She said, "Don't feel bad about it. You made enough to get you some shoes. Now, you got a telegram here."*

It was from the same guy that had the band, Wilson, and it said, "I want you to come to Hot Springs. I can give you some of your back money and give you a job." I was fifteen. She say, "You goin'?" So I said, "Yes, it's better than pickin' cotton," and while we were sitting there talkin', a fellow knocked on the door. "You got a telegram. From El Dorado, Arkansas, this time." It reads, "Can use you on the piano. Salary 70 dollars a week. Signed Bob Alexander." The landlady tells me that El Dorado is a boom town because they discovered oil over there, all round El Dorado, Smackover, and all those places. I said, "How can he mean $70 a week?" but she says they pay that kind of money. So I called him and told him that I'd be there.

I got to El Dorado and they were paying $10 a night at this white roadhouse, seven nights a week, and they pay you off every night. We had five pieces. Bob Alexander's Harmony Kings. There was a sax player named Louis Jordan in the band, and that's how Louis and I first got to meet. He was three years older than me. This roadhouse was out on the county line, and they bootleggin' whiskey, and that's why they pay you off each night. This went on for about three or four months, maybe longer.

From then on, it was clear sailin'. Bob Alexander had this small band with Louis Jordan playing alto sax, soprano sax, and clarinet; me; and a couple of the fellows, Leonard Parker on trumpet, Killebrew on drums. Our banjo player was named Buster Bennett; he used to play the banjo all behind his head and he'd be singing. He was a showman. Bob was the leader. He played saxophone, and he had a big band too. Then this Wilson hired the Bob Alexander band, and I wound up in Hot Springs again with that group. We played the season at Wilson's Tell-'Em-'Bout-Me-Cafe. Got there around first January. I didn't get all that back money, but I did get paid. When the season was over, Louis Jordan went to New York and I stayed there.

The next day, a guy named Brady Bryant, out of Little Rock, came in and asked me to come join his band, so I went up there and joined Brady's Peppers and I stayed with them for a while. That was like seven or eight pieces, trumpet, trombone, bass; [saxophonist] Charles Pillars, who was a brother to Hayes Pillars, and later played with the Jeter-Pillars band, he was in the band. He wound up going to St. Louis to join his brother. After I got playing around with them and we used to broadcast, I got a job playing with four pieces out to a roadhouse called Tony Barnardi's, and that's when I got my own group called the Yellowjackets.

This drummer—his name was Crump—had three pieces, and then I got out there and made it four. I was playing pretty good piano, and I knew all the tunes, which pleased people, so the fellow that owned the place said, "Crump, you don't know what you're doing. Why don't you let Chester be the leader of the band?" We was all getting the same amount of money, but they put me in charge because I knew how to talk to people and play all their requests. This place was out of city limits, where you come in and you bring a set-up and your own whiskey if you slip it in. It was legal in the county; you could bring it out.

I started out by playing piano by ear. That lady that gave me those numbers, she showed me some notes, and my girlfriend at the time, her people were giving her corresponding lessons. Every time she'd get through with one of her lessons, she'd give it to me and I'd take it home. I learned to spell that way, to read music. This was in Lexington. Then when I got in groups and I saw guys reading, like in this band in Little Rock where they were playing stocks, like Fletcher Henderson's number, "Louisiana Bo-Bo," which was a heckuva swing number, I learned to read by following them. I worked on it all the time. I bought books on reading, and I studied how to read. When I started arranging music, I got books on that and learned all about my chord system. I'm just strictly a self-made musician. I only took lessons for the first time just before I was called in the Navy for two years. I was playing then at a spot, and they asked me to play "Clair De Lune," but when you get into certain parts of "Clair De Lune," if your fingering is incorrect, it's very hard to play that thing. I took fingering lessons for nine months, which changed my whole style. Now I could finger correctly.

We broadcast once a week, and they would call us Tony Barnardi's Yellowjackets. Tony was a wrestling promoter, promoted all the wrestling matches in Little Rock, and he heard us on the radio and he said, "I'm no musician; I'm a fighter," so he told the announcer to make it Chester Lane's Yellowjackets, so that's how that happened. We did well. Particularly well. We started out with three men, and after we started broadcasting, I asked Barnardi if I could have a couple more men. That's when I got Forrest Powell; he's from Little Rock. He was in school there, and he was playing fine trumpet. He and I used to sit together, and he'd watch me making *arrangements. That's when he started, by watching me. He could write. Fellow named James Taylor* [saxophonist] *was with us—we called him Dink—he later went with Don Albert's band and wound up in New York. Monroe Fingers—he later became president of the Local in Toledo—he was a saxophone player for us. We didn't have a bass player at the start, but we got a bass player by the name of Wiley out of Hot Springs, so all that lasted at least three or four years.*

Alphonso Trent's band had just broken up over in Buffalo, and he came back to Little Rock and he heard my band. He said, "You know what, I would like to take your band on the road and add a couple of pieces." Well, we knew he would know the road pretty well because he'd booked his band, the first black band to play at the Adolphus Hotel in Dallas, into all those different places. He made it "Alphonso Trent Presents Chester Lane's Yellowjackets," and I said that was all right with me. We had two saxophones and two trumpets, didn't have a trombone, and rhythm, of course. We added a fellow named William Pate on saxophone and [Arthur] *Shelton on bass, so that made it about seven or eight pieces, and we traveled down through some of his routine routes. All over, in fact, and it was well received.*

We wound up back in his home [Fort Smith, Arkansas], *and we headed out to play from there. Then along comes Al Travis, out of New York. At that particular time, they had girls going 'round as Cab Calloway's sisters fronting bands. There was Blanche Calloway, which is Cab's real sister, and they had a Harriet Calloway, a Jean Calloway, and they had a Laura Calloway. Anyway, we got a girl out of Hot Springs and they placed her with this group, and they called Trent and said how would he like to go on the road with this girl they called Jean Calloway? So Trent didn't have anything particular for us to do, so he said OK and we joined them. The first job we played was Coffeyville, Kansas, and that's when Roosevelt closed the banks so that's why we stopped.*[3] *We stayed there two months, not working. The lady where we were staying, where we ate and slept, she knew Trent and she knew his people had money and their money was good for whatever the bill came to. She had credit so she could get food for us. Trent was prominent in the black section of Fort Smith, Arkansas, at that time. Both his parents were retired teachers, and they had nothing but money. So music was his plaything; they paid for a band for him.*

So anyway we were just sitting around this place. They'd give a little dance, and we'd go and play it for them for kitty money. Nobody had any money, so we'd just fool around until all that was over. The first job we had was in Marquette, Michigan, and from there we went to Alton and Hancock, Michigan. Now you can imagine that jumping out of Arkansas and that nice weather and up to Michigan by the Canadian border was pretty tough. This group wasn't the group that went with the Jean Calloway. This was really disaster. These guys were smart operators—but Trent would see that we got our money—and every night he would say, "Give me the money for the band," and they'd say, "We'll take care of it next time." "No, give me the money every night," so they didn't like that.

Anyway I think we were in Sioux City, Iowa, and this promoter Al Travis was one of them, so anyway they sent Trent over to the next job that's coming up, and the next morning they moved us out of there and do you know I haven't seen Trent from that day on. I never did see him again. We said, "Well, where's Trent?" "Oh, he's going to join us in Seattle; he's gonna join us in this place or that" until we found out that we'd been taken away from Trent altogether. It turns out Trent stayed around Deadwood, South Dakota, and played 'round there. He was a fine pianist, you know, and he stayed there until he got tired and went back home.

I'm still the leader and we got up there to Laramie, Wyoming, and by then some of the fellows had gone back home, from Seattle and Tacoma, all up there, and I had about six pieces left. Forrest was still with me, and Shelton was still on the bass. Jean Calloway, this girl out of Hot Springs—her name was really Callie Dill—she stayed with us, but eventually she went home when things got rough. Those who wanted to go back home, they went, and the rest of us went on to finish the dates. We got to Laramie, and that's when the promoter ran off with the money. At that time in Laramie there very few black people and there was no place to stay. This couple had rooming houses where they had train porters coming in to stay, and they told us we could have a room. So we played the University of Wyoming, and some of the fellows in the fraternity said to come over to the frat house; we gonna have a drink, and they treated us so nice. They liked our music, and they had some whiskey they made themselves so we all had drinks, and it's about 5 or 6 in the morning before we left. I think it was just the saxophone player, the tenor player, and the trumpet player—he loved to drink—and we got back to town and the sheriff says, "What's this? Is this the band here?" And one of the frat guys spoke up, "Yes, they with us; what about it?" Sheriff says, "There's nothing about it. You want to find the rest of the fellows? Well, they in jail." "What did they do?" "They didn't do anything; they just didn't have no place to stay so we told them to come around the jail. Now if you guys want to say there's no place to stay—we couldn't stay in the hotels—come on, we got some nice clean beds there. You welcome." So we went round there and went to sleep in the jail.

Around 8 or 9 o'clock, here comes Howard Messenger, the bus driver, who they picked up somewhere through Minnesota and he had a school bus. That's what we were traveling in, a school bus, in all that cold weather. "Fellows, I got some bad news. Larry left at 5 o'clock this morning. He checked out of the hotel, got all the money, everything." We didn't know what to do, so Howard says, "I tell you what, we got some more dates to do. I got the itinerary so I'll send to my wife and get some money." His wife's a *schoolteacher so he sent and got money, and we took off to play the rest of the dates. We played one date; we wound up going to Aberdeen, South Dakota, on Christmas Eve, and we're fifteen miles from town and got snowed in. We were sitting out there in the bus, cold, and waiting for them to try get to us. I said, "I'm going up here and ask this lady if we can come in and warm our hands." There was five of us. We went in and this lady said, "Sure, come on in," and she cut up her Christmas turkey and she gave us all Christmas dinner. This was one of the nicest things that ever happened to me on the road. We didn't get into Aberdeen until 1 o'clock and they said, "Don't worry about no music; go and get some sleep." They finally got us through with snow plows.*

So we loaded up the bus and headed for Hazen, North Dakota, and when we got there, cut a long story short, we saw all the people standing outside so we drove in, and the promoter came over, "Look, you didn't eat yet and I just talked to your manager—he means Howard, the bus driver—and we gave him the money. We don't want you to play. Why don't you take this money and go back where it's warm? You fellows have no business being up here in this weather." We dressed in all our best suits, and these guys got these great big Russian fur coats, boots, fur hats, all that stuff on, right there on the Canadian border.

They'd booked us all through the sticks. This was still with Jean Calloway's band. We played Christmas week and headed to Redfield, South Dakota, and this was like coming back to the summer. We stayed for a week and the people were very nice. They had us come around and play. Then we headed for home in Little Rock, and we made one stop in Napoleon, Iowa, overnight; that's where we met this girl, Margaret [Backstrom], she played tenor saxophone with the Sweethearts of Rhythm. She and her sister both were musicians, and we jammed some with them. Up in Seattle, we had met Buck Clayton and his Twelve Gentlemen from Harlem. He had been to Japan [actually Shanghai, China], and they were appearing at the Orpheum Theatre there with Roscoe Ates[4] and his daughter. We played the Trianon. Buck's guys were sharp, all in those long tails, top hats, sharp as they want to be. We were struggling. This old lady was giving a party and she invited me. We supposed to be "out of New York," and I got a chance to meet Buck and two or three of the guys. I didn't know anything about Los Angeles then.

Anyway I wound up back in Little Rock, and they were so glad to see me. This was about '33 or '34. The guy that ran the place, he says, "Look, tomorrow, I want you to get me a band together. We gonna play right here in this place. You belong to Little Rock." They called him Sweets; he ran the Dreamland Ballroom, so within two weeks, I'm back in business again. So I called the fellows and got the group together. Sweets went down and bought them all suits of clothes, uniforms. We played at the Dreamland every night. Had about six or seven pieces, still with Monroe Fingers on saxophone. For the black people, that's what it was. We were playing everything that Duke Ellington would play. We were taking things off records and writing them down. I was doing experimental with my arranging.

We had one of the swingiest bands; it was the first of the little bands, way before [John] Kirby came out. Our drummer was named Skeets [Ira "Skeets" Seville]. Ted Seville, his brother, played with us on the road, and when we came back we got Skeets. He was a heckuva drummer. Jo Jones thought the world of him. We had a broadcast on Thursday nights, and this guy could sing; he'd been on the amateur program, so he came and asked, "Chester, do you mind if I sing a number with you? Can I sing on the radio?" So I told the announcer about him. He said, "Can he sing? Well, let's put him on." So this guy sang "One Minute to One," and he sound so good, we start puttin' him on every Thursday. Then he did "Trees," and later on, he wound up with Jay McShann and from there to Duke Ellington. This was Al Hibbler, and in his biography he says he did his first job with Chester Lane's Yellowjackets in 1935. At a dollar and a quarter a night! That's what we were getting. He started to singing every night with the band, and he stayed with us until it broke up. We stayed there until Sweets got in an argument with some guy and the guy shot him. Killed him. That was the end of the regular jobs.

Then we went over to a place called the Chat and Chew. I took about four pieces, always featuring myself on piano, and Clifton Jones—he's in Chicago now—was on alto. We used to keep that place jumping all the time. That's when Basie came down and I met him. We were making regular broadcasts, but back in those days, recording wasn't a thing unless you were in the big time.

You know, Fatha Hines was my idol. That was way before I knew about Tatum. I used to sit on the corner and wait for that "Around The Town" broadcast to come in at 1 o'clock in the morning with "Fatha Hines from the Grand Terrace" when he'd hit that [signature] song "Deep Forest." I idolized that man, but I had never seen him. Then one morning—this is back in the Brady Bryant days when Brady was booking bands and he had booked Fatha Hines—Brady comes in the room, "Hey, wake up. Fatha Hines is here, up in the living room." I couldn't believe it, but I got up and Forrest got up, and I looked in there and there he was, rooming at Forrest's house. I said, "Forrest, get your horn." Fatha said, "Come on and play something." I got on the piano and Forrest played trumpet. Then Fatha sat down and played "Rosetta" and another number. Man, you couldn't hear nothing but "Chester knows Fatha. He was just by to his house." I went to the dance that night, and he was up on the stand and he looked up and he saw me and had me sit up on the stand with him. Boy, I was in heaven then. I went to see him at Disneyland when he came in there years later, and I reminded him. "Don't mention that. How long ago was that?" he said. That Fatha was something. He never did get the credit due him.

In the meantime, Forrest's mother had moved out here [LA] and he had left the band. Then Jeter-Pillars wanted me to come join them in St. Louis. Little Rock was their home; both Jeter and Pillars came from there and that's where Trent used come all the time with his famous band. But Don Albert wanted me to join him too. So there I was between the two. I played a couple of weeks with Don in his piano player's place, and Don said "You know this band; you workin' with me," and then Jeter-Pillars sent me this telegram.

Everybody knew they had a regular job, from September 9 to May 9 at the Club Plantation in St. Louis. It was literally a flip of the coin. The head was Pillars; the tail was Don Albert. Don was playing at the Dreamland that night. They'd started using [different] bands, so I was at the dance and Don says, "They tell me you going with Jeter-Pillars." When I joined them, [drummer] *Big Sid Catlett* was there, and he played with us a while in that summer [1935]; then he went to Chicago. The band was off from May until September. Three months off every year but for those nine months, you could look to work. That was Jeter's job as long as he wanted it, the Scarpellis said. No contract needed. Scarpelli says, "My word is my contract," and we used to laugh and say, "Pillars's word better be his contract, too!" They were some boys, those Scarpellis.

I was proud of the fact that Jeter-Pillars was the highest-paid band in St. Louis and I was playing at the Club Plantation, which was a regular job.[5] At that time, when the other guys around was making $8 or $9 a week, or maybe $2 or $3 a night, with Jeter-Pillars when I joined, it was $35 a week. My wife, Lucille, came in and joined the show, and she was making $50 a week. We weren't married then. I met her when she came in, and as usual, her music was short; she brought only a couple of piano copies. I said, "Honey, you need some music for your things," and she says, "Well, I had some music, but my music got burned up." So I went in there and made a couple of arrangements. She came in for six weeks, and she wound up staying two years at the Club Plantation. She was the leading lady in the show they would put on. She had just left home and was on the start of her career. So I start writing and the next thing we start going out. I took her to breakfast, and we had sausage, eggs, hot biscuits, yes indeed, coffee and all for 20 cents apiece. That goes to show how things was back then. I was only paying a dollar a week for my room, and with what I was making, we was doing pretty good.

Jeter-Pillars was one of the most popular bands in the country. They played what they call a society type of music. Dance music. When the Plantation moved up on Vandeventer and Alpha, the club seated one thousand people. Used to be a skating rink and they made into a nightclub. How they would operate, they would give you a set-up and a steak sandwich or spaghetti or whatever you prefer, and you bring your own whiskey and you paid

$3 a person. For people like the Ink Spots, the line was all the way up the street, and if you didn't get in for the first show, you'd hope to catch the second one. That's the way it would go; it really was the tops. Re jazz, we had three shows a night to play besides the dancing. Strict jazz wasn't all that popular at that time. It was society music we played, numbers like "A Fine Romance" and "S'posin'."

James Jeter and Hayes Pillars were very popular guys. They had played with Alphonso Trent's band, and when they left Trent's band in Buffalo, they wound up in Cleveland and they got a group there and played around there for a little while. That's where they met Sweets [trumpeter Harry Edison], and the next thing I know they were in St. Louis. They brought their band to Little Rock, and they played there during the summer during the old times. Charles Pillars joined them, and that's when I heard them. They were playing sweet music, but they would do some swing.

Sweets [in the band 1933–1936], Clark Terry, Jimmy Forrest, Dan Minor, J. J. Johnson, all those jazz guys came in and played through this time. They would stay awhile, but they wanted to play a different type of music. [Bassist] Jimmy Blanton, he came in with us—that was his first job in St. Louis—and played some with us that summer, and then in September he had to go back to school. When he came back the next summer, he went on the boat with Fate [Marable]. When he got through playing with Fate, as soon as that was over, which was about three weeks before our club reopened, we were going to try to get him for the winter for our job but it wound up Duke got him.

That September, Jimmy was down jamming at this little after-hour club called the 49 Club and Johnny Hodges heard him. Johnny went back to the hotel and told Duke about him. Duke said, "I'll listen to him tomorrow." "No," said Johnny. "Now, come out here now." So Duke makes this big production and runs out with his coat over his pajamas, slippers on, and he walks in and hears Jimmy play one number and he says to him, "Are you presently engaged?" Jimmy says no and Duke says, "Would you like to work with me?" "Of course." "I'll send Sweet Pea [arranger/composer Billy Strayhorn] 'round to see you tomorrow and you join us on Saturday." That's all he said, and he turned and walked out. So Strayhorn got in touch, and they came up to Club Plantation because Jimmy was a good friend of ours, and that's where Sweet Pea took him over some numbers. I was up there writing some music, and that's how I met Billy. Jimmy didn't see Duke no more until that Saturday, and Jimmy told me later on that when he got to Chicago, Johnny Hodges and all those guys were very nice to him, showed him what they could. They played a couple of numbers, and all of a sudden, Duke says, "Now we gonna feature our bass player on 'Sophisticated Lady,'" and Jimmy played that. It's history because the audience applauded for ten minutes before the band could play another number.

When Jimmy was a kid, he took cello, and at the time he was so small his sister used to have to help him carry the cello to school. He was so modest, a nice, quiet guy. You didn't notice him. His idol seemed to be Ben Webster. He wanted to keep up with Ben, and Ben was drinkin' all the morning, everything like that. He couldn't keep up with Ben. Seemed like there was TB in the family. Last time I saw Jimmy, it was 6 o'clock in the morning. "We just standing out here; we been talking a little bit," he says. He didn't drink that much or nothing like that, just wanted to hang out with the guys but he couldn't hack it. He needed sleep. His mother didn't want him to go on the road, period. His mother, his sister, all of them was musical. He had a cousin, [bassist] Wendell Marshall, he played with us and then later with Duke, too.

Being with Jeter-Pillars wasn't no problem for me, no more than playing shows. Some guys would come in and they had their numbers, and I just had to work my part out. It was three big clubs then: the Cotton Club in New York, Grand Terrace in Chicago, and the Club Plantation in St. Louis, and all the acts from New York, like the Nicholas Brothers, the Mills Brothers, the Ink Spots, they would play Chicago and then St. Louis, and that's as far south as they would go; then they'd go back east. Our show was three weeks. They'd come in for three weeks—some of them be held over—then go back. That's how I got the chance to know every musician, and of course, the musicians would come and visit us. The big thrill was when Duke came up. I'd been with the band about a year and a half, two years maybe, and Duke stopped in one night so Jeter said, "Chester, have you met Duke?" I say, "Yes," and he said, "Piano player, aren't you? You had the band in Little Rock?" I said, "You remember that?" And Duke said, "I always remember good bands!" I felt good about that, that he remembered that group. Everybody remembered the Yellowjackets. They recorded after I left.

I stayed there ten years with Jeter-Pillars. I started in '35 and stayed there until I went in the service, and when I came out I started playing by myself. Of course, I still wrote, and I used to go up there [Club Plantation] and write for [ex-Jeter-Pillars trumpeter] George Hudson who had the band. He was one of the mainstays when I first joined Jeter-Pillars, and later he got this band of his own.

I was drafted in '43. I fought and fought, man, but they took me anyway [laughs]. The first black Navy band was formed in St. Louis. The chief came there and he says, "I'd like to get a band together, a black band, because we don't have any." They had Lieutenant Griffith with a band over on the main side, but they wanted to get something for the colored boys. We recommended [arranger] Len Bowden because he knew military band music, so they organized a band, and he told all the musicians, "You've got a chance to do four weeks of boot training; then you go in the band department and you'll be in this band if you go in it now." Well, naturally, I wouldn't go, *being married, so I said no, but anyway they got me and they took me up there* [Great Lakes Naval Training Center, North Chicago]. *I was going to the sick bay suffering with my back, along with John Malachi, Sarah Vaughan's piano player, hoping we could get out, and three of the guys, Clark Terry, Jimmy Callender—he's out of New York; he also played with Jeter-Pillars—and Roy Torian, they all came over to see me. I've never seen fellows look so healthy. Everything in their complexion looked like they'd changed from that nightlife look after they'd exercised.*

Encouraged by his musician friends, Lane signed up for the band department, completed his boot training, and was put in charge of the yet-to-be formed No. 17 Band. He sat around from June 1 until November and was able to "moonlight" and play at Waukegan's White Door Club. By November, the band was scheduled to go to Pensacola, Florida, and Lane began to assemble a book of arrangements, including a Dudley Brooks's chart on "One O'Clock Jump" with its formidable high-note trumpet parts. Lane had the virtuoso trumpeter Frank Motley in his crew—"a top man for high notes"—but needed more capable musicians. Once assembled, he rehearsed them section by section, copied and originated arrangements, and earned considerable praise from Chief Stone, his senior officer, up from Florida to inspect this new band.

We played one number, started into another, and Chief Stone said, "Hold it, Lane. I'm no damn fool. I've been in the Navy twenty-six years so don't pull that thing on me. I know what this is. This band is too good. You'll send me some more musicians who can't play a damn thing." "Sir, this is the band that's going to Pensacola, Florida. Look, here's the list." And Chief Stone says, "They gonna go crazy over this band. How did you do that? Lane, do you drink? I got some Scotch in the car!"

So we went to Pensacola and played that first night. That's all you could hear, praise for Chester Lane and his Blue Jacketeers. We did so well they wanted to take the band out on the road. We stayed down there for two years, and after that we were sent up to Memphis and played there for a period, with guys coming in and out, and then I got out of the Service in '45 or '46.

Home in St. Louis, I didn't want to go back to big bands, so I went and got a job playing piano by myself. Figured I could do a little bit of good, and I was making more money that way. I started in the Stork Club, and from there we went out to the Barrel Bar [5614 Delmar] *with a girl singer, Ann Richardson. Just a duo. They called her "Caldonia." She was doing all the risqué tunes, but she had them cleaned up real nice. That place became so popular. I played around different places, just as a single, and of course, I was making good money.*

Billboard, August 23, 1947
In Short: St Louis—Ann Richardson and Chester Lane currently at the Barrel.

I worked up in Moline, Illinois, for a while, and then I came back to St. Louis and I started playing with Joe Smith's group [at the Windemere Bar on Delmar]. *That's where I learned a lot of Dixieland. Fellow named Orange, John Orange, trombone, he was in the band, and Norman Mason, clarinet player, and then for the first time they had a white boy in the band, Sammy Gardner, clarinet player. He replaced Norman who didn't want to play every night. Sammy's down in Florida now. I've never been too fond of those really down-to-earth, old solos like the guys back in 1900 played, but I liked the Dixieland tunes. I went out and played Dixieland with them, but first of all, they were playing swing. Joe Smith was on drums.*

It so happened that the fellow who lived below me—his name was John Moore; he was a tenor player—and he got a call from [tenor saxophonist] *Gene Ammons. Gene wanted him to go on tenor with him, so his wife came up and says, "Chester, John's going with Gene Ammons. I'm so happy. You don't like to travel, do you?" So I said, "Well, I wouldn't go on the road with nobody unless it was Duke Ellington, Count Basie, and Louis Jordan. Those are the only ones that's making money on the road as far as I can see. Duke plays piano, Count plays piano, so that only leaves Louis Jordan." We laughed and twenty minutes later, the phone rang: "Chester Lane? This is Mr. Jordan. I need a piano player." I say, "How soon?" He says, "Tomorrow or maybe a year from now." I said, "Tomorrow is too soon and a year is too long." "That's right—so when would you like to join me?" I said, "I see by your schedule that you due to be here on the eighteenth April. It's 'The Big Show.' I could join you then. I'll put in my two weeks' notice." "Well, all right," Louis said. "I'll pick up a piano player in Los Angeles with the understanding that you gonna join us in St. Louis. That a deal, Mr. Lane?"*

So on the eighteenth, they came to St. Louis and picked me up.[6] [Singer] *Frankie Laine was the headliner, with Ella Fitzgerald, Woody Herman, and Louis Jordan's band. Called it the Biggest Show of 1953. So we headed out from there on that Sunday and went on to play Cincinnati, Indianapolis, and Cleveland, and by Friday night, we end up in Carnegie Hall. I wrote back and told the fellows I made it to Carnegie Hall in five days!*

You look out [into the Hall audience] *and there was Teddy Wilson, Hazel Scott, Ed Sullivan, Guy Mitchell, Willie "The Lion" Smith, and all the jazz guys. Some came 'round to see Frankie Laine; some came to see Ella Fitzgerald. I told our trumpet player, Bob Mitchell, "Man, I'm nervous! With all these* [famous] *guys out there." He says, "Well, all you gotta do is play Louis Jordan's music. You don't need to worry about all them out there." Louis started down with "Ain't Nobody Here But Us Chickens"—that was the opening number—and once I got up on the stand, I was at ease and then it* was all smooth. After that, we went up to Montreal, Syracuse, Buffalo, and different places, and when the show closed finally three weeks later, we had a big dinner upstairs at one of those swank places. Anyway I wound up at Ella's house on Long Island somewhere, and as I didn't know how to get back to New York, I spent the night over there in her house. It was spring. She and I were good friends because we played blackjack all the way on the bus. Ella wouldn't fly so she would ride with the fellows in the bus, along with Nat Pierce, all of us in Louis's band, all the musicians from Woody's band, and [African American comedian] Dusty Fletcher.

Louis's band then had Bob Mitchell, trumpet; Johnny Kirkwood, drums; Sonny Jay, bass; me; Bert Payne on guitar; and Louis, of course. Later we got Count Hastings on tenor. And that was it from then on. I stayed with him until '57. Four years. Just going from one place to another. The only state I haven't been in is Hawaii. Went up to Montreal with Frankie's show, and this was when Fletcher didn't go over too good because his act was a lot of talkin' and that "Open The Door Richard" routine of his, and those French speakers, they didn't understand him. As to playing with Louis, I had always seen him when he came to St. Louis, but I never did want to talk to him about playing with his band.

See, from the time I hit St. Louis I did all right. From the time of Jeter-Pillars to when I got out on civvy-side, I was making good money. Before I went in the Service, they'd given us a raise up to $80 a week, and that was more than anybody was making. And then when I joined Louis, he used to brag, "I pay more than anybody on the road except Nat Cole and he ain't got but three people to pay." Yeah, Louis was paying us $350 a week.

Louis was strictly original. They should have given him credit for rock and roll because his shuffle rhythm was the same thing as the boogie-woogie style they play for rock and roll. He was playing that stuff way before anybody. We'd play a job in auditoriums, and you could hardly get in there; this was all over the country, wherever he played. It was terrific, with his personality and his vocals; that man could put a song over and he'd have you laughin'. He was funny, really comical, he could dance, and he could play his horn. Nat Cole said he was one of the greatest entertainers in the business. He had so many talents. I was just glad to be there.

He had me make him some arrangements, and some we got to record. We did eighteen sides.[7] I knew about chords and everything for arranging. Louis wanted a plain chord. He wanted a Bb, D, and F on a Bb chord. No 6ths. Everybody was making all those major 7ths, and he'd say just give me a plain Bb chord. He would take your arrangement and he would say, "Well, we won't use this." Now I didn't like the idea of him messin' with my arrangements, so I'd say, "You tell me what you want me to write and I'll write that." That was the best way. Maxwell Davis was his regular arranger, and he would send for Maxwell to come to meet him—Maxwell lived out here

[LA]—*and he would go back east and stay a couple of weeks and write for him.*

Unidentified St. Louis Source, ca. 1955

St Louis' own Chester Laine [*sic*] is still holding his own as one of the country's most outstanding keyboard artists. Laine's excellent showing brings remembrances of his dynamic performances with the Jeter-Pillars orchestra of yesteryear. Laine indicates that his association with the [Louis] Jordan crew for the last two years has broadened his scope on musicianship, showmanship, knowledge and experience. . . . Many of Chester's original scorings are found in Jordan's repertoire. Mr and Mrs Chester Laine (Lucille Agers) are now residing in Los Angeles, California.

Louis and I got on fine. He called me "homeboy" for years. No problems but then he wanted me to play organ. Wild Bill Davis was his first piano player to leave and take up organ, and I said, "I don't want to play organ," so that's when we kinda disagreed and I went back to Los Angeles. Next thing I know, Bob Mitchell was out here and the band had broken up. He said that our band was the longest Louis ever kept a band together.

I had moved out here so I came back here. I gave my family a trip to California and they liked it so well that I said, "When you want to move out here?" We got in touch with Bill Hadnott. Bill was the one that got me the job with Louis. He gave Louis my number and told him I was in St. Louis. I knew Bill from when he came in to the Jeter-Pillars band when we didn't get Blanton. So I told my wife to see what there was out here. She and my youngest son, they called me in Philly to say they was leaving, and she called me again in the next seven days and she says, "We here." They came to Bill's house [in LA]—*that was their first stop—and he showed them around. She got an apartment, and when I came back we were all here. She took care of all the hassle of moving from St. Louis.*

What I liked about working with Louis was that the band was strictly bigtime. All that traveling, all up in Alaska and Canada, in all the big towns. Being on the same TV show with Dinah Shore, Rock Hudson and Stan Kenton, Johnny Mercer, all those big names and then being at Carnegie Hall with all those stars standing around. Like when we played Birdland in New York the first time, we had terrific crowds; Marlon Brando came in and he stayed until we closed. Same with Johnny Ray, wherever Louis Jordan would go, he'd come hear us play. Birdland is where Diz [Dizzy Gillespie] *was playing and Miles Davis was around at that time. He said he knew me from standing in the wings at Club Plantation and watching me play with Jeter-Pillars. Miles played that night but Diz was really cooking. He had Bird* [Charlie Parker] *with him. Poor Bird had on a blue suit, a pink shirt, and a blue tie but he didn't play. He turned and walked on back. He was out of it.*

I call this a musician's rave. Couldn't ask for any more. Things were lean at that time for everyone else. Clark Terry and I used to talk when he was with Duke and they weren't doing well. [Saxophonist] *Ernie Wilkins, who was from St. Louis, had to leave Basie's band because they hadn't worked. "When we do work, we only get about $175 a week," he said. When I was with Louis, we never went under $250.*

Still, after four years, I was tired despite the fact that you got well paid. You closed on a Sunday night here, at the Sands, open up on a Friday night in Reno, and you got all this lay-off in between. You got to send money home to take care of your bills, and then you got have money on the road for your room rent. You can't get rich on the road as a sideman. Like we paid $145 for a house in Lake Tahoe, had seven of us staying in it sharing the price and sleeping on cots. When they did start letting us have cabins as the first blacks to play up there, it was $125 a week for a cabin apiece, so that's the kind of money you had to spend on the road. I said if I get to Los Angeles and I have a job making $100 a week, then I can count on still paying my bills.

I came here in December '57, and I had to wait three months for my transfer to the union. By the time I got here, [popular saxophonist-bandleader] *Earl Bostic*[8] *wanted me, so I went with him and played certain gigs in and out that I could play* [beyond the LA union's jurisdiction], *like up in Bakersfield, until he came up and he said, "I got two days in Denver. I pay you $150 a day." I said, "Bostic, I just got off the road. All that snow!" He says, "Look, I don't blame nobody that don't want it." So I turned him down and that was the end of working with him. He had* [renowned bebop tenor saxophonist] *Teddy Edwards with him. That's where I first met Teddy. Bostic had a big band at that time because he said the doctor told him to stop blowing so much, so he sat down and he had this ten- or twelve-piece band. "Fellows, I'm gonna let you guys play," and he went like that for a while, and the next day he's back on the road with his group and he's back blowing. He went east and the doctor told him to cut out all that traveling. Told him to settle down here* [LA]. *Him and his wife, Hildegarde, bought a place called The Flying Fox* [Earl Bostic's Flying Fox, 3724 Santa Barbara] *and he had a motel here. I played with him then. I played down to Redondo Beach; he took me down there on a gig.*

I played with [vocalist] *Oscar McLollie. He had a hot record out,* Convicted [Modern Records #970, released in October 1955], *then and he had Chuck Thomas with him. Called his band the Honey Jumpers. I told Chuck, "I don't know if I like it out here." Then Teddy Buckner called me: "I gotta Dixieland band." "Well, Teddy, I don't play Dixieland too well," I said. "Look, you play piano, that's what I hear. All I want is a good piano player. Now why don't you come down and listen to us, and see if you like the band?" They were playing at the 400 Club* [333 W. 8th Street, Los Angeles] *so I went down there and I sat in with them. I did know those Dixieland tunes from playing with Joe Smith back in St. Louis, and when they got to a stop to take a solo, they would start swinging. Jesse Sailes on the drums, Art Edwards on bass, and Streamline, they were playing swing music along with the Dixieland. So Teddy said, "You like it? Well, can you join us?" I said yeah. "OK, I'd like you to start Tuesday night." Gideon Honoré was playing with Teddy when I joined the band so I was replacing Gideon. I only met him then. He'd given his notice. I never did understand why he didn't click with Teddy. He was a good piano player. I guess he was spooked by* [his pianist predecessor] *Harvey Brooks.*

Roger Jamieson: *Gideon played kinda lightly, at least with us* [The New Orleanians]. *He didn't have a lot of volume.*

Then Teddy said, "As long as you gonna join us, we gotta recording session tomorrow night." This was on Monday night so I made this album Salute to Louis Armstrong [Dixieland Jubilee LP DJ505] *with "Bucket Got a Hole in It" and things like that. They ran through the songs and I just put that ear on them. We made the album right there before I even started working with the band.*

From then on, I stayed with the band because it was working all the time. We left the 400 on the Sunday night, and on the next Tuesday, we opened at The Huddle [Paul Cummins's Huddle Restaurant, 2625 E. Garvey Ave., West Covina, California]. *Stayed there five years, then three years at the Beverly Cavern, after that to the Harmony Inn for a year and a half where we only played weekends, and then we went to Disneyland and there we stayed for sixteen years. That's about twenty-four years in total, and I was on most of the albums Teddy made, too.*[9] *We would play all the summer, five or six nights a week, and we'd play all the private parties on the weekends. We played for the whole of Christmas Week, Thanksgiving, and Easter Week too.*

I never did too much on my own because that was all I needed to do, working with Teddy. Disneyland treated us well; Sonny Anderson, the music director, was a wonderful guy. The guy who was our agent, they even paid him every week, all the times we were there, even though Disneyland paid us our salaries themselves. We were successful because we played what the people wanted. We had people come in and they'd ask for a song, and I'm not bragging, but I know so many songs and we'd play whatever they wanted. I got a book in there with 1,200 songs, and I know practically every one of them. I always have a thing about remembering tunes. The guys would say, "You know it, Ches?" and they'd fall right in. You meet everybody, all the top musicians, working at a place like Disneyland. When we'd play our four hours, they'd go maybe to 1 o'clock so we'd go over and listen to them. Basie's band would come in, Diz would come in, Hamp's band; I knew all those guys. Meeting different people from all over the world every night. That was the enjoyment.

It came to an end in October '84. Teddy got to the place where he could hardly walk up on to those stands at Disneyland. There had been no changes. Why would you leave a job like that? Caughey's the only one that left the band, and that's when Chuck came in.

Buckner's desire to retire seemed to suit Disneyland. The band was given a glittering retirement party in December 1984 and then brought back for the Memorial Day weekend the following May for what turned out to be their final Disneyland appearance. Buckner never played again.

Approached later in 1985 to appear with the band on Nell Carter's ABC TV show *Gimme a Break*, Buckner had rejected the offer without informing his musicians. With Chester having suffered a broken leg in an automobile accident, Jesse Sailes retrieved this lucrative job but with Nat Pierce on piano. Buckner came in for further criticism when it became clear that the band members would not qualify for a Disneyland pension, despite the length of their employment at the theme park. This was due to an arcane calculation of total hours worked—a pitfall that might have been overcome had Buckner himself seen to it.

Teddy was a fine fellow to work with. His personal ways hadn't nothing to do with his musical ways. If he's mad about something, you could see it. He featured every man in the band. He wanted every man to play his solo. Not like Louis Jordan's band where it was altogether different, because Louis would get up there and he made a clear chorus, he sang a chorus, he blew a chorus, and then he'd sing another chorus and then he would go out. That's what the people wanted and that's what Bostic used to do as well. Bostic would play every chorus. That's the reason the doctor told him to cut down. With Teddy there was no restriction about what you play. When I first joined I wasn't playing no Dixieland music. He never said nothing. He never told me one time to play Dixieland style. On trumpet, he was terrific; only thing about it, he could have been further up. They sent for him to come over to Asia because they wanted him to follow Armstrong—you know he looked like Armstrong—but he wouldn't go. "If they want to see me, they come see me here," he said. In fact, he didn't want to travel. He didn't want to go out on the road. He wanted to stay home. Louis Jordan wouldn't go to Europe either. He said he wanted three weeks work with one week off and he wanted the money deposited over here before he went, but they didn't agree.

In August 1985, I had an automobile accident. Got my arm broken and I was out for a year and a half. I couldn't play anymore. Then [trombonist] Danny Snyder saw me at a jazz club, "Are you playing again?" I said, "Well, a little." "Why don't you come out and sit in with us Saturday night?" So I started playing with his quartet. Been with him at Casey's Tavern [22029 Sherman Way, Canoga Park] ever since. I turned jobs down because I was with him on Saturdays. They're such nice people.

I'm a versatile man. That's why I have been successful because I can play most anything. I love a beautiful melody when I play. The melody counts with me. I'm a jazz player, but I'm a man who sticks to the melody. Even when I take a solo, I never get too far away from the melody. You can deal so much around that melody.

I don't like nothing real fast. I don't like nothing too slow. Just medium.

Lucille Lane: *I left Dallas, Texas, for Kansas City, Missouri. Jimmy Rushing was working there at the Cherry Blossom Club, and one of the bosses of the Club Plantation came over and caught the show. He liked what he heard of me and he asked me if I would go, but naturally he had to talk to the management so it was all right and I left. That's when I met Chester. I opened up for the season at the Club Plantation and instead they kept me for two seasons. One of those things and we married later. Still hanging in there . . .*

In Kansas City, I was sitting in the dressing room, and entertainers there know that it's bad luck to whistle, and I used to whistle. I was lonely and I wanted to go home, and Sleepy Williams and Rose—they had a dance team— and he said, "Oh, Lucille, you should put that in your act." I put that in my act and I started to breaking up the house whistling in harmony.

In later years, I went to New York to work at the Apollo Theater with Jeter-Pillars band, and they really seemed to have liked me so much. Chester was in the Service then, and I went over well, which made me feel very good.

"Porto Rico" [Norman Miller][10] *took a liking to me when I was at the Apollo with Louis, and he was showing me around, "Look, I want to show you something." He went downstairs and there was a life-size standing picture of a lady. "You know this lady?" "That's my wife!" They had this out front in the lobby, life-size, from when she worked there with Jeter-Pillars. "This is one of the nicest ladies I ever met," he said.*

Lucille Lane: *I was with [Alphonso] Trent's band at the Baghdad [?]. That was in the earlier days. They had a full big band, along with [trombonist] Snub Mosley, and of course, the place wasn't paying off and I quit. That's when I first started out.*

Snub tried to get me to join his band when he was on the bandstand in New York. He had one of those organ attachments to play the bass. He said, "Ches, you can do that. We work all the time." I said, "I like it on the road." [Tenor saxophonist/bandleader] Buddy Tate wanted me to stay on in New York when I told him I was leaving Louis Jordan. He worked all the time and he had things at the Savoy [Ballroom], but I said no. I kinda liked California . . .

Chapter Ten

Isadore Leonidas "Monte" Easter

Trumpet and Vocals

The bassist Bernard Carrere was leafing through some of his career photographs at home in Los Angeles when he came on a Sonny Clay band photo from the late 1930s. Pointing to trumpeter Monte Easter, he said to us, "He's still around playing gigs in town. You should see him if you can." A quick call revealed that Easter, then in his late seventies, was playing two nights a week in the Sports Bar in the Holiday Inn at Crowne Plaza, near Los Angeles International Airport.

Easter's dark-suited quartet was set up in a corner, the early-evening drinkers showing only passing interest. Easter, a tall, lithe, well-preserved man, was flanked by tenor saxophonist Chuck Thomas and supported by the somber figure of Jesse Sailes at the drums. There was no bass, and Kitty Martell's electric piano added little of consequence. Even so, Easter impressed with his Eldridge-like lines and world-weary blues vocals, although it was Thomas's full-toned tenor that stayed longest in the memory, aided by Sailes's superb, show-time drumming. Easter explained that he called his combo Kansas City Jazz as a tribute to both his "birthplace" and the jazz style that it spawned.

Having arranged to meet for an interview, it took awhile before we could find a time to suit him, largely due to Easter's work as a keeper (bailiff) for the county marshal's office. Easter lived on Edgehill Drive in a quiet, well-kept neighborhood in the Crenshaw district, his spacious bungalow fronted by an immaculate lawn. As we talked, it was clear that he had enjoyed a period of popular success on Central Avenue and elsewhere in the 1940s and 1950s when his "jump-style" combo recordings sold well and he was in

Monte Easter of Monte Easter and His Orchestra, Los Angeles, 1950s. Courtesy Danni Gugolz / Opal Louis Nations.

demand for club appearances and R&B tours. Even so it was impossible not to sense his disappointment at the way his career had tailed off.

Easter was eager to show me his scrapbooks and to tell me his story, even if much of the chronology was muddled and his memory often at odds with the facts. It proved impossible to place many of his engagements in sequence or to properly document the many Easter bands and combos.

I liked him a lot, but his need for reassurance was only too evident. He lent me a few photographs and cuttings, and we kept in touch for a short time as he sought to reignite his career and promote his Intrigue record label. Monte Easter died at home on Christmas Day, 2000.

Monte Easter: Los Angeles, August 30, 1990

Easter was born on December 15, 1913, in Coffeyville, Kansas, a small town on the Oklahoma border in what used to be called Indian Territory, some 170 miles south of Kansas City. His schoolteacher mother, Clara, was described as a "high yellow" African American while his father William, an educator, was at least part Native American. Easter remembered his grandmother as "pure-blooded Indian."

Coffeyville was a place where all the bands out of Kansas City, like Bennie Moten, George E. Lee, would come and stop on their way down to Tulsa and Oklahoma City. It was a show town, back in those days. All the kids in Coffeyville played some kind of music; there wasn't nothing but musicians and show people coming through there. My cousins played saxophone; other friends of mine played trumpet. I took up the trumpet because all of the kids around town was taking up something. I just liked the trumpet. I taught myself how to read, got the music, started reading, always could, best reader in the world. When I came to Los Angeles, I started studying. I went to Chapman College [in Orange, California] *for a year, but I was making so much money playing music that I dropped out and just pursued music alone.*

I really didn't get the trumpet in Coffeyville. I wanted a trumpet in Coffeyville, but I got the trumpet in Phoenix, Arizona, when I was getting ready to graduate from high school and I bought me a trumpet. I had a teacher named Amos White.[1] *He started me off. Amos White was out of the South somewhere. He was a little, short fellow like Roy Eldridge, but he was a blowin' sucker. He could really blow. He used to tell me, when I was first there, "Blow the horn in and out—if you gonna cut a hog, cut a big one." He was a smooth, good trumpeter.*

I never had to work [as a child]. *I had a good life. I was very fortunate. I was from a small family, nobody but me and my sister, Rylva. She was killed in 1939, on her way back to Wilberforce University. I used to have a very beautiful voice; then I tried to sing like Louis* [Armstrong] *and I ruined the voice so now I just holler the blues* [laughs]. *I went to see Louis years ago in Los Angeles, down on 54th and Central. Used to be a drug store where all the musicians would meet at 2 o'clock in the morning and Louis used to come down there. He was working at the Cotton Club then. He was a regular person, just with everybody. He was just Louis.*

172   *Chapter 10*

Easter moved with his family in the late 1920s to Phoenix, where his father had taken a teaching job. Previously Easter senior had taught at Langston University, a black college near to Oklahoma City, where Easter went to grammar school before another move took him to St. Louis, where he attended Sumner High School. Eventually the family relocated permanently to Los Angeles in 1930.

I formed a band in Phoenix called Monte Easter and his Rhythm Stompers. I don't know how we sounded but we worked. Just local boys earning a few dollars. I used to work at a place called the Green House. Amos White was working out there. That's where I first met "Big Six" [tenor saxophonist Oliver Reeves] *and* [pianist] *Lorenzo Flennoy when Sammy Ketchel's Creole Syncopators came in town. They were in the band. We got to be good friends, and when I came to Los Angeles, I used to stay down in Lorenzo Flennoy's area. He was a great musician and a very nice fellow.*

I graduated from high school in Phoenix. I guess that that was '29 or '30. I'd been to Los Angeles and I just liked the town, so as soon as I graduated I was coming back here. It was so different from Phoenix. I really didn't know too many people here; there was Lorenzo and a girl over in Pasadena, but I've been very fortunate in my life that everybody I knew liked me. I didn't do nothing but practice on my horn every day and go to Lorenzo Flennoy's. I didn't do too much until my family moved over here and then I started back to school. That's when I went to Chapman College and I started a big band. I had a twelve-piece band. I had some of the greats in there. Britt Woodman, the trombone player, I had him in the band. He's the only one who comes to mind right now but I had twelve pieces. It was very good. In fact, it was good because he [Britt] *was in it. We used to play all the Jimmie Lunceford charts. A* [trumpeter] *friend of mine named Forrest Powell used to transcribe all their tunes for me.*

I liked the way Buck Clayton played. I kinda patterned myself after Buck with the mute because he was doing all that before Sweets [Harry Edison] *was doing it. Louis Armstrong, Buck Clayton, Dud Bascomb, boy, they all told a story on the horn, and that's what I try to do when I play my horn. Try to tell a story. When I arrived here, I'll tell you who sticks out in my mind the most was two trumpet players. The first one was J. T. Gipson and the second one was Red Mack. They were both young and they both could blow. J. T. Gipson was a youngster that played like Louis. He could really, really play. I knew him before I knew Red Mack. J. T. Gipson ended up being a writer for the* Sentinel *newspaper* [Gipson was actually theatrical editor of the (black) California Eagle newspaper]. *Gertrude Gipson, his wife, she was entertainment editor for the* Sentinel *too* [not so, she was a theatrical columnist for the Eagle]. *He never really pursued music like he should have. When I first came to town, I remember him on a truck down on 43rd and Central. J. T. Gipson* was on the truck blowin', and I never heard a young man blow so much horn. Then after a couple of years, here comes Red Mack. These are the two I remember. Andy Blakeney, he was always someone I looked up to. He was playing here before I started. Back in those days, my favourite trumpet players in Los Angeles was Lloyd Reese—I studied with him—that was in the forties—and Fletcher Galloway and Harold Scott, who used to play with Les Hite out here. Fletcher Galloway was a helluva trumpet player; I don't know what happened to Fletcher. They all came on about the same time.

The band that sticks in my mind the most, true to speaking the best band to me back in those days was Dootsie Williams. He had a band called the Harlem Dukes. On the other hand, I was in one of the best bands that was here, the Erwing Brothers.[2] We had a good-looking band; that was about 1932. We were working at the taxi dance down on 6th and Main. I was with them five or six years, a long time, when Lionel [Hampton] was over at the Paradise Café across the street. I was learning all the time. I met James and Harris Erwing, and for some reason they took a liking to me and they hired me in the band. I had never worked at a taxi dance before. We just played one tune right after another. Repetitive, sure. We had about nine, ten pieces up on the bandstand. The girls would be on the right-hand side and the guys would be on the left-hand side. At that time, it was ten cents a dance. Saxophones would take the first chorus; the brass would take the second chorus, back and forth like that. That went on 'til twelve every night. At that time it was a good payin' job. There was another taxi dance on 8th and Broadway, and there was one up on 3rd and Main for the Filipinos. Strictly for Filipinos. I guess most everybody in Los Angeles worked at a taxi dance at one time or another.

But we played dances too; like maybe on a Sunday afternoon, we'd play for the Mexican dances. Who I vividly remember in that band was Harris Erwing, one of the greatest saxophone players that ever was. Duke Ellington begged him to go with him but he wouldn't go. Why he was so great, he could blow; he didn't even know what key he was in half the time. It didn't make any difference—he'd just start playin'. He blew the right changes. He was a natural. The Erwing brothers came from down South, probably Alabama, down in there somewhere. The piano player was Jim Erwing, Horace Moore was on drums, and a Mexican trumpet player, friend of mine, Hernando Rotzquel; he was very good. The bass player [Joe Mendoza] was very good too. "Papoose" or "Big Chief" [Russell Moore], he came in the band on trombone later on. We were buddies. He was always up-going and he was a very good musician. Any time he had anything to say to me so far as playing is concerned, it was always encouragement. Constructive criticism. He gave me tips. See, Papoose was blowin' then. At that time, they [Erwings] were the band out here. They had the makings to make it. Their father used to put out this newspaper round here called Neighborhood News. That was before the

Sentinel [founded in 1934]. *He gave everybody publicity. It was a throwaway paper. We recorded with that band for Vocalion* [June 1933].

There wasn't that many bands here then, to tell the truth. Charlie Echols was a showman; I can't remember whether he was good or not. Sonny Clay,[3] *I was with him at the Paradise Club about 1937. Any kind of music you brought up to Sonny to play, he's gonna read it. He's the only one in the band can read anything. Sonny was his own enemy, his own destructive self. He took a band to Australia* [in 1928]—*that's before I got here—and he messed up over there. I think alcohol was his biggest downfall. At the Paradise Club, we had to play shows and for some of the shows, the music would be hard, but Sonny could play the music. He'd be about the only one* [of us] *who could play some of that music.*

The nineteen-year-old Easter was in an earlier Clay orchestra that played in 1932 for boxer Jack Johnson's short-lived Chez Paris club, located in the same building as Club Alabam at 41st and Central. He also recalled in passing that he followed Buck Clayton's Fourteen Gentlemen from Harlem in to the Savoy Ballroom at 55th and Central with his own big band, at around the time when Clayton took the band to Shanghai, China, in 1934. "It might have been after the Erwing Brothers, couldn't have been at the same time," he said, and recalled that Karl George played first trumpet. As if to further confuse any potential for chronological clarity, he also remembered fronting the band at the Brown Sister's Little Harlem club in Watts when putative blues star T-Bone Walker first hit town also in 1934.

After that, I guess I just freelanced around town. I was with Floyd Ray's band in 1939, maybe 1940. This is before the Lincoln Theatre. The trumpet section was me, Lammar Wright Jr. [*his dad, big Lammar Wright, was with Cab Calloway*], *and a boy named Eddie "Goo-Goo" Hutchinson, helluva trumpet player. Everybody's dead but me. Lammar went to New York, him and Dexter Gordon, in that summertime. He got all mixed up in drugs and stuff. Lionel* [Hampton] *sent for Goo-Goo, but when he got with Lionel, that was a case of clique, clique, and he got cliqued out of the band. That's when Hamp took Ernie Royal on trumpet because his brother Marshal was the kingpin in that band. Goo-Goo died, drinking too much.*

Then I went to Philadelphia, also in 1940. That's where I met Bardu Ali. A friend of mine, used to work with me, named Vernon Isaac, he was in Philly. So while I was in Philly over at the musicians union, Bardu Ali walked in, looking for a trumpet player. I never was the type that talked too much, but Vernon informed him, "Here's a trumpet player, blah, blah." Anyway Bardu Ali took me; he liked me and we went to Atlantic City to the Paradise Club. At that time he had some powerful guys in the band. I was lucky to be even there. Bill Doggett was playing piano, Shadow Wilson was on drums, Pearl Bailey was in the show, Bill Bailey, the dancer, was there. I stayed all the summer of 1940 with them. The first trumpet player was Bobby Woodlen. He went on back to New York, and a boy named Joe Jordan, trumpet player, came in his place. I can't remember the others.

Bardu Ali, he was the front man for Chick Webb, so when Chick died, he and Ella [Fitzgerald] *got to arguing who was gonna take over the band. The management wanted Ella so Bardu went to Atlantic City and started his own band. I don't how long he'd been in Atlantic City when I joined the band. After that summer we went back to New York and Joe Jordan got me a job down in Greenwich Village, but I had to come back to Los Angeles for the draft so I stayed here. I went down on 3rd and Spring for the draft and saw all the guys at the desks. They asked me a lot of questions and then they sent me home. They put me in 4F, which I was glad. I didn't want to go* [to the Service]. *I got me a job out to Lockheed.*

In the meantime, there was a young man around here named Leroy "Snake" Whyte, who was a very good trumpet player and very good arranger. Snake had a band on the WPA [Works Progress Administration], *and all they did was play for the USO and places like that. So he said, "Monte, come on the band but you got to come to the WPA first." So I went out to Pasadena where they were building the Pasadena Freeway and I worked three days. Then I got transferred to the music project which Snake Whyte had* [Whyte was affiliated with the Federal Music Project of Southern California], *and we played all the USO shows and all the Army bases.*

Whyte's band performed on Christmas Eve, 1941, in Pershing Square for a National Defense Bonds fund-raiser and then played a nine-month sequence of dance jobs for the Army at Fort MacArthur and for the U.S. Navy in San Pedro from winter 1942 onward, as well as their regular engagements at the New Plantation Club in Watts. The *California Eagle* newspaper praised their "solid jive and original style of swing."

Snake was a very good person. He was his own destructive self. Anything Snake did to hurt anybody, it wouldn't be nobody but Snake. He wouldn't be trying to hurt you; alcohol did that. Apart from that he was one of the best arrangers in town. All he had to do was to straighten up, and I think he did make a complete turnaround later. Somebody said he was teaching in Ohio now. I don't know anybody that disliked Snake. That was a very good experience.

In the meantime, Bardu Ali came out to Los Angeles. I really don't know when we started at the Lincoln Theatre [23rd and Central]. *Probably 1942. In New York, he'd told me he was gonna start the Apollo Theatre type of thing out on the West Coast. So he had me get the band for him as he couldn't move in straightaway. When I first tried to get the band together, nobody wanted to be in the band. So I had part Mexican and part Black* [musicians], *but after we finally opened, it got to going good after Bardu* brought *Pigmeat* [Markham] *and Dusty* [Fletcher] *and the girls from New York. Then everybody's trying to get in the band.*

I was in charge of the band—it was "Bardu Ali's band under the direction of Monte Easter"—and after everybody came out from New York, Bardu said, "Let him go," and he just hired just the guys from New York and that went for a long time. I did the hiring and firing at his suggestion. We stayed down there quite a while. In the meantime, I think Bardu fired me [laughs], *but the union made him hire me back, but they wouldn't let me be the steward. Bardu fired me because it was my own fault. I would go off between shows and come back late.*

Our best band was when we had myself, Wendell Culley playing first trumpet, and Teddy Buckner. That was the best band, I would consider, because Teddy was terrific and Wendell Culley was a terrific first man and I was there! At one time we had Avery Parrish on piano for a while and Johnny Otis on drums. I don't know how long Johnny stayed there. Floyd Turnham was on alto, boy named Prince, who's dead now, on tenor. Melba Liston came in on trombone in 1942. These are the ones that I can just remember. Melba, she was good. Alice Young played piano too. She quit playing later, but she was good.

We stayed down there like a couple of years, and then [producer] *Leonard Reed came out here from New York. I knew him back there. We were in a place called Shepp's Playhouse* [204 E. First Street]*, and I don't know whether I went in with Leonard or Bardu* [Bardu Ali moved from the Lincoln Theatre to Shepp's Playhouse in late 1944]*, but what happened, Leonard needed a band. I got the band for him and I worked for him quite a while. Eddie Myart, from the Myart family, played piano. Shepp's Playhouse was a nightclub. On the second floor they had a cocktail lounge, and on the third floor, where we played, they had the lounge and the dancing. Eddie Heywood used to work in the cocktail lounge, with Emmett Berry playing good trumpet.*

When I came out of the Lincoln Theatre, that's when I went to San Diego. Frederick Brothers [booking agents] *sent me there. Took a four-piece band. We went down for two weeks and stayed, like, a year or two. I started at the Club Royal* [3rd and C Streets]*. They was crazy about the band there, and then Mr. O'Malley told me, "I got a man coming out from Chicago—which was* [ex-Earl Hines trumpeter] *Walter Fuller—and I'm gonna put him in Eddie's"* [2nd Avenue and C Street]*. So Walter went into Eddie's. This was in 1946. We was at the club that night—we'd been at the Club Royal for maybe six months and we was packin' them in there. Walter didn't do too good in Eddie's, so Mr. O'Malley said, "Monte, we gonna switch you down to Eddie's and let Walter come up here." Nobody in the band wanted to do that, but I went in and we stayed there a few years. Of course Walter stayed in Club Royal forever.*

In my band then, I had on trumpet me, Hubert Allen on tenor, a boy named Sonny Hurd on drums, Rosetta Andrews on piano. Just four pieces. It was a cocktail lounge. There was nothing but sailors and girls and vice squad during the war. They liked slow things, and then we'd play another like it. I wasn't singing blues back in those days; I was trying to sing like Louis. Songs like "Pretty Baby" and "I'm Sorry Baby," stuff like that, songs that I wrote myself. This was rhythm and blues.

Easter's story unfolded thereafter via a plethora of club engagements in and around Central Avenue, some short-lived, others for longer periods. There were recordings for labels like Sterling, Aladdin, Imperial, and Discovery, juke-box fodder in the main, local hits at best, often with Easter's vocals and those of singers like Mary de Pina and Judy Canova. He spoke about his record of *Weekend Blues*, which he made for DJ Hunter Hancock's Swingin' label in 1960. "That was the best record I ever had out. It got really popular here." It's evident from the number of prominent musicians who worked with him that Easter was able to offer them attractive and steady employment at a time when styles were changing fast. Even so, he felt compelled to seek Post Office work at some time in the 1940s.

Among other short-term episodes, Easter recalled a coast-to-coast broadcast on the "Blueberry Hill" program with bandleader Noble Sissle on CBS; a period with George Brown's big band, which played "every Sunday afternoon at the Elk's Auditorium"; and a job with vocalist Bob Parish at Club Alabam. "Strictly Café Society stuff but oh, he could sing. I used to be featured every night playing 'I Cover the Waterfront' on the radio."

Down Beat, January 1, 1945

Los Angeles—A new band, fronted by Bob Parrish, singer currently at Bar of Music, and directed by Bill Grey, is in rehearsal here. It's a 19-piece combo, all-Negro, personnel of which includes such well-known musicians as Sonny Graven, trombone; Arthur Dennis, sax; Ted Shirley, bass; and Monty [sic] Easter, trumpet.

Arrangements are by Grey and Margie Gibson, who do scores for most of the top bands. Band is set up with two pianos with Grey sharing "88" assignments with Johnny Shackleford. Barbara Talbot shares vocals with Parrish. Booking is being handled by Frederick Bros. Agency. A deal has been set for the band to open at a local spot this month.

Down Beat, February 1, 1945

Los Angeles—The new Bob Parrish band (Bill Grey—pianist and musical director) managed by CBS Producer Gordon Hughes (F.Sinatra show) and which now represents an investment of some $10,000 by backers, was set by Frederick Bros. to debut at the Club Alabam here Jan. 26. Following Ernie Fields . . .

Down Beat, February 15, 1945
  Los Angeles—Bob Parrish–Bill Grey band heading for eastern theatre dates at close of Club Alabam run.

Easter also remembered leading "a little five-piece" at Club Rainbow in Long Beach and broadcasting every night. "We'd come on the air with 'Somewhere Over the Rainbow.' That's a long time ago."

Me and Art Farmer, we worked together with Jay McShann. Late 1940s, I guess. That's when he came to the West Coast and he got a band together to go to 'Frisco to open in Blackshear's Café Society [1739 Fillmore Street; the club closed in 1949]. *I know I was on first trumpet and Art was playing trumpet. I knew Art was going to be great because he was great then. He went to New York and studied, polished up all that rough stuff. He was doing the same things then that he does now, but it's polished now. He was bebop then. All of them in the band was bebop guys, and they had a meeting in the room when we got off. They was arguing about who had the most soul, Dizzy Gillespie or Roy Eldridge, so they say, "Here comes Monte; let's ask Monte." So they asked me. I pulled out my little half-pint and took me a swig and I says, "Roy Eldridge," and they kicked me out of the room!*

In 1951, I went on tour with [ex-Jimmie Lunceford vocalist] *Dan Grissom and Linda Hopkins for Harold Oxley. He booked us. I had a good band for that with Jimmy Delaney on saxophone, myself, Harris Erwing on saxophone; Skeets Lundy, saxophone, used to be with Lloyd Price. At that time, Oxley had T-Bone Walker. The way he booked us was "Monte Easter, Dan Grissom, and Linda Hopkins," but T-Bone Walker was the star and Harold would tell people, "You can have T-Bone but you got to take Monte Easter." So we just followed him with that, so that's the way it was. We backed him. I liked the way T-Bone sings the blues better than anybody I know. He'd sing with a lot of soul, a lot of feeling.*

Then there was Jimmy Nolen. I went on tour with a guy called Jimmy Wilson [1923–1965], *he made a blues called "Tin Pan Alley," and in Tulsa, Oklahoma, that's where I picked Jimmy Nolen up, guitar player, who was with James Brown* [from 1965 until Nolen's death in 1983]. *I knew he was going to be terrific so I brought him back to Los Angeles. I had a little six-piece band out at Club Manchester with Jimmy. Redd Foxx had the show out there. Some gangsters owned it; a guy named Danny Prolia. He worked for Mickey Cohen at that time. They had a big old gangster back in the kitchen cooking. They were friends of mine.*

I was working at Little Harlem [118th Street and Palmerlee] *when Mr. and Mrs. Brown first brought T-Bone Walker out from Texas* [Walker settled in Los Angeles and began to work at Little Harlem in 1934]. *I had the band. She come to me one night and said she got a young man from Texas that could sing the blues. So she brought him out there and he used to keep that place packed. Clara Lewis, who was a very great pianist at that time; Hubert Allen on tenor; Earl Sims, alto player; Sonny Hurd on drums; and me. That was the band. They put on a little show and when T-Bone came, he was the show. He was the attraction; he drew all the people out. Originally, I went into Little Harlem and just took the door, and we built it up so much that she took the door away and said she was gonna pay us scale.*

I was one of the original members of Local 767 [formed in 1920]. *It was all right as far as I know. I was in it, off and on. I think most of the problems with the black union were mismanagement. That's the way I look at it now. I was one of the people, with Buddy* [Collette] *and all of them, when we wanted to go over to the white union. The oldies didn't want it. They'd never get you any work and the union nowadays don't get you no work. They were just the union because they had to have their own union. I could describe the place to you* [located at 1710 S. Central]. *Mr. Johnson was the president* [in 1930]; *then Mr.* [Ed] *Bailey took over and Leo Davis took over from him, but I was there with all of them. They all liked me and I liked them. That's the way it was. The old heads always thought they was better than the young 'uns. The guys that had been playing a long time, they figured they weren't gonna help you do nothing. I didn't realize what was really going on until I went to New York in '40, '42, and I found out that if you was a musician, then you was just a musician. There wasn't no such thing as who's the best or who's this or that. I realized then in Los Angeles they had classifications. They didn't do that in New York.*

I used to work with Kid Ory. First thing, he was a very fine fellow. We were good friends. I knew him, but I had never worked with him before. I guess he just liked me. Me and [alto saxophonist] *Luke Jones was in the band, at the Vince Maur Café, right near Jefferson, at 29th and Figueroa. Kid Ory had the band there; we was playing mostly swing style. I forget what we were playing, to tell the truth. You can look on the police records because it was known that me and Luke Jones got into a fight over there. This was during the war. There was some sailors, Marines, there. Hubert Allen was playing tenor, and he came out of the place that night when we got off. The guys was trying to make him take them to Long Beach, back to their base. I walked up and I asked what the problem was. I started trying to talk to them and they said, "Here's a smart 'un" and that started the fight. He's swinging at me and we got to fightin'.*

In a separate conversation, bassist Bernard Carrere told me, "When Kid Ory returned to music around the beginning of World War II, he invited me to join his band. I remember Buster Wilson on piano, Alton Redd on drums, guitarist Bud Scott, and trumpet man Monte Easter who preceded Mutt Carey. We played in 1942 or '43 for about nine months at a club on Whittier Boulevard in East LA."

I was always the bandleader because nobody would hire me [laughs]. *I never did work in small bands too much. I mostly played in bands where they played music* [manuscript]. *I usually was the first trumpet player. I always played the hard part. Music, that's all I ever done until 1945 when I went into the Post Office. I got tired of being drunk every night.* [Saxophonist] *Bill Green came out from Kansas City in 1947, Ernie Freeman, all of these guys worked with me. In fact, they used to help me. I was the first one to employ that boy, Eric Dolphy.*[4] *I'm the one that really started him out. I used to have a piano player named Ernie Crawford. He was a young fellow and he said, "I have a young friend that plays saxophone." I used to come over to the West Side at that time, and Eric was living over here so his momma said, "I'll let him play, but you gotta make sure he come back home." So that's how I got Eric. They used to put me off the bandstand every night for one hour and they would play their bops. Then after I'd get back on the bandstand, they'd play what I wanted them to play. I knew he was going to be great because he practiced all day, every day. He ended up in such a tragic thing.*

When you're young, you're always making tests. I used to go out to Glenn Wallach, one of the guys that started Capitol Records; he used to have a place there on Vine and Sunset, making test records all the time. He heard one of my things, and he recommended me to Eddie Messner and Leo Messner. They owned Aladdin Records. I had a little combo then. I always got a combo off and on. That's how I got with Aladdin. From Aladdin I just went from one to another. I don't know how I got accepted by Lew Chudd at Imperial, but I would think that was my best recordings because I had Ernie Freeman making all the arrangements. I had the Simon brothers in my band—that's Maurice and Freddie; they're very good musicians. Maurice is something else. I had a very good band then.

I never knew if the records were selling. I didn't get nothing out of it. They sent me a couple hundred dollars. Back in those days you didn't get no royalties. I tell you, I blew my first record session for Speciality. Mine didn't turn out as well as they should. Art Rupe told me, "Why don't you go back in the studio and make the records over?" and to use his studio band instead of my guys. I'm hard-headed, see; I'm with the guys, and I wouldn't do it. The first they put out, "Ain't You Glad," that got kinda popular back there. I put out records with Mary de Pina; she was from San Diego; she was terrific. Very pretty, very talented. She died of leukemia. Jessie Mae Robinson, she used to sing with me too. She was a very good singer, went on the Playboy circuit. I used to work at the Hollywood Mad House on North Cahuenga. Teddy Peters used to be very popular 'round here—she was the MC up there. I had a little combo there—I'd always carry about six pieces.

As I said, I studied with Lloyd Reese. That was in the forties. I went to the Los Angeles Conservatory. I went under Jimmy Stamp [1904–1985], trumpet player, later on. I don't know whether you know him. He was one of the greatest guys. I stayed under him. I started out with Doctor Heiner; he taught me the basic foundation. He was my first teacher. I would advise any young person that wants to be a musician to put that first and forget everything else. Lloyd Reese used to tell me, "Study your horn, get to be a good musician and then you can go get your women. Get good on your horn and you can do anything you want." I didn't do that. I got to women instead [Easter was reputedly married six times].

I wish I had really pursued music like Lloyd told me years ago and go to New York to Juilliard and study—I had the potential. I am good up to a point, but I'm not good like I could be if I had studied more. Let's put it this way, when I went to Philadelphia and Atlantic City, I would have a tendency to crack. I'd be playing a beautiful solo and I'd crack up. When I came back I said I better go study some more and find out how come I keep cracking up. I found out from Lloyd that I was breathing wrong. He taught me how to breathe. Lloyd was teaching me a whole lot about piano chords when he died. He had a ruptured appendix and they rushed him to hospital. They took it out, drained all that poison out of him, and he came home. They told him not to come home, but he came home anyway and he got real sick so they rushed him back, but it was too late. That's when I went to West Los Angeles and they assigned me to Jimmy Stamp.

We used to have a club here called the Ritz Club [operated by trumpeter Red Mack] *on Vernon and Central; all my friends, everyone, used to go down there and jam every night. I'd stay a while, but I never was the type that'd just stay there all night. See, everybody was tryin'. I like music, but I like my health too.*

In 1945, I was working at the Brass Rail [South Broadway]. *I stayed there about a couple of years. That's where* [dancer] *La Wanda Page got her start. She was Aunt Esther with Redd Foxx. And I just decided I was going into the Post Office because every night I'd go to work there, everybody wanted me to drink something, drinks here and there, and I'd say I want to stay on the qui vive so I kinda put the music down. I played on and off, but I wasn't really into it. My family, that had lots of bearing on my decision. I got six kids, all of them grown, all of them doing good. I got a grandson going out to Loyola, started this year. He was the player of the year from North California; they gave him a scholarship. The North played the South, and he was the most valuable player on the North side. We talking about basketball. His name is Rahim Harris* [Harris played 110 games for Loyola between 1990 and 1994].

I stayed in the Post Office about ten years and then I quit. Just playing a couple of nights a week. I went up to Montreal to my auntie's, and I was supposed to start working up there at Rockhead's Paradise. Back in those days, that was a very popular café. Vernon Isaac was the one who got me the job, but then the government stepped in. I couldn't work without a permit, so

I stayed there for a while, and that's when I stopped off in Kansas City on my way back [to LA]. *I got reacquainted with Jay* [McShann], *and I worked around Kansas City with Jay for a while. Then the gigs got scarce. Jay didn't work with nothin' but a trio anyway. He was just using me to give me something to do. He had Claude Williams on the violin; Paul* [Gunther] *played drums.*

So I went back to the Post Office. I went down there to mail a letter, and they had a big old sign saying they wanted some people to start work. My family were all still in Los Angeles. I was a clerk, and I stayed there for ten years. Every year I'd say I was coming home. Every time I'd come out at night and see all that snow, I'd say I was coming back to California, but I stayed there ten years. I would come out here on vacation, and then in '75 I finally said I'm coming back. I went to the conservatory in Kansas City, University of Missouri, Kansas City; I studied under a trumpet player named Bill Trumbauer. His dad, Frankie Trumbauer, used to have a big band in KC years and years ago. I can remember him when I was a kid. No gigs; all I did was practice and study and go to work at the Post Office.

When I first came back here, Chuck [Thomas], *who'd been working with me off and on for years, they were having a big party so I went over there and I saw everybody I hadn't seen for a long, long time. I joined the Clef Club and I started a band. I called it Kansas City Jazz. Bardu Ali used to kid me, "Here's a guy comes from Kansas City, didn't like Kansas City and he gets back to California and he starts his band, calls it the Kansas City Jazz." That's what I did because that's the way I felt.*

To tell you the truth, I just started singing the blues as soon as I came back from KC. Before then I never did try to sing the blues. I started writing blues when me and my first girlfriend broke up. I composed a lot of tunes. The biggest one I had was with Amos Milburn, "Ain't Nothin' Shaking" [Aladdin 3093, July 1951]. *I never did think much of my singing, but when I was in San Diego in the Club Royal, the man used to say, "I don't like your singing, but the ladies like it, and as long as the ladies like it, the men's gonna come around so we gonna keep it." And that's how come we stayed so long. I sing a different kind of blues. I got a lot of soul because I feel it, and the way I sing is not like everybody else. I found out that people like it. Like the other night at the club, they kept asking for "Wonderful World" and I sang it. I got so much applause, it surprised me. It goes to show you never know what people like.*

I'll tell you how I got the county marshal job. When I first came back to town, I had another wife and we got a divorce. I've been married a whole lot of times! I was talking to my lawyer, and I said I've got to get me some kind of work. I'm not making enough money playing music. He said I'm going to get you a job where you don't have to do nothing. He made a phone call downtown, and now I'm the LA County marshal's keeper.

The keeper's job required Easter to phone in daily to any one of five LA marshal's offices and to go as directed to business premises or domestic addresses to request payment against a court writ or to repossess a car due to nonpayment. He was usually accompanied by deputies and made a point of letting them handle difficult clients. Easter told me that two other local jazz musicians, the drummers Sam Joshua ("I met Sam way back in the thirties when we were in C. C. Caldwell's band at Shanghai Red's, San Pedro. Caldwell played guitar.") and Gene Washington, were also working for the county marshal's office. He had previously carried a gun but did not now do so. He also said that he often picked up music gigs while out on keeper jobs.

I did so many things wrong. Not pursuing the music. Not putting it first. I'm a good musician, and I could have been a much, much better musician if I'd pursued it. Then I look at the other side. I think of my children. Most every problem I ever had I brought on myself. Norman Bowden always says, "The thing about Monte, he always wanted to be on top." See, he never felt like that himself. If I'd followed my dad's advice—like going to Juilliard. That's how you meet people. Now, I'm not myself. See, I'm an outgoing person. I've got a very good wife, nice lady, but she doesn't understand. I've got this place here. I wanted to get young girls and boys and try to do something to help them. Make them some money with music and singing and dancing. I couldn't do that with her.

I'm about as happy as the next man, but I have those regrets. I look back on it, and it could have been so different, if I'd stayed in college. I still say I'm a very fortunate person. Anytime you ask anybody about Monte Easter, nobody will have anything hard to say about me. So, I'm all right, I guess. I had a heart attack about five years ago, and I haven't had any problems since then. I'm gonna carry on playing my horn 'til I die. Singing and playing. Play for kicks and just try to enjoy life. If I could just be myself, I would be happy.

To me, I like all kinds of music. Most of the guys I work with don't like all kinds. I like the raps; a lot of them don't like it. I don't care for bop, but I admire it. I wish I had studied long enough to be able to play that type of stuff, but since I don't, I have to do what I do best. I've always been what they call a stylist. I try to tell a story with my horn when I blow. I enjoy playing. I like the blues and I like jazz, conventional jazz, like Count Basie, stuff like that. I like Dixieland, but I have never played it too much. I could fall right into it if I had to. I don't see nothing wrong with it. I don't feel I'd fit in, but I could fit in if I'd learned some of the tunes. Most of the time over the years, if I get a group together, Chuck Thomas will be the person I try to get. Although he knows a lot of people, for some reason or another he and I have stuck together over the years. I'm crazy about his playing.

Did my friend Norman Bowden tell you how we started off together at the Club Alabam with a band called Fess White? We were the only two trumpets in the band. That was back in '31 before the Erwing Brothers. That was a nice experience. We did the job; a lot of other people was trying to get that job but me and Norman had it. He calls me "trumpeter" and I call him "trumpeter." Then there was Florence Hoskins and Her Troubadours; he didn't tell you about that, did he? She was the mother of Li'l Farina [Sunshine Sammy's playmate in the Our Gang films] *in the movies, and me and Norman was on trumpets in her band. I forget what year that was. There's been so many bands.*

Chapter Eleven

William King "Billy" Hadnott

Bass

For a period in the 1940s and 1950s, Billy Hadnott was one of the most sought-after bassists in Los Angeles, his grounding in Kansas City swing and conservatory training allowing him to fit comfortably into a great variety of musical situations. He played with the best musicians and recorded with some of the most prominent artists on the wider Central Avenue scene, moving easily from big bands to small group swing and R&B while performing at the highest level on the early Jazz at the Philharmonic concerts. He appeared on no less than twenty-one LA recording dates in 1947 alone and might have continued to tour and respond to calls for studio and sound-track sessions but for a stubborn desire to put his family first.

His decision to pursue a childhood interest in electronics and train as a technician brought him a settled life as an aviation industry employee and ensured that the family values he prized so much were kept uppermost. Thankfully for music fans, he continued to play, mostly locally, and it was in these circumstances that I was lucky enough to encounter him when I was staying with clarinetist Joe Darensbourg in 1979. Trombonist Roger Jamieson had hired Joe to play for a poolside Republican Party fund-raiser held at an upmarket property in the Hollywood hills. The other musicians in this rather lively pick-up group included trumpeter Mike DeLay, the marvelous guitarist Everett Barksdale, drummer Sylvester Rice, and Billy Hadnott. Billy told me then that he had spent twenty-two years with McDonnell Douglas and had received $12,000 as a settlement after he fell and broke his arm.

We met for the first of these interviews at Joe's house in Woodland Hills and continued briefly during the interval when we heard Billy play again, this time at Paul's Le Petit Montmartre restaurant in Burbank where he backed

Billy Hadnott, Los Angeles, 1993. Courtesy Bob Allen.

the rather intense but very gifted pianist Kenny Watts, a transplanted New Yorker. When I returned to Los Angeles in 1990, Roger and I sat down again with Billy when he welcomed us into his comfortable family home in Inglewood. His delight in recalling his formative influences and telling us about his experiences, in particular his association with Charlie Parker, made the whole interview process a joy. By then he was playing less, only taking occasional jobs with Nellie Lutcher or performing with local country and western bands among others. He was busy composing a trombone piece for Streamline Ewing when we called. "I have a lot of ideas, things I want to write. This is something I long to hear," he explained.

Billy struck me as a principled and thoughtful man who had achieved a great deal. His calling card spoke of a "Professional Discrete Service By A Musician Who Cares." What more he might have accomplished had he moved, say, to New York is a moot point. Whether he was entirely satisfied with the way his music career had turned out, I wasn't quite sure, but he was certainly proud of his family and the security that he had provided for them.

By the time we spoke again in 1995, Billy had retired. "I've got a pinched nerve in my back. The bass is just too heavy. I sold my instruments more than a year ago. I couldn't practice. I can't stand up, can't sit down. Can't walk long ways, either. My time is up—time to take it easy. I'm tired of it. I'm over eighty. That's time enough to quit."

Billy Hadnott was born in Port Arthur, Texas, on November 30, 1914. He died on December 1, 1999, in Los Angeles. He was eighty-five.

Billy Hadnott: Woodland Hills, October 18, 1979; Inglewood, August 24, 1990

My father's people was from around Beaumont, Texas, and my mother's people came from a little town further south called Caldwell, Texas. That's where my grandmother lived. I was raised an orphan; my daddy died when I was nine months old. My mother was sick and she was trying to raise us three kids plus two of my daddy's children by his first wife until her people— that's my youngest aunt, I should say—carried us to Oklahoma. To Tulsa. She and another of my aunts lived there.

Tulsa was a small town. I'd say it was about sixty-five or seventy thousand people then.[1] *We got there in 1917 when I wasn't quite three, and then in 1918, either the spring or the summer, my mother passed away. She had the influenza. In order for my aunts to work, my grandmother came up from Texas, and then she passed away in 1923. I was nine years old. She was really my friend but I caught hell. I grew up with an inferiority complex because I never got any affection as a child. I never had the proper clothes to go to school. I went barefoot in the summertime until I was fifteen years old. What shoes I had, I had to save them to wear on Sunday. Then when the frost* would fall, naturally, I'd have to wear shoes. I was mistreated as a child. They made a difference between the other kids and me.

I have always been a person that's inquisitive. I always want to know why certain things happen, just like any child. Back in them days, you didn't ask old people why; you didn't ask them nothing. You just did what they said else they'd knock hell out of you. I have friends that are still living, that I went to school with, they had mothers and fathers, and to me, they lived better than I did, but talking to them, they was catchin' hell too. That Depression was something else.

So I was raised there in Oklahoma and that's where I got my musical training, my foundation, at Booker T. Washington High School in Tulsa [1514 E. Zion St., established 1913]. I started music there. [Saxophonists] Earl Bostic and Hal Singer, [bassist] John Simmons, and Robert Lewis, the bass player that was in the Ernie Fields orchestra—that was the local band—we was all in high school at the same time. John Hope Franklin [1915–2009], the great historian, he was in the high school band when I was there.

I've always been interested in music. We were so poor we didn't have a piano, so I used to prop up cans and buckets and play drums. My first instrument was the bass drum, and that's where I started in the high school marching band. First I wanted to play the cornet, but back in those days, you had to buy a method book and a mouthpiece. They had the school furnish the horns and I got my thirty-five cents ready to buy the book, but the class was starting and I didn't want to be left out, so I started on the bass drum instead. The next semester I was on the snare drum, and just about 1930 or 1931, they got a violin teacher came there; he was well versed on the violin. He was quite an athlete and a tennis player; his name was Charles Graham and he started the string orchestra and teaching strings. He started me out on the bass. It was my idea.

All the other kids was getting the violins and the violas, and I took the bass violin. For one reason, I knew back in those days there was a transitional period going on, away from the tuba. I thought if I learn this son of a gun I would be able to get a job and get in the school big band. In my last semester at high school, in '34, I got a job washing dishes for $5 a week. There weren't many jobs then. I used to go downtown, six days a week, twelve hours a day, and I saved my money. I wasn't too far from the music store, Jenkins' Music Store, and every Saturday when I'd get off at six and the lady would pay me, I'd run about five or six blocks down to the music store when they was just fixing to close and I'd give the guy my $5. I worked a month. The down payment on the bass was $20—I think it cost about $115 in all—and I got that bass. As luck would have it, the guy that had the job before me, he begged the woman and she gave him his job back. But I had my bass by then. I was nineteen. Naturally, I had to get somebody to sign for me, but *none of my family would sign so I begged the guy. I told him I had a job and he let me have the bass.*

I started working at a little roadhouse out on the highway making seventy-five cents a night pay, but I was making $20 to $25 a week from tips. They called it Baby Moore's Orchestra. She was a girl singer out of Memphis; her husband, Shorty Moore, was the alto saxophone player. They'd been traveling on a carnival, one of them black shows. Oscar Clark was the drummer, and the piano player was named Art Bronson. He was out of Kansas City and he'd had a band.[2] Henry Grey was the little trumpet player, and they added me on bass. Henry had a brother, Hunter Grey, that played alto and his sisters played. They had a family band. I played jobs with other guys too, older musicians around there. Nobody could play a bass fiddle around there then but they wanted it. I couldn't play but I could hold it [the bass]! I had an ear—I thought anything I could hear I could play which I did.

I worked that job for about five months and I was beginning to get the wrinkles out of my belly. I'd bought me a suit and I was getting myself straight. Then in the last part of November '34, somebody came up and burned the place down and burnt up all the instruments including my bass. I went and told the guy at the music store what happened. I imagine he had insurance but he got kinda peeved, naturally. The drummer Roy Milton and Roy Randall—he was a piano player and he's a preacher now back there in Tulsa—they were working at another roadhouse about three miles down the highway. Called themselves The Melody Boys. We was doing more business than they was because Baby was quite an entertainer and we had a nice little group. She knew all the tunes. We had a kitty in there. You'd go down there and buy a set-up. Liquor wasn't legal then, but there was plenty of bootleg whiskey in Oklahoma. All them bad-shooters, Pretty Boy Floyd, all the bad guys, they used to come in there. They'd like to shoot up the top of the house. It was wild back in those days, but they didn't bother us.

Tulsa was a hillbilly town. All the bands used to come through there. They'd play the Dixie Hall dance hall. Then they had Berry's ballroom, run by a colored feller. He had a swimming pool and a dance hall out there. Only thing I can tell you about is the black part of town; everything in those days was segregated. Bob Wills and his Texas Playboys, they was on the air every day. They were big. They called it Western swing. They'd be copying Bennie Moten, playing "South" and all those Moten things. The Original Blue Devils was a band I remember, the band that Walter Page had, with Hot Lips Page, and Buster Smith, and Jimmy Rushing. Lester Young was with them too. Clyde Hart was playing piano. That was before Basie. Earl Hines would be playing on the radio about 10:30, 11 o'clock, and I made me a crystal set so I'd lay in bed and listen to him.

One of my biggest inspirations was when I heard Louis Armstrong in 1932. Oh man, that was the greatest inspiration. I went down there; it was at a place where they used to have ice skating [The El Torreon Ballroom?]. *He was fronting his own big band. That was one of the biggest thrills, and the next biggest was when Duke Ellington came to Tulsa in about 1932 or '33* [probably October 1933]. *On bass was* [Wellman] *Braud. This was the old band with Cootie Williams, Tricky Sam, Otto Hardwicke, Lawrence Brown, Ivie Anderson, that whole group. Fletcher Henderson came there in 1929 or '30* [probably January 1930], *and I remember slipping in to the dance. Of course, I didn't have no money. Fletcher had three trumpets and two trombones and he had four saxophones. Coleman Hawkins was with him then. Coleman was from up by St. Joseph, Missouri. I heard the older musicians talk about Coleman Hawkins and how he went to New York in the early twenties. These were the biggest thrills.*

This was back when Ernie Fields was the only band that was headquartered in Tulsa. Robert Lewis was one of the younger ones in his band. Luther West was on alto saxophone; Harrington Ham was on tenor; fellow by the name of Scotty was playing—he was around New York last time I saw him. He came to Oklahoma with the Ida Cox Show and he stopped here. Another guy by the name of Jeff Carrington was a trumpet player and Ernie himself played trombone and there was another guy played piano. His drummer man, I can't think of his name, [Eddie Nicholson] *he'd smoke anything, he'd drink anything. He was from back east, worked later on with Billie Holiday. He kept her fixed up, if you know what I mean. Back then we didn't know what marijuana was 'til he came there and we found out. You could go down on a creek bed and it would be growing wild.*

I stayed around Tulsa about two weeks after the fire; this was just before Christmas. I was down downtown one evening, at the pool hall on Greenwood and Archer; that's the main street in the colored part of town. That's where all the black businesses were. These two guys was going to Kansas City and I said, "Carry me with you." I had about $10 and they had $2 between them. They didn't do nothing but hobo. I imagine they'd been in prison. They said, "Yeah, you can go with us," so I went home and I put on my blue suit, turned it wrong side out, put on my bib overalls, put me an extra shirt and a couple of pairs of underwear underneath there, and we met up in the yard. All the colored people lived on that side of the tracks so it wasn't no problem getting to the railroad tracks. So that night, about 10:30, I went down and caught the freight train to Kansas City. I hoboed there. I'd already lived there in '28, went to school there.

In Kansas City, you could live off fifteen cents a day. Every club had gambling in the back room, open twenty-four hours. Every other door was some kind of joint with music, with whores on the street. I'd never seen anything like that. It was just wide open, man. I couldn't hardly sleep anyway, and for a couple of weeks I didn't have no place to stay. Then a friend of mine that I went to school with, Isaiah Griffin, I met him down on 18th one night. I told him I'd just got into town, didn't have any place to stay. He said, "Come on, stay with me." He was living right down on 18th and Paseo in a rooming house with a girlfriend, so I'd go up there and sleep with them. I'd slip up the back stairs, ease the window up, and crawl through the window, but I didn't know the landlady's room was on the back too and she heard me on these old rickety wooden stairs. So one night she caught me and she made me get out. I think she had a shotgun [laughs]. So after that I was staying around the pool halls and gambling places, sleeping on the pool tables for two or three days.

Every Sunday night, they gave a social upstairs at the Lincoln Hall on 18th and Vine. They had this young band there and they didn't have no bass. All kids, some from high school, some had just graduated, all around my age. Naturally with me being just turned twenty, I hung out with them. Gus Johnson was in the band on drums, Winston Williams was playing guitar, Freddie Culliver was playing saxophone, guy by the name of Pugh was a trumpeter, James [Lawrence] Keyes was the piano player, and Earl Jackson was on alto. Bill Maupins was the leader—he didn't play nothing—and Lillie Mae McFadden was the vocalist. Later on she was my first wife. Both of her brothers was dancing and she could dance too. She wanted to be in show business. We married and that lasted about nine months. Then I met my wife, Gwendolyn, the one that I'm married to now; I was courting her in Kansas City so that was it between me and Lillie Mae. She would go off with them shows, dancing, and I didn't like that. A woman in the band with a bunch of men! Well, the reason why me and Lillie separated, I just didn't like her runnin' around. She'd get a job, she'd go up to Saint Joe [St. Joseph, Missouri], dancing, and one time after I joined Jeter-Pillars, I saw her up in Cincinnati. That was the last time.

So I went up to the band and I said, "Man, I blow bass," and they said, "Go get your bass; we need a bass player," so I said, "I don't have no bass. I've just got into town." So Freddie Culliver, he asked me, "Where you stayin'?" and I said, "Man, I ain't stayin' no place," and he said, "Come on, go home with me," and he carried me home, and him and his mother treated me. I've never been treated that royal in all of my life. She had three boys at that time; the oldest one was in the hospital and he passed away in January 1935. I never will forget that. Lawrence, the middle one, was in CCC camp [Civilian Conservation Corps, a New Deal work relief program], so it was just me and Freddie. Every time they ate, I ate.

After about three or four weeks, we located a bass from a man had a three-string bass in his attic. He sold it to me for $15. Mrs. Culliver bought it and I paid her back $2, $3, at a time until I got it paid. Along about February, March, of 1935, Ida Cox was starting a road show so six pieces out of Bill Maupins's band went with her. That's Lillie Mae, Freddie Culliver, Gus Johnson, Earl Jackson, Winston Williams on guitar, me on bass, and the piano player was Jesse Crump, her regular pianist. He was left-handed. He was queer. There was a trumpet player too. I was with that group for about two or three weeks, and we got on the road down through Oklahoma, played all down through Kansas, little towns, then we played Topeka, Garden City, Wichita, down to Coffeyville, Kansas, right on the Oklahoma line. Back in those days, they had dust storms, and we were traveling in an old raggedy bus. Jack Skeet was the manager, and I think Fergusson Brothers was booking us.

I'd say Ida Cox was in her late forties or fifties then. She was the youngest of the [great] blues singers. There was Mamie Smith and Ma Rainey and they were much older than Ida. Of course, Ida made records and she was very, very popular. She was a wonderful person and a fabulous singer for colored audiences. Back in those little towns, there were very few colored people. You go out there and any kind of show will draw. They had comedy and dancing; she had four dancing girls, she had three boys dancing, and she had my wife, Lillie Mae McFadden as the vocalist—she had a lovely voice—and she had comedians. "Boll Weevil" was a black-face comedian. I never will forget one time we played out in Garden City, Kansas. Down in the theater they didn't have no water and Boll Weevil didn't have the cold cream or whatever it took to get that cork off. We had to go to the next town, and he still couldn't get that doggone stuff off.

That was the last part of an era of black men doing black face. Black-face comedians came from the minstrels. Back in those days, long years ago, the American white man wanted to see the black man at his worst so you got comedians and you got Stepin Fetchit[3] type comedy. That's what these kind of guys did but they were clever. It was just popular for them to do that. Now, they didn't crack no "nigger" jokes or anything like that. Boll Weevil didn't. He was funny; he'd tell down-home jokes and he'd do his little funny dance.

The show got down to Oklahoma City to the show ground, and Bennie Moten's band was there. [Moten bassist] *Walter Page decided he was going to stay home in Oklahoma City with his family. He didn't want to stay, but I think he was forced to stay. He'd been gone and he had three kids, I believe. So when he stayed home, Bennie Moten hired me. They took me in his band. There wasn't no other bass players around so they found me. Well, Lips knew me, Herschel knew me, and Rush* [Jimmy Rushing], *all the guys, said, "Get 'im."* I figured back in those days anything I heard I could play, but I couldn't really play with those guys in the Bennie Moten band, but they accepted me. I had learned a little, but I didn't read fast enough.

They had to come back to Kansas City to put me in the union. That was the nearest black union local. Bennie had a helluva band. That was fast company. It was the nucleus of Basie's first band. He was the piano player. Jo Jones was the drummer; Cliff McTier was the guitar player; then there was Dee Stewart, Hot Lips Page, and Joe Keyes on trumpets; and Dan

Minor, George Hunt—they called him "Rabbit"—on trombones. They put me with Joe Keyes as his roommate, but I wasn't glad to be with him. He wouldn't take no bath; he wouldn't brush his teeth. He would use a hard gum and rub out the dirt from his teeth and use it to rub all 'round his collar to take away the dirt. But there's a man who could pick up a piece of music and play his ass off. He was technical; he could read anything, but he stayed drunk all the time. He'd drink whiskey like a pig. He joined Fletcher Henderson's band in 1941, and he would hit those high notes just like that. He had strong chops, but put him near a barrel of whiskey in a nice ballroom on a Saturday night and he'd be stone drunk. Fletcher would fire him and then hire him back as nobody else could read those [difficult] first parts.

Sax players were Buster Smith, Herschel Evans, Jack Washington, and the fourth sax player [Tommy Douglas?] who could come in and just read the music right off. Bennie was playing the piano when there was two pianos. Bennie was usually manning the door. Basie played more or less when Bennie didn't want to play. He was the second pianist; he was a cog in the band. A lot of the arrangements were Basie's ideas. Basie couldn't write, but Eddie Durham, which had left the band and joined Jimmie Lunceford, he'd written a lot of things as did Buster Smith.

All the guys would work around the Sunset in Kansas City; that's Piney Brown's place. They'd go up there and work. Lips was always there, every time he was in town, like an extra job. Pha Terrell would sing and Rush would sing. Piney'd give 'em all $2½ a night and tips. He would hire two musicians, [pianist] Pete Johnson and Murl Johnson, the drummer, but by 10, 11 o'clock, all the musicians would be there; a lot of the big bands laying up, they'd be there jamming so he said, "Hell, I don't need no band," but Piney was good for musicians. A lot of musicians, entertainers too, he'd take care of them. Joe Turner, he used to take care of him. Joe Turner was working there too. He was tall and skinny then.

I'd be up there every night when Bennie's band was in town. Summer of '35. I found out that Walter Page—"Big 'Un," we called him—liked whiskey. See, that bootleg whiskey was forty cents a pint, twenty cents a half-pint, so I'd bring him a half-pint and ask him to let me play. When the intermission was due, I'd go sit up on the bandstand and wait. I knew they'd got to come back and he'd see me, so finally he would go away and I'd get to play. I learned to slide up and down the bass like Page, just by sitting there and watching him. I used to hang out with him for what I could get out of him.

Page was a great musician. He was playing tuba, bass fiddle, and baritone saxophone. He'd learned himself more or less, like most black musicians. They'd get in a band, just like [tenor saxophonist] Buddy Tate, who came out of Sherman, Texas. He'd played with Terrance "T" Holder until T went south with the money and they fired him. Buddy played in a lot of bands down there in Texas, like Troy Floyd, and when he joined Basie's band, he couldn't read no music, but he picked it up being the type of guy he is.

Walter Page's conception of rhythm, in my estimation, was terrific because back in those days, there wasn't anybody walking the bass. Al Morgan played good bass, only he was such a helluva showman, slapping and all that. Page could slap too, but what Page did do with the rhythm, the beat, had the bass moving all the time. They call it the Kansas City style.

So then we [the Moten band] started out. We played Topeka, Kansas; Wichita; jumped into Denver—this was the spring of '35—where we were going to be at the Rainbow Room for two weeks. Bennie didn't go with us; he stayed in Kansas City because he was going to have this operation. He had this tonsils problem and one of his very good friends [Dr. Hubert W. Bruce] operated on him [at Wheatley-Provident Hospital], and he cut something back in there and Bennie just bled to death on the operating table [on April 2, 1935]. He was healthy, but they couldn't stop the bleeding after they cut him up. Bennie passed about two weeks after I got in the band.

We finished in Denver, and we went back to Kansas City and we played the Coconut Grove there for about three months, still called the Bennie Moten band. Bus Moten played the accordion and directed the band. We had a show and everything, chorus girls. Bus was Bennie's nephew, not his brother. It was Bus Moten that wrote "South," but he didn't get the credit for it. It says Bennie Moten on the record. I learned a lot about Bus because I played with him after, but a lot of the guys in the band didn't want to play with him. The guys didn't care for Bus because he did have peculiar ways.

After Bennie died, later that summer, first thing Basie did was he went down to the radio station in Kansas City and got a job. He made about $15 playing organ for fifteen minutes every day. It might have been WDAF. That was a big station there. He was doing that as we was working out at the Coconut Grove. We worked out there for about three or four months, and when that job closed, there wasn't anything new. Jack Washington, the alto and baritone player, went to Oklahoma City; his wife was teaching school down there, in Boley. Herschel Evans came out to Los Angeles; his brother was living out here. Buster was still around Kansas City and Lips was there. After Basie quit the [Moten] band, they got Leslie Sheffield out of Oklahoma City. In the meantime, Basie went down to the Reno Club and got that job down there. He sent to Oklahoma City and he got Big Page to come back; Edward Hale, saxophone player—"Popeye" they call him—he came out to LA later; another guy named "Tatti," Carl Smith, trumpet player; and Mack Washington [Willie McWashington] who was Bennie's old drummer, they all went in the Reno with Basie and Slim Freeman, the guy that wrote "Until the Real Thing Comes Along" on tenor.

So Basie got the nucleus and they had this broadcast, I never will forget it, about 1 o'clock in the morning, W9XBY, and they also had a broadcast *just an hour before at Sunset. They was broadcasting every night. Here's the thing, the whole Bennie Moten band would go down there and play, especially be there for the broadcast. That's what John Hammond heard in Chicago. That's how he got Basie's band.*

What had happened after we closed out at the Coconut Grove, Buster Smith and the guys weren't doing anything so they'd go down there just to be on the broadcast—that's George Hunt and Dan Minor, all these guys. Basie would have them bring the whole band down. Enough hasn't been written about Buster Smith. He was one of the greatest musicians I've ever seen. He learned himself to play; he could play piano and he wrote tremendous arrangements. We called him "Professor" because the point is he was the most knowledgeable guy in the band. He was a brilliant man. What I didn't like about Prof was he was so technical to the extent where when he'd write an arrangement he'd write two beats [for the bass] *and I wanted to "walk," play four beats to the bar like Big Walter Page. Prof wouldn't want four beats, but back in those days, I was young and I wanted to improvise. Basie's* [later] *band was the only band that had a walking bass like that, an even four-four beat. I wanted to play like that.*

I'd played in the Reno, me and Gus Johnson and Earl Jackson, and Margaret Johnson[4] *played piano; that was Lester Young's heartbeat. Young girl, she played good piano, and her brother was named Roy Johnson, turned out to be a bass player. Then we worked a place called the Bar Le-Duc* [12th and Charlotte], *right across from the jailhouse, down on 5th and Main. Some gangsters ran it. They had a show there, and we had a white girl doing a strip and they had this fag doing a strip. He looked better than this white girl. She had a big old scar across her head where she'd been cut open, and I guess the poor girl needed the work. They made her get buck naked, and they had this faggot and he come out there with all the feathers and things around him. One night some guy grabbed him and boy, was he surprised!*

That was just before the election in '36, and they always pretended to clean up the town. They'd go around on them so-called raids. They raided this joint, and they let all the customers out the back door. The help, the cooks and the waiters, all the band, they carried us right across the street and they put us in jail. That's the only time I've ever been put in jail. They kept us in the holdover about an hour and a half. I had my head gassed. Back then it was popular among blacks, imitating the white feller. If a fly would have lit on my head, he would have slipped and broke his neck it was so slick. In that jail, it was hot, man; you had to sit on the floor and I was sweating. The judge said, "Boy, what's wrong with you?" See, when you gas your hair, they call it conk, man—it's some kinda preparation with lye in it—and you put that on your head and you comb it through. First you have to put plenty grease on you, rub that Vaseline down your skin, and you put the stuff on your head. When it start burnin', you got to be ready to get to that water to wash it out. It straightens your hair, makes you hair conk good [laughs]. And I had that stuff on my head, see.

In the meantime, I was working around Kansas City, just gigging here and there and I was hot. There wasn't no bass players doing nothin' then. Just Jack Johnson and maybe two or three other guys. Gene Ramey was going to Western College in Kansas City—he was playing; he came up from Texas—and Lowell Pointer was here. All of us was learning. After I left Ida Cox, she bought Winston Williams a bass, and he started to playing bass and that's how he got started. He stayed with her about three years. He's out here in LA now.

When Basie started his group, he sent and got Lester Young. Lester went up Minneapolis; he was living up there. So Basie got Lester, Jack Washington came back from Oklahoma, and Walter Page came. Well, Basie didn't like Dee Stewart so he took Joe Keyes and Carl Smith on trumpets; then he sent out to California and got Buck Clayton. [Agent] Joe Glaser had got Lips. Dee Stewart was left out, and he went down to the College Inn and he was working on a little job there, with Jesse Price.

After Basie left, Bus Moten carried the band into the Reno. I was with that band, me and Jesse; Odell West was playing tenor; Edward Hale, he was on alto; and an old boy around Kansas City, had both of his legs amputated, his name was Robert Hall, played trumpet. He used to be with Andy Kirk. We went into the Reno after Basie and then Dee went down to the College Inn. This guy, [Eddie] Spitz was his name, him and another went in together and they had opened the College Inn at 12th and Vine. That used to be the old Gaiety Theater, and they took it and made into a nightclub, right down the street from the Muehlebach Hotel. Dee got that job so we carried about seven pieces down there.

Actually it was Buster's band. I went in with Dee Stewart on trumpet; Jesse on drums; Edward Hale, Buster Smith, and Odell West on sax; and Bob Hall. Later on we sent for Fred Beckett. I don't know how we got Beckett, but boy, could he play. Beautiful tone, beautiful trombone player. Came originally from Tupelo, Mississippi. Very, very good, but he drank himself to death. Fred left Kansas City when Lionel [Hampton] was forming his band [1940] and he went out to California. For the piano player, we got a boy out of Denver; his name was John Reagor. We had a nice band. Then we had Emile Williams on piano, but he was used to working by himself so he quit. We stayed down there I don't know how long. That job paid $3 a night and we'd get $2½ at the Reno. The Sunset paid 2½—well, Pete Johnson got 2½; we got $2 a night. That's top salary but you workin' seven days a week.

After Emile quit, here's what happened. While we were in the Reno Club one night, I saw this guy coming in with this great big old overcoat on and it was Jay McShann. He came in—he's smiling, you know how friendly he is—and he came on 'round to the back of the bandstand. He didn't know nobody in there but me because we'd worked together in Oklahoma. He used to come over to Tulsa every summer. We had a little old band, Al Denny's band, and he used to play with us.

Jay was on his way to Omaha. He'd been living in Kansas, and then he got a job in Albuquerque, worked out there for a while. He had four hours layover on the bus and he heard about 12th Street so he decided to walk down 12th Street, saw the Reno Club, and he walked in. I'm back there playin' bass, so when we took a break, I introduced him, and I said, "Stay here, ain't nothin' there in Omaha; this is where the action is. Right here. Come on, stay with me." So he stayed. Me and Jesse, Popeye and West, we was rooming with a lady called Mrs. Walker. She was charging $5.50 a week for a room and we got a meal a day. She and her husband were sleeping in the dining room, and I was living up in the living room. At first me and Jesse were sleeping in the room; we had twin beds and if you know Jesse Price, rooming with him is just like rooming with a hurricane because man, he was loud; he was right out of Memphis and he would say anything at any time. Jay told me he didn't have much bread [money] so anyway, I told Mrs. Walker, when we eat, can he eat too, and I'll pay in for him. He stayed there and after about a week or two, he'd go 'round the joints and play, and there was a joint called Wolf's Buffet, down on 18th and Purcell, at the northwest corner, and he got a job working there. Joe Turner used to go down there and sing, and then he'd go up on 12th Street and sing up at Piney Brown's place.

So after Emile left we got McShann to come down there with us.[5] I didn't know he couldn't read! He's got an ear as big as this building, and anything he heard, classical or anything, he could play it. Now we had shows in there and these acts would come in, like adagio dancers, he would play for them, just beautiful. Hell, I thought he was reading because I couldn't do much reading myself and yet it sound good. When you playing a show, you depend on the piano player and he had never played no shows.

And then Buster left to join Claude Hopkins in New York, and West left and went down to Texas. He inherited a lot of property down there near Temple, Texas, so he went home, and that's when we sent for Bob Barfield. Buck Clayton or someone told Prof about Bob Barfield, saxophone player. He lived up in San Francisco and we sent for him. Him and Beckett, they was buddies. You talking about good buddies. They'd stay juiced up.

When Buster left, that's when Dee took over the band and we got Charlie Parker. He was about seventeen years old. We couldn't do nothing with Charlie Parker. He wasn't on hard stuff then—he just smoked pot—but Charlie always did have a head of his own. He came to work when he want to. I remember we were working in tuxedoes and he didn't have no tuxedo, so one of the dancers there, Joe Palmer from an act called Penny and Joe— he used to live out here in LA; he was working at a liquor store the last time I seen him—he gave him one of those old, full dress, frock-tail tuxedoes. Charlie would put on a shirt and he had on a waiter's plastic tie [laughs] and he was wearing gaiters and his pants was about this much too short, and wearing this coat which is too small for him, he'd lope across the floor with the saxophone under his arm. I can see him now. An hour late. He never came to work on time. Beckett looked at him and sniggered. That would upset Charlie so he started carrying a razor: "I'm gonna cut that feller." He never did cut him.

I remember one night it snowed, a good ankle deep, and I looked up and this colored woman, she come down there. It was Charlie Parker's mother. She was looking for him; now, mind you, his wife, he'd gotten her pregnant. She had the baby. This is the last part of '36, and she come looking for Charlie. He hadn't been home in about three weeks. He was shacking up with a girl used to be on the Ida Cox show. Dixie was a dancer, and she smoked pot and he smoked pot.

Back in them days, we knew all about pot. For ten cents you could get a joint as big as your finger. Being around Oklahoma, 'round them Indians, these guys out here in Los Angeles, they don't know how to cure their pot. What the Indians used to do, they'd dig it up, wait for it to go to seed, wash that root off, and then take a big thing of scalding hot water. You cut all them little hair roots off of it, you stick that root down in that hot water, and all that sap will run up into the leaves. I see the guys here, they just pull the leaves off and that ain't the way to do it. You take it out after that water cools, hang it up, separate the seeds from it and the leaves, and you talkin' about some strong stuff. That's the proper way to cure pot. Police in LA didn't know anything about no pot. I remember one time T-Bone was talking to me about it and it just brought the memory of how we used to stand on the corner in Kansas City and smoke it. You go in the Sunset and you get contact high from people sittin' in the corner smokin' pot. That's all we knew—we knew nothing about no heroin or cocaine.

Charlie didn't care about nothing but that horn. If he wanted to go someplace, he'd call a taxi and go, and when he do, if he's going to this house, he'd stop at another house and say, "Wait a minute" and he'd go in the front door and out the back door of the apartment building. He got beat up more times by those taxi drivers. He was a character. He had started saxophone then. In high school, he played the euphonium. He never did finish high school, and after he quit, he just picked up saxophone and he learned. When Basie started recording, Charlie bought all of Basie's records and he'd learn all of Lester's things, all his solos on the sax, all of Coleman Hawkins's. Every solo that he could learn, he was learning. You never seen a man want to know more chord changes.

In the summer of '37 or '38, he went up to the Ozarks, somebody got a gig up there,[6] and Charlie stayed up there all summer on that job, and when he came back, he was cooking, man. He was challenging everybody to come up here; he was playing. He was looking for every saxophone player in the United States. Anything he heard, he could play. Benny Carter came through there; well, Benny's so sedate, he didn't come down, but he had a bad alto player, his first alto man, and Charlie hung him up. Charlie would go down any band that come to town, looking for everybody. I guess you have to feel that way. That's the way I was when I went to Kansas City. I'd grab anybody's bass and say, "Let me play" even though I didn't know anything really!

Charlie was a natural. He was learning to read; he had a very brilliant mind. You could hear what he was trying to do. He was running all over the horn and running changes. He wasn't hard to play with; he was just hard to control. He was an exception. One night he came to work and he said, "Man, I know some stuff that's better than pot," and he began to tell me. See, back in them days, all the white shows like Earl Carroll's Vanities, George White's Scandals, all those big shows, they'd come to town and they played out at the Main Street Theatre [14th Street and Main Street]. They'd always have one or two black acts. They was stopping at the Street Hotel, so Charlie went by there and met 'em and they shot him up for the first time. He must have stayed high for three or four days. I guess it was heroin. From then on, that's all he thought about.

Buster Smith had been to New York and he came back. We worked at College Inn hardly over a year, and then he formed a band with Emile Williams on piano, Jesse Price on drums, I was on bass, Charlie and Edward Hale on altos, I forget now who else, and we went into a place called Lucille's Band Box on 18th Street. Lucille owned a restaurant and she owned the hotel. This was May '38. [Drummer] Jo Jones had been in St. Louis and he'd been talking to Jeter-Pillars[7] over there and they needed a bass player. Jimmy Blanton had worked with them, and he had just joined Fate Marable's band on the boat. The Plantation Club job was nine months long. Fate was working on the boat, and they would leave St. Louis and that job was six months long. Jimmy was making $40 to $45 a week and the job at the Plantation paid $25 a week, so they could make more money in six months and then come back at the end of the six months. Jo Jones told them to call me, so Pillars called me and I went over to St. Louis to join the band, and I stayed with that band two years.

I didn't hear Jimmy Blanton in person until about six months later. The boat would leave St. Louis and go down Fort Howe and they'd play all the way up to Pittsburgh; take 'em three months to get up there and three months to get back, playing excursions. By the time Jimmy come back to St. Louis, he hadn't spent no money because they was getting room and board on the boat, so he'd have six months to gig in St. Louis. I'm playing and I know there's nothing I could play in that band that sounded right at all. I'm hittin' and missin'.

I never heard nobody play bass like Blanton. He was a youngster, about two, three years younger[8] than me, and I said, "Ain't nobody younger than me can outplay me." I was arrogant and I was wrong. He was one of the most talented musicians ever. Music just flowed out of him. He had already studied the violin. He had been going to Tennessee State University. He was from a wonderful home; his people were wonderful people. Man, he bowed "Stardust," "Sophisticated Lady," everything. He could bow anything. There was a guy in the St. Louis Symphony that had a cork leg and Blanton used to tell me about him; he studied with him. Jimmy played so much bass, I just felt ashamed of myself. He stayed right down the street from where I was living, about a block away, and he invited me down, "Come on up, let's practice," so I went up there and this guy, he's studying the tenor clef and the treble clef on the bass! He was so far advanced.

To top it all, Cab Calloway came into St. Louis and Milton Hinton was with Cab. I went backstage and met him to see what he was doin' with that bass. He was an advanced bass player then. In between shows, he'd go way up in the top dressing room and he was practicing, practicing. He was another one practicing up in the tenor clef and so forth. It hurt me to my heart. I had tears. He said, "Do you really want to learn?" I'm there, cryin', and he said, "The first thing you do, do you know any bass teachers?" and I said no. I knew some black bass players here, but I don't know nobody could teach me, so he says, "You go down to the music store"—the big store was the St. Louis Music Company—"and you buy your method book." He told me to buy this book, the Simandl Bass Method from Germany. I bought it in 1938. I went through that book and I concentrated on things I can't touch now. I used to play all of these things.

In that Jeter-Pillars band, George Hudson was a good trumpeter and he later had a band. Madeline Green was the vocalist. Chester Lane was a helluva piano player and writer, but he never would leave St. Louis; just like he's with Teddy Buckner's band now and he's as stagnant as he can be, but he ain't gonna leave. His wife, she was singing, not with Pillars; she worked places mostly up in Springfield. She went up there for years and begged Chester to come up and get together to make an act. Wendell Atkins, little short fellow—we called him "Skins"—he was the drummer. We had Merle Tarrent, trumpet; John Orange, trombone; and there was Hayes Pillars, James Jeter, and Charles Pillars, saxophones; and another fellow by the name of Eugene Porter on saxophone—he was from Jackson, Mississippi, but he'd lived around New Orleans. He died out in San Diego where he'd been working with Walter Fuller, but he had been working before that with Don Redman and on the boat with Fate Marable. And when I got out here [LA] he was working with Benny Carter. Eugene Porter was an outstanding musician. Floyd Smith was in that band when I joined, and he was quite a guitarist, we thought. It was a good band, a club band. We made no records in my time. Jimmy Blanton made their recordings.

The Plantation Club didn't have air conditioning, so it'd get so hot they'd close up for three months. That's when we'd play one-nighters and club dances round St. Louis, go up to Cincinnati, play the Cotton Club, and we'd travel down through the South and back, and play day excursions on the boat. They had a boat that would leave out of St. Louis, go up to Alton, Illinois, twenty-six miles, and come back, and we'd play on that.

After two years to the day, we went back to Kansas City, the summer of '40. Tony and Jim Scarpelli owned the Plantation Club in St. Louis, and they opened up a club in Kansas City, way out, but business wasn't too hot. It lasted about two to three weeks; then mysteriously that place burned down. I missed going to work that night, but Wendell Atkins, he saved my bass. He took my bass out of the place because he said it was burnin', back there in the kitchen. The guy said, "You guys better get out of here." but they had time to get the racks and their music out of there. They was going back to St. Louis. I didn't go.

[Bandleader] Harlan Leonard came back to Kansas City from New York, and I knew all the guys in that band so I joined Harlan's band. That was around May '40. Winston [Williams] had been playing bass with them, so they wanted me and I joined them. I was glad to get back to Kansas City. I was with that band until March 13, 1941, when I was inducted. Jesse [Price] was on drums, Stanley Morgan was the guitar player, William Smith was the piano player, and there was another William Smith in the band, trumpet player. Winston did their first recording sessions. I think they recorded three times and I made the last two. Twelve sides [only six were released evidently]. *Myra Taylor on vocals.*

It was a good band and Harlan was quite a good leader, but he wasn't liked by most of the musicians in the band because of his attitude. He wasn't that great a musician when you took the paper away from him. When they wanted him to get up and direct the band, he couldn't do that. Ernie Williams was the director, and he didn't have any natural ability. What hurt me was Harlan putting his name on all the guys' arrangements, like those written by Tadd Dameron and James Ross. I had some original tunes in there, two or three of them, and he put his name on them and that isn't right. He's getting credit now he's a member of *ASCAP* [American Society of Composer, Authors and Publishers] *and he couldn't write. He couldn't blow his nose.*

Down Beat, April 1, 1942
    Draft Takes Many K.C. Musicians; Kansas City—The draft is hitting Kansas City musicians hard, particularly colored musicians. Already called to the colors include Henry Bridges, Charles Goodwin, William Hadnott, . . . et al.

I was inducted into the band of the [all-black] *9th Cavalry down at Fort Riley, Kansas. I played the alto horn; later I played the euphonium and the tuba. In '42, about September, they transferred the whole 9th Cavalry outfit, the Second Cavalry detachment, and the full Cavalry Brigade down to Fort Clark, Texas, way down about ten miles from the border. I was there about two weeks and they made me a staff sergeant and sent me on a cadre to form the 10th Cavalry band, me and another guy that was a regular Army sergeant. Sergeant Persiany. They made him a technical sergeant. At that time that was the highest rank you could get in the band. That was three* [stripes] *up and two down. Mine was three up and one down. They sent the two of us out here to California. Once the two outfits was together, we formed the 4th Cavalry Brigade, and then they split us up and they sent one down to the Mexican border, the 9th, and they sent the 10th out here, fifty-two miles east of San Diego. They needed a band for the 10th, and I was fortunate enough to be selected.*

The musicians they sent to us from the reception centers, they didn't have enough experience. We had to have guys who could function, so we came down here [to Los Angeles] *and we got those good musicians. We got some music; we got guys who were A-1, fixing to be drafted; and our general made some arrangements with the draft board down there, and we just took the guys straight on into the band. I gave them their recruit training. Marching in and all that sort of stuff. We got Bill Douglass, he's the treasurer of the union* [Local 47] *here; Elmer Fain, the union business agent now; Jake Porter, he's got a band around here; and* [trumpeter] *Loyal Walker. We got a whole band, a heckuva band. Lloyd Reese was quite a musician. I put him in the class of Benny Carter because he could play all the horns. He taught music; he had a studio. He was the same type of guy as Benny. Very, very astute and very knowledgeable. He was a staff sergeant under me. After we got here, Persiany went for officer training and he became an officer. Well, that promoted me to first sergeant* [three up, three down]. *I wasn't a musician like those LA guys were, but I got there before they did. I told them, "I don't want to be here and you don't want to be here, so the best thing we can do is work and do what we have to do because we got to be here. Make it as easy as possible," and we did. I made friends with all of them.*

I was discharged out in California. No choice about that. I got out of the Service, July 29, 1944. This was up at Santa Barbara. I'd been in the station hospital up there for six months. I had bronchial problems. My wife had been living in Los Angeles to be near me. She had an aunt out here. I got a medal and no, I didn't go overseas. Stayed three years and three months in the Service.

I came here to Los Angeles. Of course, I knew a few fellers already. My first job was down in Wilmington, California, with a fellow by the name of Winslow "Winnow" Allen in August '44. He had a group down there. I can't think of the name of the joint. Nellie Lutcher was the piano player; Sam Joshua was the drummer; and there was a saxophone player, Charles Waller, who I first met with a band [George Morrison] *that used to be in Denver, Colorado. Winslow Allen was a well-seasoned trumpet player. He was a lot older than me; he lived up towards Victorville.*

I bought me a '37 four-door Buick sedan. I was living on East 25th Street. We were fortunate enough to get a house over there, and I'd go by Nellie's—she lived at 43rd and Wordsworth; that's about a block this side of Central. I'd pick her up and we go straight out on Avalon all the way down to Wilmington. We'd work there 'til 12. Joint would close at 12 and then we'd go to Long Beach. They had an after-hours spot over there; that's Crip's, a colored guy running it, at Anaheim and California. Just a trio, we had a guitar player used to be the leader named Louis Speiginer. He's passed on. He used to get on the Red Car; he'd meet us down there. I made more money down there, I'm telling you. I'd come home with gallon jugs, one for quarters, one for pennies, one for nickels, one for dimes, and that's just all my change, not my bills.

So that's how I first met Nellie. She was working on her [original] *tunes then on little spiral nickel writing pads. She'd say, "Someday, Hadnott, I might be able to use these things." She'd be writing them down at the end of the show. I didn't pay her no mind. I didn't enjoy working with Nellie due to the fact that I'd heard the Nat King Cole Trio and I wanted to play with a guitar and a piano player, just like them. They used to broadcast those C. P. MacGregor transcriptions. We'd receive them in Kansas City, and man, I'd never heard anything like that, but Nellie just wanted me to play backgrounds. Every time I started playing four, she start stomping her foot.*

The Capitol, October 1944

Great Bassist With Illinois Jacquet Ork—Billy Hadnott, rated as one of the greatest bass players in the business before he entered the army, has returned to civilian life after three years in the cavalry and has joined Illinois Jacquet's band at the Swing Club. Hadnott hails from Kansas City.

Metronome, December 1944

Hollywood Periscope—Billy Hadnott's bass playing in Illinois Jacquet's combo is one of the group's big assets.

That spring of '45, Illinois Jacquet had asked me to join him up at the Swing Club, at Las Palmas and Hollywood Boulevard. I worked there about nine months. While I was there, I met Norman Granz. When I was in the hospital up at Santa Barbara, [disc jockey] Al Jarvis used to bring shows up there. About once a month. He'd bring the Andrews Sisters up there, Nat Cole's trio, and Frankie Laine used to come up. That's how I met Frankie; he was a good friend of Al. After I got out of the Service and I started working at the Swing Club, Frankie used to come by. Now back in those days, they were making a lot of pictures where they used a lot of dancers. Well, they came down the Swing Club too and I'd see those kids and they'd be dancing the Lindy Hop. Frankie used to come in, and he didn't know nobody but me. We were good friends, and we remained friends. One night he come in there, he wanted to sing and he sang and the bartender cut the PA system off. That didn't stop Frankie; man, he just kept on singing.

Norman had started out at the Trouville with jam sessions before I moved out here, and then he got this idea of giving these concerts, like they did the symphony concerts. He asked me to play with him down there, so I started playing on those things and they got bigger and bigger. He would present the program like they did the symphony. He had a list of the tunes; he sent for Coleman Hawkins, Lester Young—he was here—Willie Smith, and Lee Young was the drummer.

Down Beat, December 1, 1944

LA Bash Nets Neat Earning; Los Angeles—Boosted by numerous plugs from co-promoter Al Jarvis, the platter-chatter man, Norman Granz's third jazz concert at the Philharmonic Auditorium here Nov. 13 packed the 2,670-seat hall to capacity with ducats from $1 to $2. Despite the rainy evening and the competition from Hampton's band at the nearby Orpheum theater, the co-promoters pocketed a nice profit.

Biggest names on the program were Buddy Rich, Roy Eldridge and Shorty Cherock, though Illinois Jacquet, formerly with Cab Calloway and now fronting his own band here, is building a reputation fast. Others who took part were Barney Kessel, guitar; Chubby Jackson, bass; Flip Phillips, tenor; Duke Brooks, piano; Slim Gaillard, guitar; Red Callender, bass; Bob Ross, drums; Maxwell Davis, tenor; Russell Jacquet, trumpet; Louis Gonzales, guitar, and Billy Hadnott, bass.

Musicians were split into groups and staged a series of jam sessions. Biggest surprise was the unscheduled appearance of Frankie Laine, white, formerly of Cleveland who bobbed up in Hollywood a while back as an agent and on this occasion did some of the best blues singing heard here for quite a while.

Down Beat, December 15, 1944

Al Jarvis Using Live Talent Unit; Los Angeles—Al Jarvis, disc jockey, is using a "live" combo on his KFWB Saturday shows. The group, tagged the "Make Believe

Ballroom Four," in a mixed combo, supporting Frankie Laine, white blues singer discovered by Jarvis and is comprised of Winnie Beatty, piano; Slim Gaillard, guitar; Billy Hadnott, bass; and Ray Raymon, drums. Winnie is regarded by her local fans as the hottest gal 88-er discovery since Mary Lou Williams.

Jarvis is bankrolling the innovation out of his own take from his sponsors. He has used live talent before on his shows but, in such cases, instrumentalists have always been paid by the niteries in which they were playing.

Down Beat, March 15, 1944

Al Jarvis Airer Sets Jazz Group; Los Angeles—Now a permanent feature on the Al Jarvis "Make Believe Ballroom" program, Frankie Laine and a four-piece mixed group are drawing acclaim after 14 weeks on the popular west coast Saturday airer.

Featured are Laine's fine blues vocals, and the 88ing of Wini Beatty, "Slim" Gaillard's guitar, Billy Hadnott's bass and Ray Hutton's drums.

Despite their excellent air shots the group has found difficulty in club bookings because of the racial angle involved in the mixed group. Setup includes two colored and three ofays, and it will be interesting to find if this group can break though the Jim Crowism so strong out here.

Illinois had Russell Jacquet on trumpet, Arthur Dennis on baritone, Kenny Bryant was the piano player, Robert Ross was the drummer, and I was on bass. That made it six pieces; that's all we had. This was in the Swing Club [1710 Las Palmas Avenue, Hollywood]. When we first started out there, Teddy Bunn and the Spirits of Rhythm was working over the bar. Zutty [Singleton] was on drums, Teddy Bunn's on guitar, and I can't think of the other guys. They lasted there quite a while, and then Nellie brought a little group in there.

Charlie Parker came out here with Diz in December 1945, and they worked six weeks at Billy Berg's. I know Diz paid them all off, and the rest of the guys went on back to New York. Norman called me one morning and he says, "We're going to start [with JATP] *down in San Diego, go all the way up to Vancouver," and he was naming all the people going to be on the tour and he said Charlie Parker. This is about four to six weeks after Dizzy left. I thought he'd gone. Norman says Charlie's at the Downtown Hotel; that's down on First and San Pedro. So I called him down there, took Charlie about ten minutes to get to the phone. He say, "Hadnott, I'm sick." I say, "Sick? You don't have to stay down there; you can stay with me." It didn't dawn on me that the man's habit was down, plus he had got second-degree syphs. He got nickels and dimes and quarters all on his arms, all 'round his neck, in his tongue, in his mouth. If I'm lyin', I hope God'll kill me.*

So I got in my car and went down there and got him. Now we lived at 1479 E. 25th Street. We had two bedrooms, a living room, a bathroom, and a kitchen. After I looked at him and saw what condition he was in, I say, hell, I can't carry this man to my house, but I'd already promised him. So I carried him home. I told him, "Man, I'm going to try and get you in the hospital and get you medical attention." There used to be a county clinic up at 54th and Central upstairs, so I called them and said I got a friend that's very sick. He needs immediate medical attention and they say, "You got to have an appointment here. We only treat people by appointment." I say the man is sick and you got to do something for him. Then the doctor said bring him up, and I'm glad because I don't want him sleeping in my bed. They took Charlie in the minute they seen him. He had a scab, a hard scab, all the way up his arm. You ever see Billie Holiday's arm? She had a scab that ran all the way up there. Big hard scab where she stuck needles. That's why she wore them long gloves all the time. Well, that's the way Charlie was.

I didn't see him again until about nine, ten months later. They sent him out to Camarillo, and he stayed out there all this time. They dried him out, got rid of that disease, and he come out again. He was fat, he looked good, and he'd been eating regular. He came right back to me. He didn't know nobody but me, so he stayed there with me. Naturally, we knew him in Kansas City, so he was just like somebody in the family. So during the day Gwen would go in there, clean up his room, make up his bed, take the sheets off, wash them, and all that sort of stuff, and she looked underneath the bed in his sax case. Incidentally, he didn't have no clothes. Well, he had a suit in pawn and I got his suit out of pawn. $12.50. So she saw this jar in his sax case, looked like a cold cream jar, had all this white powder in it. And there was a spoon, there was a needle, and a rubber band you put around your arm. I was still working at the Swing Club. All the clubs would close at 12 midnight, but the after-hours spots—that's where he was playing—they'd open up at 1.

I'd get home around 12:30, didn't take me that long to drive. I didn't go 'round no after-hours clubs then because I didn't drink and I didn't smoke pot. These guys would come to my house and visit Charlie and they'd go in the bathroom. Well, this is a room right next to me, and one night they must have been in there about forty-five minutes, real quiet. Gwen said, "What are they doin'?" These two guys and Charlie, at 1 o'clock, they came out. Charlie grabbed his horn; he's loaded by then so after she found this coke, she asked me what it was. I said I didn't know what it was; it looked like baking soda, but I knew what it was.

So I waited on him one night. I stayed up and I talked to him. "Man, you gonna get me busted, you bring that stuff here. You welcome to stay here but you can't do that." He start cryin'. I never felt so sorry for a man in all my life. He told me he'd been in every federal institution in the country: he'd been down Fort Worth, he'd been down in Missouri, he'd been two or three places back east, and he'd been in Camarillo out here. He say, "Every time I *get out, they come around and they give it to me. You don't know what it means being a dope fiend. I'm a dope fiend and I can't help myself. My bones ache when I don't have it." That ain't no monkey on his back; he got a gorilla on his back, that's what he's carrying around. But he said, "I'll leave" and he left, and you know who he started staying with? There's twin fellers that come up here, one plays trumpet, the other plays bass; they were from Phoenix, Arizona* [Art and Addison Farmer]. *They were just about nineteen or twenty, and he was sleeping on their couches. Anyway I was glad to get rid of him. He stayed around here for a few months. Then I looked up and he was gone.*

After I got out of the Service, I studied seriously. I went out to Mr. Reinschagger's house. He'd been forty years with the New York Philharmonic. He lived in Universal City, about two blocks from Universal Studios. I was living at 55th and Central by then. I'd get on the U Car with my bass and go all the way downtown. There was an interchange down there, about 4th Street, and I'd change, get on the Red Car with my bass, and go all the way out, right down Sunset, like you going to the Valley, and get off at Universal City at Lancashire and then I'd walk about two, three blocks up with my bass and take my lesson. I was working with Illinois Jacquet then. I'd practice all day. An hour's practice does me no good. You got to live your instrument, fool with it all day long. I had started studying in Kansas City and I continued studying concert bass out here. I went to the conservatory here, and I got to be a member of the Los Angeles Symphony Club.

I played jobs around, with Benny Carter, and I did an awful lot of recording for Capitol. I knew Dave Dexter;[9] *he was the big shot at Capitol. I met Dave in Kansas City, and every black musician that come from Kansas City and got any recognition, they owe it to Dave Dexter. He was the one that got us in the polls. While I was working with Illinois, I was doing the Jazz at the Philharmonic* [JATP] *things for Norman Granz and I then went on a road tour with him, but I was so engrossed in my schooling that I quit Norman in St. Louis and came back to Los Angeles to continue in the conservatory.*

Billy Hadnott played bass for the all-star Down Beat Award-Winners concert held at Philharmonic Hall on Tuesday, January 28, 1946, organized by Norman Granz. The line-up was Dizzy Gillespie, Al Killian, trumpets; Charlie Parker, Willie Smith, Lester Young, Charlie Ventura, saxophones; Mel Powell, piano; Lee Young, drums; and vocalist Anita O'Day. Recordings were issued on Granz's Clef label as were later recordings from the JATP concert featuring Hadnott, held on April 22, 1946, at the Embassy Theatre also in Los Angeles. A further cross-country tour for JATP followed, featuring Young, Coleman Hawkins, and trumpeter Buck Clayton.

Billy appeared on eight of Nellie Lutcher's Capitol sessions between 1947 and 1957. He's present on many of her hit recordings, including "Hurry

On Down," "He's a Real Gone Guy," and "Fine Brown Frame." He also recorded for Capitol with singer-pianist Julia Lee, blues guitarist T-Bone Walker, vocalists Kay Starr and Kitty White, drummer-vocalist Jesse Price, and vibes star Red Norvo, from 1946 to 1949, as well as taking part in many other freelance sessions for smaller labels, often with prominent jazz stars.

I went on the road with Louis Jordan in '48, January 1948, replacing Dallas Bartley. In that band was Bill Doggett, piano; Aaron Izenhall on trumpet; Louis Jordan, of course; Ham Jackson, guitar; Chris Columbus in drums; and I was on bass, and we had a tenor player from Denver—he's dead now—Paul Quinichette. Paul left Los Angeles with Louis and Louis fired him in New York. Paul was a handsome cat, and he was fooling around with Peggy, the little vocalist, and Louis didn't like that. Louis caught him so he fired him. We used to laugh about that.

I stayed with Louis Jordan two years. I went with him for the simple reason that I had some tunes I wanted him to record. I'd written some things, but he didn't record them. After Paul left, he got Josh Jackson on saxophone, so me and Josh put this "School Days" thing together [recorded for Decca on April 28, 1949], *but we couldn't get credit for it on account it uses all these nursery rhymes and Aesop's Fables. Diz had a big record on that idea.*

Bill Doggett had recommended Hadnott to Jordan, the ill-at-ease Quinichette joining at the same time. Billy's periods with the Tympany Five included high-grossing theater bookings (often with the Will Mastin Trio and Sammy Davis Jr.), crossing the color line in 1949 to appear in Las Vegas, an appearance in the all-black movie *Look Out Sister*, the donning of "wild-colored clothing," and regular Decca recording sessions. He's present on Jordan's famous recording of "Saturday Night Fish Fry," an enduring hit for the altoist.

When Jordan temporarily disbanded early in 1950 due to exhaustion, Billy opted to stay put in Los Angeles and resume his busy studio schedule. Jordan used Billy again for recordings in 1957, and he briefly rejoined the band in 1974 for a truncated engagement at the Golden Nugget Casino in Sparks, Nevada.

So I came back here after two years and I said, "Hell, I'm going back to school," and I went into the engineering school. I went to Los Angeles City College and got an AA in radio engineering. TV was in its infancy then, and then in '51, after my daughter was born, I went out to McDonnell Douglas Aircraft and got a job. That's a hard transition to go back to school fifteen, twenty years later, but that's what I always wanted to do.

Thinking about my background, I said that my children would never come up the way I grew up. I know being on the road isn't conducive to raising a family. See, when you play music and you get with a band, you expect to travel. I used to leave and be gone maybe eight or nine months, maybe a year before I'd get back. That's not conducive to raising children. I decided I'd get a first class FCC license, with radar and telegraphy endorsements, and so I started work. I was still going to school. I started having a family. I'd got a job so I stopped my wife from working. We was buying a house, and I started working around [in music]. *I worked down in Sterling's, a place here in Santa Monica on Ocean Avenue, with Howlett Smith, little blind fellow. He put together this* Me and Bessie[10] *thing later on with* [vocalist] *Linda Hopkins. He was her* [piano] *accompanist and traveled around with her. He and I worked together for five years down there, and then I worked with other guys, just small groups, on the weekends. Recordings and so forth.*

Back in those days, I did a lot of records with [pianist] *Lloyd Glenn and T-Bone Walker, a lot of the blues singers. I'd met Lloyd before; he used to be with the Don Albert band out of San Antone. I loved T-Bone; he was a guy where the only harm that he ever done was to himself. He would actually give you the shirt off of his back if you ask him. I've seen T-Bone make so much money, and then he would just give it away. That's how T-Bone was. I never did work gigs with him, only recordings.*

I worked a little bit on Central, but I mostly worked in Hollywood. I worked at the Down Beat down there at 42nd and Central with [pianist] *Marl Young. He had a group down there. I worked with Lee Young—he had a group at the Down Beat—then across the street there was a place called the Last Word, and I worked over there, three or four of us. Nat Cole used to play there; he had the darndest trio. Oscar Moore, his guitar player, oh, he was a very arrogant, egotistical guy. He thought he was the greatest guitar player that ever lived. He was* good, *but Nat made him better because of the way he played behind him. I never did get involved with bebop. Teddy Edwards came out here with Ernie Fields, and he played all up and down Central Avenue. I wasn't part of that.*

Down Beat, September 18, 1958
  Hollywood—Reedman Bill Green took a group into Ollie Jackson's Club Intime with Marl Young, piano; Billy Hadnott, bass and Melvin Young, trumpet . . .

Down Beat, November 9, 1961
  Los Angeles—Billy Hadnott, bassist with Dizzy Gillespie's big band [sic], is working at Douglas Aircraft here and playing casual engagements evenings.

After I'd been with the company a long time, I went back to school again, to Pacific State [Pacific States University, 3450 Wilshire Blvd., Los Angeles] *to study electrical engineering. I don't know why I didn't go to study music, but I always wanted to be an electrical engineer from a kid on up. I stayed with that until 1973. Then I had an accident. I fell one day and broke my arm.*

Broke both bones. It was just a pure accident. I wasn't an electrical engineer; I was a technician. Senior electronic technician. I didn't have a degree, but I did that type of work. I was out a year and a half and then I went back in September '74. I was fifty-nine then so they retired me; I got a medical retirement. I was glad to get out of that place. Glad to get away from it. After I'd been there so long, I said I might as well stay to get a little retirement, such as it is, but I wasn't thinking about that when I broke my arm.

Since then, I've just been playing around here, playing jobs, haven't been doing any recordings. It's different now. All the while I was in the plant, I lost my technique. I didn't figure I'd ever lose it, but when you don't practice, boy, you lose it. I think I was at my best in the early fifties because I could read anything then, but if someone like [composer] *David Rose or Nelson Riddle would call me on a session now, I wouldn't accept it. I wouldn't do him credit and I wouldn't do myself credit. In order for me to get that down, I'd have to woodshed for six months, five or six hours a day. That's the way I used to practice. I was sharp, see.*

Billy Hadnott recorded with Howlett Smith in the mid-1960s [for Tunesmith] and with singer Banu Gibson and the World's Greatest Jazz Band in 1974 [for World Pacific]. In September 1971, he appeared at the prestigious Monterey Jazz Festival with the Jesse Price Blues Band and with Jay McShann's Kansas City Six in a set entitled "Kansas City Revisited," alongside blues vocalist Big Joe Turner and a host of old KC and St. Louis friends including pianist Chester Lane.

By the 1980s, Billy was playing three nights a week with pianist Kenny Watts's Jazz Troup at Paul's Le Petit Montmartre in Burbank. He was back to his propulsive best on what was probably his last recording date, with Johnny Otis and His Orchestra on their evocative *Spirit of the Black Territory Bands* album, cut in 1990 for Arhoolie Records, just before our second interview, with Streamline Ewing in the personnel.

I did three nights at the Vine St. Bar and Grill with Nellie Lutcher. We closed there on August 4, 1990. We just work when she works. We were down in New Orleans at the Hyatt Regency Hotel in December 1977, and she hasn't done too much of anything since then other than just playing a lot of small jobs around town. She won't work by herself. See, if she don't get $750 to 800 a night, she don't work. She's got a [apartment] *building over there, near where she lives, and ASCAP pay her. Capitol never paid her no royalties. She worked at the union* [Local 47] *for seventeen years, and I guess she gets a check for that.*

Nellie's very set in her ways. She has an act, music written; she's got a couple of hundred arrangements. All the things that she's recorded. She still uses all those. She's very interesting because she really can sing. She's very, very talented. She's such a perfectionist, that for fifteen years, Nellie wouldn't call me. I didn't want to be regimented. I've learned better now. She's one of my best friends.

I work out at Casey's now on Saturdays with Dan Snyder, the trombonist. Ted Higgins is the drummer, and we have Chester Lane on piano. Otherwise, I do casuals. I play with anybody. For instance, last night I worked with Bob Allen's traditional band. I gig with some guys; they call themselves the Big Boys. I don't fool with no rock; that's not my bag. It'll be four years this coming spring [1991] *since I left* [pianist] *Jim and Martha Hession's group. I had to leave Jim—he'd play such long sessions. I had a good rapport with them, but they worked the hell out of you. You worked five hours. The Lindy Hoppers would come in and people like Curtis Peagler and Buster Cooper came out there to jam and it would go on for hours. I'd be exhausted.*

Chapter Twelve

Norman "Norm" Leland Bowden

Trumpet

Norman Bowden hardly ever troubled the discographers or made it into the trade papers yet had a substantive and highly varied career that encompassed traveling big bands, Central Avenue clubs, and lengthy periods as a taxi-dance and show-band player. To be able to speak to him about his musical life and more to the point to hear him perform during my visits to Los Angeles was a great privilege for me. His welcome and that of his wife, Levetta, was warm, and his ability to recall long-forgotten musicians stretching back to the 1920s and their playing locations was quite remarkable.

Along the way, I heard him with the Backyard Swingers, a group of mostly retired musicians who met regularly and played in the late bassist George Mason's garden and then again in rather more impressive surroundings, when he appeared with the Teddy Buckner Reunion Band at the Los Angeles Classic Jazz Festival in 1995. It was clear that Norman was highly valued by his peers and that he was a soloist with something to say.

We have stayed in contact via mail and telephone ever since. Although he has not played in public since Labor Day 2007, Norman evidently enjoys the company of his family and is always happy to reminisce. Born in Canada in 1915, and having outlived all his musical contemporaries, he celebrated his ninety-ninth birthday on September 23, 2014, and continues to live on West 60th Street in Los Angeles with Levetta, his elder by four years. "The Lord's been good to me," he suggests and adds that they are "still having fun" after sixty-five years of marriage.

Chapter 12

Norman Bowden of Harlan Leonard and His Rockets, Los Angeles, 1942. Courtesy Norman Bowden.

Norman Bowden: Los Angeles, August 28, 1990; phone interviews in 2007, 2008, 2009, 2013, and 2014

The way I understand it, my grandparents on my father's side were originally from Virginia. For some reason they migrated to Nova Scotia. That's where my father was born. Born and raised in New Glasgow, Nova Scotia. His name was Norman too. So during the [first] *war time, somehow my father came to British Columbia. He was working. He knew all about the "mother country"* [UK]. *I used to hear him talk about the king and the prince of Wales when I was two or three years old. I remember the parades; those bagpipes were wailin'. Scotch soldiers hitting the drums on both sides. Right by my house.*

He served in France in World War I, and I have a picture of my father right here in the Canadian army uniform. He was a Canadian citizen, oh yes. I don't remember when he left for the war, but I do remember when he came back. All the time he was overseas, my mother used to constantly show me a picture of "your father." When the soldiers came back, they're all in a mess hall—this was 1918—all there drinkin' coffee, and I took one look and I could recognize him from the picture that my mother kept showing me.

My mother, Della, was the oldest of thirteen children. She was the type of person that was a go-getter and they all depended on her. She was originally from Texas, but she could see there was no future at that time for black people in Texas, so she got out and went all the way to Canada. From San Angelo, Texas, to Victoria, British Columbia. That's where she met my father. He was a bootblack in a saloon, working for some Scotch people. They ran a saloon downtown on Hughes Street. He was their porter. Sixty black families there at that time. Every Sunday the black families, we would all go to somebody's house. Everybody would have a get-together on Sundays. Our immediate neighbours were Irish and Englishmen and we got along real well. Oh yeah, we were very good friends.

If I went back now to where the boat comes in to the Empress Hotel [the Fairmont Empress Hotel on Government Street overlooks the Inner Harbour], *I think I could find my way back to where I lived on Fourth Street. The beauty of the waterfront is you can sit right there on the bench and look out over the ocean where the boat comes in. You go down Front Street and way down the hill to Fourth Street. I lived right on the corner. I've never been back, but I'd love to. I'd like my wife and family to see it.*

About the move to Los Angeles, that's kinda hard for me to say. My mother had got her mother and her baby sister up from Texas to take care of them in Canada. Then we all left and came to the States. This was December 22, 1921. My auntie and her mother came here first, my mother and I came second, and ten months or a year later, my father came last. We all came at different times. When my mother and I got here, her younger sister was already here and married and was established so we lived with them until we sorted ourselves.

I didn't see very much difference between Los Angeles and Victoria because everybody was English-speaking, but strange as it may seem, I'd never gone to school with black children before. This was a strange thing for me.

All my playmates in Victoria were Englishmen and Irishmen, see, and Scotch and a few Chinese. When I got here I was living in a strictly black community, so it was a different experience for me, but other than that I didn't experience any problems. Back then the black community was located between E. 9th, E. 10th, and E. 12th and Central, and 9th and Long Beach—that's way back north of here; we're at 60th West now. Lionel Hampton lived on E. 10th Street. The first school I went to was Nevin [Nevin Avenue Elementary School, 1569 E. 32nd St.]. *Grammar school. Then I went to McKinley Junior High School, which is called Calvary now. Then from Calvary I graduated and I went to Jefferson High School* [Thomas Jefferson High School, 1319 E. 41st].

I played the violin from the age of eight until the age of seventeen. My mother found me a teacher, and she gave me half an hour, might have been an hour at that time, for seventy-five cents. When I went to high school, I played violin in the orchestra, and that's when I started to learn the trumpet by going to what we call instrumental training. I studied out of books: I never had a private lesson on the trumpet in my life. My folks didn't have the money for lessons. It was Red Mack who taught me my first C scale in 1929. We played together in grade school. He was different, really unique, played with a whole lot of soul.

No one in the family played music. No one I know of, anyway. I can just remember at an early age going to theaters when they used to have vaudeville and the violin would play. It would just do something, give me a feeling inside of me, how you get filled up. It does something in your soul. That's what the violin music used to do to me, so I got after my mother to get me a violin and I studied it for a while. I played it up to high school, but then I got tired of being in bands where they drowned me out. I liked trumpet. That was the time when Louis Armstrong came here, for the first time. I used to sit all night long until he'd come on the radio at 12 o'clock at night. I stayed up to hear Louis Armstrong and that was the beginning of the trumpet for me. By that time I was maybe fifteen, sixteen years old.[1] *See, Frank Sebastian's Cotton Club, where black patrons didn't go, they had a nightly broadcast so you could hear everything. Every night they'd come on the air with the theme song, then came the announcement and the first tune . . .*

Before me at Jefferson High School, Marshal Royal and Caughey Roberts and Teddy Buckner had played in the band. Then along in my era came Dudley Brooks, Oscar Bradley, Austin McCoy, and me; that's the next group I can remember. John Ewing and I played together in that band, too. When Marshal and Teddy and Caughey were there, you couldn't play jazz in high school. That was a no-no. When we came along, we were the first group to get permission to play jazz on stage. We played Duke Ellington's "Rockin' in Rhythm" and the house came down. They just went mad. We were about ten pieces. I don't remember who was in charge of the band, could have been

Dudley Brooks; he was playing piano. His brother was a trumpet player, Alford Brooks, and he and I were the two trumpets. We had a white boy named Richard Sibley; he played trombone. Dick Sibley was crazy about Lawrence Brown. Oscar Bradley was the drummer, a very good one. That's all I can remember about the band.

The music teacher was a guy from Wales, John Davies, a helluva violin player. He was a man approximately sixty years old at the time, but he still played. He'd take a violin and make it sound like magic. Oh, he played. A wonderful teacher. I didn't get along with him too well because I was wanting to improvise and play jazz. He didn't like that. He'd tap me on the fingers and say, "That kind of music you play, you'll never amount to a thing; you'll never amount to nothing." He was always telling me that. He didn't want to let jazz into the school.

When I was growing up there were several good black bands around in Los Angeles. Ed Garland, "Montudie," had a band at a taxi-dance hall, the One-Eleven. His band was called the One-Eleven Band. I knew about them, but I didn't hear them play. He was still there at the time I was old enough to join the union [in 1934], but I never went to the dance hall. Then you had Dave Hendricks at the 401—he was like a local band, never went anywhere but always had a job. He was a saxophone player, not a very good one. I remember one of his trumpet players; his name was Rosanda Myers. Of course, Dave and I played together after those days in other bands. And then we had Buster Wilson. Paul Howard had a band at the Montmartre Café; that was a big job in Hollywood. That was the Quality Serenaders where George Orendorff came out of that band. Lawrence Brown was in that band too. Then we had the Les Hite band, which was the most successful of the larger bands. Before him there was Curtis Mosby. I used to listen to them on the radio. Those guys inspired me. I wanted to be like those guys.

I'll tell you who I heard before those guys. I heard the Sunnyland Jazz Band. This was in 1922 to 1924. That was a great band, one of the forerunners. Matter of fact, the drummer in that band, Ben Borders, invented the brushes that they use today. He used to use flyswatters on the snare drum. My mother was with the Eastern Star,[2] and they would give their affairs at the Rose Hill community and they would hire the Sunnyland Jazz Band to play for them. I would tag along with my mother to listen to the band. They had a good band, for that time. In those days, there wasn't any of that Michael Jackson–style showmanship. They used to sit down, flat-footed, and then just play, but the sound was good. Trumpeter James "King" Porter was in that band with a trombone player by the name of Ash Hardee. He would be like the Jack Teagarden or Lawrence Brown of his time. He and Porter didn't get along off the bandstand, but they could play good together. On the bandstand, they didn't speak. They used to sit right next to each other, and the leader Jesse Smith would call a tune and say, "We're gonna play 'Tiger

Rag,'" so Porter didn't hear him and he hollers all the way down the bandstand, "What's the tune we gonna play?" He won't ask Hardee yet he's sitting next to him. Ash used to come to work with a pistol in his trombone case. My wife, Levetta, didn't like Porter too much, but I got on fine with him.

At that time, there were only two black bands in Los Angeles, the Sunnyland and Harry Southard's Black and Tan. That's before Les Hite's time. By the time I met Harry Southard, he was a barber. He was cutting hair, and he was a businessman. He had a shop on Central Avenue. I never heard his band, but I knew about it. But the best big bands here were the white bands, people like Gus Arnheim at the Coconut Grove or Jimmy Grier at the Biltmore Hotel. Could we have gone to hear them? Oh, sure, all of them. I'd never encountered segregation in my life until I grew up and went south.

I never had that problem in Los Angeles at all. One time there was an incident when I was with the Orson Welles show. We went to some little town in California, and we were traveling by bus. So we stopped to find somewhere to eat. It was Zutty's band; Barney Bigard was in the band—Jimmie Noone had passed away and Barney had taken Jimmie's place—and I took Papa Mutt's place. Kid Ory had left. Anyway, we found this place and they told us they couldn't serve black people. We had to go out. It got back to Welles, and when he got through talking to management, we were welcome to sit back down and that was it. I don't know what he said or what they said to him. But they accepted us and we ate and went on our way. Orson Welles was one of the greatest human beings I ever met in my life. I don't think he had a treacherous bone in his body. He was a down-to-earth man.

The greatest inspirations to me to start to be a musician were Louis Armstrong and Duke Ellington. Those were my favorites. That's what I'd like to be like. Not just as musicians. Those guys had class; they were gentlemen. I ran across a lot of dogs in the music business, but these guys were human beings. They had something on the ball besides music. Of course, Duke had a little more formal education than Louis Armstrong. Louis had a lot of mother wit, but Duke Ellington was an educated man. He was a class man.

I heard a band from Detroit in 1930 called McKinney's Cotton Pickers. That's one of the greatest bands I ever heard in my life. They played a dance for black people at the Elks Hall on Central Avenue [4016 So. Central Ave.]. I was there. It was crowded. They had a drummer named Cuba Austin, a helluva drummer, and this guy used to have, like, a hillbilly's old coffee can and he'd make a drum break and put the spit right in the can! He was a showman, see. The Speed Webb band had been here in 1926 and [trombonist] Parker Berry came here with them, but I didn't see them then, but I went with Parker Berry's sister a little later on so I knew him and they used to talk about it. Webb went to a place in Pico to an open-air pavilion. That's where they played.

I got a horn for Christmas before the '31 year and played my first gig in June for an Italian neighbor of mine named Henry Salerno. He came and got me to play for his wedding, which I couldn't play anyway, but I had enough brains to go with some guys who could play. I got Oscar Bradley, "Big Six" [saxophonist Oliver Reeves], *Luke Jones, and a guitar player named Willie Johns. They were all older guys; they had professional experience. I played trumpet and violin. I was so bad on trumpet, they* made *me play the violin. I wanted to play the trumpet because it was my band, but I sound so bad, bad, bad! I could handle myself on the violin. I knew what I was doing. But on the trumpet . . .*

I was just determined that I was going to learn to play. When Louis Armstrong and different bands like Duke Ellington would come to town, I would always make a point to go to meet the trumpet players. I'd already heard them on records, but I wanted to meet them in person. I hung out with them daily and I asked questions. I used to take my horn along, and it paid off because I'd learn something from each and every one of them. They'd take a liking to me and they would tell me things. "How do you do this?" and one guy would say one thing and another guy would show me something else. Russell Smith, Pops Smith—he helped me quite a bit—and Snake Whyte, that was the guy that instilled the [necessary] *confidence in me. He just said, "You can do it. Get on!" I was sitting next to him in the band and he'd just kick me and say, "Get on!" He'd be playing like hell and I always had a pretty good ear and when he said that, I'd just start right with him, but I was kinda timid. He'd say, "Hit that. If you make a mistake, hit it loud. Go on, let's go."*

Snake was a trumpet player that didn't like other trumpet players but he liked me. He was good enough to compete with the other good guys and he knew it. He could read anything you put in front of him. He was a nice arranger, too. He'd make arrangements and liked to listen to bands playing his stuff. I couldn't even touch the other guys. "You can play better," that's what he used to tell me, and he just kept on until I kept improving and getting better self-confidence. Then they'd hand out some first parts to play and he'd make me play 'em.

Snake hit the bottle, but he was the kind of guy that couldn't handle it. Two or three drinks and he was shot to hell. That was all the time. Lester Young and I, we took him home one time at 2 o'clock in the morning, and when he got to his house he stumbled and took a swing at Lester because he thought Lester had knocked him down. Next morning, he'd forgotten everything about it. When Earl Hines was in Los Angeles for the session where he made "Jelly, Jelly" and "Falling for You" [Bluebird, December 2, 1940], *they called me to replace one of the trumpet players. I hung around the studio, went out to the liquor store, and Snake Whyte walked up and he made the records! I think he went to Washington, D.C., later.*

I was having a little problem with my reading, and Britt Woodman's father, William Woodman, would have me come with the book to his home and just help me by himself. He was very instrumental in showing me how to read this music. He worked with me, so I stayed on the job for a year. I should have been fired, but he stuck up for me. Helping each other, it's always been like that.

When I passed by the front of the Dunbar Hotel, they'd be hanging around talking. On my way back from school, [trumpeter] Claude Kennedy—he came from Houston—would say, "Where are you going to give somebody a headache with that horn?" When I was a twelve-year-old, I'd go and hear Andy Blakeney every Sunday at the Elks Hall for the matinee. He'd be playing "West End Blues" with Leon Herriford's band. When Louis came here the first time, he played with the Herriford band. A lot of musicians from New Orleans were already established here, but I didn't even know they were from New Orleans. I wasn't aware of their origin, but I knew all of them. Like, I played with Papa Mutt Carey when I was about sixteen or seventeen. He took me 'round with him. I'm a youngster coming in when he was going out. He's like sixty, but in his prime, I didn't know him [trumpeter Thomas "Mutt" Carey died in 1948; he was fifty-seven].

I continued to play, but at the beginning my ambition was to be a professional baseball player. That was my thing, but during those days black people weren't allowed into anything. We had these old Negro leagues, and they weren't making any money, so when I started hanging around with musicians, I finally got away from baseball. By hanging around with musicians and with determination, I began to improve a lot and one thing would lead to another. A guy would give me a job and then someone else would. I had met Monte Easter in 1932. He was walking down the street with his horn, going in one direction, and I was coming down the street with my horn the opposite way, so we quite naturally introduced ourselves to each other. Although we were both students at Jefferson, we didn't really talk to each other up to then.

I decided to be a professional musician while I was in high school. When I left school in '33, I went to play with Florence Hoskins and her Troubadours with Monte. Didn't come to anything but rehearsals. We were kids. Hoskins's claim to fame was she had a son in the movies, in the Our Gang comedies [Allen "Farina" Hoskins (1922–1931)]. We thought by her son being famous, she had connections, but it never came to anything.

Another guy I should tell you about was J. T. Gipson. He was the same age as me, but he was way ahead of us on trumpet. He couldn't read a note, but he could play every Louis Armstrong solo. He became tubercular at a young age in his twenties, so he started writing for Negro newspapers. He was very aggressive, into everything. He'd crash a party, hang in for a while, and get away with it!

Then I got with Reb Spikes and we went on the road. That's the first band I left home with. I'd gone to San Diego with Peppy Prince a year before, but I went there and came right back. With Reb, we went up to the Northwest. Montana, Idaho, Utah. Did a whole lot of one-nighters. Boise, Idaho, was our base. I'd never been that far before. That was in 1935. Austin McCoy was playing piano; Alford Brooks was the other trumpet player; Leslie Bisco was playing trombone. The guitar player was named Ernest—I can't remember his last name—he didn't go very far; he dropped out pretty early. We had a saxophone player from Detroit; his name was Bob Rousette [or Rousseau]. He was a very good arranger, and it was his book that we would play, which was a very interesting book. There was a lot of McKinney's Cotton Pickers arrangements in there. I don't know how he got them, but he had them, so we were playing all Cotton Pickers stuff in this band.

Reb was a saxophone player. He wasn't such a great saxophone player, but he was a pretty good businessman. He wrote this tune "Someday Sweetheart," and that sent him straight to the top. That was his chief claim to fame. He wasn't playing at all with us, but he knew how to handle the money. I didn't get very much of it [laughs]. I got a little bit but not very much. We were kids. He got the bulk of the money. In fact, it wasn't a helluva lot for anybody, but he wasn't lacking; he did all right for himself. His brother Johnny Spikes was a good trumpet player, but he ended up being a wonderful music teacher. People like Lloyd Reese, all the trumpet players that came along, took lessons from Johnny Spikes. He taught me. They had a music store at 12th and Central, and these fellows went down there and he taught them how to play.

I don't remember Reb being active in the union [Local 767 AFM]. It was Leo McCoy Davis who got me in the union in 1934. He was a saxophone player. He had been to Australia with Sonny Clay's band in 1928. He was helping me as a youngster too. He worked with me to show me how to read music. He heard me play around here as a kid, and he said, "Look, you got a good tone; why shouldn't you learn how to read? You got good potential. Come on, I'll teach you how to read." If I heard something, I could play it, but if you put the music up there . . . ! He had me come by his house and just worked with me. He had a band; matter of fact it was Sonny Clay's band, and he wrote the arrangements for the band, so naturally he wanted them well played. I had the sound, but I couldn't play 'em. I was in that band with Monte, playing at Jack Johnson's place on Central Avenue. We had guys like Jim Wynn and my school friend Rodger Hurd on saxophones. I was maybe seventeen years old then.

Then I was at the Danceland taxi dance [between 2nd and 3rd on Main Street] for over a year; that was with Atwell Rose. He was a violin player. He sat in the center with us, but he was the leader. That was 1936. William Woodman was in the band, Fletcher Smith was on piano, Everett Walsh on drums. As for bass players, well, we had two. Bill Boles was there when I came in the band, and then it was Bert Holiday. He quit music altogether. He was the first black highway patrolman on a motorcycle out at Laredo. They thought he was Indian so he got the job. Leo Davis was on alto saxophone and Leonard Davidson—we called him "Big Boy"—he was on tenor. That was the band. Yes, that was a good band. I replaced Rosanda Myers.

At the Danceland, I could tell you what time of night it was by the song we were playing. We always played the same tune at ten minutes after 11. I knew when it was almost time to go home by what song we played. I was making 18 bucks a week. That was the Depression time. I had just got married for the first time, January 14, 1936. We both worked and there was no kids from that marriage. Wasn't no one to feed but she and I.

There was anywhere from seven to ten taxi-dance halls in Los Angles then, and they all had black bands. Lorenzo Flennoy was at the Rose Room, and the Erwing Brothers was at the Palmorena; that's on 6th and Main next to the Burbank Theater upstairs. The latter part of '36 and '37, I was with the Erwing brothers. Lionel Hampton was just getting started then. He had the band across the street from the taxi-dance hall. Krupa and Benny Goodman used to come and sit in with Lionel, and that's where they first heard him, and that's when Lionel left his band to go with Benny Goodman [1936].

In that band I was with Monte Easter, Chief Moore was on trombone— he's the one who got me in the band—and we had a bass player by the name of Edgar Mason. The saxophones were Rodger Hurd, Harris Erwing, and Arthur Dennis. We had a trumpet player named Calvin Temple, and Horace Moore was the drummer. It was the Erwing Brothers band, about ten pieces and there were three brothers—Harris, Dorchester, and James. To be sitting next to guys you'd heard on record, that was a big thing to me. And getting paid! To a great extent they were carrying me. They were pros. They knew what they were doing—I was just learning. I was a novice.

In the taxi dance, you had about twenty hired girls, so the guy pays and he chooses the girl he wants to dance with. Then he goes buy a ticket. Like the song says, "Ten Cents a Dance." You give the girl the ticket and she dances with you. The taxi dances were pretty popular. I'd say about three of the whole ten was all Filipinos. White girls, Filipino men, and a black band. You had a chance to solo, but they were mostly written. In other words, you had a book to play. There wasn't any improvising. You had to play the music. You turned the pages. Not like a jam session; you couldn't come in and just start hollering like a hot trumpet player. It wasn't like that. Two choruses: saxophones turn the first chorus; I'm playing the second, and when you turn the book over, it's backwards forward. In other words, whoever leads off, the saxophones play the last chorus on this one, the brass would play the first on the next tune. Backward and forward. Sometimes there wasn't no last chorus because it only lasts two choruses. You were doing the same thing every night. I thought it was great. I thought I was fortunate to have a job. There were better trumpet players than me and they didn't have a job.

The Erwing Brothers was a pretty good territory band. They never worked out of Los Angeles. They didn't go anywhere. On a Sunday afternoon, they'd pack the Elks on Central Avenue. Everybody played there: Les Hite, McKinney's Cotton Pickers, Duke, Cab Calloway; they all played the Elks. The first time Cab came to Los Angeles—that was in 1936—they played the Elks. They played the Cotton Club, and then they played a dance for the black people at the Elks. You couldn't get in there. Lammar Wright, Doc Cheatham, Pops Smith, I knew all those guys in that band.

I left here with band called Jimmy Gibbons on 10th October 1938 and I was gone until 4th February 1940. A little, jumped-up band. I was traveling the whole year of 1939. I was on the road on tour. We got down to Houston, Texas, and things were pretty bad, and a road band came through there called Jimmy Westbrook's—a little band out of Waco, Texas—and Parker Berry, Harold Scott, and I, the three of us that was the brass section of the Jimmy Gibbons band, we bolted. We all left and went with Jimmy Westbrook as a unit.

Jimmy Gibbons, I would call him a sell-out bum. He was a guy with a lot of guts and a nerve. A personality. No musical ability at all. He wasn't an instrumentalist—he didn't play any music but he had an ego. He wanted to be a Cab Calloway type—he'd dress up in white tails and be directing, then do a little dance. He had a lot of nerve. He'd walk into a town, announce himself, with no money, and the next thing you know, he'd be in a big café and have the man feed the whole band on credit and the man never got no money. This guy was a pistol. He was the best con man I ever met in my life.

We were in Great Bend, Kansas, hungry, broke, and Jimmy Gibbons talked to this guy that had a diner. We all waiting outside, hungry as kids, and he says, "Come on in; quit being so beggaring and sit down." We all go sit down and we eat, so I guess he told the guy that after we played the show, he'd pay the bill. We played the show, and there were more people on the bandstand than there were in the theater so no bread, see. So after we all got through eating, we getting ready to leave town. The guy that runs the café, he was a character too; he's nicknamed "Whisper" because he never spoke above a whisper. Jimmy comes in and says, "Whisper, I would like to speak to you a minute," so he took Whisper in the back of the diner and they were conversing. I heard Whisper say, loud this time, "Damn that, man. I need to have my money," and he didn't get a dime. We left there, owing that man. The next town, the same thing. Another time, we broke down in St. Louis, no transportation; he's gone a couple of hours and comes back with two automobiles for us to leave in. Two brand new cars. We're gone; the guy never gets his money.

Jimmy Gibbons was originally from Seattle, and he came out here [LA] and organized this band and we all went with him. The Jimmie Lunceford band was very popular, and we'd all be standing in front of the Dunbar Hotel and he'd walk up to Jimmie and tell him, "Ah, Jesus Christ, my band, we'll blow you to pieces. You can't play no music." That's what he's telling Jimmie Lunceford. He was that kind of guy. We were raggedy—we didn't even belong in the same place as Jimmie Lunceford! So he gets this band and takes us all over the country. We starved to death. We didn't make no money.

At the time I was out of work and so was Parker Berry. He had just left Les Hite. He wasn't doing anything, and this guy is painting a picture and he's offering you a salary. The trumpets was Pee Wee Brice—that's Bernice Brice—Harold Scott, and I; Parker Berry was on trombone with Leslie Bisco. That was the brass section. Saxophones was Dave Hendricks, a guy named Alfonso George, and a good tenor from Sacramento named Bob White. He could play. Piano player was Leslie Franklin. He kinda had a nervous breakdown behind a woman and he moved off. Very good piano player too, unknown, but he could play. There wasn't anybody else in that band of renown; they were local guys.

Jimmy Westbrook had been in Honolulu working with a guy called Dizzy Derricott and with Happy Johnson. A bunch of guys from here had gone to Honolulu to work at the Royal Palms Hotel. Dizzy Derricott, from Louisiana, was very eccentric, a real character. He stayed here [LA] quite a while, maybe five or six years. He had two rows of teeth, looked like an alligator. Westbrook was a steel guitar player and a drummer. He conned me to leave Gibbons to go with him so I did. Well, somehow, I don't know what happened, but Jimmy Westbrook fired me in Ville Platte, Louisiana. He gives me that two weeks' notice, and when that was up, we were in Shreveport, Louisiana. We came through Shreveport about 3 o'clock in the morning, so he let me out of the bus then. I'm standing there thinking, "I'm through; that's the end of me."

I'm out in Shreveport, don't know a soul; I got my horn in my little suitcase, and I see a sign, "Big Dance, Friday Night. Boots and His Buddies." Charlie Anderson had been in Los Angeles to play with Willie Bryant and the Ethel Waters Show. He and Harold Scott were buddies, so Harold had introduced me to him. So it comes to me I know this guy and he's in this band so I go by. It's about 3 o'clock in the morning. Some guy comes down the street from eating at one of those all-night cafés and I ask where the band is staying on Wilton Street. They were staying right around the corner. I go 'round to this rooming house, and the guys had been playing a gig and they had just got off around 2, so they were still up. So here I come and I ask for Charlie Anderson. I didn't know nobody in the band but him, and when he sees me he says, "Jesus, this is my buddy from California. Norman, what you doin'?" He told me Thaddeus Gilders had just walked out—he had a death in *his family—like an hour or so ago and was going home to Texas so there was a trumpet chair open.*

I walked in as this guy walked out. Charlie told Bumps to hire me: "Don't worry; he can play." McHenry, the bass player, said, "Boots, you don't know nothing about this man. He might not be able to play 'Yankee Doodle.' Make him play." So at 3 o'clock in the morning, I take out my horn and blow some variations just for this guy's approval. Now I don't like this guy, but in two weeks he's my best buddy. Of course, Charlie and I always were buddies. That's how I got with Boots. I had about fifty cents in my pocket.

I stayed there with Boots about a couple of years.[3] *From Shreveport to Los Angeles—that's a pretty tough walk! Jimmy Westbrook sees me about six months later with Boots and we're doing good, and he tries to bribe me to come back. Well, no way. First thing, Boots had a much better band and a better organization than this guy did. That was out. Boots was a nice person but a little on the lazy side. Not very much initiative, not much of a go-getter. He could sleep all day long.*

I can remember we were in Houston. We had played a few dates, but we weren't working at the time. Boots's room was right next to mine, and there was a fellow by the name of Dupree who was opening a club called the Eldorado Ballroom in Houston so he comes to talk to Boots. He wants to hire the band to open up the ballroom. He's knocking on Boots's door, and I can hear the man; he wants to talk to Boots, and Boots is telling the man he's asleep and to come back later. He don't want to talk to the man, and I'm so damn mad, I get up. I say, "Damn it, Boots. Get up out of the bed; go talk to the man. I got no money, no job." So I finally make Boots go talk to the man and he hires us. We got the job. We stay there for two or three weeks. He's got fourteen guys depending on him and he's telling the man to come back later! We would have had nothing.

I got Al Hibbler for the band.[4] *He was stranded in Memphis. On a Sunday afternoon, we had a little session going down at the Church Park Assembly Hall about five blocks from where we lived. I'm going down there to meet the guys and see what's going on. It's a local band named Doug Jenkins, a Memphis band, that's playing there. Hibbler's singing "Trees," and I was fascinated. I get up and go along to get Boots. "I want you to hear this singer, man. Come now." And he lays on the bed and he don't want to get up. This is 4 o'clock in the afternoon. So I keep insisting until he gets up and puts his clothes on and he comes to hear the guy. "Jesus Christ, man, you want go with us?" he says. That's how Al Hibbler got with the band.*

Al Hibbler's special quality? Between whiskey, women, and singing? Oh boy, he loved whiskey. We'd get ready to do maybe a 150-mile or 200-mile jump, and we'd buy a bottle, a pint or a fifth, he and I. We used to sit together on the bus. He could tell you how much was in the bottle—he'd shake it and put his hand down there to mark it. He and I would drink the whiskey, and I'd try to cheat him, which was pretty hard to do. So one night we stopped by the beach. There was empty old crab shells laying on the beach, all hollow, so I picked up this crab shell and brought it back on the bus. Al had the bottle between us and I told him I had a live crab, and every time he reached for the whiskey, I'd prick him with this crab and boom, he's scared to death. I drank all the whiskey, got drunk, and Hibbler got none. I drank it all.

Our band wasn't recorded, but our style was better than the group that made the records. Charlie Anderson came up in the Jenkins Orphanage Band. I remember once we had a little skirmish, and he blew Erskine Hawkins away. Charlie was phenomenal. This guy could play anything. He's the type of musician, like Benny Carter, he could play in a jazz band and he could sit right down in a symphony band and take the first chair and play that too. He was the complete trumpet player. He could play high; he could solo; he could read notes like fly specks. He was just a good man. He could have been in anybody's band. His character wasn't too good—he was the kind of guy, he might get drunk and goof off. But at his zenith, he was a top man. He got killed, got stabbed to death. He was arrogant when he drank, see.

I missed the fire with the Walter Barnes band [all but two members perished in a fire at the Rhythm Club in Natchez on April 23, 1940] *by two weeks. I was hanging out with a saxophone player named Jimmy Coles, and he was with the Barnes band. A trumpet player was getting ready to leave, and he was trying to get me to leave Boots to come with him. I talked to Walter, and he sounded very nice. He was a pretty sharp guy and a gentleman. I was impressed, and I was just about to leave Boots, and this was in Natchez, Mississippi. We used to go down to this place and jam all the time. That's how they heard me, but someone told me, "Norman, you better stay where you are. You're established; you're doing all right. Just stay." Two days later, the whole band was burned. Jimmy Coles, who was trying to get me with the band, my buddy, he got burned up sitting in his chair. Never moved out of his chair.*

Eventually, in 1940, I left Boots to come back to Los Angeles. My parents were getting a little elderly. They had a property on the East Side and somebody had to take care of things, and there wasn't nobody but me. I'm their only child. My wife and I had separated by then. I had been gone so long over the years, and things weren't the same. When I left, she was living with my folks. When I came back, she had her own place and she was with some other guy. That was the end of that. Last I heard of Boots, he was living over on 21st or 22nd on the East Side. He's the kind of guy when he's eighty years old, he probably looks like he's sixty because he never drank or smoked in his life. No pot, no nothing. I imagine he's still living, all dried up. He never dissipated, slept all day. He'd get plenty of rest.

I came down Central Avenue. See, I'm back home now. I knew a lot of the guys. The Memo [4264 Central Ave.] was just opening up across from Club Alabam. A fellow named Clarence Moore was running the Memo, and he had a good band in there. A girl named Kathy La Marr had the band and she was playing piano; Big Six was playing saxophone; a guy we called "Juicy," Clifford Owens, was on the drums. The bass player was Eddie Williams, and me, that was the band. The place opened up in February. I was in the band at the very beginning when it opened up. Kathy was in charge of the band, and we stayed there maybe six months on this job and they let her go. Something happened with her and the management.

Big Six left to get his own band, so they brought in another piano player named Walter Johnson—an old-timer, used to be with Curtis Mosby—and they made him in charge of the band, but Clarence Moore made it specific that he was to keep me in the band. I stayed there with Walter Johnson with the remainder of the guys that were there. Juicy and I were staying. That probably lasted for six months, so then they fired Walter Johnson and they hired another piano player named L. Z. "Elzie" Cooper and they put him in charge. So I'm there with three bands but I'm never the leader. "You get who you want, but Norman stays. He's gotta play the trumpet," Clarence Moore used to say. So I'm a fixture. We worked there, I'd say, for about a year after that. Then Clarence Moore and his wife were having problems, and they ran out of business and they closed the place down. It only lasted about two years, and I was there from the beginning to the end.

Elzie was a nice guy—we got along real nice. He used to be the piano player with Leon Herriford's band. He worked the Cotton Club. Elzie was a good, experienced piano player, the kind of guy that knew all the songs. He could play for any singer and he could read. He wasn't a bum. He could play; he could hold down a job. He knew his way around. You'd hire him.

The Memo was a nightclub. Regular hours. Had a bar and a dance floor. One side's the bar; then you went through a little doorway and there were the tables with booths and then the bandstand up here and they served the food on the side over there. We had a show and we had a lot of different acts, like the Four Covans dancers. Two shows a night. I really enjoyed that job. It was a classy place. Had crowds every night.

Ben Webster and Rex Stewart would come in to jam when Duke Ellington was in town. They didn't like each other, but they were both my friend, so I'd let them play a few tunes. White guys would come over and jam with us until 4 o'clock in the morning. Everybody got along real well. They'd call me up whenever they visited because I had a car so I had to drive. J. C. Higginbotham was another friend; he and I were like brothers. He loved to drink and everything to him was a party. He'd crack up even when it wasn't funny.

When Duke came here and played the Paramount Theatre in March 1934—this was about four blocks from the dance hall where I was working—

so between shows Art Whetsol, Duke's trumpet player, would come and sit in with me with at Danceland. We were buddies. We were hanging out together. He was a real class guy. A handsome guy. I always liked to be around the guys who were trying to make something new. I gained experience from those kinds of guys.

During those days, I was getting a big sound. I could always get a big sound if I could do anything. By being young I had more range; I could play much higher, but I didn't know as much as I do now. I can still get the big sound, but I may not be able to play as high, but now I know where I'm going. After Louis Armstrong, I would say my main guys would be Harold Baker, Jonah Jones, and Clark Terry. These are my boys, and I was crazy about Roy [Eldridge] too. I never met Roy personally, but I used to hang with Harold, Taft Jordan, Jonah, and Charlie Shavers.

I joined Harlan Leonard's Rockets[5] *in 1942 at Sweets Ballroom in Oakland. Chief Moore and I had worked together with the Erwing Brothers. Harlan needed a trumpet player, and Chief spoke to him and recommended me. They sent me a ticket, and I got a train, left here, and joined them in Oakland. The trumpeters were Miles Jones, James Ross, and me. I took Charles Johnson's place; he was known as "Little Dog." Chief was on trombone with a guy named "Harpo" [James Wormick]; that was the five brass. The saxophones were Merrill Anderson, James Keith, Harlan, and Earl Jackson. For my first trip in the band, the drummer was Ellis Bartee. The bass player was Rodney Richardson. Then he left, and George Bledsoe played bass. Soon after that, Bartee passed away and Jesse Price came in.*

We came back to Los Angeles and played the Hollywood Café [in May 1943]. We was there for about six weeks with nightly broadcasts over on CBS, and then we went on to Shepp's Playhouse. Harlan left Shepp's in 1945 when they cut the band down, and he got the job at Club Alabam, but they couldn't use a bigger band so that cut me out. Johnny Otis replaced Jesse Price at Club Alabam, and after that he formed his own band. That's when I stayed at Shepp's with [bandleader] Leonard Reed.

The California Eagle, December 9, 1943
    Christmas Cheer at Bronzeville's Newest
    THE PALMS BREAKFAST CLUB, 131 No.San Pedro St.
    FEATURING NORMAN BOWDEN'S QUINTETTE
    DICK BARROW Blues singer
    QUEDA British Torch Singer
    TOMAGO British Motion Picture Star Your Host

Harlan Leonard had a nice band, and he was a real nice guy to work for, but he was so easy that the guys would take advantage. He was not a strict disciplinarian, and the guys would turn up late, drunk, and he couldn't find them. I remember one night in Phoenix we were supposed to go on the air at 7 o'clock in the evening to broadcast, and here comes James Ross, trumpet player, and when it came time to play a solo, he's slumped on the bandstand, staggering. After the Alabam, Harlan got out of the business and took a job with the Inland Revenue, and that's where he retired from. He was a family man. He wanted security. That was good for him. The big band days were waning.

Then I went to the Lincoln Theater with Bardu Ali. This was in 1944. In that band, the trumpets was Monte Easter, Snake Whyte, and me. Trombonists was Melba Liston, the girl, and Henry Sloan, used to be with Lionel Hampton. That was the brass section; that's five. The drummer was Henry Green, but we all called him Tucker. He went with the Trenier Twins later. A guy named Prince Robinson was on tenor—that's not the tenor who played with Fletcher Henderson; this was a much younger fellow—and Vernon Slater was on alto. The piano was Charles Brown, the guy that was married to Mabel Scott, the singer. Bardu was the director, and Pigmeat Markham was in charge of the show. It was his show so we played the show and always had to do two band specials. Bardu used to feature me on "Sunny Side of the Street." He'd introduce me as "The Canadian." It was every night, like the Apollo in New York. I stayed there, I can say, about six months; then I left when Leonard Reed came and they opened Shepp's Playhouse.[6] I quit Bardu to go down there.

I stayed at Shepp's with three bands, with Leonard Reed, and with Harlan Leonard and Sammy Scott until the place closed. Sammy Scott was a guitar player and good arranger. He was the first one to have the band at Shepp's Playhouse. In other words, the whole band would leave and I would stay on trumpet with the new band coming in. It was a good job, and the band personnel stayed steady. Walking distance from where I was living at the time, too. We came out of there when the war was over and the Japanese came back. See, the Japanese had this territory, all these places. They call it Little Tokyo now. Where we were playing, Shepp's Playhouse was [originally] a hotel owned by Japanese people. They retrieved everything around '46, and that was the end of Shepp's Playhouse. There was a lot of bands down there in the territory, and then the whole thing pitched in. When the Japanese came back, the blacks were out. It all closed up down there.

It was good while it lasted. Capacity crowds every night. You couldn't get in there. At Shepp's, we played in sharp company. Coleman Hawkins had a good band [Hawkins played Shepp's for four weeks starting April 19, 1945], and Eddie Heywood was down there with us, too [Heywood opened at Shepp's in January 1945; his engagement ended on April 17, 1945]. They played the lounge and we played the main ballroom. I was really impressed by Eddie, him and Vic Dickenson and Emmett Berry, Keg Purnell on drums, and Lemuel Johnson on saxophone. Oh man. They had about six, seven pieces. They were wailing. You know, I played with Eddie Heywood Sr. at the burlesque theatre in downtown Los Angeles. Must have 1933 or '34! Leonard Reed's band had Eddie Davis on saxophone, Preston Love also on saxophone, and Jap Jones was playing trombone. He was married to Betty Hall Jones. We had a good band.

I played at Club Alabam with a bunch of bands. This was way before I was with Harlan Leonard. I worked there with Curtis Mosby at one time. He had the place twice. Second time around, I was with his band. I worked there with Marshal Royal, and I worked there with Kid Ory. He and I were members of Marshal Royal's band. That's Marshal Royal and myself; Alton Redd was the drummer; Kid Ory was playing trombone; and I was playing trumpet. Might have been '38, because Marshal had left Les Hite's band. Kid Ory put a band in there himself, sure, anywhere from '32 or '33 to '35, '36. Somewhere in that time. Later, he went to Union Station to work as a Red Cap. He quit music altogether for a spell. This was before he was a Red Cap.

I can remember in 1934, I was there at Club Alabam in a band called Fess White when Central Avenue was the main drag for black show people. Club Alabam was in the Dunbar Hotel, and we worked there for about a year. Monday was the only dark night. The guy that brought those arrangements from Detroit when I was with Reb Spikes, that's his book we was playing at Club Alabam with Fess White. Fess was a bad musician, but he got lucky and he had good musicians in his band. He played bass horn but so badly, the guys put apples in his horn to drown him out. He held it up and all those apples fell out. He called himself a businessman, and we did have a good sounding band. All the guys could play. One time we went to a big golf club to make an audition and we made it to the janitor! Later on Teddy Buckner came in, at the end, and he took the band over. We left Club Alabam and we went downtown, but that didn't last.

Fess was just a territorial band; he'd never been nowhere. Monte Easter was in that band, he and I, with Jap Jones on trombone. Actually there were no names in the band, but it was a band that fit that place. We were well liked; the people were crazy about us. If we had went to challenge other bands, we couldn't make it, but in that place we were like top dog. Club Alabam was a big nightclub. Oh God, we had people like Myrna Loy, George Raft; Loretta Young; they were down there all the time. All the big people came down to Club Alabam. I worked there with Lorenzo Flennoy's band as well. We're talking about the late 1930s now.

Barney Bigard and me worked with Zutty Singleton in '44, and Ory was playing trombone. He had a beautiful tone. A good sound. Yeah, he fit good because he could play his parts. It was swing, but he was playing it. He could play that. In June of 1944, Zutty was playing at the El Capitan with Kern Murray's Blackouts of 1945. He had the band there and the show closed, and that's when he got with Orson Welles. Originally that band was Papa Mutt and Jimmie Noone and Ory. Zutty did something with Capitol Records, so there was a sort of split up there. There were two factions. So Orson Welles let Mutt go and Jimmie Noone died, and then they hired me and Barney. I wasn't acquainted with Zutty, but I knew who he was. There was a trumpet player named Irving Randolph, a good friend of mine who had been with Cab Calloway. They called him "Mouse." He and I were buddies. Mouse had left Cab to go with Snub Mosley, and Zutty was trying to get Mouse to take the job with Welles, and Mouse recommended me to Zutty. That's how I met Zutty.

I did the show in June and July of 1944. This was on CBS. The sponsors were the Mobil Oil Company. With Zutty we played strictly Dixieland, things like "Royal Garden Blues." It was all right. I broke in on it. I started listening to Louis Armstrong in the Savoy Five with all those records. This was after the radio show had ended. That was the end of the band. Not the same personnel. I played some more with Zutty at the Streets of Paris. The piano player was Wilbert Barenco from San Francisco, and we had Gene Porter on saxophones, me on trumpet, Zutty playing the drums, and Wesley Prince playing bass. That was the band at the Streets of Paris. Everybody was tight, no problems, but Zutty would be harder to get along with than the rest of them. He was a character, a funny guy. The first record [Zutty's Creole Band, June 30, 1944] I made was with Zutty and Barney. That was a Dave Dexter session for Capitol records. We made "Crawfish Blues" and "Oh Didn't He Ramble." Dave was so amazed that a Canadian-born musician could relate to the blues, which was easy for me as I was born with the blues. Fred Washington on piano was from New Orleans. He used to play piano with Montudie at the One-Eleven dancehall. He was the piano player in that band. Time, old age, and sickness got him in the end. He wasn't a dissipater, and he wasn't a big man, a little taller than me. He could play, for those times, but he wasn't no Art Tatum or Oscar Peterson. Nothing like that.

After the Welles show was over, I went with Nellie Lutcher. We're working in a club called Club Royal on Florence and Broadway. Stayed there quite a while, almost a year. That was [drummer] Monk McFay, [bassist] George Mason, me, and Nellie. Four of us. It was a nice place. Nice job. We used to jam in Nellie's house through the 1930s even before we ever worked together, so I already knew her. All the bands that would come to Los Angeles like Earl Hines, Duke, Ernie Fields, they used to come to Nellie's house to jam, so everybody knew everybody. We were very good friends. She introduced me to my wife, Levetta; she was crazy about her. Nellie had a few original tunes that she did, like "Hurry On Down," and she knew what she wanted. All four of us sang and she'd sing the lead and we'd do the back-up. Everybody in the group had to sing. Can you imagine that?

We left the Club Royal and we went into the Swing Club [1710 Las Palmas Avenue] in Hollywood, stayed there for a few weeks. They had two bands, us and Illinois Jacquet. [Trumpeter] *Benny Bailey used to hang out there every night. They were good times. Jack Teagarden was 'round the corner at the Famous Door—now there's a helluva nice guy. I was crazy about him as a person.*

Me and Jake Porter rehearsed with Jelly Roll Morton,[7] *might have been late 1940. He was through winning by then. That's the most sophisticated man I ever met in my life. Jelly Roll Morton didn't open his mouth unless he said the word "I." "I am the great Roll. I am still the master," he used to say. He never spoke unless he spoke of himself. At all times. You wouldn't count, only "me." He was trying to get something going again. He still had a little name. That was here in Los Angeles. We used to rehearse at the Elks Hall, in the ballroom. He was a ragtime player. Scott Joplin style. In his day, he was king, sure. Still had the diamond in his tooth. He was kinda tall, wasn't a bad looking feller. I imagine in his younger days, he was a pretty nice-looking guy.*

Jake Porter put that band together for Jelly Roll. I don't remember Ed Garland being the organizer, although he played bass. It was Jake Porter, Hugh Bell, and I, trumpets. I don't remember the rest. The music was all Jelly's. I remember "Jelly Roll Stomp," nothing else. We never worked, only rehearsed.

Jake was in the Snake Whyte band, and Jake, Snake, and I were the trumpet section at one time. We rehearsed all the time, but we never worked. Back in '38, Snake was in Happy Johnson's [big] *band. It was me and Snake, Andy Anderson on tenor, Bob Dorsey on tenor, a whole bunch of guys. I wasn't in that band at first. I took the place of a trumpet player, can't remember his name; he went back to Detroit. Trumpets were Snake Whyte, Forrest Powell, and me. Trombones, Leslie Bisco and Jap Jones. Streamline* [John Ewing] *had gone by then. I played with Streamline in the high school band and in the Curtis Mosby band at Club Alabam. That's a long time ago!*

Jimmy Witherspoon was rooming with a girl I was going with. I was working at the Little Harlem [11812 Parmalee Avenue] *with* [guitarist] *T-Bone Walker at the time, so when I would go back to pick up the girl to take her with me, Witherspoon always wanted to go. I wouldn't take him because at the time I was courting the girl and I didn't want to be bothered with Witherspoon. One night I decided to take him. He kept saying to me, "I can do that; I can sing like that," so I said, "OK, come with me; I'll put you on," just so we could get out there. I told T-Bone, "I gotta friend of mine; let him sing." T-Bone put him on. He got a big hand, never looked back.*

We played at Little Harlem every night, down there in Watts. That's, I would say, in mid-'45. Zutty Singleton was with T-Bone with me; Charlie Mingus on bass; and the tenor player Karl Jefferson—he could read and play his parts, but he wasn't no hot soloist—Henry Sloan, trombone; and Garland Finney on piano. It was good. Mingus was a character. A very talented musician. Good bass player. Very temperamental. He used to tell me that something would come over him when the moon changed to affect his mind and make him act like that. I remember one night he drew a gun on Henry Sloan on the bandstand because Sloan was drunk. Made him get off the bandstand. A friend of mine comes looking for a guy and he has a gun; he shows me the gun, and Mingus sees it and says, "Can I see your gun, man?" Just cool like that. He gives Mingus the gun and Mingus commands Henry Sloan, "Get off, go." Made Sloan get off. Gave the guy his gun back and he took off. No big thing. Mingus was talented but very erratic.

T-Bone Walker was fine. He was a happy-go-lucky man. He was always happy. He lived every day like it was the last day. He loved to gamble. He'd bet the blue cockroach would beat the white cockroach. A top blues player. He was one of the best I ever heard. Like Elvis Presley putting the guitar behind his back—T-Bone was doing that before Presley was born. He used to do the splits, go out on the floor, and be playing. He was doing all that kind of stuff as long as I remember. He never did get the credit. He had no enemies. Everybody loved T-Bone.

Norman recorded with the popular King Perry combo [Perry had played Shepp's Playhouse in May 1945] as a one-off, with Happy Johnson on trombone, for Melodisc in 1946. He also recalled playing with Floyd Ray's band as did many Los Angeles–based African American musicians in the postwar period: "Yes, I can give you some names: trumpets, Eddie Hutchinson—we called him 'Goo-Goo'—Red Mack, me; trombones, 'Hambone' [James Robinson], [Herbert] Mullins; saxes, Harris Erwing, James Nelson—called him 'Hawk'—and two others I can't remember. Arthur Twine played piano. I can't remember the bass player, and Lee Young was on drums. We played the Orpheum Theatre in the late 1940s or the early 1950s."

Norman also played with his old friend Rex Stewart, then living in Los Angeles, possibly in the late 1940s again: "We played a place on Hollywood and Bronson, the Stadium Club. Didn't last long. Elisha 'El' Herbert, he started out with the band on trumpet, but Rex didn't like his playing so he went." With the gradual collapse of Central Avenue as a focal point for black entertainment, the gig scene dwindled, and Norman then took a variety of day jobs, while still playing "a bunch" of casual engagements. As he explained, "Things got slow at that time and I'm not going to starve to death so it's whatever I can do, but I never did stop playing."

He joined Sears Roebuck in 1949 and stayed until 1961. Initially Norman was a janitor: "The only job you could get for black people then would be a janitor. They wouldn't give you anything else. They already had a [company] band and there was a trumpet player—he was a janitor also—who was leaving so they said if I wanted a job, I could play in the band. The guy hired me more or less because of the trumpet, not because I was a good worker! The band played for all the company functions. I did that for seven or eight years.

Later he returned to the company and worked as a salesman in Glendale from 1968 to 1972. After Norman left Sears the first time, he took a job shining shoes out at the Beverly Hills Hotel and made more money than "I ever made playing in my life." He worked in their hair-styling salons and was a porter in the barber shops before resuming with Sears in 1968. When the organist Earl Grant[8] called him, Norman took a leave of absence and worked with Grant from July to September 1968 at Harrah's clubs in Lake Tahoe and Reno.

"Unfortunately Earl didn't record during my stint," he said, citing his period with Grant as a career highlight. "We'd do three shows a night and on the last show I was feeling a little tired. A few years before, it didn't mean anything. I'd be ready to go somewhere else and jam for the rest of the morning, but with three a night, by the end of the third show, I was ready for the sack."

Back in Los Angeles, Norman resumed his freelance role, often taking extended residencies with a quartet formed in the 1950s and led by his drummer friend Red Minor Robinson. "We grew up in the same neighbourhood, from 1924, as children. We had no idea we were going to be musicians." They worked at Daisy's in Beverly Hills for six or seven years in the 1970s and later at Homer & Edie's Bistro on S. Robertson Blvd. for fifteen years. Originally Red Minor and George Reed alternated on drums, and Reed was playing with the quartet at the time of his death. Norman was also well placed to take extra work in movies such as *St. Louis Blues* [Paramount, 1958] and had an on-screen role as Charlie Shavers in the Tommy Dorsey Orchestra (under trombonist Bill Tole as Dorsey) as depicted in *New York, New York* [United Artists, 1977].

I got quite a few calls like that. That's where the bread is, sitting in the middle of the brass and playing. I had a local agent, a woman; she was in on everything. It was a very competitive thing. Just because you got a call it didn't mean you got the job because when you got there, there's more people, probably a hundred trumpet players. When you're doing a video, regardless of your ability to play, it's going to be a certain type that they're looking for, and if you fit the prescription, you got a better chance of getting the job whether you play well or not.

Aside from the quartet jobs and occasional video and movie calls, Norman was a longtime member of Gordon Mitchell's Resurrection Brass Band alongside other veteran players like Andy Blakeney and George Orendorff, performing regularly at local festivals. He was on hand to play "Mood Indigo" with Benny Carter's special band at Rex Stewart's funeral in September 1967 and finished out his music career with a weekly gig at La Louisiane on

Slauson and Overhill, with Louis Thomas, tenor; Louis Collins, flugelhorn; Mickey Cochran, drums; Al White, keyboard; and Roy Brooks, guitar. He retired finally on Labor Day 2007.

I never fooled with any dope. Back in the old days, I was drinking a pint or a fifth every day. Now I just take a little taste now and then. I had a lot of interesting experiences, and I've met a lot of wonderful people. And a lot of bums too! I met two governors, Governor Brown and Governor Knight. Rewarding? I should say so—if it wasn't for jazz, I wouldn't have had my family. I never had any desire to be a bandleader. I just wanted to be an instrumentalist. If I had to do it again, I would do it again. For sure.

Chapter Thirteen

John Richard "Streamline" Ewing

Trombone

John Ewing enjoyed a far more wide-ranging career than many of the other musicians who settled in Los Angeles. He had already been a key sideman with the big bands of Earl Hines and Jimmie Lunceford before he settled in the city and was to dabble with bebop, play rhythm and blues with Johnny Otis, and move successfully into Dixieland with Teddy Buckner. He also developed an attractive sideline in film work and turned up on a great variety of recording sessions, valued by leaders and sound-track contractors as an able section player and occasional soloist. He appeared with the Johnny Otis Rhythm and Blues Caravan at the Nice and North Sea jazz festivals in July 1985, toured Switzerland a few years later, and had returned from Japan shortly before we met.

We called at his comfortable home in Altadena and talked at length about his career while his wife bustled around making us very welcome indeed. Unaccountably we failed to speak about his lengthy tenure with Lunceford or to pay much attention to his long association with the distinguished composer and bandleader Gerald Wilson. It was a pleasure to hear him play with the Teddy Buckner reunion band at the Los Angeles Classic Jazz Festival and to know that he was valued by leaders like trumpeter Bob Allen and Joe Rucker in his later years until his retirement. It was Allen who told me that John had been affected by Alzheimer's disease, a cruel affliction for someone so animated and talented. He died on February 1, 2002, at a health center in Pasadena.

John Ewing, 1990. Courtesy John Ewing.

John Ewing: Altadena, California, August 28, 1990

I was born in 1917 in Topeka, Kansas, and I stayed there, I guess, until I was about high school age. My father, Wiley Ewing, was a minister, and my mother, Willie, well, she didn't work too much. I had a pretty good youth really. My mother was interested in gospel and spirituals; she didn't think much of jazz and blues. I thought about it but she didn't. She had me taking piano lessons. In fact, she was my teacher. I didn't care for piano; I didn't have the hands for it, but I did learn to read. That's a good foundation for anybody. I was hearing church music, but I didn't hear too much jazz although I heard some records by Bessie Smith, people like that. My sister used to get records; she'd sneak 'em in and play them on what they called a Victrola in those days.

We came out here [Los Angeles] in 1932 after my mother died. That's my father, my brother, and me. We stayed here a year living with my elder brother. I enrolled at Jefferson High School in 1932, and I took instrumental training. That's where I grabbed trombone, but I didn't play jazz until we moved back to Kansas in 1933. I wasn't a whole year at Jefferson High School—I'd say from October to June. I can remember Jack McVea—he's working at Disneyland now—Oscar Bradley, a terrific drummer; and other guys like Vernon Gower and Fuzzy Gower at Jefferson. Vernon played bass and Fuzzy played saxophone. Very good musician.

Mr. [John] Davies was the band instructor. He wasn't very tall, but he had a sound on that trombone that I still remember. He was a heck of a musician. Then he had an assistant that was going to the school as a student at that time. His name was Austin McCoy. He was around until recent years, but somebody said he moved back east. He could play all the instruments [McCoy later became a pianist and record producer]. *He's the one that showed me the positions on the trombone. He could play every instrument in the band. He was really something else.*

Trombone always kinda fascinated me; even back in Kansas when I used to go to the band concerts on Sundays and listen to the brass bands. Trombone seemed kinda mysterious to me and I liked the sound of it. It's an instrument, as far as I'm concerned, where you don't see anything; you just hear something. You see a guy moving his arms—you don't see no guy pushing any keys or anything. It seemed to be a challenge. Anybody who grabs the trombone, he's grabbing the challenge. A trombone player knows what he's got to go through. Any guy that goes to it, he's got it for life really. I know guys play it until they fall out. I'm old now but guys older than me are still blowing.

While I was here [LA] I heard Les Hite's band at the Lincoln Theatre [23rd and Central] down on Central Avenue. Oh man, that's the first live [swing] band I really heard on stage. I was shook up about that band. I remember Lionel Hampton playing drums, doing the same things he's doing now. Throwing his sticks up in the air, playing vibes, everything.

My father really didn't like it out here, so when school was out, we packed up and went back to Kansas. This was in 1933, the year of the big earthquake.[1] March the 10th, 1933. Between five and six. I never will forget that. I was going to Jefferson at the time, and it demolished the high school, all but the gym. We got instrumental training under the bridges on Hooper Avenue. I was afraid. The worst feeling I ever had to this day. I remember seeing my nephew and niece running out of the house and the chimneys coming off the house. Everybody was running. I tried to run, but it didn't help much; the ground was shaking. I don't remember my father being afraid.

The first dance band and jazz band I played with was in Topeka, Kansas. It was, I guess, an eight- or ten-piece band. I remember they had two trumpets, trombone, probably three reeds, something like that. The bandleader was [trumpeter] Richard Harrison. I was about seventeen. We played a lot of stocks. That's the first time I played stock arrangements. Why "Streamline"? That comes from when I was in that little band. We were going up western Kansas on a gig one night and this Streamline train came whistling by and the drummer said, "That looks just like you!" Long and thin and bony! So that was it; I was Streamline from then on. All over the world.

I wasn't happy in Topeka. It's the capital of the State of Kansas, and it's still a funny town. I had a plan: "As soon as I can get out of here, I'm going." [Bandleader] Gene Coy came to Topeka to play the Kansas Free Fair [previously the Kansas State Fair]. Guess they said, "Kid here plays a trombone," something like that. It's easy to find out who's who in a town like that—only about twenty people altogether playing music. The black community weren't all in one place; they had different areas. The area I came up was a mixed area; I remember six black families on the street where we lived, the rest filled up with whites.

See, I took Allen Durham's place. He was coming out here [LA] to join Lionel Hampton's big band. So Gene Coy asked me to join him and he took me out on the road. First time I'd left home. It was exciting. That was a band that had some fine musicians, all youngsters, most of them from the Middle-West. Guys like [guitarist] Junior Raglin, [trumpeter] Howard McGhee, and [saxophonist-arranger] Maxwell Davis. Gene Coy came through the Midwest and he grabbed each one of them. He'd say, "Come on with me." He was like a father when everybody's a teenager. Maxwell was from Wichita, Kansas; Junior was from Omaha, Nebraska; Howard was from Tulsa, Oklahoma; and I was from Topeka, Kansas. A whole bunch of greenhorns. Some of the other guys, they didn't get much of a name, but they were very good musicians too, fellows like Lester Taylor and Slits Byars.

Howard McGhee was another very good musician; I think he'd started arranging and writing at that time. Looked like he was searching for something then; he didn't seem to be too satisfied. He'd say, "Oh, nothing's gonna happen if you stay here. This is nothing. Got to move on." In other words, he was in a hurry and he evidently got what he wanted because he got a big name. He was exciting, but I don't know about him being a stylist. His execution was very accurate. He was writing arrangements then, and the band did a pretty good job playing them. It wasn't easy music. I don't remember him ever writing anything and saying [to me], *"Here's a whole lot of whole notes for you to play."*

Red Kelly from Peru, Indiana, was another very good trumpet player in the band. He had a style but he never did record anything, but he was different from any trumpet player I ever heard. He could play lead and he could also solo. Beautiful but yet it was jazz. So pretty. He finally wound up in the Post Office. He started raising a family, and his wife, she told him, *"You never gonna be nothing of a musician."* I think he still gigs around town, sometimes with Spanish bands. He didn't get a name which was due him, but I think it was his own fault because he had something to offer.

Gene Coy was a very smooth drummer. Very rhythmic. He wasn't a great soloist, but as for rhythm, he had that down. Matter of fact, I think he had a lot of influence on Jo Jones because he used brushes a lot. His wife, Andrus Coy, she was the pianist in the band, good piano player. It seemed strange for a woman to be in those bands. Seemed out of place. They settled in Fresno, California, later. I think they both died up there [in 1966]. We worked on the road. Little one-nighters, wasn't very much money, I'll tell you now. That was the first time I learned to starve. I missed meals, nothing to eat. We had to split up what we'd make at night. Sometimes, Gene would say, *"We have to pay for the gasoline and the bus."* We had a funny old bus, so we paid for the gas or a new tire or something. Then he'd say, *"Well, fellows, here's fifty cents apiece"* or whatever. I never saw a dollar or a dollar and a half.

I was the only trombone until one time they got a guy named Manzie Shannon [?] that was from Amarillo, Texas [home base for Gene Coy's Happy Black Aces]. I remember him playing, but most of the time I was the only trombone. That was good experience because Maxwell began writing then. I was the first trombone player that he ever wrote a note for. *"Where do you make B flat? Where do you make so-and-so?"* and he'd write it down. I remember an arrangement of *"Supposin',"* he had the notes up so high for the trombone, I thought I can't play them up there. I could make 'em but I wasn't sure. I'd never seen anything hardly over a B flat. *"So where can you play 'em? Can you play 'em an octave lower?"* So he'd finally found out the range for a trombone. Hard work maybe, but it was good for me. [Saxophonist] Ike Young—he was a little older—he helped me musically quite a bit. Mostly we had to find out for ourselves. Like I say, that was a band with so many young guys.

Each day was some sort of experience. We rehearsed all the time. Maxwell would want to try out a new arrangement. *"Come on, guys, let's try this arrangement out."* He was learning then, but he turned out to be a very fine writer and a big conductor. He backed a lot of singers, Dinah Washington, B. B. King; he had a lot to do with these people. I made a lot of those dates with him in LA. He never forgot me. And that was really because we were kids together.

I was with Gene Coy, I'd say from about 1935 to 1937. I left him in Seattle, Washington, and came down here [LA] on a freight train. Me and [Douglas] Slits Byars, the trumpet player. We had no money to get down here so we hopped a freight train. Well, there wasn't much money [with Coy] and I'd had about enough. I didn't think nothing of Seattle. Slits was going with one of the chorus girls, so one night we're out on the lake and him and this girl they got in a big argument. "You know what, I'm leaving; I'm cutting out. I'm going to LA tonight. I'm going to hop a freight train," he said. I says, "If you that bold, I'll hop that freight train with you," so sure enough that night we packed our little bags and set out for LA and oh man, what a ride. I think we asked somebody in the freight yard which train is going to LA. That's a long ways from Seattle. So we hung around the yard until about ten or ten-thirty until this train came through, just regular box cars and we just had the idea that this was the right train to take. We didn't ride the rods; we were like the hobos in the box cars. We were bums too.

Los Angeles was the first stop. When we finally got here it was Sunday morning. Although I had relatives here, we made for Maxwell's address. He'd been trying to get us to come down here; he kept writing to us in Seattle: "I got jobs for you." He was working and conducting at the Follies Theatre [337 Main Street, downtown]. So we went out to his house and we had dinner. We were really worn out, so the next day he took Slits down to the theatre and he wanted to take me out there, but I wanted to rest a while. I wasn't too much excited about playing at this burlesque house because that's what the Follies was. "If you want the job, you got it," he said. Slits took the job and I didn't.

I started hanging around the musicians union [Local 767] and I met a whole lot of people there. Nat Cole, Paul Howard—he was the secretary of the union—Marshal Royal, oh, Papa Mutt [Carey]—he'd be down the Union. At that time, Mutt was a Dixieland player, pretty big name too. I never played with him. Nat wasn't even singing at that time. He was just a piano player. He'd come out here with a show. He said, "C'mon, I'm gonna get another band and I want you to play with me." He could write too. I don't think a lot of people know that Nat was a good writer. We used to play gigs. He was just another musician then. I worked with Phil Moore, big arranger, and there was a little band out here in Pasadena called George Brown. He had a big band, but we only used to work Sunday afternoons. George played piano and his brother played bass. I don't think there were any guys there that had too much of a name but they could play. Anybody had a gig, I played with them. I used to work with everybody who gave me a call. Almost like it is today. I wasn't with anybody really steady.

I played with Happy Johnson. He was a trombone player. This was before I went to Chicago. He had a big band. Good players in that band like Red Callender on bass—I work with him occasionally now—and saxophone player Sam Allen from the Midwest and Forrest Powell, one of the trumpet players. I played a few gigs with the band, like at the Vogue Ballroom [formerly Solomon's Penny Dance Hall]. Happy was the leader; he got his own work. He had his own way of playing. He liked blues a lot; that's what he played mostly. When he soloed, it would be on blues. I don't think the band lasted very long after I went to Chicago.

I got a job working in the movies, sideline things, and I made $200—a whole lot of money for me then—so there was a bass player here by the name of John Simmons who had recorded with Teddy Wilson, and he said "I'm going to Chicago; won't you go along?" I said, "Yeah, I'm making enough money to pay my own fare," and he says, "Let me know when you go because I'll get the money from my mother for the train fare." So that's how I left here and went to Chicago. I was in Los Angeles from, say, the spring of '37, and I went to Chicago in 1938.

On the way to Chicago, I stopped in Kansas City. I had a sister living there. One night, a friend of mine from Topeka, he happened to be there so we went down to this club, guys down there blowin'. I had my horn and I was energetic at that time. I don't remember the name of the club, but I'll tell you who was playing there. Charlie Parker and [drummer] Jesse Price and a piano player, but they said, "Come on up and blow, man." I went up there and I thought I had never heard nothing like that sax player in my life. What is this? Anyway I stood up there and I jammed with them. To make a long story short, I went to Chicago the next day. I met a lot of musicians there. In the meantime, I joined Horace Henderson's band in Chicago. That's Fletcher's brother. In this band there was Ray Nance, [Louis] Ogletree, Leon Scott, trumpet players; Ed Fant and me, two trombones; and Scoops Carry. Now Scoops could play [alto] like mad so I said, "Scoops, I heard a sax player in Kansas City like I never heard before." He said, "He can't play anything." He'd never heard Charlie Parker—he'd never even heard of him—so I said, "I sure wish you could get a chance to hear him." See, Scoops thought he was the only sax player who could play. Truth is he really could play.

A little later Jay McShann came to New York [February 1942]—this was when I was in New York with the Earl Hines band—and Charlie Parker was in the McShann band. Scoops walked up to me and said, "Listen, I heard this guy you was talking about—that's the greatest saxophone player I've ever heard." Well, history tells you he was right. Parker had never made a record when I played with him! But people knew *about him. Out here [LA] there was a saxophonist named Shirley Green and he said, "Man, there's a guy in Kansas City, you ought to hear him play. They call him 'Bird.' His name is Charlie Parker." I said, "Maybe someday I get to hear him," and a couple of months after that I did meet Charlie.* [His reputation] *was spread out amongst musicians way before he made a record. They knew who he was, but in that time, if you weren't on a record, how is anybody gonna know you? Wasn't but a few people made records then. Only the names. Gene Coy, a lot of them bands, they didn't make records. They weren't big enough.*

Horace Henderson, oh, that was a very fine band. I never recorded with Horace, but I know what he could do. A lot of those numbers that Fletcher got credit for, it was Horace's music. At that time, we mostly played clubs and things like that. I went to Detroit with him; we played three weeks over there, and we played in Chicago, different places. Horace was a very serious musician, him and Fletcher, both were serious. He didn't like to get anything wrong. He'd call you down for it, "Do this" or "Take that out," whatever. He didn't want any strings attached. If you couldn't play it, take it out. That's the way he built his band. On what you could do.

Horace and Fletcher, other than that they were fine musicians, I don't think they had much to do with each other. I don't think they were close. I don't remember them arguin' or fussin'. Fletcher wasn't close to anybody really. He was the most deadpan piano player I ever seen. Most guys would be scared to play with him; he was so tough. He was a trailblazer, no question about it. I didn't stay with Horace very long. Maybe six weeks. Then I went to Earl Hines. I joined in November 1938. A lot of the guys that was in Horace's band went over to Earl's band. Walter Fuller, Omer Simeon, Milton Fletcher, Alvin Burroughs, me and Ed Fant—the trombones—and Ray Nance, that was about it. Actually, those guys, they'd play with this or that band a while and go over to whoever had a job. "Earl's got the job at the Grand Terrace; that's where we going," and they carried me along with them.

Down Beat, October 1, 1940

Walter Fuller Ork on Stand As Grand Terrace Reopens by ONAH L. SPENCER; Chicago—When the once-famous Grand Terrace reopened here in mid-September most of the old Earl Hines-Fletcher Henderson boys were on the bandstand as of old, except with Walter Fuller as their boss.

Fuller, trumpet-playing scat-singer and writer of *Rosetta,* is making his debut as leader of a full-sized jump band. And he's got some fine men with him. There are Omer Simeon, clary; George Dixon, doubling trumpet and alto; Robert Crowder and Moses Grant, [sic] tenors; John Ewing, George Hunter [sic] and Edward Burke, trombones; Milton Fletcher, Edward Sims and himself, trumpets; Rozelle Claxton, piano and arranger; Carl (Kansas) Fields, drums; Claude Roberts, guitar and the dependable Quinn Wilson, bass.

Band is rough, but it's ready, too. And plenty of musicians flocked to the black and tan spot to catch it.

According to trumpeter and vocalist Walter Fuller, these musicians had left the Hines band earlier because Ed Fox, the proprietor of the Grand Terrace in Chicago, where the Hines band was resident, "wasn't paying right." They joined the Horace Henderson orchestra, stayed a year, and then moved back to Hines in 1938, just in time to enlist John Ewing.

That's one of my favorite bands because Earl was a terrific guy. He always let the band take over. He was the leader, but the band, the guys, they would write the arrangements; they had a lot to do with the band. All he had to do was to sit up there and be the leader. That's what happened on all the hit records like "Boogie-Woogie on St Louis Blues." I think that was his biggest hit; Budd Johnson scared up an arrangement on that and it hit. "Jelly, Jelly," another big hit, Budd wrote most of the arrangement on that. Actually Earl would let you do what you wanted to do, but he knew when he was coming in. He knew he was gonna say something when he got in there.

If you could do something in Earl's band, you had the opportunity. When I joined the band, I wasn't all that certain of myself. I was kinda leery. Earl made you feel at home. "If you can do something, go on, take a shot." I had a little more confidence after I got to Earl's band. When you get that kind of feeling, that's when you realize that, why, you can just do whatever you can do.

Down Beat, November 1, 1940

And Here's Earl's Lineup; Chicago—The new band which Earl Hines took out on the road, by bus, on Oct. 20 includes Madeline Green as chirper. Also in the lineup are LeRoy Harris, Willie Randall, George (Scoops) Carey [*sic*], Franz Jackson, and Bud Johnson, saxes; PeeWee Jackson, Rostelle Reese, trumpets; John Ewing, Joe McLewis and Ed Fant, trombones; Alvin Burroughs, drums; Charles (Truck) Parham, bass; Hurley Ramey, guitar, and the leader, piano.

Earl is using five saxes for the first time. Helping him with arrangements, and in charge of rehearsals, is Bud Johnson. Billy Eckstein [*sic*] also will do vocal chores with the crew. A third trumpet is to be added.

The money was better than what I'd been getting, but I wasn't getting rich. I wasn't starving either. I just didn't think you made any money 'til you got, maybe, to Duke Ellington's band, but I found out some of the bands wasn't making any more than we were. When I got to Lunceford's band, I said, "Well, heck, I was making this much in Earl's band." I remember one time Count Basie wanted Rabbit [George Hunt]—he made the first solo on [Basie's record of] "One O'clock Jump"—when he was over in Earl's band. We were both there together so Count Basie told Rabbit to bring me along too.

"I want both you guys in the band." Rabbit said, "I'll go if you'll go," so we got to talking about that. "Well, Count Basie pays $8 a night and we

make $12 over here," so we didn't go to Count Basie's band. I wish I had because I liked that music. That was the flowingest rhythmic band I'd ever heard in my life as far as a big band was concerned. I often think about that. Maybe I should have gone just to have that feeling. You got more exposure with Count Basie, but I liked Earl Hines's band too. I would say his was the only band I was ever in where I felt it was like a family. This was because of the young guys. We were a family. The older guys were OK, but we were the fire-eaters. We were the spark plugs. We used to jam; that was popular in those days. Wherever you were, somebody says, well, there's some guys from another band over there playing, so we'd go over and jump on in there. Right here in Los Angeles, during the war, we jammed; there was a place up on Vernon. Wherever you went, somebody had a place where you could go jam.

I was with Earl, I'd say maybe three years. One of the highlights was when we heard Billy Eckstine singing on the floor show there in Washington, D.C., and then he came to Chicago and joined the band. We had a record date and Billy had never recorded before. So we made those records and he came over, "How did that sound? How did that sound?" He'd never heard himself on a playback. In those days, you made a record and they'd play it back. If it didn't sound right, you could make it over. He didn't get a hit out of that first set [of records]. The hit that put him on the map was "Jelly, Jelly," and I was on that record. We made that right here in Los Angeles.

I'd got married and that's one of the reasons why I left Earl. And I just got tired of road traveling. I was still young then. Benny Green, another fine trombone player, took my place. So I'm in Chicago and playing around with different people like Red Saunders, whoever. Then I went to work with Cab Calloway at the College Inn, Hotel Sherman [West Randolph St. and North Clark St.]. I had already played a night with Cab here in LA quite a while before that. Anyway, I went down to the union and [Calloway bassist] Milt Hinton said, "Hey, Cab looking for you so come on down to the club tonight," which was the College Inn. I'd never been there before in my life, so I went down there with my horn and Cab said, "Hey, I gotta uniform that will suit you," so I went on the road with Cab and I guess I was with Cab maybe five, six weeks.

He wanted me to go to New York and he said he would give me $50 a week, but I'm working in these trombone player's places at night so altogether I'm probably making $100 or $100 and a quarter a week. I would have to join Local 802, the New York Local, and I didn't want that. They wanted me to go, Milt, all the good guys, Jonah Jones, Ike Quebec, Shad Collins. The trombones were Tyree Glenn, Quentin Jackson, Keg Johnson, and me. Doesn't sound bad, does it? That's a beautiful trombone section. Anyway I went back to Chicago and I stayed around there for a while, and I was doing all right playing casuals. I did a lot of work at the Regal Theater with King Kolax, trumpet player.

One time, I played with a guy named Lee Collins; he was a New Orleans–type trumpet player. Good, too. Sometime in the forties. I was so surprised he called me one night. He was downtown in the Loop somewhere. He says, "Can you come down and work tonight?" I didn't even know who he was, so I went down there and tried to do what they were doing. You don't fight the tide; you go along with the scene, whatever it is, as much as you can. That was the first time I ever played any New Orleans–type music, and he liked what I did, but I never saw him again in life. I used to read about him in Down Beat. *During that time I played with another New Orleans type of player, Red Allen, when J. C. Higginbotham took off one night. They called me to fill in and I went down there, and like I said, I used to do what I thought I could do. I knew I wasn't at home there either. Up until that time I hadn't really gone all out for Dixieland, but if they called me, I'd play it.*

Down Beat, August 1, 1942

Changes in the Les Hite band in reorganization in Los Angeles include Gerald Wilson, trumpet man, over from Jimmie Lunceford; John Ewing, ex-Earl Hines trombone; William College [sic], alto; Fred Trainer, trumpet; and Jimmy Robinson, trombone.

Chicago Defender, September 14, 1946

The Wagon Wheel Café (formerly Cabin in the Sky) 3252 Cottage Grove Ave will present musicdom's latest sensation Saturday night when John "Streamline" Ewing's Sextet makes its bow on the Southside. Previously Ewing's aggregation has confined its local appearances to the Loop district. A red hot floor show is being prepared for the opening.

The Jazz Record, June 1947

The Hot Club of Chicago staged its April concert at Moose Lodge on Easter Sunday, April 6, 1947. It was a musical success with its Easter Parade of Jazz Stars featuring Mama and Jimmy Yancey plus Bertha "Chippie" Hill's 57th Street Ramblers: Bill Ogletree, trumpet; John Ewing, trombone; Mike Walker, clarinet, Charles Carrington, piano; Bill "Pops" Johnson, bass and Pork Chops, drums.

Then for some reason I wanted to come back to California. I was doing all right in Chicago, but I just made up my mind that I was coming back out here so I came back. That was 1950, and I've been here ever since. There was plenty going on at that time, and I was getting into recording. I wasn't making a lot of money, but I was doing all right. At that time, there was three of us guys, three bachelors; that's [saxophonist] Buddy Collette, [trombonist] Jimmy Cheatham, and me. We got an apartment together [at St. Andrew's Place], and I never had so much fun in my life. Well, naturally, there was a lot of women coming in and out of that place, so some woman would call me and I'd say, "Can you make it next Thursday because that's the only open date we have?" That's the way it was [laughs]. *Jimmy was going to Westlake School of Music, Buddy had a job on the Groucho Marx TV Show, and I was out in the wind but I was making it.*

Charlie Parker came out here and was working at a club [The Tiffany Club]. *He had heard about Buddy Collette, and well, he knew me too. So he came up to the house one night, but I had to go play somewhere. Charlie tried to get Buddy to play:* "Man, I just want to hear you play." *Charlie was like that; he wanted to hear what* you *could do. By that time, I had been around Charlie several times; we were very good friends, even up to the day he died. I was glad to know that I was one of the first guys that knew of him.*

These guys, Jimmy and Buddy, they were doing something steady. Jimmy learned how to write at Westlake, and Buddy was the great guy; he had the TV show. I was still with Maxwell [Davis] *making records. Rene Hall was another guy who started hiring me, and I did a lot of work for him. We put Sam Cooke on the map. Rene was one of the top arrangers around here at the time. He told me one time that when he joined Earl Hines, he played trombone and guitar; they gave him the first book. He said,* "This was Streamline's book, and I never saw so many C's and B flats. I was supposed to play your book." *Rene was more of a guitar player than a trombone player. Trombone gave him a little trouble. He said when he got that trombone book, he never forgot it.*

Bebop? Well, I was around it, when it started, but I never had a fast execution on trombone. To me, you had to kinda move [fast] *and I wasn't much at that, but neither was Miles Davis but he went on trying out certain notes; he'd check out certain notes and put some stuff on it. I knew bebop was gonna hit because the young guys were playing it, but I didn't think it was for me, not that I didn't like it.*

They were playing changes that were much different than they had been. There was no melody, and as far as rhythm was concerned, they didn't care much for people patting their foot. They thought that was old-fashioned. They didn't intend that; they didn't want that. We talking about [pioneer bebop trombonist] *Jay Jay Johnson? I played on a show with him. He was with Illinois Jacquet, and I was with Howard McGhee's band. That was probably around '48, when Howard had a big band behind Sarah Vaughan. She was the headliner. Illinois Jacquet had a small band, and Jay Jay was in that band. That's the first time I met him. That was at the Paradise Theatre in Detroit. The bass player with the Modern Jazz Quartet, Percy Heath, was with Illinois, and his brother Jimmy, the alto player, was with us in Howard's band. Illinois's band was organized; who didn't he have in that band? There was Shadow Wilson on drums, his brother Russell Jacquet playing trumpet, and Jay Jay. John Lewis was playing piano. That week was beautiful. That stage was on fire between Sarah Vaughan; you can imagine what she was doing. She was a great musician too. She could walk over and tell the horns* to change this, do that, go to the piano and show them a chord. She wasn't just a vocalist. I always thought of her as a musician really. I guess that's because I was around her when I saw her do these things. Howard didn't have no organized band. He just got a band together for that engagement. He was stationed in New York then and he was on his way. He had developed a good style, the modern style; he never was a way-out type of player to me. He was influenced, I think, by Dizzy but he wasn't exactly Dizzy Gillespie.

I joined Teddy Buckner in 1956. That was enjoyable, very enjoyable. We played around different clubs, the 400 Club, the Beverly Cavern, and then we went to Disneyland. We were down there fifteen years. I never dreamed I'd ever sit anywhere fifteen years. I didn't even think I'd be alive fifteen years! One reason why I liked Teddy was because he reminded me of Louis [Armstrong] but he still wasn't exactly Louis. When he hit that horn, brother, he would be really saying something. Teddy was a live wire. He was very easy to follow as far as playing New Orleans style goes. I miss him very much, to this day. You never was in doubt with him. I knew Teddy before I worked for him. He was in the band at the Paradise Club [6100 South Main Street]. That was the club that Lionel Hampton had left to go with Benny Goodman [in 1936]. Teddy was a trumpet player in that band, so when Lionel left, they made Teddy Buckner the leader. Teddy's trombone player, Leo Williams, he liked to lay off so I used to go down there and work in his place at the Paradise. Leo didn't want to work really; he liked to gamble. That's how I first met Teddy.

We retired from Disneyland in '84. Well, that's a funny story. They contemplated getting rid of the band because we weren't the easiest guys to get along with; oh no, you didn't tell Teddy what to do. They were stuck with him because he made that job at this café just outside the French Market in the French Quarter. Now when we went there, that place was dead, and we went there for thirteen weeks. That was in 1968. When the thirteen weeks was up, they had different nights out there so we played them and kept on and the next thing we know it was Thanksgiving. "OK, you be here tonight" and finally we was in. Like I say, we weren't the best humans in the world. Finally, they caught themselves getting rid of us. That was late '83. No sooner had we'd been out of there when they asked Teddy to come back five days a week. Teddy said, "No, I'll play three days a week." That's what killed it. I was kinda glad to get out of there. I'd lost certain contacts. It was a job, so I can't say I'm sorry about having a job, but Teddy had gotten to the point where he didn't want to do anything. He didn't care whether he played good or bad. There were no new numbers, things like that. It kinda took a little fire out of him when they wouldn't go for three nights and he wouldn't go for five.

Before Teddy, I had played very little Dixieland, but I did go out and play with [cornetist] Pete Daily on Sunday afternoons. He had a guy playing drums that I used to work with named George Jenkins. He was Dinah Washington's first husband. I'll tell you who he played exactly like: Lionel Hampton. He liked to throw his sticks in the air. He played like that. He wasn't what you called a traditional Dixieland player, but he could play it. He was my type of guy, kinda like Big Sid Catlett. He'd likely play with Charlie Parker the first part of the evening; then the last part he's going down there where there's nothing but Dixieland. He didn't care what it was. So George said, "Man, why don't you come right in and play some Dixieland?" I said, "I don't even know how to play it." So I went out and jammed with them. I know it was a different type of music, but it didn't seem like it was a big hurdle to me. I always figured out that the one bunch of people who would be working all the time would be the Dixieland guys. They would always have something going.

I worked with the Young Men of New Orleans out on the boat [the *Mark Twain*] at Disneyland too. Made a recording with them. They couldn't hire me regularly because they didn't have but five pieces, but if [banjoist] Johnny St. Cyr would lay off or [trumpeter] Mike Delay couldn't make it, they'd put me in there. I work now with this band [the Tin Pan Valley Jazz Band] out in the Valley every Thursday, and I'm due at their rehearsal right now! I'm with Bob Allen's band [aka Chris Kelly's Black and White New Orleans Jazz Band] too. He's a lawyer, but he still gets jobs. He called me for a thing this week. Of course, I play with Johnny Otis. He plays what they call rhythm and blues, and we just made an album. In Chicago, when he had a big band with the Ink Spots, right after the war, he always liked a lot of people, musicians, singers. He still likes a lot of people. I still do a few commercials; did one for AT&T about two weeks ago. Whatever call I get, that's it. I've had groups of my own, but right now, things are so much less certain. I don't know if I want the responsibility, but I guess I would if I had to.

I don't think jazz is as popular as it was. I think it's the record companies' fault. It's not jazz's fault. Record companies are interested in rap or whatever you got that sells records. I don't care how good the music is, if it doesn't sell . . . Record companies don't care what's good. Just how much will it sell? I'm optimistic to the point that jazz will return someday, but whether I'll be around, I have my doubts. But it will return.

When I play, I like to be with a good rhythm section first of all. I like tunes people can recognize, and I feel good playing 'em. I'm not into modern things. People know that I'm not a Jay Jay Johnson, but they expect me to play kinda melodic-like and swing. I only do what I think I can do. I just call myself a freelance player. I have no idea what I'll be doing next week, but I know I'll be doing something. It could be Dixieland, it could be swing, or it could be a commercial. I'm connected with that, movies too.

Richard Boone (ca. 1962): *Streamline Ewing called me several times to take a job for him when he had so much work he couldn't make it. He'd got the studio thing in Los Angeles sewed up.*

I still think the trombone is a great instrument. They're doing some terrific things on trombone now that they didn't do in my time. They wouldn't have dared ask you to do what some of these guys are doing now. I got to give them credit. I always thought Tommy Dorsey was tops, but to this day I don't think I really play like that. There's a whole lot of guys I like. There's Dickie Wells, Jack Teagarden, and Trummy Young, of course. I played with Fred Beckett in Lionel Hampton's band. I was in Chicago and they were a trombone short so I worked a week with Fred Beckett. He had some hard knocks; well, at that time everybody was drinkin', but he might have drunk too much. I know he had rough times. I saw him in New York one time and he just looked like he'd been up all night. I guess he was on his way then. I just didn't know it. [Beckett, known as the black Tommy Dorsey, died in 1946 aged twenty-nine.] *I liked him playing melodies more so than jazz because he had a style I liked very much. I used to try to play melodies, but I couldn't do it like he did. Oh boy, he was something. I remember him in Chicago at the Regal Theater. He stood there, playing one of the pop tunes of the times—and Lionel had some good musicians in that band—but as far as I'm concerned, that was the best. Fred was a real standout man. Beautiful, beautiful player.*

Even now, I don't think that I've actually done my best, but on the other hand if I don't do anything else, I'm not sorry about what I did.

John's modesty is at odds with the general appreciation of his talents that led him to be employed by, among others, Milt Larkin at Chicago's Rhumboogie Club in 1941, Les Hite in 1942 in Los Angeles (alongside Buddy Collette), Louis Armstrong (for a week at the Regal Theater, Chicago, in 1943), Jimmie Lunceford (1943–1945), Jay McShann (Regal Theater again, in 1948), Cootie Williams, Louis Jordan, Earl Bostic, Onzy Mathews (at Virginia's in LA in 1962), and Big Jay McNeely in addition to those leaders highlighted in this interview. He toured with the revived Horace Henderson orchestra in 1962 and was regularly called by studio contractors and arrangers to record commercials, movie scores, and pop tunes, often for Motown artists including Stevie Wonder and Marvin Gaye. He was also a member of the backing orchestra for Lucille Ball's *The Lucy Show* in the 1970s.

His jazz and blues recordings are legion as are his movie credits. He solos rewardingly on "Swingin' on C" (1941) by Earl Hines and on "Jeep Rhythm" (1944) by Jimmie Lunceford. He recorded with Buckner and a host of Dixieland units and was a regular member of the Gerald Wilson Orchestra in the 1960s for both its live dates and Pacific Jazz recordings, evidently at ease in these parallel yet apparently incompatible worlds. He played for his old friend Johnny Otis on his big band swing album in 1990 just weeks before we met, soloing in plunger-muted style on "Creole Love Call."

Chapter Fourteen

Charles L. "Chuck" Thomas Jr.

Tenor Saxophone

It was another musician who told us that Chuck Thomas and Monte Easter were on for two nights a week at the Holiday Inn on West Century Boulevard in August 1990. The two veterans were playing with their quartet for the early evening drinkers in Strings, a strangely funereal place, just one of many public rooms and bar areas, dimly lit and quite impersonal.

Although they struggled to make an impact, the dignified, white-haired Thomas was singularly impressive on ballads and blues originals, his tenor evoking the swaggering tone and phraseology of mid-period Coleman Hawkins but underpinned by a stimulating run of ideas of his own.

At the break, we arranged to meet a few days later at his West Los Angeles home to talk about his career. Thomas lived in an attractive area where every lawn was immaculate, largely populated by black professionals. His home was in the Spanish Colonial style, with sparkling white paintwork and perfect gardens back and front. He said that he did "all my own yard work," and it was clear that he was determined not to let standards slip. The Thomases were only the second black family to move into this section of town back in the 1960s, and Chuck remembered white people driving by and calling out, "Nigger, nigger." He would reply with the same words but resolved to keep the house up so that nobody could criticize.

The living room interior was cool, shaded, and spacious. In the corner was an organ with a hymnal placed on the music stand. Otherwise there were very few signs of Chuck's musical world—just the artifacts of a happy and settled family life, of children and grandchildren. Arcelle, a schoolteacher and his wife for over fifty years, was equally welcoming and provided deli-

Chuck Thomas, Los Angeles, 1980s. From the author's collection.

cious lemonade, made with lemons from their garden trees. Outside, it was very hot.

Later on, I was able to hear Chuck play at the Los Angeles Jazz Festival with trumpeter Clora Bryant and then with the Teddy Buckner reunion band. Here again, his playing was forthright and vigorous, full-toned and focused on swing, this underlining one's regret that his solo recording opportunities were so few. A contented man, always in work and valued by his peers, Chuck Thomas was keen to tell me his story, even if his recall of its chronology was sometimes uncertain. Born in St. Louis in 1917 but raised in Albuquerque, New Mexico, he died in Los Angeles on November 3, 2000.

Chuck Thomas: Los Angeles, August 21, 1990

My father went to Albuquerque for his health. He had TB. They told him to either go to Albuquerque, Tucson, or Phoenix. I was aged five when we moved, but I still used to go back to St. Louis every year, every summer. In St. Louis we lived in an all-black community. That's where my mother was born and her sister was there. Her husband was the first black man to graduate from Harvard as a doctor. In later years he became the first black doctor to work for the federal government as the doctor for the Zuni Indian reservation. Later he moved back to St. Louis and started working for the school system there, a separate system then.

My father was a dentist and my mother was just a housewife. He had studied at Ohio State. Albuquerque was a real prejudiced place then, but there were very few black people there so my father's clientele was Mexicans, Indians and whites, and blacks too! John Lewis [later the musical director for the Modern Jazz Quartet] *and I went to school together, and we started out in music together. There was a fellow there in Albuquerque—fact is, he was my wife's cousin—and he knew how to play all the instruments, so he wanted to get a little band together to give the young people something for to do. His name was W. C. Echols, and he was a Pullman porter.*

I wanted to play trombone or drums, and he had all that, so he showed me this pretty saxophone in a magazine and he said, "This is what I want you to play." I liked him so I said OK, and we got started. That was the beginning of me. Twice a week, we'd meet and rehearse at his house. He had John on bass horn. Four weeks out there and I was marching up and down the street in the band. Making money. I was about thirteen. We had a marching band and a dance band.

Later on, we got a thing of our own. In fact, I got the band together and John Lewis played the piano with me. We'd play around little nightclubs and for dances in Albuquerque, and we made a dollar a night. That was a lot of money then. This was Charlie Thomas's Orchestra. One time I had Jay McShann play piano with me because he was there stranded and Howard McGhee too; they both played with me in the band. I was maybe about seventeen or eighteen then. Carroll Houston—that's John Lewis's cousin—

he was on trumpet, Omer Player was on saxophone, and James Selcow [?] was on the drums. I think that's about it there. James Selcow eventually came out here [LA] and started being a jitterbug dancer, and Houston became a bass player, moved from trumpet to bass, and traveled with the band I was with, Eddie Carson and His Hot-Ten-Tots, out of Albuquerque. 1937, that's when I really started playing professionally, traveling with that band. Since then it's always been the tenor for me.

So I had my own band for a long time 'round there, and then Eddie Carson wanted me to go with him. He was going to Grand Junction, Colorado, and he was working two nights a week up there. I was making $15 for the two nights, which was good money because the room rent, I think, was $2 a week so that's what made me go with him. I'd just got married that same year.

Eddie Carson was a real tall fellow to look at him. He was six foot seven and three-fourths. I'll tell you who played with that band was [bassist] Joe Mondragon. Carlton Smith, trombone player from Detroit, he was with the band, and I guess you heard of [alto saxophonist] Roscoe Robinson. The others were John White, Henry Gray—he played trumpet—Hunter Gray played saxophone—that's his brother. Oscar Clark was the drummer; Fred Maxey, the other trumpet player, he was from Memphis. Carson was the piano player. He was born in Albuquerque. He and [guitarist] Ted Brinson were very good friends—they started out playing banjos together so Ted was with that Carson band; he went with Andy Kirk later on. Eddie could play a [musical] saw, really play it! He started the band, called it Eddie Carson and his Hot-Ten-Tots, playing in town for dances and we'd go out on the road too. From Grand Junction, we traveled all 'round Colorado, over to Gunnison, up to Steamboat Springs.

It was a swing band, just a plain swing band. I thought it was very good for the time. I was the only tenor player in there so I got a lot of the solos. I used to listen to Cab Calloway and Duke Ellington on radio, every Saturday night, I think it was, so I felt I was working my way up to being with Duke and Cab and them. That was my ambition. My model then was Lester Young. I lived by my father's office in Albuquerque, and Lester used to live next door. Right next door to me. He and his father and his brother and his sister and his mother. They had a band called Billie Young and his New Orleans Strutters. Lee was playing drums, Lester was playing alto, his sister Irma was playing alto, Ben Webster was playing tenor,[1] his mother was playing piano, and his father was playing cornet, and they had a little guy in there called Bull Frog Shorty. He played violin and he was a dwarf. They were playing strictly Dixieland then, more or less. Ben left them and went to Cab Calloway. I left town and went to St. Louis like I did every year, and when I came back they were gone. That was in 1933. I know Lester came through Albuquerque with Andy Kirk later on. He was playing tenor then. I didn't hear anything special with Lester until he got with Basie. That's when I started hearing something different. I used to try to copy him, and then in some sort of way I drifted over to Coleman Hawkins with his sound and Ben Webster with his sound. I don't even know when it happened.

Eddie Carson was in demand. One time we went out for about nine months. We stayed in Grand Junction for quite a while, and then we went out on the road working for some guys on a percentage; we'd get 60 percent, they'd get 40 percent of the door. Every time we got into a town, they'd say, "You should have been here yesterday"; like in Driggs, Idaho, they said, "The pea-pickers are all gone: you should have been here last week" and all that. I remember one Saturday we worked in Pocatello, Idaho, and I made thirty-five cents. I don't know how we even paid the hotel bill. We kept going—just by the hair of our chinny-chin-chins [laughs].

We had a big old Pierce Arrow car with jump seats in the back; that's what we traveled in. There was nine of us although the band was the Hot-Ten-*Tots*. My wife was traveling with me then, and the trombone player's wife was with him too. That was Pete Collins; he and Eddie did the writing. Pete's brother Booker played bass with Andy Kirk. In fact Andy Kirk tried to get Pete, but when I left Eddie Carson's band and came out here [LA], I sent for Pete and he came out here instead of going with Andy Kirk. Joe Mondragon was with the band when I quit; this was in Pocatello, at the end of one of those tours.

Eddie tried to get me back, but I wouldn't go. I guess we had a lot of fun, but we weren't making any money really. So we went back to Albuquerque, living with my father. He was doing all right. I started working around Albuquerque again with my little groups, with Mexican guys and black guys and one or two white guys. Had a white piano player, I can't remember his name, but he used to have epileptic fits. I remember that. I got a job playing at a place up in the mountains, about thirteen miles from Albuquerque, called Silvers, and pretty soon the war started and I left Albuquerque.

My wife and I came to Los Angeles. See, I knew Los Angeles because I went to school here. I ran away from home and came out on a freight train— I did this several times—the first time when I was fourteen. I just wanted to get away from Albuquerque, and I liked it out here. The oranges and lemons fascinated me. In 1934 I stayed until my father sent word out that he was sick and dying! He sent me a ticket and I came back home. Then in '36, I came out on a freight train again and I started shining shoes down on 5th and Hill. Jack Webb, the Dragnet *actor*, and I were going to Belmont High School [1575 W. 2nd Street] together. We were very good friends, Jack and I. In the school band—you heard of Joe Howard, trombone player? He and I were in that band together. That's the way I kept the music up.

My father brought my girlfriend—she wasn't my wife then—John Lewis, and my wife's brother out here for my graduation from Belmont in 1935, and *we all went back* [to Albuquerque] *in the car. That's when I started at the University of New Mexico under pre-med to be a dentist. I couldn't be no dentist as I was still hooked up in this music, so I quit and went out again with Eddie Carson, back to Grand Junction.*

I finally left Albuquerque on a section gang, putting ties in for the railroad, to get a free ride out here [LA]. *That's how I came out. You had to charge everything we got, and they was taking all the money from us in the company stores, but I stayed two weeks and made enough money to get a bus back to Los Angeles. I sent for my horn, and I started playing out here with different guys. This was 1939. I got myself a little established, and I'd play with people like Jack McVea's father, Mr.* [Satchel] *McVea; Henry Lloyd, he was a drummer; and Percy Williams, another drummer. With Mr. McVea, every piece of music you wanted to hear, he had it, in stock arrangements. He didn't belong to the union, but he'd hire the secretary of the union or the president of the union to work with him on Saturdays. He used to have three, four bands out at different places on Saturdays.*

I'd been out here about two months, I guess, when a guy called me up to work out at the Cricket Club [1571 West Washington Boulevard] *with Doug Finis, and that's when I worked with Kid Ory. Our bass player left town and went to Texas, so the leader went to the Hall of Records and got Kid Ory, who was a janitor there. At that time nobody knew anything about Dixieland. It was all swing then. So Kid Ory came in to play bass fiddle with us. I didn't even know that he played trombone, to tell you the truth. We had Teddy Buckner on trumpet; Leo Trammel and Edward Hale—they called him "Pop-Eye"—they were the two altos; Doug Finis was the pianist; Alton Redd was on drums; and Kid Ory played bass fiddle. As a bass player, he was just so-so. He wasn't no exceptional player but he'd keep up with things.*

It was an all-white club: blacks couldn't come in there, only to work. We played shows. An ex-prize fighter owned it. Doug Finis wanted to let me go, but Teddy talked to him and I stayed. Maybe I wasn't playing good enough for him. My reading? Just so-so. Doug was writing the arrangements. I don't know his background—I think he was from here. Tall fellow. Anyway, he finally ended up being a mailman. Illinois Jacquet played with us, and he went to Cab Calloway after that. He's the one that started people standing up playin' all the time. That used to kill me when I first started doing it because we'd sit down all the time. Just standing up to play a solo. Illinois was playing the heck out of the alto at first; then Lionel [Hampton] *moved him over on to tenor. He made the right move. Arthur Walker—he took Teddy's place—used to down me because I drank; me and Kid Ory, we used to drink a lot. Never got stinking drunk but we'd drink a lot. Arthur was a lot younger than me, and I'd say, "Man, one of these days, you gonna drink too." He'd say no, but when I came back from the Army, he wasn't drinking; he was on heroin. He was with Earl Hines by then. He had taken Billy Eckstine's place—he could sing like that too. I went down to the Orpheum to see him backstage. He came out, "Man, you sure were right. I'm worse than that; I'm a dope fiend now."*

Kid Ory, Teddy, and I, we would go up to the bar and get an eight-ounce glass of whiskey and say, "OK, bottoms up" and drink the whole eight ounces down. At that time we played 8 p.m. to 12 midnight, and by 11 o'clock, Ory would say, "Let's get another one, with me, man." I didn't know who he was; I'd be so drunk. There'd be people buying us drinks, and Teddy would say, "I can't keep up with this cat." He was a lot older than Teddy and me, but he could really put that stuff away.

I stayed there a year and a half, and then the war came up and I was drafted. While I was waiting, I was making pictures. They'd call me up and I'd go out [to Hollywood]. *I'm in* Cabin in the Sky, *with Lena Horne,* [MGM, 1943]; I Dood It, *with Red Skelton* [MGM, 1943] *and with Lena again, and Hazel Scott, as a musician. I made an audition to play in* Stormy Weather [20th Century Fox, 1943], *but by the time it started, I had to be in the Army. Just before that time, I went with Buddy Rich's Quartet; that was me and* [trumpeter] *Jake Porter, Meade Lux Lewis, and Buddy Rich. We worked at Billy Berg's Trouville club* [Beverly Boulevard and Fairfax Avenue] *for maybe two months. I remember one time Buddy called "Bugle Call Rag" so fast, Jake Porter couldn't make it. He won't admit that now.*

In May 1943, I went to Fort Huachuca in Arizona. When you were finally drafted, you went to the union and told them whether you wanted to go to Camp Lockett, Campo, California, or Fort Huachuca, and they would see to it that you went to the band. I picked Fort Huachuca and the trombones in that band were Henry Wells, Chester "Butch" Burrill—used to be with Noble Sissle—and Booker Christian—he became a barber in Denver. Tiny Roberts, Walter Williams, George Orendorff, Raymond Tate, Allie Grant, those were the trumpets. The saxes included Elwyn Frazier; he was a very good player. We write to each other; we were very good friends. He lives in Keyport, New Jersey; he doesn't play music anymore. Years back, he used to arrange for Duke. Sharkey Hall was the drummer.

We played for soldier advances; we were at a place called the Old Post, a forwards check-in post. We just played music, that's all we did. This was just strictly a dance band, no marching, no taps. We'd rehearse band music about one o'clock in the afternoon for about an hour and then we're on our own, and at night we'd play for dances in service clubs and things like that. It was easy. That Fort Huachuca band was a heck of a band; we came down here [LA] *and made an Army film called* G.I. Joe.[2] *Austin McCoy was the leader of that band.* [Dancer] *Fayard Nicholas, he was in there.*

Down Beat, May 15, 1944

Ravings at Reveille by "SARJ"—There's a mess of fine jive, whenever the former musicians, among soldiers quartered at Fort Huachuca, Ariz., get together for a session. Henry Wells, former Andy Kirk and Lunceford alto [sic], is leading one of the post bands. Irving Ashby, former Hampton guitar is matching riffs with musikers like Wesley Prince, Hampton bass; Booker Christian, Noble Sissle trombone; Robert Rudd, Sissle bass; Earl Jackson, Sissle reed; Walt Williams, Benny Carter trumpet; Jimmy Ellison, Erskine Hawkins sax; and arrangements by Jimmy Mundy, who scored for all the names.

I was home on furlough, and when I went back all the other sax players were gone on furlough, and the 37th Special Service unit was going overseas and they needed a sax player, so that's how I got in that. We stayed overseas eighteen months with the 37th. Six months in North Africa, Casablanca, and a year in Italy. We just went 'round playing for the soldiers. No combat, just Special Services. Ananias Berry of the Berry Brothers [dance team], *he was in there, and we had Lawrence "Pepper" Neely; he was quite an entertainer. Special Services consisted of people who took care of the PXs, of the athletic equipment, libraries, and entertainment, so every day at one o'clock we'd go to the hospitals and play for the patients. We'd get paid extra for that. I never even went through basic training, but I learned to read pretty good. I was a Musician Second Class.*

It was segregated, sure was. We were only playing for black troops and regiments; that's the way it was. Fort Huachuca was an all-black camp. Camp Lockett too. They turned the guys in Camp Lockett into a Port Battalion, used them to unload the ships. They went to Italy too. I saw them there—some of the guys were friends of mine.

I came out in January 1946. My wife and I had bought a home over on the East Side. So I started playing around, started out with a fellow named Felix Gross, made recordings with him. "Six Eight Boogie" and all that kind of stuff. I think I made some recordings before with Eddie Smith and his trio. He was a drummer, and in that band was [trumpeters] *Forrest Powell and Jesse Perdue; Monroe Tucker, piano; Arcima Taylor, saxophone; and Eddie played drums. We didn't have a bass. When I came out of the Army, the first record I made was with Austin McCoy* [Sterling Records, 1945]. *I forget who was on those records. Then I started making records with Jimmy Witherspoon; this was during the record strike. He was making records for three different companies. "Cain River Blues"* [Supreme Records, October 19, 1947], *"Ain't Nobody's Business"* [Supreme, with Jay McShann's band, November 15, 1947], *I was on all of those.*

Felix Gross had the band at the Senate Club in San Pedro. That was an all-black club. In that band we had Eddie Cane and me on tenors and "Smitty"—that's Vernon Smith, trumpet player; he was married to Dolores Parker, and he was with Erskine Hawkins for a while—Ernie Freeman, piano; and Bernard Carrere on bass. Felix played drums, and that band stayed there maybe six or eight months, a year at most. Played weekends, Fridays, Saturdays, Sundays. Strictly blues. Then Felix left and I took the band over, and we stayed for about two years, I guess. I had Orville Austin Jr. on piano; a guy named Joe, drummer; Buddy Floyd, he was playing tenor; and Al Williams was playing trumpet.

I went home to see about my mother, down in Albuquerque, and when I came back, the owner says, "I've let Buddy Floyd take the band. You can still work here but you gonna work under Buddy Floyd," so I said, "No, that's OK; he can have it." Buddy Floyd didn't last for very long. I had made a big name down there. I did a lot of publicity with the people. I was playing like Illinois Jacquet then, walking the bar, walking all over the place in fact. I was doing pretty good. Big Jay McNeely used to come in there and look at me with disgust because he was playin' bop. Next thing I know he was doing the same thing.

There was a club 'round the corner called the 409, and if we didn't have any business, I'd call "Flying Home" and I'd get up on that bar and walk that bar—it was a long bar, real long—playing that song. Pete Collins, the trombone player, and Jimmy Marvin, trumpet, they'd get up there with me, and we'd draw all the people out of the 409. "They're playing it," they'd say and they'd come around fast. Billy Eckstine came down to the 409, and we outdrew him because we did "Flying Home" and all those kind of numbers. Billy said, "Man, I don't understand it."

Then I got with Floyd Ray's band [in 1947, according to Fletcher Smith]. In that band there was Charles Mingus, Chico Hamilton, Al Killian, Buddy Collette, Jewel Grant, Fletcher Smith, Tex Thomas, trumpeter and arranger. One time we had Britt Woodman in the band; another time we had Wild Bill Moore. We traveled with Sammy Davis's uncle's trio, the Will Mastin Trio, and Sugar Chile Robinson playing the piano. It was a package. We traveled all 'round small places in California and played the Lincoln Theatre and the Million Dollar Theatre in Los Angeles.

Then we went into a club down in Los Angeles on Vernon Avenue called the Brass Rail [on South Broadway] with [drummer] Peppy Prince. There was five of us. Christine Chapman, Willie Jackson, Warren McOwens, Peppy, and myself. We turned that white club into a black club. The man made more money with us than he ever made in his life. He'd been there for years. He's called Pops Davis, the owner, and he had stage shows there. He had [dancers] Leroy and Skillet—Leroy at that time was called the Chattanooga Shoeshine Boy—and Redd Foxx, Arthur Adams, they all worked there. We stayed there a year and a half or maybe two years. This was in the fifties, maybe early fifties. We made records under Peppy's name, and then we recorded with the Platters under Peppy's name. Their first records in fact. We made "Only You" with them, but [producer] Ralph Bass shelved the things and then Mercury came out with the same things and it was a big hit without us. We were playing certain Joe Liggins licks because Peppy and Little Willie had been with Joe, so we became like a sort of Honeydrippers. Peppy was a funny person to get along with, but he was a real good drummer. Years back, he had taken Lionel's place with Les Hite.

Then I got Christine, piano; a fellow named Fats Theus on tenor; bassist Warren McOwens; and [drummer] Bert Brooks to go into the Riviera Hotel when they opened it up, in Las Vegas. [The Riviera opened on April 20, 1955.] We went there for two weeks and stayed there nine months. The band was called Oscar McLollie and his Honey Jumpers, and I quit when I found out McLollie was making all the money and we were doing all the work. He was a vocalist, and we were backing him. I'd get his bands together for him. That was a jumping combo—we kept all the Riviera crowds happy.

I took Plas Johnson's place with Ernie Freeman. Plas didn't want to go out on the road. Ernie had made that "Jiving Around" record [for Cash in 1955]—that was his hit—so Irving Ashby, Joe Epps, Raymond Martinez, Adolphus Allsbrook, and me, we went out on the road with Ernie. He would get so drunk; we just couldn't make it so we came back here. That's when I went with Horace Henderson's big band.

That was a good band. We had Bumps [Myers] on tenor; Russell Jacquet, Freddie Hill, trumpets; Pete Collins and Streamline on trombones; the drummer was George Reed. He's the one that got me in that one. I played a gig with George somewhere—I didn't even know him before and he said, "Man, how'd you like to work with Horace?" Next thing I heard, Horace called me and he asked me did I want to play with him. He wanted to be like his brother Fletcher, and he wasn't like that. He wanted to be a perfectionist. He was good, but he wasn't as professional as his brother. We were supposed to work in the Casino on Catalina Island until his wife, Angel, told the man over there what Horace would do and what he wouldn't do, and the man said, "Well, forget it" and he took Russ Morgan in there instead. That man lost his home behind all that, and some more things, trying to build up Horace into a big conglomeration. Horace was on his way until Angel messed that up. We played maybe fifteen gigs around Los Angeles with the big band and that was it.[3] So then I started working with Horace with a quartet. George Reed, McOwens, Horace, and myself. We stayed on a job at the Amber Light here in Los Angeles for about a year. Swing music.

I quit Horace and went into the mountains, up there to Buckhorn. Made more money than with Horace, playing up there with a quartet in the skiing country. I was walking 'round the dining room playing real soft to people eating. McOwens was up there with me, and Lady Will Carr was playing piano. She could play, but she was an alcoholic. I got mad and quit up there because the man was trying to tell me how to play. The band that I followed up there, his son would tell them to play "Louie, Louie" [composed by

Richard Berry and released in 1957] *and all that kind of stuff. I said, "I'm not playing that kind of music," so I quit and went to Anaheim and started working with Tommy Hearn. He was playing organ. I got Alton Redd in that trio later on; at first it was Rabon Tarrant on drums, who was also a very good vocalist. He got me in the band, and when Tommy let him go, I got George Reed in there and then I got Red Minor. He and I had been in Manhattan Beach with a fellow named Charlie Martin. We stayed there quite a while until Tommy got sick. He had a sissy playing the organ in his place—Dick?—and the owner couldn't stand sissies so he let us go.*

I've left out a lot of guys I played with [laughs]. *Like* [blues pianist/vocalist] *Little Willie Littlefield; I was on the road with him. Buddy Floyd, myself, and* [trumpeter] *Douglas Byars—they call him Slits—and* [drummer] *Cake Wichard. We were all with Little Willie Littlefield and traveled down south with him. Early 1950s, I guess. I made just about all his records with him. I traveled too with Dinah Washington for about nine months* [starting in autumn 1950]; *that was with Calvin Boze's orchestra. He was a trumpet player; band was Clyde Dunn, Sheridan Black, and myself, saxophones; Charlie Davis, piano; Al Bartee, drums; and Warren McOwens, bass fiddle. Warren was my buddy, and I used to get him in all these things. Dinah was crazy, but she was all right. Traveled quite a bit with her. I enjoyed that. No other acts with us as Calvin was being featured as he had put out these hit records, like "Safronia B"* [Aladdin, January 13, 1950] *and the others. I quit that band in New York when we had to go to a job in Newark and they never showed up. I'm standing there all day waiting, but they never called me or told me the job was called off. It was the principle of the thing, so I said to heck with it, I'm going back to Los Angeles.*

I went to Disneyland with Teddy Buckner in 1977. I took Caughey Roberts's place. He had played clarinet, and I said to Teddy, "I don't want to play clarinet, man. I'll make the soprano sound like a clarinet. Just stay in the upper register all the time" and I did. I never could play clarinet. I've had 'em but I couldn't play 'em! I stayed there seven years until Teddy let the whole band go.

The Dixieland repertoire wasn't easy for me. Teddy would call a number I'd never even heard of before. He'd play the first chorus down and then point to me, so I've got the solo chorus and I'd never heard it before. Boy, that was hard, but I made it. Then he'd say, "You got the idea of how it goes?" and he wouldn't play it again for maybe two months, honest to goodness. So that was steady for me, nothing else for seven years. Teddy played both Dixieland and swing: the first hour he'd play Dixieland; the second he'd play swing. So I played soprano on the Dixieland things, and on the rest of the night, I'd play tenor. I enjoyed playing with Teddy.

He's OK, but he doesn't play his horn anymore. I don't think he even listens to music anymore. He's got bad knees. That's the reason he didn't want to play Disneyland anymore because we used to have to help him on and off the stage. He didn't want people to see him like that. When they let us go, Teddy said, "Well, I'll come back for three nights, but I won't do five nights." He could have told people he'd do the best three nights and let some other trumpet player do his other two nights, but he wouldn't do that. After we left that, he never played again. That was it.

People used to call Teddy up for jobs like when Frankie Capp wanted us to go on the Nell Carter show. Teddy didn't even recommend us, so Capp called Jesse Sailes and he got hold of the rest of us for the show. Norman Bowden played the trumpet, and Nat Pierce played the piano because [Buckner pianist] Chester Lane had broken his arm in an automobile accident. We got residuals on that show for four years. Just from that one time. I used to get about $600 every two months, I guess. After four years, it cuts out. And I got a great big one, $1800, when they showed it overseas. And I just did a TV show for Jackie Collins—I guess that was for her company—about a book she'd written called Lucky Chance. I'm in that Wild at Heart [Hollywood, 1990] movie with Streamline, Jesse, and [trumpeter] Herb Permillion; we're all in that. David Lynch was the director. It just came out and we should be getting some money out of that. We made up a tune that we play; I don't know what they named it, but we made it up.

After Teddy, I started playing with the Angel City Jazz Band [1984–1988] and then the Surfside Jazz Band and now I'm with this Tin Pan Valley band. We play half Dixieland, half swing. The Surfside band was getting rid of [trombonist] Danny Snyder, and I told them about Streamline and I got him in the band, and that's when they changed the name to the Tin Pan Valley band. Good band. I do like the piano player with the band. He owns a club downtown called the Redwood Room on 2nd Street between Hill and Broadway, and about every month or six weeks we go down and play Friday nights for him. He has a big feed for everybody, and they like us down there. We play more swing down there. In the meantime, I'm with Monte Easter, and it's lucky it doesn't conflict. I hate to tell anybody no.

Monte just seems to like the way I play. I've known him for years, but I never played with him way back. First met him in 1939. Now we're here at the Holiday Inn. We had two weeks with a two-week option, and then we had three-week options so we did seven weeks, laid off two weeks, now we're back to two weeks, two-week options. We'll see what happens.

The tenor players now, I don't care for the new ones and I don't care for modern music. Bebop? It doesn't say anything. My men were Hawkins, Webster, Young, Ike Quebec, Illinois, all those guys. The tenor players now, all they do is play a lot of notes to me. They're seeing who can play the most notes. I used to be on Central Avenue jamming all the time, playing swing not bebop, with J. C. Higginbotham, Dexter [Gordon], a fellow named Little

Hawk, Art Tatum, and Tiny Grimes, all those people. This music you should play it from the heart.

Peppy Prince told me years ago, he'd say, "Man, when you're playing a solo, you're playing to those American people out there; don't talk Chinese to them. They won't know what you're saying." I never forget that when I try putting my message over to the people.

Arcelle and I, I guess we've been together all our lives [laughs]; we're fifty-three years married now. We got a boy and a girl and four grandchildren. We started going together in junior high school. Arcelle went to Lincoln High and I went to Washington High—that's in Albuquerque—and I used to run all the way from Washington High to Lincoln High just to carry her books home for her.

I've had fun, made a pretty good living. Been around some good guys, some rotten ones too. Being around the good guys and being happy playing with them, that's what counts. Making people happy makes me happy. I can't imagine putting the horn down. I wouldn't know what to do. I used to play tennis, got to be pretty good. My hobby now is making canes; I call them tree lamps. Come on, I'll show you some . . .

Chapter Fifteen

Jesse John Sailes

Drums

For a period in the postwar 1940s and 1950s, the drummer Jesse Sailes was hardly ever out of the Los Angeles studios, sometimes taking part in three sessions a day as one of a rotating group of premier sidemen who were on call to record with gospel groups, blues shouters, and R&B combos.

By the time we met him in August 1990, just hours after leaving another drummer, Monk McFay, he was "retired" but still taking gigs with Monte Easter and Bob Allen's traditional band. His house on East Colden Avenue, set between Avalon and Central, was comfortable, and there was a substantial RV (recreational vehicle) in the driveway, Jesse explaining that he and his wife liked to escape the city and drive out. The room in which we sat featured her rather startling collection of crystal pieces, the chairs and settees plastic-covered, an indication, doubtless, of a well-kept home. It was good, too, to meet Mrs. Laverne Sailes, who turned out to be the niece of the pianist Ann Coy, the wife of the drummer and bandleader Gene Coy, a key figure in many of these oral testimonies.

I had heard Jesse play with Easter's neat combo twice and again with a Teddy Buckner reunion band at the Los Angeles Jazz Festival and been bowled over by his vitality and swing. So how was it that an artist of his caliber seemed so little known? There were no *Down Beat* profiles or interviews that we could locate, and even now he does not figure in any of the recognized jazz encyclopedias. A burly, dignified man, whose reminiscences were punctuated by peals of laughter, Jesse enjoyed several long-term musical associations in and around Los Angeles, apparently happy to stay off the road. He probably never sought (or needed) much publicity, seemingly always in demand, secure in his family life, and devoted to St. Paul Baptist

Jesse Sailes, at Follies Theatre, Main Street, Los Angeles, late 1940s. From the author's collection.

Church on W. 49th Street, where he became a deacon following his "retirement" from music.

Once the market for blues and R&B had subsided, Jesse found a safe haven in trumpeter Teddy Buckner's traditional band, working out at Disneyland until Buckner retired in 1983, still taking record dates and making the occasional movie appearance. His recording career credits were as eclectic as could be, ranging from Little Richard to Kid Ory, from Big Jay McNeely to Cher, from Elmore James to Doris Day, from Jimmy Witherspoon to Louis Armstrong; the companies involved both big and small. His sole "name" release was a 45-rpm pop single for the Felsted label entitled "I'm in Love with the Drummer" and billed as by Jesse Sailes and the Waves.

Jesse Sailes was born in Denver, Colorado, on December 3, 1919, and died in Los Angeles on September 5, 2007.

Jesse Sailes: Los Angeles, August 27, 1990

My mother, Della, was out here [Los Angeles], *but I was staying with my grandmother in Denver. My father, John Sailes, was a drummer and a very good one. In fact he was the one who showed Jo Jones how to play with brushes. He was one of the greatest brush men I've ever seen in my life. He was a good singer too, always played and sang. He was in Omaha, and he used to have a band of his own there.*

I started playing in 1934, and my first job was with a band in Denver. I was still goin' to school. This older man was a trumpet player who had a band and he needed a drummer. My grandmother let me make it, so that was my first professional job. I didn't know what I was doing, but he asked me if I wanted to play and I said, "Yeah, I'll try." I was nervous on the first job, but I made it. He liked my playing, so I played with him for two or three gigs. That was nice.

I had a brother; he's a piano player. Two years older than me. He's in Omaha now. He's still playing, piano and organ. Mostly organ now. His name is William Asher Sailes,[1] *but they call him "Big Daddy" in Omaha. He's twice as big as me* [laughs]. *He used to work with Rex Stewart, and he was playing in Boston with Earle Warren; they used to have a band* [in 1946]. *He was a good musician. My brother used to live here* [LA]; *then he went to the Navy, and after he left the Navy, he went back to Omaha.*

My father was my inspiration for playing the drums. I had a little old snare drum I used to bang on. Something my grandmother had around the house. I just found it and start beating on it. Then my father came through town and he gave me a drum set, and I started playing from there. I was doing high school then, and I played with the school marching band.

I didn't do too much playing in Denver, but when me and my brother came out here to live with my mother, we got us a little group together. This was in '34. We went to Jefferson High School. Quite a few musicians came out of Jeff. You remember Chico Hamilton; I started him out, too. There was Leo Williams, trombone player; Streamline [John Ewing], *he went to Jeff; and Walter Murden, drummer, he was a good buddy of mine. He passed. Mr. Davis, he was the music teacher, and Samuel Browne was one of my teachers too. Our little group, we done what you call house parties; you know kids had house parties so we played them and we built on up. Me and my brother, a kid by the name of Terry Cruise on clarinet, just us three. It was fun. Terry Cruise*[2] *went up north; he went to Seattle. I never heard from him since.*

When Terry left town, that broke us up, so me and my brother quit playing together. He went one way and I went another. He got jobs on his own. I was still going to school then. A little later, about '36, '37, I started working with the Woodman Brothers.[3] *I worked with them quite a while. That's Britt, Coney, and "Brother"* [William Woodman Jr.], *and Buddy Collette was with* us sometimes. Joe Comfort played bass or Nutty Mingus sometimes [laughs]. He was a gas, crazy, but he was a good fellow. I loved that bass. They was all out in Watts.

I used to go 'round Central Avenue and try to see the bands when I could, but being young you could just go so far. I used to hear all the big bands like Basie, Andy Kirk, and Jimmie Lunceford and Les Hite and the local guys. You remember Sammie Franklin? He used to work at the Elks;[4] they used to have dances there all the time and I used to go to those dances. Then the Muslims bought that Elks. So that was what I was mostly used to, listening to big bands. My two favorite drummers were James Crawford and Jo Jones. That's who I tried to pattern my style after. Every time Jo was in town, he'd always come by the house. He knew my father, so that's how we come to be such good buddies.

I got the job at the Follies[5] when I was about eighteen. Just come out of high school. Went straight to the Follies. Sure, that was awful young. One thing about the Follies, the man down there, Gordon Harrison,[6] who was the leader, you probably never did hear of him but he was one of the greatest. He knew music. He taught me. He used to make me mad: I wanted to quit that job, but I said I was gonna learn. That was a million dollars' worth of experience I got, and it taught me how to play a show. It was great. I used to beat up a show; I'm not bragging on myself, but I loved to play a show.

I think the Follies building is gone now. The Follies was a burlesque show, on 3rd and Main. It was a big theater, had upstairs and downstairs. Strippers. The band played behind the strippers and the dancers. It was a regular show. It was nice. It was a white show; no blacks. They just had a black band there. The acts on stage would be white and the audience was whatever; it wasn't segregated at all. There was another burlesque house called the Burbank, which was up on 7th and Main too. When the Follies closed up, the Dalton brothers—that's the ones that had it—they bought the Burbank and used the Burbank.

How I got the Follies job, I was working at my church and Woody Woodman was working down there too. He asked me did I want to go to work. I said, "Yeah, I'll go down there." He said, "OK, well, Gordon's looking for a drummer." So I auditioned and he liked it and I got the job. The band was Woody Woodman [William Woodman Sr.], trombone; Maxwell Davis, tenor; and there was a trumpet player by the name of Slits [Douglas Byars]—he came out here [LA] with Maxwell—Gordon Harrison, that was the piano player; and me. There was an alto player, Jewell Grant; he played there for a while. There was six of us. No bass. It was rough, but after a while, Chuck [Ralph "Chuck" Hamilton] came in and played bass and Gordon stayed until my brother started playing piano with us. Happy Johnson came in on trombone after Woody quit.

We worked seven days a week, day and night. Monday to Friday, we worked three shows; Thursday night, we rehearsed strippers; and Friday night, we rehearsed the show. Saturdays we done five shows, and Sunday we done four shows. Sometimes a show would last an hour or hour and a half; sometimes the people would stay in and they'd have pictures in between. At first, I couldn't stop looking [at the girls]; then after I got used to it, I started reading funny books [laughs]. What would kill them, the girls up there would be trying to do bumps and things and show me up. They couldn't get me: I'd catch everything they'd do. If they'd blink a toe, I'd catch it and I'd read my funny book at the same time.

At first, it was exciting. Like any new job is exciting, but after a while, I just got used to it. Sure, I had to read. Definitely. Different acts would come in and bring their music. When Gordon, our MD [musical director] passed, they gave the job to me, but I didn't want it, but they said if you don't take it, we gonna get another band and that threw the guys out of work, so I said, "OK, I'll take it." Which was a hassle. I was sure glad to get rid of that. You had to buy music, you had to rehearse the acts, and you had to contend with their personalities. It was something else. Two of the acts was real good. That was Tempest Storm, she was one of the greatest [striptease artists], and Lili St. Cyr. Those were the two best stars. In fact Lili St. Cyr wanted me to travel with her to be her drummer. I said, "No, thank you—I'm gonna stay right here with Momma."

It definitely limited my jazz playing because you just had to play show music. Mostly stocks [arrangements] and that was it. I was doing quite a bit of rehearsing for recording jobs, but it knocked all that out because I never could make 'em, working three shows a day.

About 1942, we just decided to form a band, all of us. Just wanted to get out of there [the Follies], so we had to join the union and they fined us for being in a non-union house [laughs]. Everybody was non-union but my brother; he was already in the union. Maxwell was the musical director and Happy [Johnson] was the leader. He took care of finding work. Happy was OK, a good leader and a good businessman. He took care of business.

So we had Happy on trombone, Jewell Grant played alto, Woody Woodman Jr.—we call him "Brother"—he played trumpet and baritone saxophone, Maxwell on tenor, Chuck Hamilton playing bass, my brother, and me. And Carolyn Richardson singing with us. That was one of the greatest bands you want to hear, and Maxwell was one of the greatest arrangers. Oh man, he had this band sound like Duke, like Basie, you name it, he had us sound like that.

You talking about a bass player, Chuck played some rhythm that make you blow your mind. He remind you of "Hoss" Page [Walter Page]. "Fat Boy," that's what we call him. He was from Chickasha, Oklahoma. That was my boon coon. We was runnin' buddies. People saw us together, they'd think *we was policemen coming through. Two big guys. In fact Chuck was the one who caused me to meet my wife. This was when I was trying to stay out of the Army while I was working at the Follies. My wife's aunt was Ann Coy; that's Gene Coy's wife. She played piano in Gene's band. We used to go to the fair to see him all the time. Streamline came out of that band; Maxwell; this guy Slits; guy by the name of Lester* [Taylor], *saxophone player from Fresno, California; and bassist Junior Raglin, they all came out of that band. He had some good musicians in there. Gene Coy was lots older than me. He done more traveling up north; he didn't come out here very much. Seattle, Fresno, Washington state, up in that area he used to play. The whole family's gone now. My wife just has a couple of distant cousins.*

Maxwell, me, and sometimes my brother, we used to record quite a bit. Maxwell was always in demand, but he died young [in 1970]. *He went to the doctor for a check-up and he came back OK, and doggone, the next day he had a heart attack. He sure was a workin' dude. He had put the horn down, went to playing piano, and he was an excellent violin player, too. That was his first instrument and he could still play.*

Happy got in contact with a man in San Diego who first started the Creole Palace[7] *club down there. We started working there for a while and then we went to the College Inn* [1st and C] *and worked there the longest. See, we were supposed to work there for two weeks with an option, and we worked there for at least a year and a half, two years maybe. The Creole Palace was a black club, and the College Inn was a white club. Mostly down there, it was those Marines. They were wearisome. Marines and sailors, they loved to drink and fight.*

Then we came out here [LA] *and went to the Club Alabam and played for the shows. From the 'Bam we went out to the Hollywood Café; this was later on in 1943. The band stayed the same all this time and didn't do no recording at all. The popularity of that band was due to the sound and the musicians. All of them was good musicians and it was a good band. The people, they wouldn't dance; they'd just sit while we were playing. So one night, Happy asked how come they wouldn't get up to dance and they said, "We didn't come here to dance; we come here to listen to the band." Yes, sir. You heard of the Savoy Sultans? Well, this band I would put up against the Savoy Sultans; that's just how great it was.*

I went to the Army on January 11, 1944. Zutty Singleton took my place at the Hollywood Café. I was in an ammunition company. I couldn't get in a band; the quota was full. Well, if I had of went when they was asking for musicians, I could have made it, but I stayed out as long as I could and those days was gone. I went out to Germany. I stayed over there for a while. Being in ammunition, I wasn't far behind the front line. Made Staff Sergeant. When the war was over in Germany [May 8, 1945] *and it was the end of ETO* [European Theatre of Operations], *they was sending us over to the South*

Pacific. I prayed the war would stop and we'd come home, and that's when they dropped this bomb on Hiroshima [August 6, 1945; Japan surrendered September 2, 1945], *and the next morning, they sent word on our ship we would dock in the U.S. and we didn't have to go over there. I said, "Thank you, Lord"* [laughs]. *I always will believe in the power of prayer! Got out about '46, just stayed until they processed our discharge. They asked me if I wanted to sign up. I said, "Not on your life. No way." I was away from home two and a half years. That's a long time.*

I started playing again, and then me and Chuck, we had a trucking business. First of all, we got us a truck and we started hauling watermelons, and then we started hauling scrap iron. At that time, music jobs was sorta scarce, but then I started doing gigs with Jake [trumpeter Jake Porter], *just pick-up things, playing swing music. I was doing quite a bit of recording too around that time, so that kept me going pretty good.*

I done a couple of things with Kay Starr and Percy Mayfield with Ray Charles playing piano and B. B. King. He was my man. In fact, I used to do all his Los Angeles recordings. I like his style. He had a nice style. One of the greatest guys I ever worked for—you can't say anything wrong about him; if they do, they'd be lying. He's a great cat. I just made records with him. Never went on the road. All my time playing music, my road experience was just San Diego for those eighteen months. That was a steady job. All my jobs have been right here in Los Angeles. I didn't have to go on the road; if I could make money here, why travel? That's just how it worked out. That's why I didn't do no drugs because I wasn't on the road. I believe that's one reason that causes musicians to get on that junk. They get away from home and get to messin' around and the first thing you know they get on that stuff. I never fooled with it, never wanted to, and never been enticed to. Never will.

Maxwell used to write for B. B. all the time. Maxwell liked my style of playing, I guess. He always used to call me to play. He was my buddy, too. I liked to work with Maxwell because I listened and I learned. I learned a whole lot from Maxwell. He'd teach me rhythm, different kinds of styles. He let me be free; he let me do what I wanted to do. The main thing he liked about it, my time was good.

I try to play everything. I didn't have no certain thing I play. I play it all. If Wayne King wanted me to play waltzes, I could do that all night. If you stick to one thing, you lost. Do everything. That's what you gotta do if you want to make it. There's only one thing I never did like, that's this modern jazz. I hated that. I still don't like it. If I have to play it, I play it, but I just don't see no sense to it. I dropped by and heard Charlie Parker, never sat in with him. It don't say nothin' to me.

Max Roach, he's a heckuva drummer. I used to hate his playing because a man would be taking a solo, and doggone, he's soloing right with the man. I mean, where's the beat? What's the man [soloist] *got to go on? That used to kill me to hear him. But now he's changed; he's playing more like a drummer should play and I love him. Now, my teacher Dick Shanahan was a very good drummer. He used to work with Stan Kenton and all the big bands. He was great. Sid Catlett, don't forget him. I used to go see him here at a club. Him and Zutty Singleton. One drummer I sure wish I could have seen playing in person and never did was Chick Webb. He was something else, too.*

I played with Slim Gaillard's big band. Remember Billy Berg's? He used to have a club over on Vine Street in Hollywood and Slim had a big band in there. Me and Chuck worked with that band. Teddy Edwards, saxophone player, and I think Bobby Bryant was in that band too. Just after the war. Not too long, didn't last too long. I never did play with a big band again.

As I told you before, I patterned my style between Jo Jones and Jimmy Crawford, so I put them both with what I wanted to do and that's the style I come up with. I just hear something crazy in my ear and I try to see what it sound like. If it sound OK, then OK, just like this boogaloo going around this town. I started that. I was doin' a commercial with a group so they said, "Do something funny; do something different," so I said, "OK, I'll think of something." I started doing that and they liked it, and the fellow at Capitol Records, A&R man, called me in for a session. "I want you to do what you done on this demo" so I done that, and that's what started me out on my recording career.

The Billboard, September 3, 1949

Burlesque by UNO—Gordon Harrison, pianist, is rounding out 20 years as musical director at the Follies, Los Angeles. Others in the ork are Michael DeLay, trumpet, Jewell Grant, sax and clarinet, and Jesse Sailes, drummer.

The biggest one I ever done which was a hit, because it was made good, was "The In Crowd,"[8] *with Dobie Gray. That was me on that. That's what sorta made my hit, and that's when I did a whole lot of recordings.*

It's evident from the Billboard reference that Jesse had rejoined the band at the Follies once he had returned home although his reminiscences tended to highlight his recording experiences. It's impossible to document all of his recordings. Many were made for obscure local labels, and the personnel details have never surfaced. Others were for large commercial dates where Jesse was strictly a hired hand. Those that we do know about include sessions with blues shouters Big Joe Turner, Jimmy Witherspoon, and Crown Prince Waterford, invariably with Maxwell Davis and Chuck Hamilton involved, often under the leadership of pianists Jay McShann or Pete Johnson.

He also recorded many times with Percy Mayfield, Lloyd Glenn, Amos Milburn, and Ike Carpenter, and less often but in more eclectic surroundings with Woo Woo Moore, Pat Valdeler, Willard McDaniel, as well as Eddie

Cochran, Cecil Gant, Johnny "Guitar" Watson, Frankie Lee Sims, Phil Spector, Shirley & Lee, B. B. King, Elmore James, Gene Vincent, Lowell Fulson, Oscar McLollie and His Honey Jumpers, Little Richard, Louis Armstrong, Duane Eddy, Doris Day, Chris Montez (*Let's Dance*), The Easy Riders, The Coasters, Brother Joe May, Cher, Barbara Dane, and for the sound track of *Lady Sings the Blues* (with the Teddy Buckner band) in 1972. There were doubtless many more dates, some for the Los Angeles–based MoTown team, the details now lost in the mists of time.

In 1955, Jesse Sailes joined trumpeter Teddy Buckner's newly formed traditional jazz band, a wise move as it turned out. Buckner had lately left Kid Ory's Creole Jazz Band, then hugely popular, having learned the traditional repertoire from scratch and impressed critics and audiences alike. Buckner's band was to undertake a series of long-term residencies that endured until Buckner decided to retire and disbanded in December 1983.

Along the way the Buckner band achieved considerable acclaim and starred in numerous special concert presentations including the seventieth birthday celebration for Louis Armstrong held at The Shrine in Los Angeles in 1970. They appeared in the films *Four for Texas* (1963, Warner) and *Hush . . . Hush, Sweet Charlotte* (1964, TCF) and played three times for the long-running KABC TV series *Stars of Jazz* in the 1950s and for *Stars of Jazz* in 1962 while recording regularly for the Dixieland Jubilee label. After his Buckner days, Jesse performed in the 1990 David Lynch film *Wild at Heart* in a group with Streamline Ewing and Chuck Thomas and was co-credited with their composition "Streamline" as listed in the film's credits.

I had met Teddy Buckner, but I didn't know him personally. That's when Woody Woodman asked me if I wanted to join the band because he was playing with him. I was working at my church where I was the custodian and janitor. So I said, "Yeah, I'll go." I was replacing George Jenkins, and Teddy had been organized about three months then. I was with Teddy twenty-seven years to '83.

I never played Dixieland before. No, sir. I didn't even used to listen to it. See, I had been studying drumming with Dick Shanahan, so I said, "Hey, Dick, I got a job to join a Dixieland band. How do you play Dixieland?" "You just play, that's all," he said [laughs]. *I just went in and played. Been doin' it ever since. I knew Ram* [Ory drummer Minor "Ram" Hall] *and all of them because I used to meet them at the union hall and we used to talk. But I never did hear them play. But like I say, when I get into something, I want to learn it to make sure I'm doin' it right but I still do it my way. I have my own style of doin' it. It's the way I feel.*

A drum is a metronome of a band. Where you gonna get that pulsation from, the bass drum, right? Three-fourths of those drummers, they don't even have no bass drum. You can't even hear it. My idea is that you let them hear the bass drum. That's why I keep my bass drum muffled down so you can hear it and feel it, more than it being a big boom. It helps the band to move. Now maybe I'm wrong but that's my idea. A band don't swing without a bass drum, without that beat. Even on records you can hear my bass drum.

Teddy's band was beautiful. Great. Pud Brown, he was playing saxophone at first; Woody Woodman, trombone; Harvey Brooks, piano; Teddy; me; and Art Edwards playing bass. Very good bass player. He was with Nellie Lutcher for a long time. He had started with Teddy right away, and when Teddy retired, Art quit playing altogether. Harvey was a very good piano player, nice fellow. He wrote quite a few songs. His hit song was "A Little Bird Told Me." I made that with Paula Watson.[9] *Maxwell wrote [arranged] it; we was on that together. Harvey was a nice little drinker; he used to drink a lot. Teddy used to get in about that drinking too.*

Teddy was beautiful. He was good-toned trumpet player. He had a style that no other trumpet player had. That's what made him. That's why everybody loved him. Him and Louis [Armstrong]. Teddy didn't have no right [need] to be tough. He wasn't dealing with a bunch of kids. We knew how to handle ourselves. First it was Joe [Darensbourg] on clarinet, then Caughey [Roberts]; then after he left, Chuck [Thomas] came in and Streamline [Ewing] after Woody. Joe was a very good musician. We had a nice time together.

The Buckner band stayed at the 400 Club [3330 W. 8th Street] for three years starting in 1954 before moving on to the Beverly Cavern [Beverly Boulevard and Ardmore Avenue, Hollywood] to which they returned a number of times, playing five nights a week, also fitting in an engagement at the Hangover in San Francisco for three months in 1955. They played the Huddle in West Covina for five years before eventually landing the Disneyland residency that made their name. The Teddy Buckner Dixieland All-Stars, as they were billed, with vocalist Jewel Hall, were located in New Orleans Square from 1967 through to December 1983.

In 1959, Jesse recorded with New Orleans trombone pioneer Kid Ory for the Verve label up in San Francisco.

One day when we were playing at the Beverly Cavern, he came in and asked if I'd make a recording with him. He was a nice fellow, enjoyed working with him. He had his own style, definitely. He really had a style of playing. He just called the numbers and said, "Let's do it." We'd run 'em down, get 'em set, and then do 'em. No hassles, none whatsoever. Caughey was on the date, too; he was a very good musician. I think that was one reason that the [Buckner] band was so together was because of him and Stream. They could work together so good. They had everything solid and together, and they could back Teddy up. Caughey left the band and he retired. He may do gigs, like me, but he's not even teaching anymore. He put that down too.

Down Beat, September 27, 1962
  Caught In The Act—Teddy Buckner—The Huddle, Covina, Calif.—The Lane-Edwards-Sailes rhythm team does its job thoroughly and with maximum effect.—John Tynan

Those were very good years. The fellows all liked each other; they liked to play together, which means a lot. Wasn't no drunkards in the band and they were all down to business. When they go on a job, they went to do the job, not play around. The fellows were never late; they always on time, early, ready to go. Every place we played, they wanted us to stay. That will show you how good a band it was. We all acted more like brothers in a family so that helped. There wasn't no discord among the men.

  We played the year round at Disneyland. I was working at the Los Angeles Herald-Examiner *at the same time. I had started there the first of the year, and about two months later, they called me to come and work at Disneyland. I retired in January 1983 at the* Herald-Examiner *and at Disneyland too. We didn't have enough hours at Disneyland to get a pension.*

  I broke my leg, my left leg, the one I play the bass drum with, but I said this ain't gonna stop me playing, so I just start playing right-handed. See, I was a left-handed drummer. I was acting stupid. The first time, I was going down to pick up my wife at work, and I was getting out of the car and some fool went across and hit me and cracked the fibula bone. The second time, I was coming across the train track and my foot got tangled up in the track and I cracked it. That was my fault. Me and Streamline was walking together and he said, "Come on, here comes the train; I can't carry you." "Man, my foot, I can't make it." The train was coming down, but I made it.

  I went to the doctor and he X-rayed it; it got swoll' up and there it was, cracked. That ain't gonna stop me, so I bought me one of those practice pads and start practicing with the right hand. They didn't want to let me work out at Disneyland, but I got paid anyway. We were on salary. Got sick pay. Disneyland was a very good employer then, but now the new regime that took over they say is something else, but when we were there, it was beautiful. The director of entertainment was beautiful, and there was another guy who was crazy about Teddy—I forget his name—and they threw a birthday party for Teddy. That was one of the most expensive parties you ever want to see. They closed down the whole French Market where we played for a surprise. Everybody went out and Teddy didn't even know it, and then they all came back in again. It was beautiful—that's what they thought about him up there at Disneyland.

  I was the foreman of the custodians [at the *Herald-Examiner*]. *I just like to be doing something. The job wasn't hard. I was working the daytime there and the evening at Disneyland. It keeps me going, plus when you don't drink or smoke and get your rest, you can do things like that. See, you can't be going to all these jam sessions and all the parties and do that stuff, so I say, "No, forget it." It's one or the other.*

Now, we didn't want to retire from Disneyland. We could have still been working there, but Teddy just got tired. His knees was messin' up, and he was embarrassed the way he was walkin'. He didn't want to work no two- or three-hour days. He just wanted to work one or two, but you can't tell Disneyland when you want to work, so the man said, "Hey, we'll just retire you." That's how what it was. Now, Teddy just sits there at home. He don't want to do nothing.[10] *The band could have gone on, but they wanted that name. Teddy's name. We could have got somebody, but it wouldn't have done no good. Looking back, working with Teddy at Disneyland was most pleasurable, the greatest job I ever had playing music.*

Now I do what I can do, working with Bob [Chris Kelly's Black and White New Orleans band] *or working with Monte every now and then, and I get a few recording sessions. I knew Monte for quite a while personally. He just called me up and asked me to work with him one night. I did and he told me if I wanted to join the band, well, I hadn't nothing else to do so I said yes. He liked my playing and this has been about two years, and with Bob, about four years. Now, that's two different styles. Bob sends me tapes about the different drummers in New Orleans, so I listen to what they're doing and do some of those things that Bob likes. I'll try to please him. Streamline plays in Bob's band, and Mike Baird is on clarinet; Buddy Burns on the bass, he's OK; and the piano player is Reggie Evans. He goes to my church. We had a concert at the church, so I told Bob to come down and listen to him. He heard him and he asked him if he wanted to join and Reggie said he'd try. He never played no Dixieland before.*

A guy named Ernest Dodson used to have a group of his own here and he quit playing. He's a very good fellow. Awful good Christian. Still around. He said, "Got a set of drums at the house; you can have them if you want 'em." I went over there and got 'em and there they are. I brought 'em home, cleaned them, fixed them up, and that's what I use. They're light, got a good tone, and easy to carry. He gave me the case, bass drums, two tom-toms, and a metal snare and cymbals. The whole works. For nothing. I've got three sets now. I used to have to have this many sets because of the way I was recording. I had to have a collection service. I'd use one set and finish and then go to another studio and pick it up from the collection service and take it to another. I would go all day recording so one set wouldn't do it. It would kill too much time, packing up and unpacking. I had to get me some more drums, and then Louis Bellson, he talked me into endorsing Pearl drums, so I got two sets from them. One of them I gave to the church; the other's in the garage.

My church is St. Paul Baptist Church at 100 W. 49th Street. I'm a deacon; that's somebody who takes care of the church and helps the pastor do different things around the church. Plus I work down there during the day. After I retired, I just decided I'm gonna get more in the church. It's been interesting. I play at the church too. I play with the choir. Baptist is more like the Holy Roller black church. You should come down there; you'd enjoy it. Reggie plays piano and organ and we got a bongo player. We really get something goin' [laughs]. *That's a challenge to you because you don't know what the choir director is going to do, the numbers she calls, you never played 'em before so you out there and you gotta guess what she gonna do. That's what doing shows taught me: watch your director, and be alert at all times.*

I don't think none of the music is gonna change. There's always gonna be rock, always gonna be jazz, always gonna be progressive jazz. Me, I like swing. Count Basie, that's my style. My biggest of dreams was to play with the Count Basie band. Never did. I loved the way it played and I loved the dynamics.

One of the musicians I would like to put on a pedestal is Maxwell. You know what was most phenomenal about him? We'd be on a bandstand and he'd come to work with about eight bars of a voicing for the band. "Hey, fellows, play that for me." If it sounds OK, the next night he'd come up with the arrangement and he'd make an arrangement like that without even a master sheet. Like you writing a letter . . .

Maxwell was a great tenor player, too. Beautiful. I remember one jam session. They used to have a place over here on Vernon, and Lester Young, Maxwell, Jo Jones, Hoss Page, Art Tatum, and another tenor player, they all tied up there. Oh boy, that was the greatest thing you ever want to hear. Art Tatum and Maxwell were the only two left, so Art was trying to play in different keys Maxwell couldn't play in and he couldn't do it. Maxwell followed him every place he went! I was there. Lester Young packed up his horn and Maxwell outblew 'em all. He was something else.

I didn't do too much on Central Avenue. I played the Elks with the Woodman Brothers, and I used to work at Club Alabam with Happy Johnson. I worked at the Down Beat with Earl Grant, piano player. Just for two weeks. He needed a drummer. After the riot, Central Avenue went down; the places weren't hot no more, and there's just nothin' there now. At 10 o'clock, you can take a rock, throw it, and you wouldn't hit nothing. As time goes, everything goes. Pitiful.

It's fun to play with a good band when they're happy and they enjoy playing. That makes you feel good. See, I like to be happy. I'm gonna play until I can't do it no more. I don't never intend to give it up. That's my life.

Chapter Sixteen

"Red" Minor William Robinson

Drums

It was my host, Roger Jamieson, who arranged for us to talk to Red Minor in August 1990. Red had been playing with Roger's New Orleanians band for some time by then, alongside Roger on trombone and the trumpeter Clora Bryant. Red and Rose, his wife—they had married in 1947—made us very welcome at their home on South Genesee and found an interesting selection of photographs for us to use.

Well known on the local music scene, Red proved to be an articulate, thoughtful man whose ability to maintain an active playing life alongside his day job with the city had given him great satisfaction and genuine financial security. Now retired and evidently contented, Red was about to set off on a golf trip with the New Orleans–born tenor saxophonist Lee Allen and was doubtless looking forward to more gigs when he came back.

A boyhood associate of the likes of Charles Mingus and Buddy Collette and brought up like them in Watts, Red chose early on to eschew the capricious life of the full-time jazz musician. Yet the more we looked into his career, the more obvious it became that here was an accomplished player who had kept good company musically yet unaccountably had made very few issued recordings as far as we could discern.[1] He continued to play with the New Orleanians until the work ran out.

Red Minor died in Los Angeles on March 6, 2008.

Minor Robinson: Los Angeles, August 21, 1990[2]

It began for me in Port Arthur, Texas, in 1920. The first of February.[3] *My family moved to Los Angeles, January of the same year. My father didn't*

Minor Robinson, Los Angeles, 1960s. Courtesy Steve Isoardi.

want us to grow up under segregation in the South, and we already had family here. At first we lived between Adams Boulevard and Compton Avenue. I went to Nevins Avenue Elementary School, and then we moved down to Watts in 1927. That's where I grew up.

Watts was one of the most cosmopolitan communities in the country at that time. When they talk about bussing, they were trying to get the same racial balance that Jordan High School [2265 E. 103rd Street] automatically had, which was one-third Caucasian, one-third Latin, one-third Blacks, and 1 percent Asian. Watts was quite a community then. In fact, the reason why my folks moved to Watts was to get into a quiet community, more an ideal spot to raise children. To find a better place, to get away from hustle and bustle of the city. We had lots of vacant lots so we'd grow our own vegetables, had chickens and rabbits. Lady in the back had a cow so we'd get our milk from her.

Watts was actually a city at one time until it was incorporated in Los Angeles in 1926. We called it "Plum Nelly" or Plumb Nearly. That's Plumb out of the city and Nearly out of this world! 103rd Street when we moved down to Watts was Main Street. A lot of musicians came out of Jordan High School at that time, like the Woodman brothers, Buddy Collette, Mingus, Eddie Davis, Charlie Martin, and Joe Comfort. We had a pretty good climate for musicians in Watts then.

My father, James Robinson, was in business for himself. He bought a truck and he had a moving business. He died in 1937. My mother, Clemmie, was just a housewife. She stayed home and brought us up. My brother, James Jr., passed on early this year, and I have a younger sister, Lois. You might have heard of Leslie Drayton?[4] My sister is his mother. She married Charlie Drayton, who was the bassist with Benny Carter and Lena Horne. He's dead now.

The first thing that brought my attention to music was when I was a youngster at elementary school and they wanted someone to play a bass drum. A little girl that I kinda liked said, "Why don't you try it?" So I went over there and tried it. When I got to high school, I looked into it, and we had a good music program at Jordan High School. We had a good teacher, J. Louis Lippi; he kept us interested. It was an all-white faculty. We'd go over to Buddy Collette's house and jam as kids. Like me he lived in the Central Gardens area; that's from 99th up to 92nd Street. It would be Buddy, Vernon Slater, Charlie Martin, Elvin Coger, and Kid Crosby [Lewis], who decided not to follow music and dropped out. He was a good trumpet player at that time.

At school, when you take band or orchestra, you have to learn to play bass drum, snare drum, both the drums, and you have to learn a few things like bells or the vibes or marimbas, for those half notes, quarter-note tunes. You playing at assembly and the next day some kid says, "Oh, I didn't know *you could do that,"* and it motivates you to try and do better. That inspires you.

The music we liked then was Benny Goodman and Count Basie, Lunceford, Louis Armstrong, all those people. During that time, music was easier to hear. We could go downtown into the theaters, and they'd have Count Basie there, so we'd see one bad movie and wait for the show and listen to Count Basie and then see the same third-rate movie again. I'd see it three times so I could see Count Basie three times. Every week we could see a band downtown at the Orpheum or the Paramount Theatre. Other times they had Fats Waller and Jimmie Lunceford or Duke Ellington. Every time they'd change bands, we'd go downtown and stay all day through.

For drummers, for me, back then, it was Sonny Greer, Crawford, Big Sid Catlett, Gene Krupa, and Buddy Rich. Later on, Joe Morello. There were so many drummers. The one I think was outstanding at that time was Jimmy Crawford. I liked the way he played with Lunceford. He had a good solid beat. Jo Jones had another good solid beat, but his was just a little lighter, smooth, with the cymbals. He had the kind of beat I followed after that. Krupa was a soloist; his beat wasn't as great to me, but his solo work was sometimes unbelievable. He's the one that brought drums out front. He made people realize that drums was a musical instrument. All drummers owe that to Krupa because he made people look at a drummer.

At Jordan we had a swing band. In fact, Jordan was one of the first schools in California that introduced swing in the schools because at that time some principals thought swing was bad. They preferred John Philip Sousa. And we organized a band called the Jordan Hep-Cats. Buddy Collette was the leader of that, with Vernon Slater, tenor; Crosby Lewis played trumpet; Theodore Collins played trombone; I was on drums; Charlie Martin, piano. There was another band out there too. Ralph Bledsoe, trombone player—he ended up being a doctor, gave up music to practice medicine—he had a band in school. We started out with his band and we had a little disagreement, so we switched over to Buddy Collette. I think one of the main reasons why was because Ralph Bledsoe's brother played a tuba in the band and we wanted a bass fiddle. So we talked Charles Mingus into buying a bass. That's how Buddy Collette's band started because Mingus always used to say, "No cat can slap a bass horn."

Mingus was about three or four years younger than I am [Mingus was born in April 1922]. When I associated with him, he was kinda childish because he was younger. He had an enormous appetite, I know that. Buddy would pick him up first when we were going on a gig, and he'd stop at everybody's house and they'd offer him a sandwich. Charles would have a sandwich at every house. He was about sixteen then, maybe fifteen. Talented? Always. He start playing bass like a duck went to water. He started right on in. See, he was a cellist at first. He played cello in school bands, so he already had musicianship and a savvy about music. His sister Grace played violin, and he had another sister, Vivian, played the piano, so he had music in the home all the time. When he started playing bass, he just grabbed that fellow like he's going to teach it. I always admired what he did. I'm proud to say that I was there at the beginning of Mingus. He's progressed much further and faster. He went into another dimension while I was still back with the straight-ahead!

After a gig we would always either stop at the drug store at 54th or stop at a restaurant called Finley's on Central. I was always trying to play like a practical joke. We had this thing with Mingus, and I remember one time I was betting him he couldn't eat a certain amount of food. Every time I offered him something, he said, "I'll take another," and in the end he had all my money. I'd made my little two bucks. Malt was a dime, spaghetti was fifteen cents, and he went through all my night's pay. Buddy and those guys, they laughed at Charles's eating ability. "I'm dining sufficiently on your pay," he says.

So we had this school band, but the same personnel would go out and play other gigs under Buddy Collette's leadership all over Southern California. We used to go as far as Buena Park, which was quite a long ways, or Santa Ana or Garden Grove, and we'd go as far as Monrovia. Buddy had an old Dodge sedan his grandmother gave him, so we had transportation. After he found out he could take care of his old Dodge, his dad gave him an old Auburn car. That was our transportation. He carried about five or six of us, three rhythm and Buddy, Vernon Slater, and Crosby Lewis. Then we had Theo Collins, one time. That was about it. We were an all-black group, interested in music. The music was swing style. We used to play a lot of Benny Goodman, a lot of Count Basie, from music stocks plus Buddy got some music from [trumpeter/bandleader] Dootsie Williams.

We were like little gangsters at times. We'd buy a Benny Goodman stock, but we didn't have the six pieces, so we'd go in the music store and we'd get our six charts, put them in a little folder, get another six, had about five arrangements in there, until Mr. Harper, he got pretty smart. He caught us but he didn't say anything. "We got it mixed up," we'd say. We did that a couple of times.

Buddy Collette always played good. He started out on piano, but he was always ahead of us. He's about a year younger than I am. [Collette was born in August 1921.] Music-wise, he was the leader. We always wanted to be musicians. We used to discuss that, coming from gigs, what we wanted to do. That's the way I started. I wanted to make that my aim in life: to be a musician.

After I graduated in 1938, Charlie Martin, my pianist friend and I, we started working downtown at the Look Café. That was the first job I had, in 1939, I think it was. This was on 4th and Hill, had a long bar where sailors hung out. We worked from seven to two, and all the musicians used to come round there and jam. Charlie worked with the Stanley Morgan Ink Spots later, and he, Chuck [Thomas], and I had a trio together.

From then on I started working with Papa Mutt Carey in the taxi dance. I was non-union at the time. The lady wasn't too happy with the [previous] band, all Mexican guys, so she called the union and they sent Papa Mutt there, but she wanted me for some reason because I was singing and doing other things. The taxi dance was in downtown Los Angeles on 4th Street, off of Hill. I can't think of the name, right round the corner from the Look Café, so that's how they came 'round and saw me. That's how they got me.

It was upstairs because all the taxi dances had to be upstairs. City ordinance say you can't walk in off the street into a dance hall of that type; you had to walk up. Can't be at ground level. That was the dance hall detail. If you was going there, you had to know where you goin', up a flight of stairs. In the taxi dance, we had just local musicians. I think the sax player was Joe Walker, L. Z. Cooper on piano. I think it was Elzie or Bernard Banks, one of the two. Papa Mutt always bragged about he brought me into the limelight, made me a union musician [laughs]. "I'll make something of you yet," he said. He took me down to the union in 1940, had him the money. He was a friend of Paul Howard, who was the secretary of the union then. I think I put $5 down and paid so much a week.

This was before Pearl Harbor, about a year before, last part of 1940, early 1941. Playing just strictly commercial stuff, straight melody, one chorus and out, then another dance. When Papa Mutt came in, we stayed there about a month or two; then we went to Bakersfield, California. He formed a new band, with [altoist] Joe Lutcher and myself, Bobby Burge, piano, and we stayed there about six months. It was called the Rooster Club, on the Edison Highway, a bar and nightclub, dancing and entertaining.

Papa Mutt, he was just like a father to me because at that time I was young, and he started telling me how dumb I was doing silly things like boys do. The way you treat a girlfriend, how you date someone, this girl you like but you're afraid to talk to, you do it a certain way; he'd tell you different things like that. Did I respect him? Yes, indeed. He, Joe Lutcher, and I, we had a good relationship. Joe was fun, too. That was before Joe turned Seventh Day Adventist. Now, he's a minister. He's in religious music now. We used to have a lot of fun. We were all young and wild at that stage. Joe always did play good sax. He used to come out to the Look Café too.

Then when the war broke out, I walked into the club and I told the manager I was 1-A,[5] and he told Papa Mutt he might as well give up on the band now because "Red's going and I think Joe's going too." Papa Mutt told me how dumb I was. "You're dumb; keep your mouth shut." He was having a problem with the piano player anyway. We had this young piano player, Bobby Burge. He was coming in drunk and acting up.

Papa Mutt, I respected what he was doin'. After all, I was just getting into the game. He was in it. Sometimes we'd brag, "Man, I'm more important to the band than him." Just kidding, and he says, "Man, I made history; now get your name in jazz history, then you'll be something." We'd kid along. He's talking about how his name was in a few jazz history books. He'd played with quite a few respected people like Kid Ory and Oliver, all the famous guys. I'd say, "Man, these guys are old now." Mutt was playing about 50-50 muted and open. He'd do a lot of wa-wa with the plunger. I figured, just like the kid I was, "I say, man, you ought to be playing like Roy Eldridge," and he says, "I made history; just you try to make it" [laughs]. We had a lot of fun. He had his way of playing, and he had his own sense of humor and he had his way of kidding. You didn't think he was that old when he was talking to you. [Thomas "Papa Mutt" Carey was forty-nine in 1941.]

Papa Mutt told us once he didn't have to worry about the modern way the guys are playing; all he needed was to just surround himself with a bunch of young guys. "That's why I got you guys here. That's your job. I'll play my style." One other thing he told me when I was leaving, "When you come out, just like you talking now about swing or old jazz, there'll be another style of music waiting for you. Either you guys gonna go in the Service and come up with something new or somebody out here, I don't know who, going to do it." And he wasn't kidding either because everybody was playing bebop when I came out. Music just keeps going along.

About singing, just prior to working with Papa Mutt, somebody called me up for a job and they wanted the drummer to sing and the guy asked me could I sing. I just told him yes because I desperately wanted a job. So I went down to the book store and bought about four or five song books, with Top Ten numbers in them. Just the words. I knew the melodies. I made the job, and I was good enough to stay for a while. I sing with Roger now. You can get over if you can sing in tune and if you do it a certain way. Papa Mutt used to say, when I used to sing sometimes, "Put a little more soul in it. That's the way you supposed to sing it." He's the one that kinda started me freeing and styling.

I went in the Service right from the Rooster Café in May 1942. I was with the 93rd Division Band, went straight in a band. We had a pretty good band. Eventually, we did have some name guys in there. [Tenor saxophonist] Eddie Chamblee came in later; [trombonist] Jimmy Cleveland was in it; Bill Douglas, saxophone, he used to play with Nat Coles, he was there. He was a good alto, good tenor. He was out of Kansas City; he had a brother played saxophone named Buck. We went to Fort Huachuca for basic training and from there we went to Louisiana for maneuvers and from there we went overseas, to Guadalcanal, Dutch East Indies, Treasure Island, Indonesian Islands, right there with the band. It was a regular fifty-six-piece marching band, and we had an eighteen-piece jazz band and a six-piece combo.

Bill Douglas ran the eighteen-piece band. I ran the combo. I picked up guys for that. Some that wasn't in the main band. At one time, I had [pianist] Billy Kyle, [bassist] Herman Monsanto, Richard Davis, out of Chicago, good tenor player. He died. And we had this guy Hackley [trumpeter], Hoffard Hackley, that was it. We played officer's clubs, enlisted men's clubs. The big band played mostly for shows; they had outdoor theaters, so they'd play until dark. They assigned us [the combo] to Special Services, and they would send for us. I was in the big eighteen-piece band, but when we were stationed out here in the Californian [Mojave] desert, out in Needles, California, just three hundred miles from Los Angeles, and they wanted us to play every weekend out in the desert, I wanted to come home. So I got out of the big band. When I got overseas, they was gonna punish me so they wouldn't let me get back in the big band so that's when I formed the combo. As soon as we got this together, Special Services put their hands on it and made it official. We got all the good gigs.

Actually, what we'd do sometimes, we'd go over to another company, another outfit and put a hat on the floor and we'd charge them a buck a song. It's wartime so we had to wear uniform, but we made out like a band and we'd go out and make 20, 30 a night back then. We'd save that money, send it home.

My musicianship improved a lot in the Service. I learned to read. I ran into a good drummer in the band, Jim Herndon,[6] out of Chicago. I was a better jazz drummer than him at the time, but he was a very well-taught drummer, and he turned out to be a very good jazz drummer later on. He won the Iowa State Rudiments Contest. He's from Council Bluffs, Iowa. He was a young kid and he went right into the Service. Just because I was a better jazz drummer, I wasn't afraid to let him show me a paradiddle, an open roll, or a flam and how to do it. I'll never forget the first time we played together on a tune, he said, "You know, we just not getting this part right"—it seems like he's using a five-stroke roll and I'm using a seven-stroke roll—"I think it's better to use a seven-stroke roll." I didn't know a five-stroke from a seven-stroke so after we finished, I said, "Jim, what did you mean about that?" He taught me a lot. Later on he was teaching in Chicago, and I went there about twelve years ago and I went by his gig and sat in and played with him. I played a couple of tunes. He really is a very good drummer. In the Service, he couldn't swing a beat. He came out and went to school on the G.I. Bill and furthered his education and became great. He did a lot of work with Oscar Brown Jr.

I came out of the Service in '46. Did three years, eight months, eight days. That's what they put on my discharge. When I came back [to LA], I hooked up with [tenor saxophonist] Wild Bill Moore. I think he was the first one I was with. He was in Fort Huachuca with that band, so when he saw me and he said he had a band and he wanted me, I went with him. He was more or *less a jazz player. We had [trumpeter] Jack Trainor, Perry Lee on piano, Bill Cooper, bass, and "Hambone" [trombonist James Robinson]; he used to play in the movies, too. We used to work the jam session after-hours at Jack's Basket Room on Central Avenue. Bill would take one or two guys out of his band, and Charlie Parker would show up or Errol Garner would come in. One time, we had [bassist] Slam Stewart, Errol Garner, and myself at the session.*

Marshal Royal: *There was a place called Jack's Basket Room. Thirty-Third and Central, with jam sessions every night. The guy that used to be in charge of hiring the musicians was a fellow by the name of Wild Bill Moore. And he tried to always keep a rhythm section there, and then the guys that came in would play according to the way they wanted. They'd just jam up there all night having cutting contests. You were liable to have Charlie Parker up there one night, Teddy Edwards, Lucky Thompson, and a lot of good players.* (quoted in Bryant et al., *Central Avenue Sounds*, 1998)

Was Wild Bill Moore the first one or was it Bardu Ali? When I worked with Bardu, it was at the Lincoln Theatre. That lasted about two or three months. They had jazz and they had amateur nights similar to the Apollo in New York. Bardu had a big band, not much I can say about him. Two people came into national prominence in that band. [Trumpeter] *Arthur Farmer was in Bardu Ali's band at the time, he and his* [twin] *brother, Addison, bass player, and then we went with Floyd Ray's band. Floyd at that time didn't have a band but he had a name, so when he had a few gigs to make right quick, he took Bardu's band as Floyd Ray's band. Put his charts in there, same group of musicians. Chuck Thomas was in it, I think. Floyd Ray had a good book, good band. Real interesting book. My forte at that time was to be able to walk right in and sit in on a book. Bardu was there quite a while. He was a nice gentleman. He had formed a band, and then Gerald Wilson moved in and took most of those guys.*

Then I guess I went to the Cricket Club with [vocalist] *Bixie Crawford; Freddy Simon, tenor; Fletcher Smith, piano;* [bassist] *Herman Washington; Louis Speiginer, guitar; Joe Walker, alto; this was trumpeter Geechie Smith's band. That was a good band. Bixie Crawford sang with Basie at one time. This was on Washington and Vermont. It was owned by Paul Ruben, who was an Italian so you can't say it was a black club. During that time they were getting away from this "black club" idea, so it was just a nightclub. They had a floor show and everything. Singers, dancers, and Pot, Pan and Skillet, the dance team that used to be in Duke Ellington's* Jump for Joy. *They started having jazz after we left there, bands like Dizzy Gillespie.*

Up to 1948 this was my livelihood. That year we were trying to buy a home, and I just couldn't make enough money to do what I wanted, to live the lifestyle I wanted. It was Paul Howard who advised me to find a day job as well as keeping my music going. Music wasn't payin' that much for me, so I took another position with the City of Los Angeles. I was a street maintenance supervisor in charge of Hollywood street maintenance. I started out as a truck driver and I wanted to quit and then I went to supervisor. I worked thirty years for the city, but during all this time I was working the nightclub scene around town too.

If you want to do a certain thing, then you have to make a change. Some of the guys was hanging with music, and they were probably driving an old car, renting a too-small apartment, and they just wanted to die with the [music] *business. Guys like Buddy* [Collette], *he did exceptionally well, but how many of those guys do you have? I couldn't have accomplished what I did with the one job. I know that. I'm not rich, but if I never work another day, I'll be OK.*

Thereafter Red became a jobbing freelance musician, picking up odd gigs, many short-lived, working weekends and weekdays, while pursuing his day job with its early start. "Sometimes, I'd be playing five or six nights a week and at five or six in the morning, it's like at night, and I'd put on my tuxedo and go into the day job. Wearing the wrong outfit!" he laughed. Red played in the Metropolitan Orchestra alongside William Woodman Sr. for Sunday concerts in the city's park, as well as in the Shriners and Elks bands, and recorded with bluesman Floyd Dixon, playing local dates with him, but turned down road offers. He ran a quartet with saxophonist John Griffin, another veteran of the 93rd Division Band, and Frank Johnson on piano in 1949 and 1950 and worked with organist Clyde Washington, in Club Novo on 6th Street in San Diego.

One of his most enduring associations was with trumpeter Norman Bowden, pianist Art Hillery, and bassist George Mason in a quartet that he ran with Bowden for something like thirty years. "We did a lot of work together." He worked with both Chuck Thomas and Eddie Davis in trios, usually completed by pianist Charlie Martin. Roy Milton used him occasionally at Club California [1957 W. Santa Barbara Blvd.] with tenorist Eddie Taylor, trumpeter Romie Lewis, and James Jackson, the old Honeydrippers' tenor saxophonist. "Wasn't anything exciting," said Red. He also covered for Jesse Sailes at Disneyland for six months with Teddy Buckner's band while Jesse's broken leg was mending.

I had a good stand with Carl Perkins,[7] *We worked the Down Beat* [4201 Central]. *I think we were the last group that worked there. After that, there was no more Down Beat. I closed up the Alabam the same way with Joe Liggins's Honeydrippers at the tail-end. This was the early 1950s when Joe had changed bands, and the only guy from the original band was Weepin' Willie* [Jackson] *and the only other guy I can remember is Gene Smith on bass. I think he quit playing. Only thing I can remember about being the last* band that played in Alabam when it closed up, it's the only time I worked in music that I didn't get paid.

I worked with Carl and his brother, Ed, who played bass. He was a good bassist, too. That was fun. Just a trio. I don't know how long it was, but we played several jobs. If he needed a drummer, he'd call me. His way of playing, with his arm at an angle, that's just the way he learned to play. He wasn't deformed. He was a self-taught musician; he didn't read anything. They drank quite a bit, him and his brothers. I used to call them the Guzzle Brothers; they'd drink brandy like water. That's the only thing I knew he was on. Just brandy. Ed's dead too; his brother died shortly after. Carl was a distinctive player and a nice guy, a little on the bop kick. He played tempos I liked. He carried me apace. After playing with Carl, fast tempos were nothing to me. Sorta like that guy Duke Burrell out there in Long Beach at Trani's. Very exciting. What I like about Duke and playing up tempos, he's not playing chords; he's playing sixteenth notes, with all that piano technique. He's not sustaining notes at all. I worked with him a couple of years ago, and he had a drummer, George Griffin, very good drummer used to be with Lionel [Hampton], so I'm his number one relief drummer, which I really like.

I worked with Ben Webster. I don't know the year [ca. 1962?]. Bill Hadnott was in the group. That was quite an experience. I thought Ben was about the smoothest tenor player ever. One night [violinist] *Stuff Smith came in and sat in so we had quite a session. This was at Club Intimi at 50th and Western. Ben Webster was living here* [LA]. *In fact he was living around the corner* [in Wilton Place], *not too far from the club. Living here with his relatives* [his mother and aunt]. *Quite a few celebrities used to come in. They were good times.*

Ben didn't have much to say. I was just the local drummer they hired, and he just went along with it. Not too much drinking then because he was really cool. In fact, the piano player had had a stroke one time so he wasn't cutting it, and Ben was very diplomatic about telling the guy, "Look, I like to stroll sometimes. I just call it strolling. I just want the bass and the drummer to play. You stay out for a little while." I heard about how crude he could be, but he was real diplomatic about that. We'd do that for about a whole set, just Bill, Ben, and myself. Boy, you talking about sounding good. That was quite an experience. Right after that Ben went to Europe.

By living in Los Angeles, guys would come into town and I'd work. By not being attached to certain bands or working regular with a band, I was available where other drummers were tied up on the gig. Like doing a thing with [singer] *Helen Humes. It's a weekend's work. You come in; you do it. Wasn't nothing outstanding.* I worked with Big Joe Turner and I worked with Charles Brown in different places. I did a couple of weekends out at the Morocco with Eddie Heywood. By me being freelance like this, I got quite a few gigs. I guess I was doing the job. It's like being a house drummer. Floyd [Dixon] was looking for a drummer, and I knew [guitarist] Chuck Norris from several other gigs during that time. It was through Chuck that I got with Floyd. I did a few things with Percy Mayfield the same way. Irving Ashby. I worked with his trio. He had just left Nat King Cole, and he had this little legal problem at that time. He was drinking a lot. He was a very, very exceptional guitar player, but he started drinking and it turned him a little bit around. We went to San Diego with him. Played a club there. I can remember the pianist, fellow named Lionel Reason. On the way back, Irving was drunk and Lionel made him get out of the car, his own car, and he put him on the back seat. "I can drive. This is my car," Irving says, but Lionel said, "I'm gonna drive."

I guess the most fun was working with [organist] Tommy Hearn's Trio, with Chuck Thomas. And the Eddie Davis Trio. Two good moving groups, I thought. We worked in Orange County at the Maple Inn; this was a club adjacent to a bowling alley. Stayed on that job two years. Tommy and Chuck are a lot of fun. Chuck's a beautiful person to work with plus a very good musician. Then I worked with Eddie Davis, who was also a very good tenor man, at the Palms in Santa Ana. Stayed on that job for two years. Played a lot of cocktail lounges. That was the highlight, financially.

I retired from the day job in 1978 with my pension. I decided to play golf and play music. That's it. Among the golfers, Teddy Edwards is about the best one I've played with, him and Ernie Andrews are the best. Cleanhead [Vinson] was nice too. He had a beautiful golf swing. We used to get together in the mornings and play quite a bit. Roy Milton was pretty good, but he wasn't quite there with Teddy or Ernie. He was more or less in my class.

The best thing about playing music, what I've always admired about it, is there's a certain gratification after you do something that's particularly difficult and you sail through it. It's a gratification you can't get except from hitting one of them 200-yard-long drives straight down the middle!

I've had a lot of good experiences, but I think the best part is now. When you reach financial independence, you don't have to get into situations you don't like. I don't really want to work three nights a week anymore. I don't want to go to the same spot week in, week out. A regular Sunday gig, maybe catch two this week and then one over there, that's good enough for me. The New Orleanians suit me fine. I hadn't played Dixieland very much prior to joining Roger. I used to go to quite a few sessions and sit in and play, but I never did play with a Dixieland group for money. When we have our charter members there, all of them, it's a good groove. Sometimes when one of the regulars is off, I can feel it. The other guy does a good job, but there's just something missing when one of us is not there. It's like putting on somebody else's shoes. They may fit but it still feels wrong!

Regrets? Sometimes it seems like I wish I'd have tried harder. That I didn't give it all that I feel I could have. But I'm glad I didn't take the gamble with music. In fact I don't regret going to the city at all now. As I look on it I'm glad I made that step. I see so many good guys that they have to have a benefit for, really good musicians. That helped me make my decision to follow another career because I saw some guys that I thought was just out of this world and they were just as poor as I was or poorer. I made up my mind if I can't make x dollars per month, by a certain time, then I was gonna find another way. Working nightclubs around town was a little below x amount of dollars; in fact, even going on the road with some of the bands wasn't making x amount of dollars. I know what sort of money those guys was making. $150 a week and keeping up two homes wasn't what I wanted.

We have two daughters. Sent one to college; the other could have went to college if she wanted. I'm a great-grandfather now. If I could have hung in there like Buddy and those guys and made $30 or $40,000 a year, I'd have stayed with it. Britt [Woodman] and those guys make that; they make good money. Sitting around here working nightclubs just wasn't enough. It was fun, and I feel satisfied I accomplished something in music. It's just hard to let go of music when you find out you can do something you like doing and also you getting paid for it. I couldn't let go for two reasons. Love of it and the mercenary part of it.

Central Avenue has completely changed. It's Latin there now. Where you had bands coming in from Kansas City or New York City, they're bringing in bands from Mexico City. It's a whole new scene now. It's run-down; it's different. I drove up and down, and I ain't seen a single nightclub on Central Avenue. A place we had, about a mile from Central Avenue, we lived there at 451 East 48th when I was a kid, and I used to walk from there to Central Avenue. Sometimes when I'd take my car up on Central Avenue, I'd be so stoned that I'd forget where I'd parked my car so I'd just walk on home. I'd come back the next day, walk two or three blocks, forget where I put it, and I'd finally run into it. I wouldn't think about walking down those streets at 2 o'clock in the morning now. Wouldn't be safe.

Appendix

Snapshot

Name	Instrument(s)	Place of Birth	Born	Died
Andy Blakeney	trumpet	Quitman, MS	1898	1992
Gideon Honoré	piano	New Orleans, LA	1904	1990
George Orendorff	trumpet	Atlanta, GA	1906	1984
Nathaniel "Monk" McFay	drums	Wichita Falls, TX	1908	1994
Floyd Turnham Jr.	tenor saxophone	Spokane, WA	1909	1991
Betty Hall Jones	piano	Topeka, KS	1911	2009
McLure "Red Mack" Morris	trumpet	Memphis, TN	1912	1993
Caughey Roberts Jr.	alto saxophone	Bodell, OK	1912	1990
Chester Lane	piano	Lexington, MS	1912	2004
Monte Easter	trumpet	Coffeyville, KS	1913	2000
Billy Hadnott	bass	Port Arthur, TX	1914	1999
Norman Bowden	trumpet	Vancouver, Canada	1915	
John Ewing	trombone	Topeka, KS	1917	2002
Chuck Thomas	tenor saxophone	St. Louis, MO	1917	2000
Jesse Sailes	drums	Denver, CO	1919	2007

Red Minor Robinson	drums	Port Arthur, TX	1920	2008

Notes

2. GIDEON JOSEPH "GID" HONORÉ JR.

1. The Century of Progress International Exposition was held in Chicago from 1933 to 1934 to celebrate the city's centennial. It ran from May 27 to November 1, 1933, and resumed from May 26 to October 31, 1934.
2. Ginger Smock researcher Laura Risk confirms that Gid Honoré played with Smock and Williams at Mike's Waikiki Inn in July and August 1949, replacing pianist Lloyd Glenn as advertised in the *Los Angeles Sentinel* newspaper. His appearances there the previous year when he succeeded Walter Johnson were unpublicized but can be dated between July and November 1948.

4. NATHANIEL JACK "MONK" MCFAY

1. Dallas-born Herbert "Kat" Cowens [1904–?] traveled with revues and shows, eventually moving to New York and recording with Hot Lips Page, Fats Waller, and Stuff Smith. He toured widely with his own bands before retiring to Dallas in 1980.
2. A. G. Godley [1903–1973] from Fort Smith, Arkansas, was a mainstay of the celebrated Alphonso Trent Orchestra from 1924 to 1933 and rated as one of the Southwest's finest big band drummers. He moved later to New York and worked with trombonist Snub Mosley's popular group before settling in Seattle.
3. Texan drummer-bandleader James Henry "Jimmy" Westbrook [1910–1972] was with the Happy Johnson band, which followed Buck Clayton's Harlem Gentlemen into the Canidrome in Shanghai, playing there between August 1935 and February 1936. Westbrook continued to lead bands in Texas and LA until his death.
4. McFay left Little Rod's band in 1934 and joined Joe Brantley's Spotlight Entertainers at the Ritz Ballroom in Oklahoma City. By 1935, pianist Leslie Sheffield had taken over as bandleader at the ballroom, with McFay and Charles Christian among his Rhythmaires. At some point, trumpeter Leonard Chadwick became the leader of the Rhythmaires, and McFay sat in with them while on vacation from Hawaii.
5. John "Cappy" Oliver [1880?–1968] performed with Floyd Ray in the late 1930s and recorded with Jack McVea in LA. He died in New Jersey.

6. Banks and company left Los Angeles for Honolulu on October 22, 1935. Following his accident, Bernard Banks left Hawaii with his family to return to LA on October 19, 1936, and continued to work in nightclubs.

7. Harold "Slim" Jenkins [1890–1967] founded his Slim Jenkins Supper Club at 1748 7th Street in West Oakland in 1933, an area known as the Harlem of the West. The club attracted all the greatest stars in African American blues and jazz and incorporated a banqueting hall, market, and liquor store. It closed in 1962.

8. Joe Liggins [1915–1987] was an Oklahoma-born pianist and bandleader based in Los Angeles whose recording of "The Honeydripper" for Exclusive became a multi-million-seller, staying at number one for twenty-six weeks in the Billboard charts in 1946 and making his Honeydrippers band a national attraction.

9. Art Foxall [1925–2008] was born in Houston and moved to Los Angeles in the 1950s where he formed his trio. Foxall performed with many top R&B acts and later toured extensively in Europe from his base in Seattle.

5. FLOYD PAYNE TURNHAM JR.

1. The influential alto saxophonist and music teacher Frank Dordan Waldron (1890–1955) taught several generations of Seattle jazz musicians, black and white, including tenor saxophonist Dick Wilson, bassist Buddy Catlett, and trumpeter-arranger Quincy Jones.

2. The Orpheum Circuit was a chain of vaudeville and movie houses founded in 1886 by Gustav Walter that stretched across Canada and the United States. It operated until 1927 when it merged with the Keith-Albee circuit, later becoming part of the Radio-Keith-Orpheum [RKO] Corporation.

3. Alexander Pantages (1897–1936) was a Greek American impresario, and at its height his circuit comprised eighty-four movie and vaudeville houses, mostly based in Canada and North America west of the Mississippi River. All Pantages Circuit tours started out from Winnipeg in Canada.

4. In addition to Floyd on alto, his Cricket Club Orchestra included John Anderson (t), Britt Woodman (tb), Coney Woodman (p), and Oscar Bradley (d). Floyd appeared in the 1937 Louis Armstrong movie *Every Day's a Holiday* as part of the Local 767 marching band along with Red Mack, Caughey Roberts, and Streamline Ewing. He made his first records with popular singer Maxine Sullivan in 1939.

5. Turnham's recall seems to be at fault here. Woodman dates the Chicago episode to 1940 and says it lasted four weeks, not six months. Gerald Wilson only joined the band in 1942, so it seems unlikely that he was with Floyd when they confronted the Chicago union.

6. The California Shipbuilding Group (one of the "Six Companies" headed by Henry J. Kaiser), known as "Calship," was established in February 1941 on Treasure Island between Los Angeles and Long Beach to build all-welded Liberty Ships. Calship eventually closed in September 1945, its forty thousand men and women employees having built some 467 ships for the war effort.

7. "Soundies" were three-minute musical films produced between 1940 and 1946 in New York City, Chicago, and Hollywood for display on Panoram machines. These coin-operated jukeboxes were located in bars, restaurants, and nightclubs. Many African American artists including Hite, Duke Ellington, Count Basie, Louis Jordan, and Louis Armstrong made "Soundies," and they constitute a precious archive of live musical action.

8. Britt Woodman recalled that Johnny Hodges had recommended Kansas City alto saxophonist Tommy Douglas as his replacement, but Douglas had been too nervous to play properly, so "in an emergency they had to call Floyd Turnham, a very prominent alto player, but Floyd didn't have a chance to rehearse before we went to Las Vegas to play the Thunderbird [for two weeks starting February 15, 1951]. Floyd came in and played the gig at the Thunderbird but Duke didn't like his sound. Floyd didn't have the velvet sound Duke wanted so he made an arrangement to get Willie Smith from Harry James's band."

9. Lorenzo Flennoy was born in LA on June 26, 1910, and died in LA on October 4, 1971.

6. BETTY HALL JONES

1. Clarinetist and saxophonist Orville Demoss was evidently an accomplished instrumentalist. He was featured with the pianist Edward "Sleepy" Hickox's trio in Kansas City in 1942 as well as with Bus Moten's band earlier.
2. Betty appeared in Sweden and Norway in 1986 for impresario Michael Gelardi and made a second visit to Sweden in 1987 accompanied by her husband Dick Beresford, performing in Reisen in Stockholm and other locations. The Swedish jazz authority Bo Scherman remembered Betty as "a fantastic entertainer, very lively, with a great sense of humour, and an excellent singer and pianist. Of course, she had to play stupid requests from drunken people, but she always managed to make something good of it."
3. Richard Beresford died on December 2, 1997; Betty was residing in Carson when she died in 2009.
4. "Gossip, Gossip" by Betty Hall Jones and Jester Hairston (1959) is the best known of Betty's many compositions along with "This Joint's Too Hip for Me."

7. MCLURE "RED MACK" MORRIS

1. The great stride pianist Joe Turner, born in Baltimore on November 3, 1907, worked first in New York before traveling to Europe as singer Adelaide Hall's accompanist in the mid-1930s. He relocated to Paris in the 1950s and died on July 21, 1990, at Montreuil, France.

8. CAUGHEY WESLEY ROBERTS II

1. Boley, in Okfuskee County, was the largest of the more than fifty all-black towns of Oklahoma founded in Indian Territory after the Civil War and one of only thirteen that survive. Started in 1903 by the daughter of a Creek Freedman, it attracted African American settlers from a wide area. The advent of the railroad brought prosperity, but its later failure helped to bankrupt the town in 1939. The present-day population numbers 1,126, and its downtown business district has been designated a National Historic Landmark.
2. John A. Gray, an African American who was a graduate of the Ecole Normale de Musique de Paris where he studied with Nadia Boulanger, founded the Gray Conservatory of Music at 1106 E. 38th St. in 1931.
3. The Eubanks Conservatory of Music and Arts is at 4928 Crenshaw Boulevard. The then proprietor was Ms. Rachel Eubanks (1922–2006).
4. Earl Dancer was a Broadway producer who had toured in vaudeville with his common-law wife, the singer Ethel Waters. On arriving in Los Angeles in the early 1930s, he formed an orchestra known as The Fourteen Gentlemen of Harlem, appearing with them in a number of films and later opening the Club Ebony in the Dunbar Hotel. In Buck Clayton's words, he was a "bit of a con man and gambler."
5. Buck Clayton and His Fourteen Gentlemen from Harlem arrived in Shanghai on April 9, 1934, for their Canidrome Ballroom engagement, later transferring to the Casa Nova. The band comprised Buck Clayton, Jack Bratton, Teddy Buckner (trumpets); George "Happy" Johnson, Duke Upshaw (trombone); Hubert "Bumps" Myers, Arcima Taylor (alto saxophones); Caughey Roberts (tenor saxophone, clarinet); Eddie Beal (piano); Frank Pasley (guitar); Reggie "Jonesy" Jones (bass); David "Babe" Lewis (drums); Joe McCutcheon (violin); Thelma Porter (Mrs. Upshaw; entertainer). Howard Rye's research shows that Roberts eventually arrived back in Los Angeles on October 13, 1935. For Clayton's later Los Angeles engagements, Bert Johnson replaced Happy Johnson, Herschel Evans was added on tenor saxophone, and Callend-

er and Hackette replaced Jones and Lewis. Callender recalled that "Caughey Roberts played marvelous tenor and clarinet."

6. "King Happy and His Synco Boys," led by Happy Johnson, left LA in late 1935 to appear at Shanghai's Casa Nova Ballroom, returning home on March 14, 1936.

7. Trumpeter/bandleader Elisha "El" Herbert was born in Maddison, Mississippi, on March 4, 1898, and died in LA on January 3, 1963.

9. CHESTER C. LANE

1. Lexington is the county seat of Holmes County, Mississippi. In 1920, the *county* population was 34,500; in 2000, the *town* population was 2,025, of whom 72 percent were African American.

2. Prohibition was repealed on December 5, 1933.

3. The Emergency Banking Act was passed in March 1933, and the banking system was closed down for four days.

4. Roscoe Ates (1895–1962) was a successful movie and TV actor in later years, who used his pronounced stutter to comic effect.

5. The Jeter-Pillars "Club Plantation" Orchestra played for the opening of the club in 1933 and stayed on for a decade. Their only recordings were made in Chicago for Vocalion in August 1937 and featured Lane on piano. They were joint winners of the Fitch Shampoo Band Contest in 1942 and broadcast on the Fitch Summer Bandwagon show from the Opera House in St. Louis.

6. For more detail about Lane's period with the Tympany Five, refer to John Chilton's superb Louis Jordan biography *Let the Good Times Roll* (1992).

7. Louis Jordan's Tympany Five with Chester Lane on piano recorded thirteen sides for Decca, twenty-four for Aladdin, and twelve for RCA, during the 1953–1956 period.

8. Alto saxophonist Earl Bostic (1913–1965) died aged fifty-two following a heart attack.

9. Teddy Buckner's band with Lane is seen in the 1963 Warner movie *Four for Texas*. They also appeared in the popular *Stars of Jazz* TV series in September 1962 and played for movie sound tracks.

10. Porto Rico was "the crazy stagehand, the gruff enforcer in charge of sound, who served as the Apollo audience's hitman on Amateur Night" (Fox, *Showtime at the Apollo*, 1985).

10. ISADORE LEONIDAS "MONTE" EASTER

1. Cornetist Amos White (1889–1980) was born in Kingstree, South Carolina, and began playing while at Jenkins' Orphanage in Charleston. He toured extensively with blues singers and circus shows before settling in New Orleans and working with prominent local bands. He then moved to Phoenix in the late 1920s and on to Oakland in 1934, where he gigged locally and ran his own print shop.

2. The Erwing Brothers Orchestra originated in Birmingham, Alabama, and was active in Los Angeles as a taxi-dance hall dance band from 1927 through to 1935 when the Erwings became involved with religion.

3. Texan William "Sonny" Clay (1899–1973) was a drummer-turned-pianist and bandleader who was active in Los Angeles from the 1920s until he retired from full-time music in the 1940s. Clay took a band including future Local 767 President Leo McCoy Davis to Australia in January 1928 to appear in the all-black vaudeville show *Sonny Clay's Colored "Idea,"* Their visit was aborted after four weeks when some of Clay's musicians were accused of consorting with local white women, although all charges against them were later dropped.

4. A Los Angeles native, Eric Dolphy (1928–1964) studied with Lloyd Reese and was renowned as a virtuoso of the bass clarinet, also performing brilliantly on flute, alto saxophone,

and clarinet. He was admired for his improvising prowess and is ranked among the most influential exponents of avant-garde jazz.

11. WILLIAM KING "BILLY" HADNOTT

1. Tulsa's population in 1920 was 72,079. Today it is the forty-sixth largest city in the United States with a population in 2013 of 398,121.
2. Art Bronson's Bostonians were based in Salinas, Kansas, in the 1920s and featured tenor saxophonist Lester Young.
3. Stepin Fetchit (1902–1985), real name Lincoln Theodore Monroe Andrew Perry, was the most celebrated black actor in Hollywood and appeared in more than fifty movies. His persona as "the laziest man in the world" was seen by later black commentators as a negative stereotype. Originally a vaudeville artist, Perry became a millionaire and was known for his flamboyant lifestyle. He filed for bankruptcy in 1947.
4. Pianist Margaret Johnson, known as the Countess, was linked romantically with Young but succumbed to tuberculosis in 1939 aged only twenty.
5. Buster Smith remembered that Emile Williams *succeeded* McShann in the band. McShann recalled that he was only filling in for John Reagor. After playing with McShann's quintet in April 1938 at St-Martin's-on-the-Plaza, Hadnott was replaced by Gene Ramey who stayed on when McShann formed his successful big band.
6. Kansas City bandleader and vocalist George E. Lee secured a summer-long engagement at Lake Taneycomo in the Ozarks in 1937. The band played for dancing at night in a pavilion overlooking the lake. During the day, the pianist Carrie Powell and guitarist Efferge Ware worked with Parker, giving him instruction in harmony. Early in October, Lee paid off the men and Parker returned to Kansas City, ready to take on all-comers.
7. The Jeter-Pillars Recording Orchestra, co-led by saxophonists James Jeter and Hayes Pillars and formed in St. Louis in late 1933, was resident at the whites-only Plantation Club, billed as the "Largest Nite Club in St. Louis," from 1934 to 1944. Owned and managed by Tony and James Scarpelli, the Plantation was originally located at Vandeventer and Enright and moved to Delmar Boulevard in 1940. The Jeter-Pillars recordings made in 1937 featured Vernon King on bass, not Blanton.
8. James Blanton was born in Chattanooga, Tennessee, in October 1919.
9. Dave Dexter Jr. (1915–1990) wrote first for the *Kansas City Journal-Post* and then for *Down Beat* and was a tireless champion of African American jazz musicians, especially those who performed in Kansas City. In 1943 he joined Capitol Records in Hollywood and became an extremely influential producer, signing Frank Sinatra, Peggy Lee, Stan Kenton, Nat King Cole, Duke Ellington, Woody Herman, and Kay Starr to the label and recording many local jazz artists. Count Basie recorded "Diggin' for Dex" and Jay McShann "Dexter Blues" in tribute to him.
10. *Me and Bessie*, a music revue about the life and career of blues singer Bessie Smith, was a one-woman show, conceived and written by Linda Hopkins and Will Holt. It debuted at Ford's Theatre in Washington in November 1974 with Howlett Smith and Lenny Hambro as the co-musical directors. The later Broadway production ran for 453 performances.

12. NORMAN "NORM" LELAND BOWDEN

1. Louis Armstrong appeared at Frank Sebastian's New Cotton Club in Culver City, California, from July 1930 to March 1931 as a featured artist backed by the house band. This was led, initially, by trumpeter Vernon Elkins and later by saxophonist Les Hite, with trumpeter George Orendorff in the personnel.

2. The Order of the Eastern Star is said to be the largest fraternal organization in the world that is open to both men and women. It was established in 1850 and has ten thousand chapters in twenty countries. Male members of the Order must be Master Masons; women must have a specific relationship with a Mason as wife, widow, sister, or daughter.

3. Drummer Clifford "Boots" Douglas was born in Temple in central Texas on September 7, 1908 (or 1906), and formed his Buddies orchestra in the early 1930s after playing with local bands around San Antonio. The Buddies recorded forty-two sides for Bluebird and continued to tour until Douglas relocated to Los Angeles in 1950. After working for the county authorities, he retired in 1974 and died in Los Angeles on October 27, 2000.

4. Vocalist Al Hibbler (1915–2001) was blind from birth. He is best known for his work with Duke Ellington, with whom he was associated from 1943 to 1951.

5. Saxophonist and bandleader Harlan Leonard (1905–1983) played with George E. Lee and Bennie Moten in Kansas City and formed his Rockets band in 1937, touring extensively and recording for Bluebird. He relocated to Los Angeles in 1942, and when his final band broke up in 1945, he took up defense work before moving to the Post Office and later to the Internal Revenue Service, from which he retired in 1975.

6. Shepp's Playhouse was opened on First and Los Angeles Streets in the Little Tokyo (Bronzeville) district by Gordon Sheppard, an African American former Hollywood cameraman, on September 12, 1944. Sheppard hired Leonard Reed to produce its floor shows. There was music on three floors and broadcasts five nights a week. The club closed in August 1946 after Sheppard was declared bankrupt. Reed moved on to Chicago.

7. Pianist and bandleader Jelly Roll Morton arrived in Los Angeles in November 1940 and lived initially at 4052 Central Avenue. Bassist Ed "Montudie" Garland had organized a band for him; they rehearsed but never played in public. Morton died in Los Angeles on July 10, 1941. He was fifty (or fifty-five).

8. Earl Grant (1931–1970) was a popular organist, vocalist, and pianist who had many hit records, including "Ebb Tide" (1961), which sold one million copies. He cut thirty albums for Decca records and was killed outright when his Rolls-Royce ran off the road near Lordsburg, New Mexico. Grant also played trumpet and drums.

13. JOHN RICHARD "STREAMLINE" EWING

1. The Long Beach earthquake, measuring 6.4 on the Richter scale, resulted in the loss of 120 lives and damaged property valued at $50 million. The Jefferson High School campus buildings (at 1319 E. 41st Street) were destroyed, causing the school to close from March 10 to April 6, 1933. Temporary tent bungalows were erected on the school's football fields and classes shortened to half days. Jefferson High School is said to have produced more jazz musicians and composers than any other school west of the Mississippi. It was eventually rebuilt in its present form in 1935.

14. CHARLES L. "CHUCK" THOMAS JR.

1. Ben Webster lived with the Young family in Albuquerque for a few months before returning to Amarillo, Texas, early in 1930 and joining Gene Coy's Happy Black Aces. He passed through a number of other more prominent bands and eventually joined Cab Calloway in 1936.

2. It is likely that *G.I. Joe* is a misnomer. Mark Cantor's researches suggest that Thomas and the Fort Huachuca band appeared in an *Army-Navy Screen Magazine* release in the Jubilee series of broadcasts under the title of *Strictly G.I.*, which starred Lena Horne, Rochester, and comedian Timme Rogers. It was aired in October 1943 and was made in Los Angeles.

3. Horace Henderson's big band began a series of dates in Southern California in December 1961 billed as the Fletcher Henderson Orchestra. They opened on December 30 at the Avalon Casino on Catalina Island, a popular vacation resort, twenty miles off the California coast, reported Leonard Feather in the *Melody Maker* dated January 6, 1962. The book included some three hundred arrangements by Horace and Fletcher.

15. JESSE JOHN SAILES

1. William Asher Sailes, pianist, organist, and bandleader, aka "Big Daddy," was born in Omaha on November 10, 1917, and died in Omaha on November 22, 2011.
2. Terry Cruise became a prominent saxophonist and bandleader in Seattle and later managed the Blue Note club before taking a civil service job. He died in 1988.
3. The Woodman Brothers were billed as "The Biggest Little Band in the World" and consisted of Britt Woodman, who played clarinet, tenor saxophone, and trombone; William Jr., who played alto saxophone, clarinet, and trumpet; and the eldest of the brothers, Coney, who doubled on piano, banjo, and guitar, with George Reed or Jesse Sailes on drums. All still in their teens, they were something of a sensation, constantly changing instruments and justifying their claim to be "4 Musicians Who Play Like 8." The band was managed by their father, trombonist William Woodman Sr.
4. The Elks Hall (also known as the Elks Temple) was at 4016 Central Avenue and had three floors, with the Elks Auditorium or ballroom on the first floor. This had a balcony and could accommodate two thousand patrons. On the second floor there was a smaller room where there were Saturday and Sunday matinee dances. In its day, the Elks was said to be the largest African American–owned building in Los Angeles. In 1973 the building was purchased by the Nation of Islam; it was demolished in 1983 as it was structurally unsound, and the site is now occupied by Masjid Felix Bilal mosque.
5. The Follies Theatre opened as the Belasco Theatre in 1904 at 337 S. Main Street. It was renamed the Follies in 1919 and became a burlesque house. By 1948, burlesque had given way to vaudeville, and then to "skin flicks." The Follies was demolished in 1974.
6. Pianist Gordon C. Harrison was born in Texas on December 28, 1901, and died in Los Angeles on May 5, 1951.
7. The Creole Palace club opened in the Douglas Hotel, San Diego, at 3rd Avenue and Market Street, in 1924 and became known as the Harlem of the West, attracting top African American talent. The building was sold in 1956 and razed to the ground in 1985.
8. Vocalist Dobie Gray made "The In Crowd" in 1964 in Los Angeles. It reached number thirteen in the U.S. Hit Parade in 1965. Jesse's drums play a prominent part in the success of the record.
9. Harvey Brooks (1899–1968) was born in Philadelphia and arrived in Los Angeles in 1923. He was the first African American to write a full film score, for Mae West's *I'm No Angel* in 1933. Paula Watson's version of "Little Bird," made in 1948 for Supreme with Sailes playing drums, made it to number two in Billboard's R&B chart and to number six in their pop chart. Covered by white singer Evelyn Knight on Decca, it made number one in the Billboard Best Seller chart.
10. Teddy Buckner died in September 1994, his final years blighted by chronic arthritis.

16. "RED" MINOR WILLIAM ROBINSON

1. Minor Robinson recorded four sides with trumpeter Geechie Smith's band for Capitol on September 27, 1946, and at least seven tracks with pianist and vocalist Floyd Dixon for Specialty on June 17, 1953. These appear to constitute his complete discography.

2. The Minor Robinson interview transcript, part of the UCLA Central Avenue Sounds project (© 2005 The Regents of the University of California), was also consulted.

3. Robinson recorded his birth date as February 22, 1920, in his interview with Steve Isoardi.

4. Trumpeter/arranger Leslie C. Drayton was a founder member of the successful R&B group Earth, Wind and Fire and went on to write and conduct for singers Nancy Wilson and Marvin Gaye. His father, bassist Charlie Drayton, died when Leslie was three years old, and Leslie was encouraged to pursue music as a career by his mother, who was singer Pearl Bailey's hairdresser. Drayton later ran a successful big band and recorded regularly in the 1980s and 1990s. More recently, he taught at Ventura College.

5. 1-A: available, fit for general military service.

6. James H. Herndon, born March 24, 1922, enlisted in the U.S. Army on November 22, 1940. He became a prominent drummer and teacher in Chicago and died October 21, 2005.

7. Carl Perkins was born in Indianapolis on August 19, 1928, and died in Los Angeles on March 17, 1958. Perkins was an accomplished bop pianist who often played with his left arm parallel to the keyboard, using his elbow to strike notes. He appeared with his trio around LA in 1956–1957.

Selected Bibliography and Source Materials

BIOGRAPHICAL STUDIES

Allen, Walter C. *Hendersonia—The Music of Fletcher Henderson and His Musicians*, 2nd edition. Highland Park, NJ: Self-published, 1974.

Bigard, Barney. *With Louis and Duke: The Autobiography of a Jazz Clarinettist*. Ed. Barry Martyn. London: Macmillan Press, 1985.

Boujot, Michel. *Louis Armstrong*. Paris: Éditions Plume, 1998.

Britt, Stan. *Long Tall Dexter: A Critical Musical Biography of Dexter Gordon*. London: Quartet Books, 1989.

Broadbent, Peter. *Charlie Christian, Solo Flight: The Seminal Electric Guitarist*, 2nd edition. Blaydon on Tyne, UK: Ashley Mark Publishing, 2003.

Brothers, Thomas. *Louis Armstrong: Master of Modernism*. New York: W.W. Norton, 2014.

Callender, Red, with Elaine Cohen. *Unfinished Dream: The Musical World of Red Callender*. London: Quartet Books, 1985.

Chilton, John. *Let the Good Times Roll: The Story of Louis Jordan*. London: Quartet, 1992.

Clayton, Buck, assisted by Nancy Miller Elliott. *Buck Clayton's Jazz World*. London: Macmillan Press, 1986.

Collette, Buddy, with Steve Isoardi. *Jazz Generations: A Life in American Music and Society*. London: Continuum, 2000.

Collins, Tony. *Rock Mr. Blues: The Life and Music of Wynonie Harris*. Milford, NH: Big Nickel Publications, 1995.

Dance, Helen Oakley. *Stormy Monday: The T-Bone Walker Story*. Baton Rouge: Louisiana State University Press, 1987.

Dance, Stanley. *The World of Earl Hines*. New York: Charles Scribner's Sons, 1977.

———. *The World of Count Basie*. New York: Charles Scribner's Sons, 1980.

Daniels, Douglas Henry. *Lester Leaps In: The Life and Times of Lester "Pres" Young*. Boston: Beacon Press, 2002.

———. *One O'Clock Jump: The Unforgettable History of the Oklahoma City Blue Devils*. Boston: Beacon Press, 2006.

Darensbourg, Joe. *Telling It Like It Is*. Ed. Peter Vacher. London: Macmillan Press, 1987.

Darensbourg, Joe, as told to Peter Vacher. *Jazz Odyssey*. Baton Rouge: Louisiana State University Press, 1987.

Dawson, Jim. *Nervous Man Nervous: Big Jay McNeely and the Rise of the Honking Tenor Sax!* Milford, NH: Big Nickel Publications, 1994.

Foster, George "Pops," as told to Tom Stoddard. *The Autobiography of Pops Foster New Orleans Jazzman*, 2nd edition. San Francisco: BackBeat Books, 2005.

Gelly, Dave. *Being Prez: The Life and Music of Lester Young*. London: Equinox Publishing, 2007.

Giddins, Gary. *Celebrating Bird: The Triumph of Charlie Parker*, 2nd edition. Minneapolis: University of Minnesota Press, 2013.

Gushee, Lawrence. *Pioneers of Jazz: The Story of the Creole Band*. New York: Oxford University Press, 2005.

Hampton, Lionel, with James Haskins. *Hamp, an Autobiography*. London: Robson Books, 1989.

Hawes, Hampton, and Don Asher. *Raise Up Off Me: A Portrait of Hampton Hawes*. New York: Da Capo, 1979.

Hershorn, Tad. *Norman Granz: The Man Who Used Jazz for Justice*. Berkeley: University of California Press, 2011.

Lipsitz, George. *Midnite at the Barrelhouse: The Johnny Otis Story*. Minneapolis: University of Minnesota Press, 2010.

Lomax, Alan. *Mister Jelly Roll*. Berkeley: University of California, 2001.

Love, Preston. *A Thousand Honey Creeks Later: My Life in Music from Basie to Motown—and Beyond*. Hanover, NH: Wesleyan University Press, 1997.

Martyn, Barry. *Walking with Legends: Barry Martyn's New Orleans Jazz Odyssey*. Ed. Mick Burns. Baton Rouge: Louisiana State University Press, 2007.

McCusker, John. *Creole Trombone: Kid Ory and the Early Years of Jazz*. Jackson: University Press of Mississippi, 2012.

Miller, Mark. *High Hat, Trumpet and Rhythm: The Life and Music of Valaida Snow*. Toronto: Mercury Press, 2007.

Mingus, Charles. *Beneath the Underdog*. London: Weidenfeld & Nicolson, 1971, Penguin Books, 1975.

Otis, Johnny. *Upside Your Head! Rhythm and Blues on Central Avenue*. Hanover, NH: Wesleyan University Press, 1993.

Pastras, Phil. *Dead Man Blues: Jelly Roll Morton Way Out West*. Berkeley: University of California Press, 2001.

Pepper, Art and Laurie. *Straight Life: The Story of Art Pepper*. New York: Schirmer Books, 1979.

Poindexter, Norwood "Pony." *The Pony Express: Memoirs of a Jazz Musician*. Frankfurt: JAS Publikationen, 1985.

Porter, Lewis, editor. *A Lester Young Reader*. Washington, DC: Smithsonian Institution Press, 1991.

Porter, Roy. *There and Back*. Ed. David Keller. Oxford: Bayou Press, 1991.

Priestley, Brian. *Mingus: A Critical Biography*. London: Quartet Books, 1982.

Reich, Howard, and William Gaines. *Jelly's Blues: The Life, Music and Redemption of Jelly Roll Morton*. Cambridge, MA: Da Capo Press, 2003.

Royal, Marshal, with Claire P. Gordon. *Jazz Survivor*. London: Cassell, 1996.

Russell, Bill, compiler. *Oh Mister Jelly: A Jelly Roll Morton Scrapbook*. Copenhagen, Denmark: JazzMediaApS, 1999.

Santoro, Gene. *Myself When I Am Real: The Life and Music of Charles Mingus*. New York: Oxford University Press, 2000.

Scherman, Tony. *Back Beat: Earl Palmer's Story*. Washington, DC: Smithsonian Institution Press, 1999.

Selchow, Manfred. *A Bio-Discographical Scrapbook on Vic Dickenson*. Westoverledingen: Self-published, 1998.

Stratemann, Dr. Klaus. *Louis Armstrong on the Screen*. Copenhagen, Denmark: JazzMedia ApS, 1996.

Terry, Clark, with Gwen Terry. *Clark: The Autobiography of Clark Terry*. Berkeley: University of California Press, 2011.

Vacher, Peter. *Jazz Greats: Kid Ory*. London: Marshall Cavendish Leisure, 1998.
Vail, Ken. *Bird's Diary: The Life of Charlie Parker 1945–1955*. Chesssington, Surrey, UK: Castle Communications, 1996.
Ward, Geoffrey C. *Unforgivable Blackness: The Rise and Fall of Jack Johnson*. London: Pimlico, 2005.
Wilkinson, Christopher. *Jazz on the Road: Don Albert's Musical Life*. Berkeley: University of California Press, 2001.

BLACK LOS ANGELES

Bryant, Clora, et al. *Central Avenue Sounds: Jazz in Los Angeles*. Berkeley: University of California Press, 1998.
Cox, Betty Yarborough. *Central Avenue—Its Rise and Fall (1896–c.1955) including the Musical Renaissance of Black Los Angeles*. Los Angeles: BEEM Publications, 1996.
DjeDje, Jacqueline Cogdell, and Eddie S. Meadows, eds. *California Soul: Music of African Americans in the West*. Berkeley: University of California Press, 1998.
Flamming, Douglas. *Bound for Freedom: Black Los Angeles in Jim Crow America*. Berkeley: University of California Press, 2005.
Hoskyns, Barney. *Waiting for the Sun: The Story of the Los Angeles Music Scene*. London: Viking, 1996.
Reed, Tom. *The Black Music History of Los Angeles—Its Roots. A Classical Pictorial History of Black Music in Los Angeles from the 1920s–1970*. Los Angeles: Black Accent Press, 1992.
Smith, R. J. *The Great Black Way: L.A. in the 1940s and the Lost African American Renaissance*. New York: Public Affairs, 2006.

REGIONAL JAZZ HISTORIES

De Barros, Paul. *Jackson Street After Hours: The Roots of Jazz in Seattle*. Seattle, WA: Sasquatch Books, 1993.
Driggs, Frank, and Chuck Haddix. *Kansas City Jazz: From Ragtime to Bebop—A History*. New York: Oxford University Press, 2005.
Eckland, K. O. *Jazz West 1945–1986: The A–Z Guide to West Coast Jazz Music*. Carmel by the Sea, CA: Cypress, 1986.
———. *Jazz West 2: The A–Z Guide to West Coast Jazz Music*. San Rafael, CA: Donna Ewald, 1995.
Gioia, Ted. *West Coast Jazz 1945–1960: Modern Jazz in California*. New York: Oxford University Press, 2000.
Haydon, Geoffrey, and Dennis Marks. *Repercussions: A Celebration of African-American Music*. London: Century Publishing, 1985.
Keller, David. *The Blue Note: Seattle's Black Musicians Union—A Pictorial History*. Orange, CA: Self-published, 2013.
Oliphant, Dave. *Texan Jazz*. Austin: University of Texas Press, 1996.
Owsley, Dennis. *City of Gabriels: The History of Jazz in St Louis, 1895–1973*. St. Louis, MO: Reedy Press, 2006.
Pearson, Nathan W., Jr. *Goin' to Kansas City*. Basingstoke, Hants, UK: Macmillan Press, 1988.
Pepin, Elizabeth, and Lewis Watts. *Harlem of the West: The San Francisco Fillmore Jazz Area*. San Francisco: Chronicle Books, 2006.
Rose, Al, and Edmond Souchon. *New Orleans Jazz: A Family Album*, revised edition. Baton Rouge: Louisiana State University Press, 1978.
Stoddard, Tom. *Jazz on the Barbary Coast*, revised edition. Berkeley, CA: Heyday Books, 1998.

COLLECTED ESSAYS

Defaa, Chip. *Blue Rhythms: Six Lives in Rhythm and Blues*. New York: Da Capo Press, 2000.
Levin, Floyd. *Classic Jazz: A Personal View of the Music and the Musicians*. Berkeley: University of California Press, 2000.
Millar, Bill. *Let the Good Times Rock: A Fan's Notes on Post-War American Roots Music*. New York: Music Mentor Books, 2004.
Vacher, Peter. *Soloists and Sidemen: American Jazz Stories*. London: Northway Publications, 2004 (includes interviews with LA-based artists Art Farmer, Britt Woodman, Teddy Edwards, Vi Redd).
———. *Mixed Messages: American Jazz Stories*. Nottingham: Five Leaves Publications, 2012 (includes Gerald Wilson, Plas Johnson, Herman Riley).
Vernhettes, Dan, with Bo Lindström. *Jazz Puzzles Volume 1*. Paris: Jazz'edit, 2012.

GENERAL JAZZ HISTORY

Blesh, Rudi, and Harriet Janis. *They All Played Ragtime*, 4th edition. New York: Oak Publications, 1971.
Chilton, John. *Who's Who of Jazz*, 5th edition. London: Papermac, 1989.
Driggs, Frank, and Harris Lewine. *White Heat, Black Beauty: A Pictorial History of Classic Jazz*. New York: William Morrow, 1982.
Fox, Ted. *Showtime at the Apollo*. London: Quartet, 1985.
Gitler, Ira. *Swing to Bop: An Oral History of the Transition in Jazz in the 1940s*. New York: Oxford University Press, 1987.
Kernfeld, Barry, ed. *The New Grove Dictionary of Jazz*, 2nd edition. London: Macmillan Publishers, 2002.
Kisch, John, and Edward Mapp. *A Separate Cinema: Fifty Years of Black Cast Posters*. New York: Noonday Press, 1992.
McCarthy, Albert. *Big Band Jazz*. London: Barrie & Jenkins, 1974.
Meeker, David. *Jazz in the Movies*. London: Talisman Books, 1981.
Yanow, Scott. *Jazz on Film: The Complete Story of the Musicians and Music on Screen*. San Francisco: BackBeat Books, 2004.

OTHER AUTHORITIES CONSULTED

Directory of Members, Musicians' Union, Local 47 American Federation of Musicians: various editions.
Musician's Directory (Musicians Protective Ass'n), Local 767 A.F. of M., Los Angeles, California: various editions.

CD/LP LINER NOTES AND BOOKLET ESSAYS

Bernholm, Jonas. Liner notes. *Roy Milton and His Solid Senders, The Grandfather of R&B*. Juke Box Lil (Sweden) JB-600 (LP).
Dance, Helen Oakley. Booklet essay. *The Complete Recordings of T-Bone Walker 1940–1954*. Mosaic MD6-130.
Elwood, Philip. Liner notes. *Kid Ory's Creole Jazz Band—The Complete 1944 Appearances on Orson Well's [sic] Mercury Wonder Show and the 1945 Standard School Broadcasts*. Folk-Lyric (LP) 9008.
Ertegun, Nesuhi. Liner notes. *Kid Ory Creole Jazz Band 1944/45*. Good Time Jazz GTJCD-12022-2.

Isoardi, Steve, et al. Booklet essays. *Central Avenue Sounds, Jazz in Los Angeles (1921–1956).* Rhino R2 75872 4-CD box set.
Lange, Charlie. Liner notes. *Joe Liggins with the original Million Seller "The Honey Dripper."* Juke Box Lil (Sweden) JB-622 (LP).
Millar, Bill. Booklet essay. *Nellie Lutcher and Her Rhythm.* Bear Family (Germany) BCD 15910 DI.
Oess, Attila. Liner notes. *Lloyd Glenn and His Joymakers: "Texas Man."* Juke Box Lil (Sweden) JB-608 (LP).
Pieper, Bill, Liner notes. *Kid Ory Live!* Vocalion (UK) LP LAE-L605.
Porter, Bob, and Ira Gitler. Booklet essays. *The Complete Illinois Jacquet Sessions 1945–50.* Mosaic MD4-169.
Rust, Brian. Liner notes. *Jazz in California 1923–1930.* Timeless (Holland) CBC 1-034.
Schaap, Phil. Liner notes. *Charlie Parker 1946 JATP Concert.* Verve 513 756 2.
Silsbee, Kirk. Liner notes. *Duke Henderson Get Your Kicks.* Delmark 668.
———. Liner notes. *Howard McGhee West Coast 1945–1947.* Upbeat UPCD 27.74.
———. Liner notes. *Gerald Wilson Suite Memories Reflections on a Jazz Journey.* MAMA Spoken Word—MMF 1014.
Szwed, John. Booklet essays. *Jelly Roll Morton: The Complete Library of Congress Recordings by Alan Lomax.* Rounder 8-CD box set 11661-1888-2.
Thompson, Bill, with John Wilby and Colin J. Bray. Liner notes. *Curtis Mosby/Henry Starr 1924–1939.* Jazz Oracle (Canada) BDW 8003.
Topping, Ray. Liner notes. *Maxwell Davis, Father of West Coast R&B.* Ace (UK) LP CHAD 239.
———. Liner notes. *Joe Lutcher and His Alto Sax "Jumpin' at The Mardi Gras."* Ace (UK) CDCHD 753.
Willard, Patricia. Liner notes. *Black California.* Savoy (LP) SJL 2215.

MAGAZINE ARTICLES

Anderson, J. Lee. "Lee and Lester: Marching to a Different Drummer." *The Mississippi Rag* (December 1992): 1–4, 6–8.
Ashforth, Alden. "The Eagle Brass Band in Los Angeles." *Footnote* (UK) (December 1983): 4–9.
Battestini, Jean-Pierre, and Claudia Battestini. "John 'Streamline' Ewing." *Bulletin du Hot Club de France,* no. 427 (May 1996): 4–9.
Bentley, John. "Sonny Clay: A Veritable Giant." Part One: *Jazz Report* 3 (December 1962). Part Two: *Jazz Report* 3, no 3–4 (January/February 1963).
Bentley, John, and Ralph W. Miller. "West Coast Jazz in the Twenties." *Jazz Monthly* (UK) (May 1961).
Boarman, Vivian, and Cy Shain. "Kid Ory." *Jazz Music* (UK) 3, no. 7 (1948): 9–13. Part Two: *Jazz Music* 3, no. 8 (1948): 19–23.
Bryant, Clora. "Clora Bryant's First Stroll Down Central Avenue." *IAOJA Newsletter* (February 1988): 6.
Bullock, Paul. "A Conversation with Eddie Beal." *Jazz Heritage Foundation* 5, no. 4 (November/December 1984): 12–21.
Burns, Jim. "Central Avenue Breakdown." *Blues & Rhythm* (UK) (July 1986): 4–13.
Cantor, Mark. "The Edgar Bergen Shorts—Almost Soundies." *IAJRC Journal* (Winter 2001/2002): 30–36.
Carr, Peter. "Leon Scott." *Storyville* 53 (June 1974): 168–89.
Cavanaugh, Inez M. "Reminiscing in Tempo: Lawrence Brown." *Metronome* (May 1945): 13, 28.
Dance, Stanley. "Buck Clayton's Story." *Jazz* (November/December 1962): 6–9, 36–37.
———. "The Independent Lawrence Brown." *Down Beat* (January 27, 1966): 21–22, 38.
———. "Red Callender." *Coda,* no. 167 (June 1979): 9–11.
Dawbarn, Bob. "Teddy Buckner Interview." *Melody Maker* (UK) (July 19, 1958).

Demeusy, Bertrand. "Lloyd Glenn—Texas Pianist." *Jazz Journal* (UK) (October 1985).
Driggs, Frank. "Eddie Barefield's Many Worlds." *The Jazz Review* 3, no. 6 (July 1960): 18–22.
———. "Floyd Ray's Orchestra: The Story of the Harlem Dictators." *Coda* (Canada) (July 1968): 2–7.
Eastman, Ralph. "Central Avenue Blues: The Making of Los Angeles Rhythm and Blues, 1942–1947." *Black Music Research Journal* (Spring 1989).
Ellison, Mary. "The Honey Dripper, A True Survivor." *Juke Blues* (UK), no. 7 (December 1985): 4–5.
Emge, Charles. "Move Grows to Scrap L.A.'s Jim Crow Union." *Down Beat* (June 15, 1951): 1, 19.
Ertegun, Marili. "Just Playing Music I Love, Says Kid Ory." *Down Beat* (August 10, 1951).
Feather, Leonard. "The Fletcher Henderson Band Lives Again." *Melody Maker* (January 6, 1962).
Finley, Alice. "Minor Hall Speaks." *Record Changer* (August 1947): 5, 13.
———. "Guitar and Vocal by Bud Scott." *Record Changer* (September 1947): 5–7.
Gushee, Larry. "How the Creole Band Came To Be." *Black Music Research Journal* 8, no. 1 (1988): 83–100.
———. "New Orleans—Area Musicians on the West Coast, 1908–1925." *Black Music Research Journal* 9, no. 1 (Spring 1989): 1–18.
Hague, Doug. "Jack McVea." *Jazz Journal* (UK) (February 1964): 7–8.
Heide, Karl Gurt Zur. "Eugene Porter." Part One: *Footnote* (UK) (June/July 1976). Part Two: *Footnote* (September 1976).
Jacobs, Irving. "Paul Howard." *Playback* (July 1949): 15–20.
Jones, Max. "'Louis Deserves a Monument': Red Mack Digs Back into Jazz History." *Melody Maker* (UK) (June 27, 1963).
Jung, Maureen, and Jack Rhyne. "Live at the 504 Ballroom—Bringing the Blues back to South Central L.A." *Living Blues*, no. 121 (June 1995).
Kaye, Harold S. "Francis 'Doc' Whitby." *Storyville* 110 (December 1983/January 1984): 50–65.
———. "Jazz in Hawaii 1935–1941." *Storyville* (UK) 129 (March 1987): 90–107.
Keller, David. "The Women of Seattle's Black Musicians' Union." *Columbia Magazine* (Winter 2009/2010): 6, 8, 10, 12.
Kochakian, Dan. "The Marl Young Story." *Blues & Rhythm*, no. 179 (May 2003): 16–20.
———. "The Joe Lutcher Story." *Blues & Rhythm* (UK) (October 2007).
Kunstadt, Len. "Some Early West Coast Jazz History—The Black and Tan Orchestra and Kid Ory's Orch. (ex Chicago Defender, February 1923)." *Record Research* 61 (July 1964): 12.
Lees, Gene. "The Ordeal of Ernie Andrews." *Gene Lees Newsletter* (June 1992): 1–7.
Levin, Floyd. "The Spikes Brothers—A Los Angeles Saga." *Jazz Journal* (UK) (December 1951): 12–14.
———. "Ed 'Montudie' Garland, Jazz Pioneer." *The Second Line* (Summer 1979): 6–27.
———. "Ed 'Montudie' Garland, Legend of Jazz." *Jazz Journal* (June 1979): 21–24. Part Two: *Jazz Journal* (August 1979): 5–6.
———. "Andrew Blakeney (Tulane University oral history transcript)." *New Orleans Music* (UK) 1, nos. 4–5 (April–June 1990).
———. "Kid Ory's Legendary Nordskog/Sunshine Recordings—A Seventy Year Controversy." *New Orleans Music* (April 1991).
———. "I Remember Buster Wilson." *New Orleans Music* 6, no. 4 (December 1996): 6–10.
Macnic, Ray. "Reb Spikes—Music Maker." *Storyville* 21 (February 1969): 100–104.
Manus, Willard. "Blues for Central Avenue: Remembering L.A.'s Storied Music Strip." *Blues Access*, no. 19 (Fall 1994): 16–22, 24–25.
McGarvey, Seamus. "'Open the Door Richard, It's Jack McVea.'" Part One: *Blues & Rhythm*, no. 59 (March/April 1991): 4–7. Part Two: *Blues & Rhythm*, no. 60 (May 1991): 10–13.
Mitchell, Bill. "Reminiscences of George Orendorff." *The Mississippi Rag* (October 1984): 4–7.
———. "A Talk with Andrew Blakeney." *The Mississippi Rag* (July 1985): 1–2, 4–6.
———. "Carrere's Career." *The Mississippi Rag* (May 1988): 1, 3–4.

Mohr, Kurt. "Teddy Buckner Interview." *Jazz Hot* (France), date unknown.
Nations, Opal Louis. "'I'm Hunched': The Monte Easter Story." *Real Blues* (February/March 1999): 38–40.
———. "'I'm Hunched': The Monte Easter Story." *Blues and Rhythm* (UK), no. 169 (2002): 4–7.
———. "The Muted Methuselah: The Norman Bowden Story." Part One: *Record Convention News* (April/May 2005): 9, 17. Part Two: *Record Convention News* (June/July 2005): 8, 10.
———. "'Dance Time': The Life and Times of Peppy Prince." *Blues and Rhythm* (UK) (April 2012).
Patch, Derek. "Teddy Buckner, Jazzman of the Year 1984." *Jazz Forum* (July 15, 1984): 1–12.
Propes, Steve. "'Man You Drop A Lotta Honey' (Joe Liggins)." *Blues & Rhythm*, no. 52 (June 1990): 18–20.
———. "Los Angeles Race Music: The Record Industry and the Roots of R&B in Los Angeles." *Blues & Rhythm* (UK), no. 213 (October 2006): 4–9.
Rusch, Bob. "Jack McVea Interview." *Cadence* (April 1986): 11–23.
Russell, Bill. "Mutt Carey." *Record Changer* (November 1948).
Russell, Ross. "West Coast Bop." *Jazz and Blues* (UK) (May 1973): 9–11.
———. "Master Drummer Jesse Price." *Jazz and Blues* (July 1973): 14–15.
Schiedt, Duncan. "Speed Webb." *Jazz Monthly* (UK) (November 1968): 2–8.
Shain, Cy. "Papa Mutt Carey." *Jazz Music* (UK) 3, no. 1 (1946): 5–6, 9–10.
Silsbee, Kirk. "Bronzeville Gypsy: How Charlie Parker Lit Up Little Tokyo." *Los Angeles Downtown News* (May 22, 2006): 1, 6–7.
———. "Memories of Bronzeville, a Forgotten Downtown Era." Date and publication unknown.
———. "Saxophone Feature." *Playboy Jazz Festival Programme* (June 2007).
———. "Jazz High—West Coast Jazz Owes Much to L.A.'s Jefferson High." *Los Angeles City Beat* (September 13–19, 2007).
———. "Yardbird in Lotusland." *Arroyo* (November 2007): 20, 22.
———. "Jazz in the Key of G-Strings: The Golden Age of Los Angeles Burlesque Had a Jazz Soundtrack." *Playboy Jazz Festival Programme* (June 2010).
———. "Radio Waves: The Golden Age of Jazz Radio in Los Angeles." *Playboy Jazz Festival Programme* (June 2011).
———. "Los Angeles Burlesque Feature." *Treats* (June 2011).
Simmen, Johnny. "'Un trompette-poète': George Orendorff." *Bulletin du Hot Club de France* (November 1967): 8–10.
———. "Bumps Myers." *Coda* (Canada) (June 1969): 9–12.
———. "Maxwell Davis." *Coda* (December 1973).
———. "Lloyd Glenn." *Coda* (May/June 1977): 22–23.
Stuart, Dave. "Kid Ory." *Jazz Information* (November 22, 1940): 5–8.
Swyer, Alan. "The Life and Death of R&B in Los Angeles." *Blues & Rhythm* (UK), no. 153.
Townley, Eric. "Lloyd Glenn: San Antonio Piano Man." *Storyville* 78 (August 1978): 220–24.
Tynan, John. "Caught in the Act: Teddy Buckner." *Down Beat* (September 29, 1962): 42.
Vacher, Peter. "Andrew Blakeney." *Melody Maker* (March 30, 1974).
———. "Andrew Blakeney—A Lifetime in Music." *Storyville* 58 (April 1975).
———. "California Dreaming." *Jazz Journal* (January 1980).
———. "Obituary: Caughey Roberts." *The Mississippi Rag* (August 1991).
———. "Andy Blakeney, An Appreciation." *The Mississippi Rag* (June 1992): 10.
———. "West Coast Survivors." *Juke Blues*, no. 27 (Autumn 1992): 24–25.
———. "Jake Porter Obituary." *The Independent* (UK) (April 29, 1993).
———. "Red Mack Obituary." *The Independent* (UK) (July 12, 1993).
———. "Teddy Buckner Obituary." *The Guardian* (October 3, 1994): 12.
———. "Los Angeles One More Time." *Juke Blues*, no. 36 (Winter 1996/1997): 20–22.
———. "Billy Hadnott Obituary." *Jazz Journal* (April 2000).
———. "The Complete Pacific Jazz Recordings of Gerald Wilson and His Orchestra." *Coda* 300/301 (January/February 2001): 52–54.
———. "Jack McVea Obituary." *The Guardian* (UK) (March 6, 2001): 22.

Vernhettes, Dan, with Bo Lindström. "Ernest Coycault 1884–1940." *VJM's Jazz and Blues Mart* (UK) (Summer 2012): 3–13.
Williams, Gene, and Marili Stuart. "Papa Mutt Carey." *Jazz* 3 (March 1943): 5–7.
Williams, Martin. "Zutty." *Down Beat* (November 21, 1963): 18–20.
Wilmer, Val. "The Lee Young Story." *Jazz Journal* (UK) (January 1961): 3–5.
———. "Texas Trombone: Henry Coker." *Jazz Journal* (October 1962): 11–12.
Wood, Berta. "The American Jazz Scene: Andrew Blakeney et al." *Jazz Journal* (UK) (September 1955): 34–36.
———. "Charlie Lawrence." *Jazz Journal* (October 1956): 6–7, 12.
———. "George Orendorff—Quality Serenader." Part One: *Jazz Journal* (January 1957): 4–6. Part Two: *Jazz Journal* (February 1957): 4–6.
———. "Paul Leroy Howard." *Jazz Journal* (November 1957): 6–8. Part Two: *Jazz Journal*, (December 1957): 13–14.
Young, Marl. "Amalgamation of Local 47 and 767." *Overture* (December 1988): 8–9.

Index

Abernathy, Marion, 73
Abrams, Ted, 67
Adams, Arthur, 261
Adams, Chuck, 77
Al Denny's band, 196
Albert, Don, 152, 157, 209
Alexander, Bob, 151
Ali, Bardu, 83, 84, 229, 289; Easter and, 174–175, 175–176, 176, 182
Allen, Bob, 3, 28, 211, 237, 250, 267
Allen, Henry "Tin Can", 12, 50, 51
Allen, Hubert, 177, 178, 179
Allen, Lee, 281
Allen, Red, 247
Allen, Sam, 243
Allen, Winslow "Winnow", 25, 81, 203
Allsbrook, Adolphus, 262
Ammons, Gene, 161
Anderson, Alfonso, 123
Anderson, Andy, 79, 88, 117, 232
Anderson, Bill, 38
Anderson, Charlie, 224–225, 226
Anderson, Ivie, 23, 80
Anderson, Kenneth, 36
Anderson, Merrill, 228
Anderson, Sonny, 165
Andrews, Ernie, 292
Andrews, Rosetta, 177
Angel City Jazz Band, 264
Angelo, Michael, 67
Apex nightclub, 9, 10, 14–15

Armstrong, Louis, xi, xiv, 37, 38, 92, 145, 166, 171, 172, 251, 268, 274; Blakeney and, 5, 10, 14, 31; *Hello Louis!* Concert, 145; influence of, 177, 189, 216, 218, 219, 228, 231, 249, 276; Orendorff and, 47–48, 53–54, 58; Red Mack and, 111, 112, 116, 119, 124, 126; seventieth birthday celebration, 275
Arnheim, Gus, 218
Art Foxall Trio, 73
Ashby, Irving, 259, 262, 291
Ates, Roscoe, 155
Atkins, Wendell "Skins", 200, 201
Austin, Cuba, 218
Austin, Orville, Jr., 260
Axton, Hoyt, 145

Baby Moore's Orchestra, 189
Backyard Swingers, 213
Bailey, Benny, 231
Bailey, Bill, 174
Bailey, Buster, 49, 51
Bailey, Ed, 9, 179
Bailey, Joe, 78
Bailey, Pearl, 56, 174
Baird, Mike, 278
Baker, Chet, 144
Baker, Harold, 228
Ball, Lucille, 251
Banks, Bernard, 19, 65, 66, 73, 286

Banks, Buddy, xiii, 92, 114, 116, 140; McFay and, 59, 61, 62, 65, 70, 71, 72, 73
Baptiste, Xavier "Tink", 35
Barbarin, Paul, 5, 40, 48
Barefield, Eddie, 115, 121
Barenco, Wilbert, 231
Barfield, Bob, 197
Barker, Blue Lu, 95
Barksdale, Everett, 185
Barnardi, Tony, 152
Barnes, Walter, 226
Barnett, Edward, 14
Barrett, Dan, 29
Barrow, Dick, 228
Bartee, Al, 228, 263
Bartley, Dallas, 40, 208
Bascomb, Dud, 172
Basie, Count, 19, 20, 21, 48, 63, 65, 73, 121, 156, 161, 165, 196, 198, 256, 269, 279, 284, 289; Moten band and, 183, 192, 193, 194; Roberts and, 139, 140, 141; Turnham and, 79, 80, 81, 88
Bass, Ralph, 261
Bateman, Ralph, 57, 89
Battle of the Trumpets, 5
Beatty, Winnie, 204
Bechet, Sidney "Pops", 40, 43, 144
Beckett, Fred, 196, 197, 251
Beiderbecke, Bix, 52
Bell, Hugh, 232
Bell, Jimmy, 37
Bell, John, 7
Bellson, Louis, 278
Bennett, Buster, 151
Bentley, Alan, 36
Beresford, Dick, 104
Berg, Billy, 56, 116, 118, 121, 259, 274
Bernard Banks and His Five Clouds of Rhythm, 19, 66
Berry, Ananias, 54, 260
Berry, Emmett, 176, 229
Berry, Parker, 13, 218, 223, 224
Berry, Richard, 262
Berry Brothers, 260
Berton, Vic, 53
Biddle, Vernon, 70
"Big Six". *See* Reeves, Oliver "Big Six"

Bigard, Barney, 5, 10, 25, 30, 48, 121, 125, 218, 230
Bigbee, Cordell Elisabeth. *See* Jones, Betty Hall
Bigbee, George Archie, 97
Biggest Show of 1953, 161
Biggs, Verona, 7
Billie Young and his New Orleans Strutters, 256
Birdland, 163
Bisco, Leslie, 221, 224, 232
Bishop, Wallace, 33, 45, 49
Black, Sheridan, 263
Black and Tan Orchestra, 10, 11, 218
Black and White New Orleans Jazz Band, 250, 278
Black Hawks, 78
Blackwell, Charlie, 72
Blakeney, Andrew "Andy", xi, xii, xiii, 1–32, 42, 58, 146, 172, 220, 234; McFay and, 66, 67; Turnham and, 75, 80
Blakeney, "Professor" Thomas, 3
Blakeney, Ruth, 3
Blanton, Jimmy, 158–159, 163, 199, 200
Bledsoe, George, 228
Bledsoe, Ralph, 284
Bob Alexander's Harmony Kings, 151
Bolar, Abe, 63
Boles, Bill, 221
Boll Weevil, 192
Boone, Lester, 3
Boone, Richard, 251
Boots and His Buddies, 222–225, 226
Borders, Ben, 10, 217
Borders, Ben, 8
Bostic, Earl, 164, 166, 188, 251
Bowden, Della, 215
Bowden, Lavetta, 213, 217, 231
Bowden, Len, 159
Bowden, Norman, Sr., 214–215
Bowden, Norman "Norm" Leland, xii, xiii, 70, 183, 184, 213–235, 214, 264, 290
Boze, Calvin, 57, 89, 125, 263
Bradford, Kirt, 20, 21, 67
Bradley, Oscar, Jr., xiii, 65, 79, 117, 216, 219, 239
Brady's Peppers, 152
Brantley, Joe, 63

Braud, Wellman, 189
Breakfast at Sunrise (film), 12
Brice, Bernice "Pee Wee", xiii, 17, 114, 115, 224
Brice, Pee Wee, 17
Bridges, Henry, 201
Brinson, Ted, 102, 256
Broiles, Dorothy, 73, 122
Bronson, Art, 189
Brooks, Alford, 117, 216, 221
Brooks, Bert, 117, 262
Brooks, Dudley, 25, 117, 160, 216
Brooks, Duke, 204
Brooks, Harvey, 11, 50, 53, 78, 276
Brooks, Roy, 234
Brown, Boyce, 40
Brown, Charles, 83, 229
Brown, Crawford, 78
Brown, George, 177, 242
Brown, James, 178
Brown, Lawrence, 14, 51, 53, 85, 189, 216, 217
Brown, Les, 26
Brown, Oscar, Jr., 288
Brown, Piney, 193, 197
Brown, Pud, 276
Brown Cats of Rhythm, 20, 67
Brown Sisters, 115, 174
Browne, Samuel, 132, 269
Bryant, Artis, 20, 65
Bryant, Bobby, 274
Bryant, Brady, 152, 156
Bryant, Clora, 31, 92, 281
Bryant, George, 15–16
Bryant, Marie, 117
Bryant, Willie, 224
Buck Clayton and his Twelve Gentlemen from Harlem, 155
Buck Clayton's Fourteen Gentlemen from Harlem, 174
Buckner, Teddy, 65, 78, 110, 200, 216, 230; Ewing and, 237, 249; Lane and, 147, 164–166; Roberts and, xiii, 23, 27, 28, 129, 136, 137, 144–145; Sailes and, 267, 268, 274, 275–278, 290; Teddy Buckner Reunion Band, 213, 237, 267; Thomas and, 258–259, 263–264
Buddy Banks Sextete, 73
Buddy Rich's Quartet, 259

Bull Frog Shorty, 256
Bunn, Jimmy, xiii, 85
Bunn, Teddy, 205
Burge, Bobby, 286
Burke, Ceelle, 80, 88, 134; Blakeley and, 10, 13, 14, 18, 22, 23, 24; Orendorff and, 53, 54–55, 56, 58
Burke, Edward, 244
"Burlesque Wheel", 6
Burns, Buddy, 278
Burrell, Duke, 291
Burrill, Chester "Butch", 259
Burroughs, Alvin, 244, 245
Busse, Henry, 52
Byars, Douglas "Slits", 240, 242, 263, 270
Byas, Don, 61, 91, 113, 115

Caldwell, C. C., 183
Callender, Red, xiv, 79, 117, 138, 204, 243
Calloway, Cab, 6, 18, 115, 153, 174, 200, 204, 223, 246, 256, 258
Calloway, Jean (Callie Dill), 153, 154
Campbell, Floyd, 38
Campbell, Paul, 141
Cane, Eddie, 260
Canova, Judy, 177
Carey, Thomas "Papa Mutt", xiii, 9, 12, 17, 24, 51, 81, 110, 144, 179, 218, 220, 230, 242; Robinson and, 286, 286–287
Carmichael, Hoagy, 47
Carnegie Hall, 161
Carpenter, Ike, 274
Carr, Lady Will, 116–117, 262
Carrere, Bernard, 169, 179, 260
Carrington, Charles, 247
Carrington, Jeff, 190
Carry, George Scoops, 243
Carson, Eddie, 255–256, 257
Carter, Benny, 30, 51, 84, 89, 134, 198, 200, 202, 207, 226, 234, 259, 283
Carter, Cecil "Count", 21, 67
Carter, Nell, 166, 264
Cary, Dick, 28
Casino Ballroom, 19, 66, 67
Catlett, Big Sid, 157, 249, 273, 284
Chadwick, Leonard, 63, 65
Chamblee, Eddie, 287
Chapman, Christine, 261, 262
Charles, Ray, 273

Charlie Thomas's Orchestra, 255
Cheatham, Doc, 223
Cheatham, Jimmy, 247, 248
Cher, 274
Cherock, Shorty, 204
Chester Lane and his Blue Jacketeers, 160
Chester Lane's Yellowjackets, 152, 156
Chicago, 1–7
Christenson School of Music, 35
Christian, Booker, 259
Christian, Charles (Charlie), 63, 64, 70, 73
Christian, Eddie, 64, 70
Chudd, Lew, 180
Clark, Fred, 73
Clark, Herbert L., 49
Claxton, Rozelle, 244
Clay, Shirley, 7
Clay, Sonny, 9, 15, 81, 109–110, 169, 174, 221
Clayton, Buck, xiv, 107, 111, 113, 126, 126–127, 155, 172; Hadnott and, 196, 207; Roberts and, 136–137, 137–138, 139
Clef Club, 59, 92, 182
Cleveland, Jimmy, 287
Club Alabam, 15, 23, 65, 78, 103, 177, 184, 228, 229–230, 272
Club Plantation, 157, 159, 167
The Coasters, 274
Cobb, Arnett, 73
Cobb, Bert, 5
Cochran, Eddie, 274
Cochran, Mickey, 234
Coger, Elvin, 283
Coker, Henry L.C., 20, 21, 67, 73
Cole, Eddie, 38
Cole, Nat King, 10, 38, 83, 116, 121, 162, 203, 204, 209, 242, 291
Coleman, Herschel, 54, 141
Coles, Jimmy, 226
College, William, 247
Collette, Buddy, xiv, 65, 179, 247, 261, 269, 281, 283, 284–285, 285, 290
Collins, Lee, 247
Collins, Louis, 234
Collins, Pete, 89, 257, 261, 262
Collins, Shad, 246
Collins, Theodore, 284, 285
Columbus, Chris, 208

Comfort, Joe, 269, 283
Compton, Glover, 4, 37
Conn, Lanier, 78
Cook, Charlie "Doc", 5, 6
Cooke, Sam, 248
Cooper, Bill, 72, 288
Cooper, Buster, 211
Cooper, Elzie (L. Z.), 9, 14, 27, 42, 227, 286
Cotton Club, 14, 17, 18–19, 22, 50, 50–51, 52, 78, 105, 159, 171, 216
Count Basie and His Barons of Rhythm, 139, 140
Courtiers, 73
Covan, Willie, 128
Cowens, Herbert, 63
Cox, Ida, 191–192, 196
Coy, Andrus, 241
Coy, Ann, 112, 267, 271
Coy, Gene, 61–62, 64, 107, 110, 112, 240, 241, 242, 243, 267, 271
Coycault, Ernest, xiii, 9
Craig, James, 40, 270
Crawford, Bixie, 73, 289
Crawford, Ernie, 180
Crawford, James (Jimmy), 270, 274, 284
Creole Jazz Band, 58, 125, 275
Creole Palace, 109, 138, 272
Crofton, Vera, 82
Crosby, Bing, 52, 88, 117
Crosby, Bob, 18
Crowder, Robert, 244
Cruise, Terry, 269
Crump, Jesse, 191
Culley, Wendell, 54, 176
Culliver, Freddie, 191
Curtis Mosby's Blue Blowers, 9, 14, 25, 82, 107

Dade, Bob, 117
Daily, Pete, 249
Dameron, Tadd, 201
Dancer, Earl, 136
Dandridge, Frank "Devil", 27
Dane, Barbara, 274
Daniels, Billy, 70
Darensbourg, Joe, xi, 1, 13, 25, 30, 33, 92, 185, 276
Davidson, Leonard "Big Boy", 15, 24, 221

Davies, John, 217, 239, 269
Davis, Baby, 71
Davis, Charles (Charlie), 23, 54, 80, 141, 263
Davis, Eddie, 70, 86, 229, 283, 290, 292
Davis, Leo McCoy, xiii, 9, 81, 115, 134, 179, 221, 240, 241
Davis, Maxwell, xiii, 22, 23, 57, 88, 89, 162, 204, 241, 248; Sailes and, 270, 271–272, 273, 274, 279
Davis, Miles, 163, 248
Davis, Mr., 269
Davis, Pops, 261
Davis, Richard, 288
Davis, Sammy, 261
Davis, Wild Bill, 163
Day, Bob, 90
Day, Doris, 274
Day, William "Basie", 70, 71
de Barros, Paul, 75
de Luce, Gus, 13
de Pina, Mary, 177, 180
Dejan, Leo, 27
Delaney, Jimmy, 178
DeLay, Michael (Mike), 29, 185, 250, 274
Demond, Frank, 29
Demoss, Orville, 99
Dennis, Arthur, 177, 222
Derricott, Dizzy, 224
Dewey, Helen, 49, 50
Dexter, Dave, 207, 231
Dickenson, Vic, 56, 229
Dickerson, Carroll, 3, 38
Dixie Aces, 78
Dixie Syncopators, 5
Dixon, Floyd, 290, 291
Dixon, George, 244
Dodds, Baby, 35, 40
Dodds, Johnny, 35
Dodson, Ernest, 278
Doggett, Bill, 174, 208
Dolphy, Eric, 180
Dominique, Natty, 37
Dorsey, Bob, 79, 117, 232
Dorsey, Thomas A., 49
Dorsey, Tommy, 26, 251
Douglas, Bill, 287–288
Douglas, Buck, 287
Douglas, Tommy, 193

Douglass, Bill, xiii, 57, 89, 202, 287
Down Beat (club), 70–71, 209, 279, 290
Drayton, Charlie, 283
Drayton, Leslie, 283
Dreamland Orchestra, 6
Duff, Hosea, 38
Dunham, Katherine, 55
Dunn, Clyde, 263
Durham, Allen, xiv, 64, 70, 79, 110, 240
Durham, Clyde, 64, 112
Durham, Earl, 64
Durham, Eddie, 64, 193
Durham, Joe, 64
Durham, Roosevelt, 64
Dutrey, Honoré, 47

Eagle Brass Band, 75
Easter, Monte, xiv, 169–184, 170, 220, 221, 222, 229; Sailes and, 267, 278; Thomas and, 253, 264
The Easy Riders, 274
Echols, Charles (Charlie), 18–19, 27, 81, 111, 113–115, 121, 174
Echols, W. C., 255
Eckstine, Billy, 70, 245, 246, 258, 261
Eddie Carson and His Hot-Ten-Tots, 255–256, 257
Eddy, Duane, 274
Edison, Harry (Sweets), 155, 156, 158, 172
Edwards, Art, 164, 276
Edwards, Teddy, xii, 124, 164, 209, 274, 289, 292
Edythe Turnham and Her Eight Knights of Syncopation, 78
Eldridge, Roy, 64, 118, 171, 178, 204, 228, 287
Elkins, Vernon, 12, 14, 52
Ellington, Duke, xiv, 17, 19, 25, 79, 85, 88, 118, 121, 155, 158, 159, 161, 189, 216, 218, 219, 223, 227, 231, 259, 284, 289
Ellison, Jimmy, 259
Epps, Joe, 262
Erwing, Chester, 134
Erwing, Dorchester, 222
Erwing, Harris, 134, 135, 173, 178, 222, 233
Erwing, James (Jim), 134, 173, 222
Erwing Brothers, 23, 118, 134, 136, 173, 174, 184; Bowden and, 222–223, 228

Evans, Gil, 51
Evans, Herschel, 61, 71, 113, 139, 192, 193, 194
Evans, Reggie, 278
Ewing, John Richard "Streamline", xiv, 89, 121, 164, 185, 216, 237–251, 238, 264; Sailes and, 269, 275, 276, 277, 278
Ewing, Wiley, 238

Fain, Elmer, xiii, 13, 202
Faire, Johnny, 147
"Fanchon and Marco's Idea", 16–17
Fanning, Manzie, 62
Fant, Ed, 243, 244, 245
Farmer, Addison, 206, 289
Farmer, Arthur (Art), 178, 206, 289
Federal Music Project of Southern California, 175
Fields, Carl (Kansas), 244
Fields. Ernie, 190, 209, 231
Filhe, Fields, 48
Filhe, George, 5
Fines, Doug, 57, 258
Fingers, Monroe, 152, 155
Finis, Doug, 17
Finney, Garland, 121, 232
Fitzgerald, Ella, 84, 86, 161, 175
Flennoy, Lorenzo, 65, 90–91, 113, 126, 172, 222, 230
Fletcher, Dusty, 161, 162, 175
Fletcher, Milton, 244
Fletcher Henderson Band, 89
Florence Hoskins and Her Troubadours, 184, 220
Flowers, Jimmy, 7
Floyd, Buddy, 143, 260–261, 263
Floyd, Troy, 193
Floyds of London, 90–91
Follies, 270–271, 274
Forrest, Jimmy, 158
Four Cheers, 144
Foxall, Art, 73
Foxx, Redd, 178, 181, 261
Franklin, Leslie, 224
Franklin, Sammie, 57, 270
Franko, Frankie, 37
Franz, William, 8, 14, 18
Frazier, Elwyn, 259
Freeman, Bud, 35, 47

Freeman, Ernie, 180, 262
Freeman, Slim, 194
Fuller, Walter, 176, 200, 244–245
Fulson, Lowell, 274
Funky London, 4, 5

Gaillard, Slim, 204, 274
Galloway, Fletcher, 172
Gant, Cecil, 274
Gant, Moses, 38
Garland, Ed "Montudie," "'Tudie", 9, 10, 17, 18, 26, 28, 30, 42, 86, 231, 232
Garner, Errol, 288
Garner, Robert, 18
Gaye, Marvin, 251
Gene Coy's Black Aces, 61, 62, 64
George, Alfonso, 224
George, Karl, 55, 174
Georgia Minstrels, 9, 15–17
Gerald Wilson Orchestra, 251
Gibbons, Jimmy, 223–224
Gibson, Banu, 210
Gibson, Lee, 13, 23, 54, 110, 141
Gibson, Margie, 177
Gilders, Thaddeus, 224
Gillespie, Dizzy, 31, 56, 82, 85, 163, 178, 248, 289; Hadnott and, 205, 207, 208, 209
Gipson, Gertrude, 172
Gipson, J. T., 172, 220
Glaser, Joe, 147, 196
Glenn, Lloyd, 124, 209, 274
Glenn, Tyree, 113, 115, 246
Godley, A. G., 63, 64
Going, Ron, 29
Gomez, Phil, 28
Gonzales, Louis, 117, 204
Goodman, Benny, 26, 39, 51, 65, 138, 222, 249, 284, 285
Goodwin, Charles, 201
Gora, Tommy, 66
Gordon, Dexter, xii, 119, 124, 174, 264
Goss, Jack, 40
Gower, Martin "Fuzzy", 132, 239
Gower, Vernon, 54, 65, 132, 141, 239
Graham, Charles, 188
Grand Terrace, 159
Grant, Alton, xiii
Grant, Earl, 234, 279

Grant, Harold, 72
Grant, Jewel, 146, 261, 270, 271, 274
Grant, Moses, 244
Granz, Norman, 73, 204, 205, 207
Graven, Sonny, 53, 177
Gray, Dobie, 274
Gray, Hunter, 256
Gray, Professor, 135
Gray, Wardell, xii
Greagor, Rafael, 21, 67
Green, Bennie, 243
Green, Bill, 142, 146, 180, 209
Green, Dodo, 49
Green, Henry Tucker, 121, 229
Green, Madeline, 200, 245
Green, Shirley, 243
Greer, Sonny, 284
Grey, Bill, 177
Grey, Henry, 189
Grey, Hunter, 189
Grier, Jimmy, 218
Griffin, George, 291
Griffin, John, 290
Griffith, Lieutenant, 156
Grimes, Herman, 19
Grimes, Tiny, 264
Grissom, Dan, 178
Gross, Felix, 260
Gunther, Paul, 181

Hackett, Bobby, 48
Hackette, Kid Lips, 138
Hackley, Hoffard, 288
Hadnott, Gwendolyn, 191
Hadnott, William King "Billy", xii, 93, 163, 185–211, 186, 291
Hairston, Jester, 104
Hale, Charlie, 199
Hale, Edward "Popeye", 63, 194, 196, 197, 199, 258
Hall, George, 100
Hall, Jewel, 145, 276
Hall, Minor "Ram", 9, 28, 42, 51, 275
Hall, Rene, 248
Hall, Robert, 196
Hall, Sharkey, 259
Ham, Harrington, 190
Hamilton, Chico, 261, 269

Hamilton, Ralph "Chuck", 270, 271, 273, 274
Hammond, John, 139, 195
Hampton, Gladys, 114
Hampton, Lionel, 36, 54, 72, 84, 143, 165, 173, 174, 196, 215, 222, 229, 239, 240, 249, 259, 261, 291; Blakely and, 3, 4, 5, 7, 9, 14, 17, 18, 19, 22; Orendorff and, 45, 50, 51, 52–53; Red Mack and, 114, 119, 123, 138; Roberts and, 138, 140
Hancock, Hunter, 177
Hanna, Paul, 132
Happy Black Aces, 111, 241
Hardee, Ash, 8, 9, 17, 217
Hardwicke, Otto, 189
Harlan Leonard and His Rockets, 70, 214, 228
Harlem Dukes, 173
Harney, Ben, 49
Harpe, Gene, 37
Harper, Buddy, 65, 102, 107
Harris, LeRoy, 245
Harris, Rahim, 181
Harris, Wynonie, 85
Harrison, Gordon, 270, 271, 274
Harrison, Lawrence, 6
Harrison, Richard, 240
Hart, Doc, 15
Hastings, Count, 162
Hawkins, Coleman, 47, 64, 70, 81, 91, 189, 198, 204, 207, 229, 253, 256, 264
Hawkins, Erskine, 259, 260
Heard, Sonny, 123
Hearn, Tommy, 262, 292
Heath, Jimmy, 248
Heath, Percy, 248
Henderson, Angel, 262
Henderson, Fletcher, 54, 89–90, 152, 192, 229, 243, 244
Henderson, Horace, 89, 243, 244–245, 251, 262
Hendricks, Dave, 217, 224
Henley, John, 38
Herbert, Elisha "El", 142, 233
Herman, Woody, xiv, 161
Herndon, Jim, 288
Herriford, Leon, 50, 53, 111, 220, 227; Blakeley and, 14, 17, 17–19, 25; Orendorff and, 52

Hession, Jim, 211
Hession, Martha, 211
Heywood, Cedric, 145
Heywood, Eddie, 56, 176, 229, 291
Heywood, Eddie, Sr., 229
Hibbler, Al, 156, 225
Higginbotham. J. C., 227, 247, 264
Higgins, Ted, 211
Hightower, Alma (Aunt Alma), 108–109
Hill, Bertha "Chippie", 247
Hill, Freddie, 262
Hillery, Art, 290
Hines, Earl, 3, 37, 54, 89, 147, 156, 189, 219, 231, 258; Ewing and, 237, 243, 244–246, 248, 251
Hinton, Milton, 200, 246
Hite, Les, 64, 67, 111, 115, 172, 218, 223, 224, 230, 239, 261, 270; Blakeney and, 4, 9, 10, 11, 13, 14, 17, 21, 22, 27; Orendorff and, 45, 49, 50, 51, 52–53, 54; Turnham and, 79, 80–81, 82, 84–85
Hodges, Johnny, 57, 85, 91, 92, 144, 158
Holder, Terrance "T", 193
Holiday, Bert, 221
Holiday, Billie, 145, 190, 205
Hollywood Café, 228, 272
Hollywood Sextete, 71
Holmes, Tommy, 62
Honey Jumpers, 164, 262, 274
Honoré, Gideon Joseph "Gid" Jr., 27, 33–43, 34, 164–165
Hopkins, Claude, 197
Hopkins, Linda, 178, 208
Horne, Lena, 23, 56, 259
Hoskins, Florence, 184, 220
Houston, Carroll, 255
Howard, Camille, 87, 88, 143
Howard, Darnell, 5, 40
Howard, Joe, 257
Howard, Paul, xiii, 12, 18, 50, 101, 102, 146, 217, 242, 286, 289; Orendorff and, 45, 52
Hudson, Armand, 138
Hudson, George, 159, 200
Huff, Wallace, 71
Hughes, Gordon, 177
Humes, Helen, 291
Hunt, George "Rabbit", 192, 195, 244
Hunter, Fluffy, 71

Hurd, Rodger, 55, 221, 222
Hurd, Sonny, 178
Hutchinson, Eddie "Goo-Goo", 174, 233
Hutton, Ray, 204
Hyner, Doc, 51

Ida Cox Show, 190, 198
Ingle, Red, 56
Ink Spots, 157, 159, 250, 285
Isaac, Vernon, 174, 181
Isoardi, Steve, xiv
Italian Village, 11
Izenhall, Aaron, 208

Jackson, Blind Willie (Willie the Weeper), 108, 290
Jackson, Chubby, 204
Jackson, Earl, 191, 259
Jackson, Franz, 245
Jackson, Ham, 208
Jackson, James, 86, 290
Jackson, Jimmy, 72
Jackson, Joshua, 40, 208
Jackson, Little Willie, 86
Jackson, PeeWee, 245
Jackson, Quentin, 246, 248
Jackson, Tony, 37
Jackson, Willie, 261
Jacquet, Illinois, 73, 203–205, 207, 231, 258, 261, 262, 264
Jacquet, Russell, 73, 204–205, 248
James, Elmore, 274
James, Etta, 83
Jamieson, Roger, 3, 29, 31, 95, 164, 185, 281, 292
Jarvis, Al, 79, 115, 204
Jazz at The Philharmonic, 185, 207
Jazz Nighthawks, 149–150
Jazz Troup, 210
Jefferson, Karl, 232
Jefferson High School, 215–217, 239, 269
Jeffries, Herb, 70
Jenkins, Doug, 225
Jenkins, George, 28, 249, 275
Jenkins Orphanage Band, 226
Jesse Price Blues Band, 210
Jesse Sailes and the Waves, 268
Jester, Helena, 41
Jeter, James L., 152, 157, 158, 159, 200

Index

Jeter-Pillars band, 152, 157–159, 162, 167, 191, 199, 200
jitney dances, 13
Joe Liggins Honeydrippers, 72–73, 86, 290, 298n8
John Kirby Sextet, 72
John "Streamline" Ewing's Sextet, 247
Johnny Mitchell and his Ebony Idols, 11
Johnny Otis and His Orchestra, 210
Johns, Willie, 219
Johnson, Bert, 65, 114, 138
Johnson, Bill "Pops", 247
Johnson, Bob, 63
Johnson, Budd, 38, 245
Johnson, Carl, 22
Johnson, Cee Pee, 114, 116, 117, 122, 138
Johnson, Charles "Little Dog", 228
Johnson, Clarence, 37
Johnson, Frank, 290
Johnson, George "Happy", xiv, 20, 67, 137, 158, 224, 232, 243; Sailes and, 270, 271, 272, 279
Johnson, Gus, 191, 195
Johnson, J. J., 158
Johnson, Jack, 174, 196, 221
Johnson, Jay Jay, 248, 250
Johnson, Keg, 38, 246
Johnson, Lemuel, 229
Johnson, Margaret, 195
Johnson, Marvin, 10, 23, 52, 54, 141
Johnson, Murl, 193
Johnson, Pete, 193, 196, 274
Johnson, Plas, xiii, 262
Johnson, Roy, 195
Johnson, Walter, 14, 42, 227
Jones, Betty Hall, 95–104, 96, 229
Jones, Callwell "King", 37
Jones, Charles (Charlie), 10, 52, 54, 141
Jones, Clifton "Snags", 4, 156
Jones, Dale, 118
Jones, Isham, 47
Jones, Jap, 70, 103, 230, 232
Jones, Jo, 21, 63, 67, 156, 192, 199, 241, 269, 270, 274, 279, 284
Jones, Jonah, 228, 246
Jones, Luke, 101, 117, 122, 123, 179, 219
Jones, Miles, 63, 70, 228
Jones, Reggie (Jonesy), 14, 18, 27, 42, 137
Jones, Richard "Mynee", 3

Jordan, Joe, 6, 56, 174–175
Jordan, Louis, 147, 151, 161–163, 166, 208, 251
Jordan, Rupert, 14
Jordan, Taft, 121, 228
Jordan Hep-Cats, 284
Jordan High School, 283, 284
Joshua, Sam, 123, 183, 203
Judkins, James, 146

Kansas City Jazz, 169, 182
Keith, James, 228
Kelly, Chris, 250, 278
Kelly, Red, 241
Kelso, Jackie, 88, 121, 143
Kennedy, Claude "Benno", xiii, 15, 108, 114, 116, 220
Kenton, Stan, xiv, 51, 275
Keppard, Freddie, 5, 47
Keppard, Freddy, 35
Kern Murray's Blackouts of 1945, 230
Kessel, Barney, 204
Kesterson, Bob, 70
Ketchel, Sammy, 172
Keyes, James Lawrence, 191
Keyes, Joe, 192, 196
Kid Ory Plays W.C. Handy, 145
Kiko, Napoleon, 35
Killebrew, 151
Killian, Al, 207, 261
Kimball, Andrew, 9
Kimball, Margaret, 9
King, B. B., 241, 273, 274
King, Wayne, 273
The King of Jazz (film), 52
King Perry combo, 233
Kirby, John, 156
Kirk, Andy, 52, 64, 196, 256, 257, 259, 269
Kirkwood, Johnny, 162
Kolax, King, 246
Krupa, Gene, 118, 222
Kyle, Billy, 288

La Marr, Kathy, 227

Lacey, Millard, 27, 146
Ladnier, Tommy, 5, 47
Lady Sings The Blues (film), 145, 274

Laine, Frankie, 161, 162, 204
Lancaster, Archie, 52
Landry, Louis, 13
Lane, Chester C., 147–167, 148, 200, 210, 211, 264
Lane, Johnny, 39
Lane, Lucille, 147, 157, 167
Larkin, Milt, 251
Last of the Line, 75
Lawrence, Charlie, 8, 23, 52, 81
LeBlanc, 132, 135, 143
LeBlanc's Boys Band of L.A., 132
Lee, George E., 99, 171
Lee, Julia, 99, 207
Lee, Perry, 288
Lee, Sammy, 92
Legends of Jazz, 1, 30, 75
Leon Herriford's Whispering Syncopators, 18
Leonard, Harlan, 70, 71, 201, 214, 228, 229, 230
Lewis, Baby (Babe), 14, 137
Lewis, Clara, 178
Lewis, Crosby (Kid), 283, 284, 285
Lewis, George, 31
Lewis, Joe, 109
Lewis, John, 248, 255, 257
Lewis, Meade Lux, 259
Lewis, Robert, 188, 190
Lewis, Romie, 290
Liggins, Joe, 23, 72, 86, 91, 261
Lincoln Gardens, 5, 7
Lincoln Theater, 9, 10, 14, 107, 229, 239, 261, 289
Lippi, J. Louis, 283
Liston, Melba, 83, 85, 176, 229
Liston, Sonny, 47
Little Hawk, 264
Little Louis, 47–48
Little Richard, 268, 274
"Little Rod" Orchestra, 62, 74
Little Teddies, 16
Littlefield, Little Willie, 263
Lloyd, Henry, 258
Long, Huey, 38
Los Angeles Classic Jazz Festival, 213, 237, 255, 267
Los Angeles Conservatory, 180
Los Angeles Jazz Festival, 1990, 147

Los Angeles Urban Concert Band, 27, 146
Louis Armstrong All-Stars, 1, 147
Lounge Room, 18
Love, Preston, 70, 229
Lovett, Leroy, 57
Lowe, Curtis, 57, 89
Loy, Myrna, 230
Lunceford, Jimmie, 20, 54, 67, 89, 123, 172, 193, 224, 259, 270, 284; Ewing and, 237, 245, 247, 251
Lundy, Skeets, 178
Lutcher, Joe, 286
Lutcher, Nellie, 79, 92, 95, 100, 102, 103, 105, 231, 276; Hadnott and, 185, 203, 205, 207, 210
Lyman, Abe, 53
Lyon, Ray, 103
Lyttelton, Humphrey, 126

Ma Rainey, 192
Mac, Baby, 52
MacGregor, C. P., 203
Make Believe Ballroom Four, 204
Malachi, John, 159
Mallett, Sax, 62
Malone, E. J. (Emmett), 62
Marable, Fate, 158, 199, 200
Markham, Pigmeat, 175, 229
Marshall, Wendell, 159
Martell, Kitty, 169
Martin, Charlie, 91, 262, 283, 284, 285, 290
Martinez, Raymond, 262
Martyn, Barry, 1, 30–31, 75, 92–93
Marvin, Jimmy, 261
Mason, Edgar, 95, 103, 135, 222
Mason, Fred, 100, 101
Mason, George, 128, 213, 231, 290
Mathews, Onzy, 251
Maupins, Bill, 191
Maxey, Fred, 256
May, Brother Joe, 274
Mayfield, Percy, 72, 273, 274, 291
McCoy, Austin, 28, 216, 221, 239, 259, 260
McCracken, Bob, 27, 28
McDaniel, Willard, 274
McDaniel, Willis, 102
McDonald, Vernon, 62

McEachern, Murray, 121
McFadden, Lillie Mae, 191, 192
McFarland, George, 5
McFay, Nat "Monk", xi, 19–20, 21, 32, 59–74, 60, 86, 231, 267
McGhee, Howard, 31–32, 70–71, 124, 240, 248, 255
McHenry, 225
McKinney's Cotton Pickers, 218, 221, 223
McLewis, Joe, 245
McLollie, Oscar, 164, 262, 274
McNeely, Big Jay, 251, 261, 268
McOwens, Warren, 261, 262, 263
McShann, Jay, 156, 178, 181, 196–197, 210, 243, 251, 255, 260, 274
McTier, Cliff, 192
McVea, Isaac "Satchel", 12, 78, 258
McVea, Jack, 12, 50, 65, 70, 113, 114, 115, 116, 119, 239, 258
McWashington, Willie "Mack", 194
Melody Maker, 28
The Melody Boys, 189
Mendoza, Joel, 23
Mercer, Wallace, 61
Merrell, Bob, 40
Merriman, Ted, 107, 112
Messenger, Howard, 154
Messner, Eddie, 180
Messner, Leo, 180
Metronome, xii
Metropolitan Orchestra, 290
Meyer, Gertrude, 97, 98
Meyer, Harold, 97
Milburn,, Amos, 182, 274
Miller, Glenn, 20, 86
Miller, Johnny, 18
Miller, Norman, 167
Miller, Punch, 37
Mills, Florence, 37
Mills Brothers, 18, 111, 159
Milton, Roy, 87–88, 90–91, 95, 100–101, 189, 290; Roberts and, 129, 142–144
Mingus, Charles, 118, 121, 232, 261, 269, 281, 283, 284–285
Minor, Dan, 158, 192, 195
Minor, Red, xiv, 262
Mitchell, Adam "Slocomb", 4, 133
Mitchell, Bob, 161, 162, 163
Mitchell, George "Humpy", 6
Mitchell, Gordon, 27, 29, 45, 234
Mitchell, Guy, 161
Mitchell, Johnny, 8, 11, 13, 14
Mitchell, Tommy, 64
Modern Jazz Quartet, 248, 255
Mondragon, Joe, 256, 257
Monsanto, Herman, 288
Monte Easter and his Rhythm Stompers, 172
Monterey Jazz Festival, 210
Montez, Chris, 274
"Montudie". *See* Garland, Ed "Montudie," "'Tudie"
Moore, Arvella, 70
Moore, Clarence, 227
Moore, Horace, 173, 222
Moore, John, 161
Moore, Oscar, 209
Moore, Phil, 242
Moore, Russell "Papoose," "Big Chief", 173, 222, 228
Moore, Shorty, 189
Moore, Wild Bill, 261, 288–289
Moore, Woo Woo, 274
Moorehead, Baron, xiv
Morello, Joe, 284
Morgan, Al, 115, 140, 194
Morgan, Russ, 262
Morgan, Stanley, 70, 201, 285
Morris, Joe, 120
Morris, Red Mack McLure, xiii, 17, 19, 54, 65, 92, 105–128, 106, 172, 181, 216, 233
Morris Brothers Show, 150
Morrison, George, 203
Morton, Jelly Roll, xiv, 6, 36, 232
Mosby, Curtis, 51, 53, 81–82, 107, 115, 217, 227, 230, 232; Blakely and, 9, 14, 23, 25
Moseley, Francois, 37
Mosley, Snub, 167, 230
Moten, Bennie, 100, 139, 171, 189, 192, 193, 194
Moten, Bus, 99, 100, 194, 196
Moten band, 183, 192–194
Motley, Frank, 160
Mullins, Herbert, 233
Mundy, Jimmy, 85, 123, 259
Murden, Walter, 269

Murray, Kern, 230
Musso, Vido, 79
Myers, Bumps, 89, 137, 139, 225, 262
Myers, Eddie, 176
Myers, Rosanda, 217, 221

Nance, Ray, 243, 244
Nat King Cole Trio, 18, 203
Navy band, black, 159
Neely, Lawrence "Pepper", 260
Nelson, James "Hawk", 233
Nelson, Louis, 30
New Charleston Cafe, 7
New Orleanians, 281, 292
Nicholas, Albert "Nick", 5, 27, 42
Nicholas, Fayard, 259
Nicholas Brothers, 159
Nicholson, Eddie, 190
Nickerson, William J., 35
No. 17 Band, 160
Nolen, Jimmy, 178
Noone, Jimmie, 38–40, 43, 218, 230
Norris, Chuck, 291
North, Dave, 36
Norvo, Red, 207

O'Day, Anita, 207
Ogletree, Bill, 247
Ogletree, Louis, 243
O'Hare, Huck, 39
O'Hare, Ray, 39
Oldham, George, 38
Oliver, Cappy, 65
Oliver, Joe "King", 5, 8, 35, 37, 43, 51, 287; Orendorff and, 47, 48
One-Eleven Band, 10, 17, 24, 217, 231
Open Air Dance Hall, 10
Orange, John, 161, 200
Orendorff, George Robert, xiii, 45–58, 46, 80, 89, 111, 141, 217, 234, 259; Blakeney and, 1, 4, 7, 14, 22–23, 23, 27, 28
Original Blue Devils, 189
Ory, Kid, xi, 268, 275, 276, 287; Blakeney and, 1, 6, 10, 13, 15, 18, 24–27, 27, 30, 31; Honoré and, 42, 43; *Kid Ory Plays W.C. Handy*, 145–146; Thomas and, 258, 259
Osborne, Will, 118, 119

Otis, Johnny, 86, 210, 228, 237, 250, 251
Owens, Clifford "Juicy", 227
Oxley, Harold, 178

Page, Hot Lips, 64, 66, 192, 193, 194, 196
Page, LaWanda, 88, 181
Page, Walter "Big 'Un," "Hoss", 189, 192, 193–194, 196, 271, 279
Palmer, Joe, 197
Panico, Louis, 47
Papke, Billy "Young", 113, 114
Paradise Club, 140, 174, 249
Parham, Charles (Truck), 245
Parham, Tiny, 40
Parish, Bob, 177
Parker, Charlie, 31, 56, 91, 144, 163, 185, 197, 198–199, 205–206, 207, 243, 248, 273, 288–289
Parker, Dolores, 260
Parker, Firpo, 49
Parker, Parker, 151
Parnell, Rich, 90
Parrish, Avery, 176
Pasley, Frank, 86, 88, 137
Pate, William, 153
Pattison, Pat, 40
Payne, Bert, 162
Peagler, Curtis, 211
Penny and Joe act, 197
Perdue, Jesse, 260
Perkins, Bill, 53
Perkins, Carl, 290–291
Perkins, Ed, 291
Permillion, Herbert, 31, 264
Perry, King, 233
Peters, Teddy, 180
Peterson, Big Pete, 124
Peterson, Oscar, 41
Peyton, Dave, 5
Phillips, Earl, 40
Phillips, Flip, 204
Phillips, Gene, 57, 89
Phillips, Melvin, 89
Pierce, Nat, 161, 166, 264
Pillars, Charles, 152, 158, 200
Pillars, Hayes, 152, 158, 200
Pinkney, Red, 36
Player, Omer, 255
Pointer, Lowell, 196

Pollack, Ben, 18, 45, 51
Pollock, Ed, 38
Pork Chops, 247
Porter, Eugene, 200
Porter, Gene, 231
Porter, Jake, xiii, 23, 30, 89, 95, 202, 232, 259, 273
Porter, James "King", xiii, 7–8, 51, 82, 217
Porter, Roy, xiv, 71
Porter, Thelma, 21
Powell, Forrest, 79, 101, 152, 154, 156–157, 172, 232, 243, 260
Powell, Mel, 207
Presley, Elvis, 233
Preston, Ed, 70
Price, C. Q., 63, 65
Price, Jesse, 196, 197, 199, 201, 207, 210, 228, 243
Price, Lloyd, 178
Priestley, Roy, 128
Prince, Henry, 11, 54
Prince, Peppy, 11, 17, 45, 57–58, 72, 86, 221, 261, 265
Prince, Wesley, 10, 121, 231, 259
Purnell, Alton, 28, 29
Purnell, Keg, 229
Pyles, Frosty, 71, 73

Quality Serenaders, 11–12, 45, 50, 52, 217
Quebec, Ike, 246, 264
Queda, 228
Quinichette, Paul, 208

Raft, George, 230
Raglin, Junior, 240, 271
Rainey, Ma, 49
Ramey, Gene, 196
Randall, Roy, 189
Randall, Willie, 245
Randolph, Irving "Mouse", 230
Ray, Dewitt T., 21, 67
Ray, Floyd, 145, 174, 233, 261, 289
Ray, Johnny, 73
Raymon, Ray, 204
Raymond, Clem, 12, 17
Reagor, John, 196
Reason, Lionel, 291
Red Mack. *See* Morris, Red Mack McLure

Redd, Alton, 27, 42, 114, 179, 230, 258, 262
Redd, Vi, xiii
Redman, Don, 200
Reed, George, 89, 90, 234, 262
Reed, Leonard, 176, 228, 229
Reese, Lloyd, 51, 65, 82, 108, 116, 172, 180–181, 202, 221
Reese, Rostelle, 245
Reeves, Oliver "Big Six", 65, 172, 219, 227
Reeves, Reuben, 5
Reinschagger, 207
René, Googie, 88
Rene, Leon, 10, 134, 141
Resurrection Brass Band, 27, 43, 45, 234
Rhythm and Blues Caravan, 237
Rhythmaires Ork, 117
Rice, Sylvester (Syl), 28, 33, 185
Rich, Buddy, 204, 259, 284
Richardson, Ann (Caldonia), 160
Richardson, Carolyn, 271
Richardson, Rodney, 228
Riddle, Nelson, 210
Rieman, Al, 27
Rinker, Al, 52
Rivers, Candy, 72, 86
Roach, Max, 271
Roberts, Caughey Wesley, II, xi, 23, 28, 54, 80, 129–146, 130, 166, 216, 263, 276
Roberts, Claude, 244
Roberts, Tiny, 259
Robinson, Bill (Bojangles), 45
Robinson, Clemmie, 283
Robinson, Curly, 61
Robinson, Dave, 144
Robinson, James "Hambone", xiv, 233, 283, 288
Robinson, Jessie Mae, 180
Robinson, Jimmy, 247
Robinson, Prince, 229
Robinson, "Red" Minor W., 234, 281–293, 282
Robinson, Rocky, 43
Robinson, Roscoe, 256
Robinson, Rose, 281
Robinson, Sugar Chile, 261
Rose, Atwell, 221

Rose, David, 210
Ross, Bob, 204
Ross, Diana, 145
Ross, James, 201, 228
Rotzquel, Hernando, 173
Rousette, Bob (Rousseau), 221
Rousseau, Milton, 14
Royal, Ernie, 56, 174
Royal, Marshal, xiv, 9, 52, 54, 108, 119, 174, 216, 230, 242, 289
Royal Gardens, 5, 7, 37
Rucker, Joe, 237
Rupe, Art, 180
Rushing, Jimmy, 167, 189, 192
Russell, Luis, 5
Rye, Howard, 59

Sailes, Della, 269
Sailes, Jesse, 88, 89, 145, 164, 166, 169, 264, 267–279, 268, 290
Sailes, John, 269
Sailes, Laverne, 267
Sailes, William Asher "Big Daddy", 269
Sammy Ketchel's Creole Syncopators, 172
Sands, Renee, 89
Sapp, Hosea, 143
Saunders, Red, 246
Saunders, Vince, 29
Savoy Ballroom, 5, 174
Savoy Five, 231
Savoy Sultans, 272
Scott, Bud, 24, 179
Scott, Emerson, 18
Scott, Ernest, 89
Scott, Harold, 52, 111, 172, 223, 224
Scott, Hazel, 161, 259
Scott, Leon, 38, 243
Scott, Mabel, 229
Scott, Sammy, 229
Sears Roebuck company band, 233
Sebastian, Frank, 12, 14, 18, 50, 52, 53
Selcow, James, 255
Seventh Annual Cavalcade of Jazz, 72
Seville, Ira "Skeets", 156
Seville, Ted, 156
Shackleford, Johnny, 177
Shadowin, Leon, 21, 67
Shanahan, Dick, 273, 275
Shannon, Detroit, 7, 49

Shannon, Manzie, 241
Shannon, Shannon, 5
Shavers, Charlie, 228, 234
Sheffield, Leslie, 63, 64, 65, 194
Sheffield Blues (record), 8
Shelton, Arthur, 153, 154
Shepp's Playhouse, 70, 84, 88, 176, 228–229, 233, 302n6
Sherman, Walt, 121
Shirley, Ted, 177
Shirley & Lee, 274
Shoffner, Bob, 5
Shriners band, 18, 290
Shroff, Brodie, 118
Sibley, Richard, 216
Simeon, Omer, 6, 244
Simmons, John, 188, 243
Simon, Freddie, 180, 289
Simon, Maurice, 180
Sims, Earl, 178
Sims, Edward, 244
Sims, Frankie Lee, 274
Singer, Hal, 188
Singleton, Zutty, 205, 218, 230–231, 232, 272, 273
Sissle, Noble, 177, 259
Slater, Vernon, 85, 229, 283, 284, 285
Sloan, Henry, 229, 232
Smith, Bessie, 99, 238
Smith, Buster "Professor", 139, 189, 193, 194, 195, 197, 199
Smith, Carl "Tatti", 65, 110, 194, 196
Smith, Carlton, 256
Smith, Eddie, 260
Smith, Fletcher, 73, 79, 117, 221, 261, 289
Smith, Floyd, 64, 200
Smith, Geechie, 70, 289
Smith, Gene, 290
Smith, Howlett, 208, 210
Smith, Jabbo, 38
Smith, Jeff, 13
Smith, Jesse, 217
Smith, Joe, 161, 164
Smith, Keith, 28
Smith, Mamie, 99, 192
Smith, Pops, 223
Smith, Russell Pops, 219
Smith, Stuff, 291
Smith, Warren "Smitty", 27, 28, 38, 260

Index

Smith, William (piano), 201
Smith, William (trumpet), 201
Smith, Willie "The Lion", 20, 67, 161, 207
Smock, Ginger, 42
Snow, Valaida, 54
Snowden, Carolynne, 11
Snyder, Danny, 166, 211, 264
Solid Senders, 95
Soper, Tut, 40
South, Eddie, 45
Southard, Harry, 11, 218
Southern California Hot Jazz Society, 27
Spector, Phil, 274
Speiginer, Louis (Lou), 203, 289
Spikes, Johnny, 9, 221
Spikes, Reb, 8, 9, 50, 81, 110, 221, 230
Spikes Brothers, 8, 81
Spirit of the Black Territory Bands, 210
Spitz, Eddie, 196
"Spotlight Entertainers", 63
St. Cyr, Johnny, 28, 250
Stamp, Jimmy, 180, 181
Starks, Willie, 18
Starr, Henry, 54
Starr, Kay, 124, 207, 273
Stars of Jazz (TV series), 275
Steiner, John, 40
Steward, Wilbur, 36
Stewart, Billy, 62
Stewart, Dee, 192, 196, 197
Stewart, Rex, 227, 233, 234, 269
Stewart, Slam, 288
Still, Willie Grant, 52
Stone, Jesse, 38
Strayhorn, Billy (Sweet Pea), 158
Sturdivant, Johnny, 14, 81
Sudler, Joe, 7
Sullivan, Ed, 161
Sunnyland Jazz Band, 7–8, 10, 217–218
Surfside Jazz Band, 264
Swan, Son, 35

Talbot, Barbara, 177
Talmadge, Constance, 12
Tapscott, Horace, xiv
Tarrant, Rabon, 262
Tarrent, Merle, 200
Tate, Buddy, 61, 62, 167, 193
Tate, Erskine, 112, 113

Tate, Raymond, 259
Tatum, Art, 43, 81, 156, 264, 279
Taylor, Arcima, 23, 27, 28, 137, 260
Taylor, Eddie, 290
Taylor, James (Dink), 152
Taylor, Lester, 240, 271
Taylor, Myra, 201
Teagarden, Jack, 217, 231, 251
Teddy Buckner Dixieland All-Stars, 276
Teddy Buckner Reunion Band, 213, 237
Teddy Bunn and the Spirits of Rhythm, 205
Telling It Like It Is (Darensbourg), xi
Temple, Calvin, 222
Terrell, Pha, 193
Terry, Clark, 158, 159, 164, 228
Theus, Fats, 262
Thomas, Ann, 62
Thomas, Arcelle, 253, 265
Thomas, Charles L. "Chuck," Jr., 89, 164, 169, 182, 183, 253–265, 254, 276; Robinson and, 285, 289, 290, 292
Thomas, Creon, 78
Thomas, Joe, 123
Thomas, John, 48
Thomas, Louis, 234
Thomas, Roderick "Little Rod", 62, 63, 64
Thomas, Tex, 261
Thompson, Earl, 52
Thompson, LeMon, 70
Thompson, Lucky, 91, 289
Thompson, Sir Charles, 88
Tillman, Pal, 63
Tin Pan Valley Jazz Band, 250, 264
Tole, Bill, 234
Tomago, 228
Tommy Dorsey Orchestra, 234
Torian, Roy, 159
Towles, Nat, 62, 67
Trainer, Fred, 247
Trammell, Leo, 79, 258
Travis, Al, 153, 154
Trenier Twins, 229
Trent, Alphonso, 65, 153–154, 157, 158, 167
Tricky Sam, 189
Trumbauer, Bill, 182
Trumbauer, Frankie, 182
Tucker, Henry, 121

Tucker, Monroe, 133, 137, 260
"'Tudie". *See* Garland, Ed "Montudie," "'Tudie"
Turner, Joe, 85, 193, 197, 210, 274
Turner, Joe (Paris), 126
Turnham, Daisy Bush, 81, 85
Turnham, Edyth, 77–78, 79, 81, 86, 88
Turnham, Floyd, Sr., 78, 79
Turnham, Floyd Payne, Jr., 22, 23, 30, 57, 72, 75–93, 76, 117, 176
Turnham, Gloria, 75
Twine, Arthur, 233
Tympany Five, 208

Ursery, John, 67
Utopia Orchestra, 3

Valadiche, Jack, 36
Valdeler, Pat, 274
Vann, George, 28
Vaughan, Sarah, 159, 248
Vincent, Gene, 274
Vinson, Cleanhead, 292

Wade, Puss, 121
Waldron, Frank, 77
Walker, Arthur, 258
Walker, Joe, 286, 289
Walker, Little Joe, 100, 101
Walker, Mike, 247
Walker, Nat, 80
Walker, T-Bone, 57, 58, 80, 124, 174, 178, 198, 207, 209, 232–233
Walker, Will, 49
Wallach, Glenn, 180
Waller, Charles, 203
Waller, Fats, xiv, 39, 43, 54, 129, 140, 141, 284
Walsh, Ellis, 12
Walsh, Everett, 24, 221
Warren, Earl, 139, 269
Washington, Al, 7
Washington, Clyde, 290
Washington, Dinah, 241, 249, 263
Washington, Fred, 10, 231
Washington, Gene, 183
Washington, Herman, 289
Washington, Jack, 65, 139, 193, 194, 196
Washington, Mildred, 12

Waterford, Crown Prince, 274
Waters, Ethel, 37, 99
Watson, Johnny "Guitar", 274
Watson, Paula, 276
Watts, Kenny, 185, 210
Weatherford, Teddy, 37, 137
Webb, Chick, 83, 175, 273
Webb, Jack, 257
Webb, Speed, 11, 13, 52, 218
Webster, Ben, 115, 127, 159, 227, 256, 264, 291
Wedberg, Lee, 29
Weekend Blues (record), 177
Welles, Orson, 10, 218, 230, 231
Wells, Dickie, 251
Wells, Henry, 259
West, Odell, 196, 197
Westbrook, Jimmy, 64, 223, 224, 225
Weston, Fitz, 13
Whaley, Wade, 9, 17
Whetsol, Art, 227
Whispering Syncopators, 49
White, Al, 234
White, Amos, 171, 172
White, Bob, 224
White, Cecil, 38
White, Fess, 230
White, John, 63
White, Kitty, 207
White, Leon, 10, 24
Whiteman, Paul, 52, 77
Whitfield, Charlie, 65
Whitfield, Smoky Joe, 123
Whitsett, Raymond, 49
Whyte, Leroy "Snake", 115, 175, 219, 229, 232
Wichard, Cake, 263
Wiggins, Anatieve, 35
Wiggins, Earl, 35
Wiley, 152
Wilkins, Professor, 9
Wilks, Ernie "Boots", 67
Will Mastin Trio, 208, 261
Williams, A. J., 114
Williams, Al, 260
Williams, Clarence, 7, 8
Williams, Claude, 181
Williams, Cootie, 189, 251
Williams, Eddie, 66, 73, 227

Williams, Eleanor, 102
Williams, Emile, 42, 196, 199
Williams, Ernie, 201
Williams, Herb, 9, 12, 17
Williams, Joe, 39, 84, 86–87
Williams, Leo, 249, 269
Williams, Percy, 258
Williams, Ray, 78
Williams, Walter "Dootsie", xiii, 83, 173, 259, 285
Williams, Winston, 191, 196, 201
Wills, Bob, 189
Wilson, Bill, 48
Wilson, Buster, 8, 18, 21, 24, 25, 179, 217
Wilson, Dick, 112
Wilson, Fats [Floyd], 78, 88
Wilson, Gerald, xiii, 83, 84–85, 86, 88, 237, 247, 251, 289
Wilson, Jimmy, 178
Wilson, Quinn, 244
Wilson, Shadow, 174, 248
Wilson, Teddy, 161, 243
Winston, Bill, 3, 21
Witherspoon, Jimmy, 72, 232, 260, 268, 274
Wonder, Stevie, 251
Woodlen, Bobby, 174
Woodman, Britt, xiii, xiv, 79, 85–86, 172, 220, 261, 269, 293
Woodman, Coney, 269
Woodman, William, Jr. "Brother", 72, 269, 271, 275, 276

Woodman, William Willie, Sr., xiv, 27, 28, 86, 144, 146, 220, 221, 270, 290
Woodman Brothers, 269, 279, 283
Woodson, Buddy, 57, 89
World's Greatest Jazz Band, 210
Wormick, James "Harpo", 228
Wright, Charles (Charlie), 20, 65, 66
Wright, Gene, 13
Wright, Lammar, 174, 223
Wright, Lammar, Jr., 174
Wright, Mel, 62
Wynn, Al, 38
Wynn, Jim, 221

Yancey, Jimmy, 247
Yellowjackets, 152, 159
Yorke, Vernell, 112–113
Young, Alice, 176
Young, Billie, 256
Young, Ike, 241
Young, Ken, 112
Young, Lee, 21, 91, 117, 121, 204, 209, 233
Young, Lester (Les), 64, 91, 117, 121, 139, 189, 195, 196, 198, 204, 207, 219, 264, 279
Young, Loretta, 230
Young, Marl, 209
Young, Melvin, 209
Young, Trummy, 251
Young Men of New Orleans, 250
Yung, J. T., 19, 67

About the Author

Peter Vacher has been writing about jazz in all its forms for more than fifty years, contributing to numerous magazines and other media in the United Kingdom, United States, and Canada. He presently writes for *Jazzwise* magazine and the *Guardian* newspaper.

His enthusiasm for the music was kindled during the UK's traditional jazz "boom" of the 1950s, which led to him leading an amateur jazz band. Once his limitations as an instrumentalist became evident, he began to write for the *Melody Maker* and the international jazz press, all the while maintaining a successful corporate career.

His collaboration with the clarinetist Joe Darensbourg led to the latter's autobiography, *Telling It Like It Is*, which appeared in 1987; more recently, he has published two critically acclaimed books of interviews with U.S. jazz musicians, *Soloists and Sidemen* (2004) and *Mixed Messages* (2013). He continues to work as a freelance journalist, runs jazz classes, promotes concerts, and evangelizes about the music wherever and whenever he can.

Peter lives in London with his wife, Patricia, and loves the company of his children and grandchildren, none of whom has emulated his interest in jazz!